R. E. Francillon

A Real Queen

A Romance

R. E. Francillon

A Real Queen
A Romance

ISBN/EAN: 9783744675581

Printed in Europe, USA, Canada, Australia, Japan

Cover: Foto ©Thomas Meinert / pixelio.de

More available books at **www.hansebooks.com**

A REAL QUEEN.

A REAL QUEEN

A Romance

BY

R. E. FRANCILLON

AUTHOR OF "OLYMPIA," "QUEEN COPHETUA," "ONE BY ONE," ETC.

A NEW EDITION.

London:

CHATTO & WINDUS, PICCADILLY.

1885.

A REAL QUEEN.

CHAPTER 1.

> . . . . I call
> This gift before all other good—
> To have the rose of womanhood
> Mine own, from bud to fall.

ROSAMOND!—why, you must have taken leave of your seven senses, my dear boy. Rosamond! do you know her age ? "

" Yes. She is old enough for me to know that the older she grows the better I shall love her. But I don't think you quite understand."

" Well, that's soon seen. I'll state the case, as if for the judges. My niece, Rosamond, was just fifteen yesterday. You are—let me see, how old are you? "

"Three-and-twenty last July."

"Quite so. And you, Oswald Hargrave, who were only her age eight years ago, actually offer marriage to a child who in eight years will be only as old as you are now ! Come—put such nonsense out of your head; and if you can't, come indoors, and I'll show you a flint hatchet—found only yesterday in Patchett's Piece, Oswald!—which will. A real Celt, my boy."

"No, Mr. Fane," said Oswald Hargrave, colouring a little at the slight put upon the number of his years, but with certainly no other sign of indecision ; " I'm afraid—or rather I'm not afraid —that the flint is still unfound that can work that miracle. You haven't stated the case quite fully, after all. It's true, Rosamond's but fifteen, and I but twenty-three. Well, I suppose most people are, at some time in their lives, either one or the other. Some day she will be twenty-three, and I shall be thirty-one. Of course I'm not asking to marry Rosamond to-day."

1

"To-day! God bless the boy!"

"But, as I surely mean to marry her some day, the sooner that's clearly understood by everybody the better it will be. I'll wait two years—three—four; but if I have to wait a hundred it will be the same."

"Bless the boy! Why in a hundred years she'll be *too* old!

"Rosamond, Mr. Fane, will never be either too young or too old. I made up my mind to marry her when she was seven and I was fifteen, and I've never changed my mind, not for an hour But now she's fifteen, I must be prudent, you see."

"Prudent? No, Oswald, the prudence I do *not* see."

"Never mind. I'll make it as plain as a pike-staff before I've done. At fifteen—well she won't be much longer a child. I know she lives out of the world down here, and it may be long before she finds a face to her liking. But then, on the other hand, it mayn't be long. All sorts of things may happen, and all sorts of faces may come in her way. And I may be out of it; her world's small, but mine's wide. I want to work my way through it with the knowledge, as fixed as fate, that I shall find Rosamond at the end—as the end. And so, if she understands, and you understand, that she is mine even as I am hers, I shall go off with a good heart, and come back when her finger's large enough for a ring."

"Bless the—you could talk the skin off that flint hatchet! Oswald, if I didn't know you better—I *do* know you, my boy, but the world doesn't yet; and what'll the world say to a man with nothing but his fists for his fortune, coolly proposing that a child, with something more than her face for hers, should be kept for him under lock and key?"

"I hate that sort of talk, and I despise it; and so do you. If Rosamond had a million a-year and I were without a sixpence, what difference would it make to me? I'm not a man in a story, to think himself bound in honour not to care for a girl unless she's got nothing. Yes; if Rosamond had twenty million a-day I'd care for her just the same. And as for the world, it won't even be troubled to tell a single lie. If in two years I'm not richer than Rosamond, then I don't love her, that's all."

"Ah, it's a fine thing to be three-and-twenty; a very fine thing indeed. I sometimes think I'd almost give my Macedonian Stater to be three-and-twenty last July. But three-and-twenty has other tricks besides faith in itself, Oswald. If I were to shut up Rosamond, in my cabinet, and label and catalogue her as the property of Oswald Hargrave, how would that shut Oswald Hargrave's eyes from seeing a prettier face before he was twenty-five?"

"Of course I shall see prettier faces than Rosamond's. I've seen scores. But what does that signify? I mean to marry Rosamond, not because she's pretty, or ugly, or rich, or poor, or anything."

"Then, bless the boy! what *do* you want to marry her for?"

"For the best of all reasons. Because she is—She."

"And for a still better, because you're an ass, my dear lad. Come in and see that flint hatchet; there's a thing that remembers the Ancient Britons and isn't changed! Think of that, an axe that links Queen Boadicea——"

"With Queen Rosamond," said Oswald, without a smile. "Yes; I'll see that hatchet. I like the thought of a thing that has cut its way through two thousand years, and found Rosamond at the end. I will take it for my crest, sir: a flint axe, proper, with the motto *Semper Idem*—'Always the same.' I accept the ass, sir. It's a stubborn brute, and knows its own mind."

"Quite so; it's naturally easy to know—nothing. Take care your heraldry doesn't turn out false, my dear lad, before you've done. But come, we've talked nonsense enough for one day. Rosamond! Bless the boy!"

This talk, whether it was truly nonsense, or whether there were on one side of it more sense than the somewhat rusty philosophy of that worthy magistrate, Æneas Fane, was carried on in the kitchen garden of a hybrid kind of house overlooking the sea. If the character of a house be any index to that of its occupants, then the character of the occupants of Cliff Cottage must have been nondescript indeed. But more probably the result was due to the conflicting views of many generations of tenants or owners. The house had really been a cottage once —perhaps a fisherman's. Then the fisherman had drawn to himself a neighbour, as was natural enough, seeing the convenience of the lofty outlook for catching first sight of a school of mackerel, and the single cottage had grown into two. But these had been prevented from forming the nucleus of a colony by their transformation into one farm-house, and as such it had for long continued, with the addition of necessary out-houses and offices. The farmer (as in former times happened to farmers

now and then) prosper d, and the occasional ruins wrought by
winter storms were repaired with brick-work that very ill corres-
ponded with the original lath and plaster buttressed here and
there with stone. In another generation or two crept in a greenhouse, a modern stable, and a yet more modern structural addition, fancifully termed Elizabethan—had it been yet more modern
it would have been yet more fancifully named after Queen Anne.
Doubtless that also would come. Meanwhile Cliff Cottage was
large, rambling, incongruous, with rooms as little on a level as
those of an Eastern palace, and with neither ground-plan or
elevation that an architect could understand. Of course it is
the fashion to admire such abnormal growths, but it was the
hereditary custom of the Fanes, a desperately Philistine race, to
deplore the inconveniences of the cottage, even while increasing
them for the disadvantage of posterity. And this was the more
inconsistent, because it would have been so perfectly easy to make
a clean sweep of the whole house, and to build another. But
then, on the other hand, the Fanes had not made their money by
investing it in bricks and mortar. They had been content to en-
large their elbow room from time to time, according to immediate
and indispensable needs. Thus it happened that the stable
which formed an actual wing of the house, was the best devised
and best built portion of the whole.

All the parish of Crossmarsh had once known, but had also
completely forgotten, that Æneas Fane—though that descendant
of the original fisherman had become squire and justice—was not
the actual owner of the cottage and the large farmlands of which
it served for the mansion. He was, in law, merely the trustee
and guardian of his two nieces, Rosamond and Sophia, the mother-
less daughters and co-heiresses of his deceased elder brother,
Anthony. Under the circumstances, it was only natural that he,
being a middle-aged bachelor, should live with his nieces in the
capacity of second father, and should in time come to be popularly
treated as if he himself were the Squire of Crossmarsh—that
delightfully unknown corner of the coast to which not even a
landscape painter had pioneered the path of iron till Rosamond
was fully five years old. He did not fall into the popular error,
however, as some men might have fallen, for the simple reason
that he was entirely indifferent to the adding of scrip to scrip and
of rood to rood, which had been the otherwise universal tendency
all the Fanes. Indifference, not virtue, made him an absolutely

honest steward. His carelessness of his own interests extended even to the future. No doubt Rosamond, or Sophia, or both, might marry some day, and the cottage pass away from the name of Fane; but, even so, he could not conceive of circumstances under which a decent sort of nephew-in-law would grudge space enough among those many rooms for a certain cabinet, and for the easy-going uncle who served the same.

For Oswald Hargrave, the son of the late rector of Crossmarsh, had, even in his babyhood, learned to connect, indissolubly, the idea of the tall, lean, hard-featured, dry old gentleman in spectacles with a wonderful cabinet of bits of stone and battered buttons. Probably Æneas Fane had not really been old when Oswald first emerged from long clothes more than twenty years ago. On the contrary, he could hardly have been middle-aged. But the child's impression had been right, all the same. Æneas, indifferent to the present, careless of the future, was absorbed in the past, heart and soul. He was a born collector ; he had really gathered a unique museum of coloured pebbles and pierced farthings, until, in maturity, Celts were substituted for pebbles and ancient coins for the disfigured effigies of the later Georges. That was his way of displaying the inherited acquisitiveness of the Fanes. He had been a pupil of Parson Hargrave, and his taste had made him something of a scholar—indeed, in these unscholarly days, what would pass for a ripe and good one. And at last, when his guess proved right that the Pix-Knoll, in Patchett's Piece, was a veritable and possibly prolific barrow, the mission of his life was found. He passed from the barrow to the cabinet, dealing justice among his neighbours by the way. No—it was absurd to dread the advent of a nephew-in-law who would break such a life in two. How could it be within the bounds of natural reason that Rosamond or Sophia would marry a fiend ?

To Oswald, that cabinet had once been a fountain-head of infinite delight and wonder. It had been a treat when his baby fingers were allowed, on days of special favour, to grasp a flint weapon or to touch the brightly-polished face of some king of Macedon. The magician in spectacles, who ruled the cabinet, would even read him lectures, fascinating with their crack-jaw words, hoping, it might be, that he was educating a pair of shoulders on which his mantle might hereafter descend not unworthily. But, alas, neither Rosamond nor Sophia cared for any of these things; especially Rosamond.   Did Æneas ever quite forgive Oswald for dropping a *decadrachma* into a chink of the floor because Rosamond tumbled down the three steps leading from the next room, and cried?   I think he did, for none but rival and critical collectors were beyond the pale of pardon.   Nevertheless, as time went on, Oswald and the cabinet fell more and more apart, and Oswald and Rosamond more and more together, until—until a schoolboy, of the mature age of fifteen, who ought to have been above such girls' nonsense, took to scrawling upon his slate " Rosamond," " Rosamond Fane," " Rosamond Hargrave ;" and all for a rather plain little girl of seven, who could not even read.   He was, nevertheless, boy enough to prefer a slate for the purpose of the inscriptions, for the excellent reason that he could at any moment easily rub them out again. He never went beyond " R " upon a wall.

What Rosamond thought of this shy but stubborn adoration, or even if she so much as knew of it, was her own affair.   The · question of how early little girls begin to discover their power has never yet been solved.   At the same time, she could scarcely, at her age and in the seclusion in which she had always lived, have learned to think of that far-off dream called marriage with her old playmate, the good-looking young gentleman farmer from the next-door parish of Windgates, who had studied at an agricultural college, and looked so grave and talked so wisely.   He was like a grown up brother, or a young uncle, or an intimate cousin ; a part of the daily life she had known.   Only, if he had been any of these, he would surely have kissed her now and then, and Oswald Hargrave had never committed such an act of sacrilege, except once, when he at twelve had been commanded to kiss the baby, and had gone through the process sorely against his principles and his will. I dare not say that her eyes had never caught a glimpse of the nature of Oswald's resolve; but I will say it as nearly as I dare. For the rest, Oswald Hargrave, though far from able to keep a wife like a co-heiress of Fanes, and with the bulk of his capital spent upon an as yet unproductive education, was worth looking at with older than fifteen-year-old eyes.   Possibly Rosamond's thought him already on the verge of middle-age ; and it may be that he really looked a little older than his by no means excessive number of years.   He was a brave looking young Englishman, stalwart, and the owner of a becoming friendship with wind and weather, whose fair face served for the clear window-pane of a very honest heart and a sufficient share of brains.   For, though Æneas Fane had called his old friend's son an ass, he did not mean anything of the kind—except so far, indeed, as a young man must needs be of that persuasion who prefers a little girl to a flint axe that had been made before Boadicea was Queen.

This was the state of things at Crossmarsh-by-the-Sea on the day after Rosamond became fifteen.

CHAPTER II.

She stood upon the charmèd height
Between the vales of Day and Night,
 And sighed. " But all in vain
My secret path I strive to seek,
While clouds conceal the mountain-peak,
 And mists are o'er the plain."

Yet, who may stand in doubtful wise,
'Twixt clouded earth and cloudier skies ?
 On moments hangs the way,
By Chance's chasms creeps the path
She dares, unknowing if she hath
 Fared forth toward Night or Day.

BUT, as well as a Rosamond, there was a Sophy—a very good little girl, with wits as quick as lightning, and two eyes which only wanted to be a little less blue in order to be as sharp as needles. It was she, not her sister, who happened to be looking out of the precise window which had a full view of the kitchen garden up and down which Uncle Æneas and young Mr. Hargrave were pacing. Somehow it always did happen so—that, when anything happened, great or little, Sophy, by the merest accident, chanced to be at the only window which overlooked them. The visitor was welcome, for Oswald had never been shy with Sophy, and she ran off to let her sister share in her piece of good news. But, on her way through that devious house, she chanced to pass another window, and that happened to be the only window with a clear view of the entrance to the carriage drive at the precise moment when Mr. and Mrs. Pitcairn, the Rector and his wife, were entering. Sophy did not care for the Rector one quarter of a straw, nor for the Rector's wife more than three ; so that it was with mingled feelings that she continued her flight, seeing nothing more by the way—whereby it was proved to demonstration that there was nothing more to see.

From the second window, she ran along a dark and narrow white-washed passage, full of bulges and beams, then plunged down three steps into a sort of lumber room with a skylight, and then struck with her fist a solemn blow upon a closed door. Counting three, aloud, she struck two blows; then counted five, and struck three blows. Then she waited to see what would come of this somewhat complicated manner of tapping at a door.

But Sophy was certainly not of the sort to wait long for anything; so, after a minute, she showered a rain of raps, and called out,

"Rosamond! aren't you there? But I know you are, for the door's locked. Let me in—I've got such heaps of news!"

Presently she was answered by the grating of a rusty key in an exceedingly stiff lock, and the door was opened, showing the interior of a loft not unlike what a prison cell of ancient times may have been. It was gloomy, being lighted only by a barred and latticed window, nearly as high as the ceiling : the walls and floor were bare, and it was furnished only with a chair, a table, and a thick heap of straw piled up in one corner.

"When will you give the signals right, Sophy?" asked Rosamond—not impatiently, but with sad reproof in her tones. "Didn't we settle that three knocks—three between the first and second, and five between the second and third, was to mean 'Everything all right, and nobody wants you?'"

"Of course I know that—but 1 made, indeed I did, five—no, three, between the first and second, and five—no, *that* was three—between the second and third; and I know that's the sign for 'Come out at once—important news!'"

"Oh, Sophy," said Rosamond, "you must be more careful—you must indeed. Just think what would happen, if the enemy—if signals were to be mixed up in a war! We might as well have none at all. Before we go to bed I'll make you go over all the secret signs all over again. But what *is* the news? And I'm so busy—*must* I come down?"

Sophy was already pretty; but Rosamond, the elder sister by a year, was not beautiful yet, although there was no reason why she should not, some two or three years hence, wake up one morning and find herself—or go out some evening and be found—beautiful. Meanwhile, it was perfectly clear that she was magnificently alive. When out of doors, as every fisherman in Crossmarsh knew, her dark grey eyes were as good as telescopes for the horizon, and as microscopes for every tiniest caprice of nature among the rock pools. She ought to have been an invaluable niece to a collector of the caprices of nature and art like Uncle Æneas; but, alas, she was nothing of the kind. She was content to see things, and disliked gathering them. Though not a downright brunette, she was by no means so fair as became her historical name, and her complexion, not as yet clear enough for beauty, had no suggestion of the lilies of her namesake, nor her hair of the gold—of the rose, about which the sea breezes had much to say, there was something; her hair was brown and heavy, not to say at present shaggy, with an undertint of chestnut; a good colour, and not too common. The lips had much of the child left in them, and had yet to form; they promised to become the outward signs of a large and generous nature. She was well grown for her age, as the phrase is, and might remain at her present height for good and all without disadvantage. For she had already obtained a graceful and stately bearing at once erect and free; Diana herself, at whatever age among goddesses answers to mortal fifteen, must have been curiously like Rosamond. Brotherless as they were, there had grown up between Sophy and Rosamond something of the relation of girl and boy, for, where but two are in company, the one must serve and the other must rule. In this case the ruler was unquestionably Rosamond. Sophy was all blue-eyed littleness and liveliness, with a suggestion of the kitten, both in its softness and in its peculiar style of mischief; but if Rosamond was in any sense femininely feline, it was in the lioness's way. And it is good for a girl to have a touch of the boy in her, just as it is good for a boy to have a touch of the nature of the girl.

"Yes, you must come down indeed!" answered Sophy. "Oswald's here!"

"Oh!" said Rosamond; "that all? Sophy, you are incorrigible! Just on the very point of raising the murderer's ghost, and to be interrupted for nothing, and the ghost rising so nicely, too. No, Sophy. If it's only Oswald, I don't think I'll come down. He can't want *me*—it's only that new flint thing that's brought him, you may depend. We'll have a new signal for Oswald. If he asks after me, tell him I'm particularly engaged."

"With the ghost of a murderer?" asked Sophy, simply; but perhaps not quite so simply as it seemed. For she represented the humour of the household in her blue-eyed way.

"For goodness sake—no!" exclaimed Rosamond, colouring to the hair. "You might just as well let him in to all our secret signs. *We* understand, Sophy, but, when you come to know the world, you'll find that people like Oswald only laugh at such things:

and it isn't nice to be laughed at.   He'd call me a witch—and—
and all sorts of things."

" Yes, I think very likely he would," said Sophy.   " And the
ghost—is it very dreadful ?   Is it really rising well ? "

" You'll see ! I only knew it haunted me all last night—at least
till I fell asleep—till I really thought I should never close my eyes.
You see, I had committed such a terrible murder——"

" The ghost, you mean ? "

" Of course—before it *was* a ghost, you know—that what came
afterwards—But I can't tell you now. No. I can't leave the
ghost now.   He's just coming out of his grave, and he might go in
again if I went away, and then I should have to begin to raise him
all over again."

It is lamentable that Sophy was not of an imaginative nature
for thus was thrown away a picture that more than one of those
few painters who had as yet discovered Crossmarsh and Windgates and all that country would have thought worth risking an
academic rejection for.   There was the witch's magic chamber—
dark,silent, secret, cell-like, as such chambers ought to be.   Only
enough sunlight came through the lattice to bring out the gloom
of the background, and, by leaving the corners untouched, to leave
an unexplored further region of darkness, in which the fancy
might work spells at will.   A veritable ghostly outline was afforded
by the heap of straw—at any rate, any ordinary brush could easily
conjure up the suggestion out of a material whereof ghosts have
been so often made.   And there, at the entrance, framed by the
black oaken doorway, stood the witch herself, with the pale day
of the skylight bearing full upon her face—a wild young witch,
disturbed in the midst of her ghastly incantations by a smiling
blue-eyed child.

"Oh ! but won't the ghost wait ? " said Sophy.   " And you've
been with him all day ! "

" No ; he *can't* wait," said Rosamond, " and *I* can't wait——"

" Then he's a selfish creature," said Sophy.   " Can't you tell him
that if there's one thing I hate in all the world, it's having to talk
to those Pitcairns ?   And you do it so nicely, and I've so much to
show Oswald.   Oh, Rosamond, I don't like your ghost to-day ! "

" The Pitcairns ?   Are they here too ? "

" Yes ; but I'm sorry I said it now.   Of course, if you wouldn't
come down to Oswald, you won't for the Pitcairns.   Well, what
shall I say about why you can't come ? "

Rosamond looked lingeringly behind her, then up at the skylight, and pushed back her tumbled mane.

"Of course it's dreadfully provoking: but—I do really want to see—the Pitcairns," said she. And she meant the Pitcairns, and did not mean Oswald Hargrave, for all that she made that pause before the name—so false a witness a tell-tale pause may be. Whatever the nature of her secret incantations, the heart of the witch was too honestly absorbed in them to desire the company of an earthly farmer who knew no magic but that of phosphates and steam boilers. But there were reasons why Mr. Pitcairn, though reputed a bore, represented to the mind of Rosamond the great, wide, unknown, wonderful world that lay beyond Crossmarsh —nay, even beyond Windgates: beyond everywhere. "I have a question," she said, "that I want to ask Mr. Pitcairn. I want to ask him if, when he was a missionary, he ever saw the upas tree."

"Oh! that will be delightful!" cried Sophy.

"I can take Oswald into the garden, and uncle can show Mrs. Pitcairn his cabinets, and you can talk to Mr. Pitcairn about the upas tree. They're all safe to stop to tea, and that will suit us all. Rosamond, you *will* get the ghost to wait till after tea?"

Rosamond looked down—some distance down—at her sister, and then, for the first time, smiled. She had, at any rate, laid one ghost—that of temper. Sophy, after all, was dearer to her even than her murderer's spirit, and the more masculine nature, as a matter of course, gave way. I have said that Rosamond was the one who nature ruled. And even so do men rule—by obeying her. If there be one grain of paradox in the relation between Sophy and Rosamond, between man and woman, between mind and matter, Science shall decide.

The scene in the witch's cave had not occupied many minutes but still, with its necessary sequence of a slight toilette, long enough to have assembled the visitors in the drawing-room. Except as regarded the stables, there was a decidedly old-fashioned air about everybody and everything about Cliff Cottage which unmistakably embraced its two young mistresses. Both Rosamond and Sophy were certainly what is called old-fashioned young people, each in her separate and different way. Indeed, it would be surprising had it not been so, seeing how completely out of the common air of the living modern world their bringing up had been—all in all to one another, and otherwise companionless, save for one antiquarian uncle and a grave, grown-up young man. Even in their talks with one another, simple and unaffected as they were, they had developed certain mannerisms, which might strike outsiders as being quaintly set and formal. Sophy, in spite of her own individuality, very considerably reflected Rosamond when in company, and the contrast between her own self and Rosamond's reflection made her often appear the more singular child of the two. The grown-up sayings and the long, sometimes even pedantic words were odder in her than in the elder and statelier Rosamond, who might at times pass almost as a real woman for an hour together. Oswald wondered sometimes whether Rosamond had ever been a real child—sometimes whether she would ever cease to be one. And nobody else ever studied her at all.

This, however, is to stray from the drawing-room, where Uncle Æneas and his visitors were gathered. The host himself was very decidedly and appropriately old fashioned, in accordance with his surroundings, for it was full two generations since the Fanes of Crossmarsh had bought any new furniture worth mentioning. The room was therefore as little like the results of modern fashion, and as much like what modern fashion fancies itself to be restoring, as can possibly be imagined. Art was utterly absent, and chance reigned supreme—that chance who alone is possessed of really good taste in such matters. Moreover, the place had its traditions, which Rosamond and Sophy accepted as matters of hereditary faith, without any insight into the æsthetics of them. The window was open, but the air of the room was mysteriously fragrant with the forgotten mysteries of *pot-pourri* instead of the stinging scent of the sea shore. The frame was ready, but empty; and, when Rosamond entered, with Sophy's hand in hers, the picture, so Oswald thought, breathed into being, and the frame became full.

Oswald was lounging in the window ; Uncle Æneas was displaying the ancient British hatchet to a plain little old lady, in a real bonnet and flat grey curls; and the Rector, a burly clergyman, evidently considerably younger than his wife, was apparently delivering a lecture to the world at large. The two girls had not seen enough strangers in their lives to have caught the shyness that only seeing more and more strangers can partly cure. Sophy at once left her sister for Oswald, and Rosamond, taking a quick kiss from Mrs. Pitcairn, and a beaming handshake from the Rector, without interrupting the discourse, settled herself quietly on an out-of-the-way sofa. Oswald could certainly have gone to her, but he was Sophy's prisoner; and, though bold enough to Uncle Æneas, that very boldness had rendered him embarrassed before the girl. However, he would speak to her presently; and, meanwhile, any common, public speech would be out of keeping with his humour. And besides, there seemed, to his eyes, always something new about Rosamond. Whenever he saw her again, after however short an absence, she had spread out some new and unexpected charm—and a new charm meant a change that required fresh study before adding to his heart's familiar picture.

For his love for this child was still childlike; he foresaw the passion that it would become some day, and meanwhile, lived in an air of conscious hope, which is the purest air that a man can breathe. He, rightly or wrongly, reverenced in Rosamond the woman who was yet to be, so soon as the unapproachable angel of the bud should give place to the visible and gracious angel of the open flower. These were not his conscious words, but they were his thoughts; and it did not end in sentiment, but in the fixed resolve he had spoken to Uncle Æneas—that he, who alone had perceived the beauty of the bud, should alone gather the flower. That he did not wholly understand what was hidden and growing in the closed petals he perfectly well knew. But he was content to be aware of mysteries, without a thought of forcing the petals apart before their time. And so, where Rosamond was, it was Oswald, for all his age and knowledge, who was shy.

"As you're so curious in axes, Fane," said Mr. Pitcairn, in his rich voice, by which an Ulster man would have been reminded of his allegiance to the pious and immortal memory of the Prince of Orange, "you must come over some day soon—drop in to pot-luck, you know—and see some of mine; *I've* got axes—aye, and some with the blood on them still!"

Uncle Æneas smiled superior, and stroked his own last new treasure gently—a singularly perfect specimen of the times before flint had wholly yielded to steel.

"I daresay you must have gathered some curious things," said he. "But they are the work of savages, after all. Now this—how old this is, heaven knows."

"And what were any of us but savages, before Cromwell?" asked the Rector. "Come, Miss Rosamond, you've learned your books well enough for that, I dare say. Now I like natives myself, because I know how to deal with them. Maria can tell you that: I forget, though—the savages were in my first wife's time. Anyhow, *she* could tell."

" Do you like Mr. Pitcairn, Oswald ?" whispered Sophy, in the window. " Because if you do——"

"The first Mrs. Pitcairn," said the second, as if the allusion, and the error, had been the most delicate and natural in the world, " was the lady who shared the earlier portion of Mr. Pitcairn's life when he was working among the South Seas. I never had the pleasure of her acquaintance, but I have her portrait among the other curiosities at home. She was not exactly what in England, at least, would be considered beautiful, but she must have been interesting, decidedly. She, her picture, has an extraordinary darkness of complexion, and there is a singular crispness about the hair which is quite unique in its way. I consider it one of my misfortunes that I was never acquainted with the first Mrs. Pitcairn."

Having thus in the sweetest manner, executed condign vengeance upon the Rector, the second Mrs. Pitcairn, whose money had paid for his presentation to Crossmarsh, embraced the whole company with a contented smile.

"Do you detest Mrs. Pitcairn, Oswald?" whispered Sophy again. " Because if you don't——"

" But the question is, Pitcairn," said Uncle Æneas, ever ready to effect a diversion in the direction of peace and harmony, " how you did deal with the savages in the South Seas. I must say it would puzzle me, magistrate as I am, and with savages enough in Crossmarsh, and in Windgates to——"

" How did *I* deal with them?" asked the Rector, upon whom the delicate satire of his richer half had been entirely thrown away —" why, as easy as I looked at them. I took the natives one by one, man to man. I kept a lot of blue glass beads in one tail pocket, and a bit of stick, with eight ounces of lead at the end, in the other. Then I preached at him just as hard as I could, till I'd done. If he gave in before I was hoarse, I gave him a handful of beads; if he didn't, I took out the bit of stick and made him feel reason. I made more converts that way than any man on the station; and there wasn't one I made but stuck to his guns and turned out well."

" Yes, Sophy," whispered Oswald back, " yes, I think I do rather like Mr. Pitcairn."

" But did they never preach back, or strike back?" asked Rosamond. " I don't think you'd have converted *me* that way."

'Certainly not, my dear; I should have begun on you with the blue beads."

"You must not take everything Mr. Pitcairn says seriously," said Mrs. Pitcairn. "Of course he does not mean that he really converted the heathen of the South Seas with those sort of things. But you know his way."

"But I do mean it, Maria," said the ex-missionary; "I do mean it, every word. I used every device but rum. To that I never would give in. I just took hold of a semi-brute, and by main force I made a man of him, or as much of a man as might be. If I'd taken any other tack I should only have made a humbug of him. Perhaps I didn't make quite so many bad Christians as some did, but I know I made a good many decent savages. And that, I maintain, is the only way to begin. Treat your native like a child, tell him to be good, and tell him how; and if he won't obey you, knock him down till he's tired."

"Didn't any native ever try to convert you," asked Uncle Æneas, "on the same lines?"

"Often—often; but the same man never tried again. But about that new old chopper of yours, Fane. What barbarians our ancestors must have been—before Cromwell. My savages would be ashamed to turn out a weapon like that. You should see my lances and knives, as I said before. It would make another chapter for your book. By-the-way how's that getting on? Have you found out who was buried in Pix-Knoll?"

"Ah," said Uncle Æneas, with a shake of the head, and a wise smile, "you've hit the question there. When the world reads the twenty-seventh chapter of the History of the Barrow in Crossmarsh, commonly called Pix-Knoll for which I am collecting the materials at this moment, I think the world will stare. Think of it—every pre-historic theory that has ever been invented, overturned in an instant by things like this that I hold in my hand! I cannot but feel myself justified in thinking that a special Providence caused such an over-flowing mine of pre-historic discovery as Pix-Knoll to be discovered on *my* land."

"Oh, Mr. Fane!" protested Mrs. Pitcairn.

"Why not? If Providence, as we believe, watches over history why not over the records also? As I was saying to Moldwarp only the other day, if he could only find in that Barrow a Phœnician sun-dial, of a certain peculiar form, my theory would be *totus*

teres atque rotundus—that is to say, Mrs. Pitcairn, without a flaw.
Yes, as sure as we are sitting here, Rome herself was a colony
not from Troy, but from Pix-Knoll."

"A strange fellow, that Moldwarp," said the Rector.

"I'm told," said Mrs. Pitcairn, "that he works in the Barrow
on Sundays. But, surely, that *can't* be true."

"I know nothing about that," said Mr. Fane, with some guilty
haste. "He is certainly an extraordinary man. With no education,
and, when he came here, without even local knowledge, he can
hardly walk ten yards without coming upon some most important
relic of antiquity. He brings me everything he finds that strikes
him as out of the way, and it's wonderful how seldom he brings me
what isn't worth its weight in gold. And yet with all his talent
for finding, he learns nothing. I reasoned out once that there
must have been a coin of King Caractacus in that barrow; *must*
have been, or else a most important piece of evidence would have
been wanting to my theory. Now nobody ever found, that I
heard of, a coin of King Caractacus anywhere. Well, about a
month after, Moldwarp finds, in the barrow, what turned out to
be a coin of King Caractacus beyond doubt or question. And yet
Moldwarp can't be got to call him anything but the King o'
Carrots to this day! If he could only find that Phœnician sun-
dial—but, well, one can't have everything."

"Too true," said Mrs. Pitcairn, solemnly. "Yes; I found
that out long ago. And it gets truer and truer every
day."

"And a good thing too," said the Rector. "A good big want's
the best thing a man can owe. I only wish I had one myself,
but with such a parish as Crossmarsh, and such a wife as Maria,
faith, I'm afraid it's past praying for. And what's the result?
I'm the only miserable soul in the room. There's you, Fane,
wanting a Phœnician sun-dial; and when you've got it, and
Moldwarp has drunk the price of it, he'll be all the worse, and
you none the better. There's Hargrave—being a farmer, he
wants wet weather, since it's fine; that's the calling for a man to
enjoy himself in, for it's all 'I want' from year's end to year's
end. There's Maria: she wants new furniture for the drawing-
room; so, as I like to make her happy, I won't let her lose her
want too soon. There's Sophy, wanting a new doll. And here's
Rosamond, wanting—wanting—no; I don't know what Miss
Rosamond wants, unless she'll tell."

" Pooh," said Uncle Æneas, remembering what Oswald wanted of Rosamond, and glad of an opportunity for once more setting his foot down, " pooh— Rosamond wanted the purple jar."

" And she got it too," said the Rector, " and made another point to my moral thereby! But she wasn't the only Rosamond, Fane. There was a fair Rosamond, who wanted—who got, any way—what she choose, and wasn't the happier for that, anyhow. And there was Rosamond who was made to drink wine out of her father's skull. And there's was Charles Lamb's Rosamond, poor thing. By-the-way, what a queer thing it is, Fane, that all the Rosamonds, in history or fiction, or drama, are always unlucky, or miserable, or no better than they should be, and come to bad ends! That's queer; and then they ask, What's in a name? Faith, I'll give old Moldwarp five shillings, if he'll find me a Rosamond that didn't come to a bad end, either through somebody else's fault, or her own."

" Oh, Maurice!" exclaimed his wife, " how can you say such dreadful things? And with the girl in the room! It's enough to frighten her!"

And, when they came to think of it, it did, as their exceedingly unpolished specimen of a rector had said, seem very strange that so graceful a name should have proved so invariably unfortunate to its bearers. It struck Oswald, though he scorned superstition, more than merely unpleasantly. Why could not that vulgar Irish parson from the South Seas hold his blundering tongue? But love and superstition are substance and shadow, and he racked his memory for a Rosamond of good omen in vain.

" Oswald!" said Sophy, pulling his arm, " is that true?"

Rosamond herself felt a curious sensation, as if a spell had suddenly been cast upon her. Of course, it is a fine thing to have a tragic destiny—people make one the heroine of its histories and romances—but she had rather liked her name hitherto, and now it seemed to turn against her, and to put out a poisoned sting. Perhaps ninety-nine girls would have felt nothing of the sort, and have taken the Rector's awkward chaff with a laugh. But Rosamond chanced to be the hundredth girl.

" Then Mr. Pitcairn, I will be the first fortunate Rosamond said she, flushing.

" And the first good one, my dear," said Mrs. Pitcairn, with more kindness than her small sub-acid manner would have led one to expect from her.

"There, then, you have found *your* want," said the Rector, feeling that he had been making some sort of mistake somewhere and somehow. "So you want——"

"There, that'll do," said Uncle Æneas, "don't tease the girl. How should she know what she wants at her age? The thing's absurd." It almost seemed as if he were out of temper about something less than an injury to a Celt. But Oswald knew why: and, feeling through sympathy that she was feeling strangely, though it was impossible that he or any other reasonable person should guess the cause, he left Sophy, and seated himself by Rosamond.

"I think I'll tell you a story," said Mr. Pitcairn, *à propos*, as it seemed, of nothing. "When I first went out as a missionary, I got acquainted with a curious kind of a customer named Green. He'd knocked about for years in those parts, and certainly knew a lot more about the tracks and the natives than any other Englishman. By the way, it was from him I got one or two of those little wrinkles we were talking about a minute ago. Some people said he was a liar, and some said he wasn't—but though he had unquestionably seen strange things, it's equally true that there were strange things to be seen. He wasn't much of a Christian, but he wasn't a bad sort for a man of the world, and we got on very well, on the whole, though I was uppish in those days, and thought—well, never mind. Anyhow, we agreed to differ : and there are worse sorts of friendship than that, by a long way. One day we were taking a walk along a cliff, when I saw distinctly, with my naked eye, an outline of coast that I had never yet seen with a spy-glass. I suppose it was some effect of refraction, and pointed it out to Green. It was a low, dark blue line with white specks of breakers here and there. I shall never forget his reply. He told me that to that coast, only visible, as I had guessed, in certain abnormal states of the air, he had once gone—I forgot from where—years ago. He had found an island, I forgot how large, where no European foot had ever stepped, but where he had found a civilization—yes, a civilization—that puts our highest dreams to shame. Everybody was good, and everybody was happy. I suppose there were no Rosamonds there."

Oswald's eyes were secretly upon Rosamond, towards whom his open declaration of his life's plan had inspired him with deeper feelings. She was listening intently, as a child to an Arabian voyage. At her name he felt her start, and he took her hand, while Sophy came from the window, and laid her head upon his knee.

"Green was not well up in theology," continued the Rector, "and all he could gather was that the people were expecting a kind of natural death, or national euthanasia, to be preceded by the reign of a woman from over the sea. Their institutions, oddly enough, were the exact contrary of ours—and yet they were happy! I'll tell you all about that later on. They treated Green well, but wouldn't let him go, for fear he should discover the existence of the island, though how it had never been discovered before was certainly a mystery: unless, indeed, Green was lying. But he got home-sick, though where his home was he would have been puzzled to say; and at last he persuaded them to let him do. But it was on condition that he would never name the place to mortal man or woman, or give the faintest clue to its discovery."

"Yet he told you?" asked Oswald, who certainly hesitated between acceptance of the general reputation of Mr. Green and a suspicion that the Rector was inventing an allegory, after the style of the vision of Mirza.

"A man must tell somebody," said the Rector. "He had no Maria, so he told me. Of course I said I'd boat over my beads and my bit of stick the very next day. Don't, said Green—the people swore like Genii in the Arabian nights, that the next foreigner who set foot on their shores, they'd kill him, and the next, and the next, and so on, taking for granted that Green had betrayed them; and they'd no more look at my beads or care for my stick, than if they were Britons—and not half so much, said he. They'd turn up their noses at our crown jewels, and were proof against words and blows. However, he'd said he teach me the language, so that if I wanted martyrdom I might go under the best advantages. I got as far as the eighty-ninth letter of the alphabet, and to my shame, gave in. Whether Green invented that alphabet, as he went on to keep me from finding out—Green, I don't venture to say. That nameless island, with its extraordinary civilization, has never, I believe, been discovered to this day: and Green disappeared, I'm sorry to say, under a cloud. But, for all that, his account of everything was beyond invention, and invariably held together: especially about the expected woman, who was to bring everything to an end. However, the most wonderful part of the story is still to come, and

2 A

the moral. One day Green was carried before the Sultan, or whatever they called him—"

Boom! It was the sound of a heavy gun from the landside.

    •   •   •   •   •   •

Mrs. Pitcairn started from her slumber over a thrice-told tale with a broken snort; Uncle Æneas rubbed from his eyes the dream of a Phœnician sun-dial; Sophy slept soundly on, with her head still on Oswald's knee. It was monstrously impolite, but the weather was warm, and the Rector's yarn was unquestionably dull as well as preposterously absurd; it was a parable that seemed likely to end in a sermon. Only Oswald and Rosamond were wide awake; Rosamond alone was listening to the Rector with all her heart in her ears, as if the tale were fascinatingly true. The heavy "boom!" seemed to mark a crisis: and she also started, and look round.

"What's that?" said the Rector. "I didn't know we had artillery here."

"It's a convict escaped from Lowmoor!" exclaimed Uncle Æneas, rising as if at a sudden call of duty. "That's what *that* means—by George!"

CHAPTER III.

He'd find you almost Everything,
From Venus' Zone to Saturn's Ring:
Each stray that ever Earth or Sky had
From Jest's lost Point to vanisht Pleiad—
The Crown that Cæsar ne'er put on;
The Crystal Shoon of Cendrillon;
Last Summer's Rose; lost Lover's Vow,
Or Lay that killed the ancient Cow;
The perisht Books that we assign
The Titus Livius Patavine,
And eke the Secret of the Rune
That's writ on t'other side the Moon
And Wand of Witch, and Drug of Hakim—
And if he cannot find, he'll make 'em.

THE inland part of the parish of Crossmarsh is not beautiful. The cliffs and bays are magnificent, but the moors leading up from them are barren and dull—at least for all those who do not understand the beauty of Nature nude. The dullest and the most barren part of all, and also the most solitary of all, is distinguished by a long mound rising sharply and clearly from the Downs, in shape and size suggesting the grave of Goliath. On a closer approach one used to find the mound cut through in three trenches, one from end to end, and two, at equi-

distant intervals, crosswise. And this was the wonderful
Barrow of Crossmarsh, vulgarly called, from immemorial times,
Pix-Knoll.

This was the centre to which the mystery which enfolds the pre-
historic history of Man was to be traced back and thus revealed.
Enthusiastic hobby-rider as he was, Uncle Æneas had been guilty
of no sort of exaggeration in stating that extraordinary, nay, incredible, results, had been already obtained from Pix-Knoll. For
full exposition Uncle Æneas, like a prudent antiquary, who for-
sees a contest with all British and all German learning, was biding
his time. He knew that Cliff Cottage contained a collection of
startling evidences of a startling theory that no museum in Europe
could approach, much less rival: but, a true collector, his own
satisfaction was all-sufficient for him until the day should come—
nay, it would be sufficient even if that day never came. For the
present his notes and materials were in too chaotic a condition
to be of use to any but the owner, wherefore there is as yet
no occasion to make a critical examination of a theory that made
Tyre and Sidon colonies from Crossmarsh, and England the mother
instead of the daughter of the world.

Rosamond and Sophy held prime places in the museum of Uncle
Æneas's heart: but Uncle Æneas's soul was buried in the barrow.
Uncle Æneas had been fortunate in his barrow, but thrice fortu-
nate in Silver Moldwarp, the man who found—Everything.

Silver Moldwarp was indefatigable in the search for evidence
that he did not understand. It was true that Sundays as well as
week days found him in or about Pix-Knoll, and it was in one of
the cross cuts that he was sitting now—not exactly searching, but
working hard, though the sun was blazing. In the corner of the
cut he had chosen he was invisible to all eyes save that of the sun.
He was a lean, wiry, undersized man, of an indefinite age, one who
could never have been really young, and seemed incapable of ever
becoming really old. He was dressed in a rough, almost ragged
suit of clothes, in which elegance was recklessly sacrificed to ease.
In spite of the heat, his head, chest, and arms were bare, displaying
a superabundance of hair and muscle. The man's strength was
evidently out of all proportion to his size, and very likely to his
age. His face was extraordinarily full of character, considering
that he did not appear to be above the condition of a common
labourer, if indeed he stood so high. Aquiline features, worthy of a
field marshal and a full, low, projecting brow, befitting a lawyer

or an engineer, were flatly contradicted by a pair of comically
twinkling eyes, suggesting that union of cunning and folly which
constitute the buffoon. The mouth, in its character, though partly
hidden by a scrubby moustache and half beard, agreed with the
eyes, rather than with the nose and brow, so far as it could be
seen. It was weak, and hung half-open, displaying teeth that were
the reverse of ornamental. Yet—to come at once to the essential
matter—he looked an honest fellow, despite his want of facial
harmony.

Sophy, with the unreasonable impulsiveness that characterised
her opinions of her fellow creatures, had said, at first sight, that
she did not like Mr. Moldwarp; and to this opinion, she
had stuck, with consistent obstinacy. In this opinion, however,
she stood almost alone. There was a tacit and mutual avoidance
between him and the Rectory, but then the Rectory did not guide
the parish in social matters. So far as these were concerned, the
" Feathers " beat the Church hollow: for even the ploughmen and
fishermen of Crossmarsh, as became the proven fathers of civilized
humanity, had certain aristocratic sympathies, and felt that the
parson was somehow too much one of themselves to take the command.   And Silver Moldwarp had proved a real acquisition
not only to the customers of the " Feathers."   He was a capital
customer himself while it would have paid the landlord to
have kept him in drink for nothing, or even to have
given him a trifle for what he consumed.   He could do
wonderful things. He could make a jack-knife disappear from a
fisherman's fist into a ploughman's hat, and play a score more
tricks, which, being coarser, were even better calculated to please
their simple minds. Better still, he could break a kitchen poker
by striking it upon his bare arm, and straighten a horse-shoe between his ugly fangs. And he could pay for other men's beer, as
well as for his own.   Finally, he had the prestige which attaches
to an accomplished stranger : nobody knew whence he came. But
as both his honesty and his good-fellowship proved above reproach,
and as he seemed, though well able to maintain a quarrel, incapable
of making one, and as he had regular employment as Squire Fane's
hobbygrubber, he speedily became a recognised institution into
whose origin nobody dreamed of inquiring. A fellow parishioner
who should make handsome weekly earnings by picking up
bits of flint and crockery would have been regarded with envy.
Moldwarp, as a foreigner, had been entitled to take a line of his

own, especially as it interfered with nobody. When he was neither in the barrow, nor at the " Feathers," nor searching, inch by inch, along the ploughed furrows, or the streams, or the sea-shore, he lived in a two-roomed stone hut in the middle of a potato patch, which Squire Fane allowed him rent free.

The most noticeable point about Silver Moldwarp, however, and at the same time the least likely to escape ordinary masculine observation, was the extraordinary contrast between his general strength and roughness and the delicacy of his hands. His fingers were long and fine enough for a lady's and were distinguished by those tapering tips that are supposed to note the artist, or at least the exceptionally skilled craftsman. Such fingers have also been observed in the superior order of pickpockets, to whom their sensibility in touch is as important as to a surgeon. At the present moment, instead of following his unlearned instinct upon the traces of an ancient coin or specimen of stoneware, he was using his fingers, with a rough file in them, upon a large piece of flint, raw from the hands of nature.

There was the absorption of the artist in the man's whole being as he crouched over his rather niggling labour, and he worked with such energy that the perspiration poured from his forehead, less from the heat than from his obvious mental strain. A separate thought seemed to enter into every touch that he gave with his file. So deeply occupied was he that he failed to hear the gallop of a horse over the hard turf that led landward from the barrow, and he started up in doubly hot confusion, as a strong voice called out :

"Holloa there, my man! Stand fast there; which way is he gone ? "

Moldwarp, with a practised hand, threw his flint and his file under his hat, in such a manner that only a professed conjurer could have been aware of the action, and saw a prison warder, in the well-known uniform of Lowmoor, reining his horse at the edge of the barrow.

" Which way ? Who's gone ? " he asked in a rough country accent which had, however, no kindred with the Crossmarsh tongue.

" An escaped convict. Didn't you hear the gun ? A youngish man, in the prison uniform——"

" I've seen ne'er a soul," said Moldwarp; " nor e'er a body nyther. No convic' 's been nigh here."

" Who are you ? What's your name ? "

"Silver Moldwarp, labourer to Squire Fane. That's who I am."

"To Squire Fane, eh? How long have you been on this hill? All day?"

"Ay—all day."

"And you've seen nobody."

"Nobody never sees nobody nigh here, but me and Squire Fane."

The warder looked baffled, and swore. With the best of reasons in his own mind for believing that the convict had made in the direction of Croesmarsh, and with the certainty that he had disappeared close by the convenient excavations of Pix-Knoll, it was hard to swallow that a man, who had been on the spot all day, and was notoriously hawk-eyed and quick eared, should have seen nothing of the Lowmoor uniform.

"Hold my horse here," said he, "I must have a look into those cuttings of yours."

Moldwarp obeyed, while the warder, cocking a revolver so that any temptation to horse-stealing or to any other tricks might be put to instant flight, let himself drop into the barrow. The search was easy enough, for the cuttings were of the simplest kind, and contained no corners where a man might hide.

"Any way, nobody's there now," said the warder, still half suspicious of Moldwarp, "whatever there may have been. He must have made for one of the caves. I'll ride on to Squire Fane's. If you see or hear anything, let your master know."

Moldwarp scarcely waited to see the warder ride off, before returning to the spot where he had left his hat, resuming his incomprehensible work with flint and file.

"That's the way with the likes o' them," he thought, or rather muttered more than half aloud, after the manner of men who live and labour alone. "A man must be sharp to get clear of Lowmoor in this sunshine—and a sharp man wouldn't make for Squire Fane's Folly, nor the caves— he'd know that's where a fool would go, because it's there a pack of fools would go straight to find him. There must be a spice o' fox about that chap there. Well, 'tis naught to me."

At the end of about an hour the careful and minute filing came to an end. He put the file into his jacket pocket, and drew from the same place a small hammer of a rather peculiar shape, with which he began to clip his flint lightly. It was curious to watch the dexterity with which he made tiny flakes of stone obey the delicate touches of his hammer ; how, if he required to remove the smallest speck in one particular point, just that speck came off in exactly the right place and the right way. Presently the flint grew visibly into the form of an arrow-head, of a shape well known to antiquaries, and the resemblance was rapidly increased when the barb also came into being under the presence of a brad-awl that took the place of the hammer. The barbed arrow-head was made quite as well as the best in the cabinet of Uncle Æneas ; and yet it was not made a bit better, which was certainly more curious still. In short, it was an exact reproduction of the real thing, and for a triumph of modern art—bearing similar signs of age and burial.

The long and ceaseless practice, the manual skill, and the ar-tistic, even scientific instinct which had gone to the production of the forgery were worthy of all admiration, and should have given Silver Moldwarp high rank in a more recognised calling. As things were, he was compelled to find for himself the admiration which circumstances denied him from others.

" There ; that's older than old King Carrots," said he, as he examined his *chef-d'œuvre* for a possible flaw. " It is wonderful what a man can find if he goes the right road to look for 'em. I wouldn't wonder if I chance upon that Fenian sun-dyle some day, after all, if I could only get hold of a big enough block to seek for'n in. Granic, now, might do. It ought to be worth two pounds——Ugh ! "

The knuckles of two fists were pressed tightly into his throat, and forced from him a strangled cry. In the same breath he was dragged and forced down backwards, while his feet flew high into the air.

Moldwarp was a strong man and struggled strongly. But, taken at this complete disadvantage from behind, his efforts were in vain, and he could only lie back panting under a knee upon his chest and the two hands that did not for a moment leave his throat free. His eyes were free, however : and they saw in his assailant a powerful young fellow, with a smooth-shaven brown face, cropped hair, and the unmistakable costume of a convicted felon.

" Murder—you're strangling me ! " gasped Moldwarp.

" Wait a bit," said the convict, coolly, and in the accent of a gentleman. " It's no use your calling for help. If we were in earshot I shouldn't have turned up quite so soon. I don't want your life, my man ; but, you see the state of things, I want your clothes."

" Ugh ! how can I give 'em when——"

The convict's fingers relaxed for a moment, and Moldwarp gave a sudden spring that almost set him free.

" None of that, my man," said the convict, giving his throat and his chest an extra squeeze. " I want your clothes. I don't want to kill you; but if I can't get them except of a dead body, then——"

There was a cool desperation about the convict that told of a man who would be as good as his word : and his plight was unquestionably at the last point of extremity. Moldwarp realised that the case was neither for feats of strength nor for sleight of hand.

" I give in—there ! Only let go my windpipe and let me up," said he.

The convict removed one hand, but only to reach a crowbar. " Then get on your knees, and off with every rag you've got on. If you lift one knee one inch from the ground till you're as naked as you were born, 'ware head, for down comes the bar."

Moldwarp rose to his knees, drawing in a great gulp of delicious air. He moved slowly, for he was calculating the odds of a sudden rush, and of a wrestler's hug with the convict at close quarters, and therefore within the reach of the crowbar. He had the discretion, which is valour's better half, but he had the valour besides. It was valour that left him the wits to study his assailant, and to avoid rashness : and so perhaps it would be truer to say that valour is the better part of discretion.

In the first place, he could see that the convict was no common felon of his own class, a forger, perhaps, at any rate, guilty of no savage or vulgar crime. Silver Moldwarp had a natural contempt for rogues who allowed themselves to be found out, and at the same time he could not feel that this particular convict, though he wore the garb of discovery, was contemptible. His artistic nature could sympathise with the cunning which, by not taking at once either to the barrow or the sea caverns, had baffled the warder. He was also unconsciously influenced by that magnetic something about the convict which distinguished the few who are born to be obeyed from the many who are born to obey. After a long look from the convict to the crowbar and back again, Moldwarp ended by smiling in a not unfriendly way.

" You're a rough customer," said he. " But I don't see why you'd a call to throttle a fellow creature, before you'd known you had a call. It's nought to me whether you're in or out of Low-moor—not to me."

"I don't want smooth words, my man—I want your clothes. I don't suppose my liberty means more to you than to anybody else, but I fancy the reward for catching me will mean a good deal. Now then—strip away. Off with your jacket, man, to begin."

He gave the slightest jerk to the bar ; and Moldwarp was conscious of an uncomfortable feeling that there was only one thing to be done. As soon as his arms became embarrassed in getting out of their sleeves, the convict whipped off his own jacket, recovered the use of his own arms the first of the two, and was again ready with the bar. The process was repeated till both men were stripped to the skin.

"That'll be a new trick for the 'Feathers'" thought Silver Moldwarp—"how to get out of your bags and your boots, without lifting a knee over an inch from the ground. Well: live and learn." The convict threw his prison clothes in a bundle to Moldwarp, and began hastily to cover himself with the suit he had just acquired. He was considerably the bigger man, and the clothes were a bad misfit ; but then they were also so much the worse for wear, that they had hung loosely about their former owner, and would not have looked conspicuously out of place on any tramp of any size. "There," said the convict, "we haven't found one another such bad fellows after all. I won't apologise—my liberty is of more use to me than your old clothes are to you. You can get another suit, but I mayn't be able to get another liberty—if I lose this one. Good day."

Silver Moldwarp made no attempt to attack the convict, while the latter was dressing, thus, it may be thought, losing an opportunity. He had either yielded to a magnetic authority, or knew a better way of recovering his own.

"Eh, but the chap's a born fool, after all," muttered he, as he watched the man striding out quickly and boldly towards the sea. "He dodged the warders, that's sharp enough, and I'd like to know how 'twas done ; but he shifts his gaol bird's feathers for clothes that's better known in Crossmarsh than the 'Feathers,' and are enough to hang him in; and he's let me see him naked, tattoos and all, so that I could swear to him when his hair's long, and his beard's grown, and his eyes under glasses. There's a fool's trick, if there ever was one : and now he's taken the straight road to Squire Fane's. Well—it's nought to do with me, barring that I'll

get a new suit for nothing. I'll wear these canvas things to the
'Feathers' to-night, and alter the twist of my mug, and give the
folks a scare. Ay, I *will* have a try after that Fenian dyle. But——"
All at once Silver Moldwarp turned absolutely pale. Mechanically he put his hand to the part of his prison jacket, where the
pocket should have been, and naturally, found that his hammer,
file, only he knew what besides, had changed hands with the exchange of clothes. But it must have been something more than
even this loss that made him groan aloud, scramble out of the
barrow like a madman, and hurry to his own hut, a good mile off,
at the top of his speed. He alone could tell what, when the convict came to be caught, would be found upon him besides a hammer
and a file.

CHAPTER IV.

When she is far, and I
 Ride o'er the meadow
Under the sunny sky,
 Over the shadow—
How it is easy then
 Boldly to woo her
While down the winding glen
 Speed I unto her.

Scant while for answering
 Love shall allow her—
Space while a wild bee's wing
 Brushes a flower . . . .
Nay, but the path hath grown
 Nearer and nearer—
Farther and farther flown
 All, save to Fear her ;

THE sudden boom of the gun, breaking the Rector's traveller's
tale off in the very middle, had fired the imagination of Rosamond—always in a state of tinder ready to be set blazing
by any chance spark that might happen to fall. She had not
often been far from the cottage in all her life—never what
Mr. Pitcairn would have called far—but she had once driven past
the gates and under the walls of Lowmoor, and these had made
upon her, though it was many years ago, an impression never to
be forgotten. "That is where all the bad people go," was the ex-
planation she had received of its existence when she was even
younger than now. But even such commonplace words as those
meant a great deal to Rosamond. Where all the bad people go—
all : not merely some, but all! Why, it must be the very main
gate of Hell, with a separate sin for every brick that had gone to
its building, and with those for warders that were not good even

to dream of. The thought was her own, for the theology that surrounded her childhood was ancient and simple, and was based largely on very realistic images and exceedingly plain words. Once again she had driven past Lowmoor, but she had not again seen it, for on that second occasion she had shut her eyes, and had not opened them again till the building was safely on the other side of the hill.

Growing older, she naturally learned more of what an earthly prison-house means, and what it is for. But, though thus enabled to build a certain structure of facts, upon her original quicksand of fancy, the sand was ready to swallow up the house upon the very smallest provocation. Lowmoor, in her mind, was still a place apart from all else, having nothing to do with the common light and air that gave light to Crossmarsh, and Windgates and the Sea. The building was to her invisible, but the idea of it was a shadow often falling over her mind when she was alone, as if it were in itself a thought of evil. One of the books she had most ardently devoured was a stitched pamphlet that had come in Uncle Æneas's magisterial way—some sort of official return, or report, giving an account of the routine, dietary, and other such interesting matters connected with Lowmoor Goal. In one sense, it half-piqued, half-satisfied her curiosity, but it lamentably disappointed her on the whole. Men, whose hands were red with the blood of their fellow-men, were confined in Lowmoor. How could the knowledge that he was allowed so many pints of soup, and so many ounces of bread, and no tobacco, help her to see into the heart of a man with such a hand? The contrast between Cliff Cottage, with its quiet garden and its changeless days, and that mansion of darkness, near enough to be felt all the more for not being quite near enough to be seen, remained a more awful mystery even than before. It had never suggested itself to Rosamond that such fathomless thoughts as these about a hideous parallelogram, used as a fold for the world's black sheep, were unshared by Sophy. Her own ways of looking at things, she took for granted, were common to all mankind—even by old Moldwarp, she supposed.

But the idea that a living man had actually escaped from Lowmoor! Such a thing scarcely needed the added solemnity of a great gun's thunder to impress her profoundly. Not only was it new in all her experience, but it was new to all her ideas, which drew their life from the original notion of the visible *Inferno* aft⋯

all. She knew something, from the old stitched report, of the difficulties, supposed to be insuperable, which stood in the way of such a deed. But something more than statistical descriptions made her feel it to be a prodigious oversetting of natural laws. The voice of the gun through the hot, heavy summer afternoon, seemed to Rosamond less a mere announcement of a marvel than some supernatural effect necessarily accompanying the return of a condemned soul to the world.

"It's an unprecedented thing," said Uncle Æneas, when that part of the afternoon arrived when its routine ordered that his visitors should inspect the greenhouses, "that a convict should escape in broad daylight, as this man must have done. The last man chose a fog, in winter—it was twenty years ago, the day before I first saw my Cretan Obolus—and he would have escaped, only——"

"Aye?" asked the Rector. "Only——?"

"Only he walked over Furnace Point—and—well, he did escape out and out, after all. You know the rocks under Furnace Point. There wasn't much of him left to take back to Lowmoor."

"Ah," said Mrs. Pitcairn, "if people only would be contented with their lot; but it's always the way. A contented mind——"

"Isn't a continual feast at Lowmoor—if you mean that, Maria," said the parson. "Poor dev—— You'll have a fine crop of grapes this year, Fane," he went on, quickly, having himself narrowly escaped a precipice, "a first-rate crop."

There were many questions that Rosamond was longing to ask; but she had not yet passed the age when, according to the primitive etiquette of those parts and of that household, young people ought to be seen, and not heard. It seemed to her, however, that she could understand how terrible and life-crushing must be the existence within prison walls, if it drove its victims to an escape more terrible still.

"Oswald," she half-whispered to her old playfellow, "what was the story of that man who was killed? What had he done?"

Oswald, grown shy with the consciousness of his new relation towards Rosamond, self-made and one-sided as it was, welcomed a chance of speech with her that came easily and without seeking. "I remember hearing of it when I was a boy—a child," said he, "and that's all. What he'd done, I don't know. . . . But these aren't things for you to think of. . . . No; you needn't

be in a hurry to run away. *I* haven't looked at the grapes yet,
you know." For the greenhouse had now been inspected, and
Rosamond, disappointed of her answer, was preparing to follow
the general progress to the cucumber frames, or wherever it might
be tending. He had not ridden over from Windgates solely for
the purpose of making a clean breast of things to Uncle Æneas;
he had come, with all the courage of a lover at a distance, to fix
his life for good and all. And, though he unaccountably had
found his courage less at the end than it had been at the beginning
of his ride, he had no notion of facing the shame of riding home
again without having said what he meant to say. It already
seemed quite shameful enough that he, a grown man of the world
had found himself at fault before a girl who was still almost
a child.

"Of course you can see the grapes, and eat them too, when
they're ripe," said Rosamond, seriously. "But you might have
told me about the man that was killed."

"I'll tell you something better than that, Rosamond."

"Better than——"

"Than walking over Furnace Point in a fog? Well, I hope so.
That is to say, I know it would be better for me—and for you—
well, that's where the hoping comes in. I——"

This was so far different from the manner in which he had
meant to begin, that he lost himself; and, besides, last night, alone
with his pipe, and this afternoon while riding over, he had never
realised all that asking Rosamond to wait for him would mean.
It is true that he saw in her the future woman who ought, of
rights, to blossom from a girlhood of perfect innocence and simplicity; and to the woman who was to be he could have made love
as easily as true love knows how to be made, and like a m an. But
seeing her in the midst of these flowers which, to his eyes, claimed
her as a sister, he could only feel, more surely even than he had
ever hitherto felt, that the woman who was to be had not yet
come. Now that he was alone with her presence, it seemed as if
it were a lighter matter to make love to that white rose whereby
she was standing, and as if a single note of the language sacred to
the purest of passion would be a stain. And yet, at the same
time, an instinct no less true told him that to make love even to a
real white rosebud as if it were nothing more is to lose one's pains.

"I wonder if you know how much I like you!" said he at last.

"I hope I do," said Rosamond, frankly. "I hope you like me

'all That,' as we used to say when we were children," she added,
stretching out her arms as wide apart as they would go.
"Ah, you can't reach wide enough yet, to measure. But—
when we were children! That's getting some way back, now—
at least to me. We have to measure liking in other ways—
now."

"True," sighed Rosamond. "I really feel getting quite old,
sometimes—as if I remembered old Moldwarp's arrows and
hatchets when they were new. And just think how many roses,
just like these, I have seen born and dying! And on they will go,
being born and dying, while I shall go on living and living—why
Queen Boadicea can't seem half so old to Uncle Æneas as I must
seem to them. Isn't it strange?"

"Very strange, indeed," assented Oswald, gravely, not in the
least following her meaning, but accepting it as faithfully as
an echo. But she took his assent for intelligent sympathy, and
was encouraged to go on. It was not often that she felt such
encouragement in the presence of a playmate of long ago who
had grown up into a man of awe-inspiring gravity and learning,
and she would well-nigh have walked, in her own person, over
Furnace Point rather than let his superior wisdom into the secret
of her magic cage—she was shy and tender over secrets that
even to her seemed to belong to a childhood that, at her mature
age, needed to be hidden away in dark corners, and she
instinctively feared the grown-up smile that would scatter them
away in shame. But there were many fancies, short of her
Grand Mystery, which belonged but to the moment, and might,
therefore, be as fearless as butterflies in sun, who know neither
to-morrow or yesterday ; and, somehow, in spite of Oswald's
unusual constraint, he seemed to have grown backwards nearer to
her own age than he had seemed to be when he had last visited
Crossmarsh, a week ago. After all, a young man of three-and-
twenty is not bound to be so very much older than a girl of
fifteen. There are other things in the Kingdom of Time besides
years and days.

"I assure you," she said, leaping over a long stretch of
thought, in forgetfulness that Oswald's wits did not share with
hers the privilege of wings, "I assure you I have thought
everything all out, and that I mean us—Sophy and me—to have
nothing to do with change. Everything, here at Crossmarsh,
is to be always exactly what it is now. Old Moldwarp is to go

on finding flints for Uncle Æneas till he has found them all—and then he must begin to find them all over again. Sophy and I will keep house, and never change a servant, nor an animal, nor the place of a chair. And——"

"Well?" asked Oswald, with more interest than the scheme called for—except, indeed, on the part of those who have as yet seen nothing change, nor known what change means.

"And—and that's all."

"Quite all? Haven't you kept a place for me?"

"Indeed I have, though, Oswald! You shall ride over from Windgates—just as often as you do now."

"Not oftener? But if you only mean *I'm* not to change— you may be as sure of that, dear, as that you are alive. Only— though not in me—change *must* come. And, since it must, don't you want ever to spread your wings and see the world?"

"No. Perhaps I should, if I were a man. But—no. I should find nothing that I want, and that I can have here, whenever—whenever I please." She coloured, though without knowing it: for her tongue, not often at liberty, had been on the point of betraying her power of raising, at will, a far larger and fuller life than, as even Rosamond knew, is to be found in the whole wide world since dragons and dragon-slayers followed in the track of the ichthyosaurus and the dodo. "If I did not wake up in the morning in Cross-marsh!——"

"Why should that be such a terrible thing?"

"I should have crossed the sea—or else the hills——"

"And then?"

"I should perhaps know what Lowmoor means. I am *afraid* to know."

"Good God, Rosamond!" cried Oswald, only kept from laughing outright by the awful knowledge that she was She, and there-fore must needs mean something, though her meaning might stand in sore need of an interpreter, "anybody, who did n t know you, would think you meant you are afraid of being sent to gaol!"

And, indeed, how could he guess, even faintly, into the manner in which, during a childhood as deeply alone as was ever passed in this world, she had evolved a world out of hints, guesses, and shadows, in which the few things she half knew were but types and forecast shadows of the vast and unimaginable unknown?

The sea and the cliffs bounded all the few realities of life that were signified by that narrow word, Home. Beyond it lay, to her mind, unbounded space and endless time, wherefrom the passing ships were messengers no less shadowy than the sea-birds whose nests she had never seen. On the other side were the hills, in the half distance, beyond which lay the world of men, with a citadel of crime for its entrance, and its end in one. Cross-marsh lay between two mysteries, dividing them: and while those who feel the mysteries of life only a little long to dare them, those who feel them a great deal can only feel, and fear.

And yet the very dread of change may be but an extreme form of the fascination which brings the bird to the serpent against its will. But of that, Rosamond could, as yet, guess nothing. Her new fancies were all that had come to disturb the melodious monotony of her days, which, like the flowers among which she stood, fell off the ear's stalk so softly and easily that, when the next came, it only seemed as if yesterday were waking again from a dreamless sleep and re-opening upon her the self-same eyes.

"Rosamond," said Oswald, with the air and all the sensations of a philosopher, "of course you can't think that you—and Sophy—can go on living all your lives just as you are now. Changes *must* come, in a world where people live and die, and never know what is to happen next—and it's a good thing they do, considering what a humdrum sort of place it would else be. One needn't talk of anybody's dying—yet: but Sophy will marry, and you—the more you will want somebody to stand by you, and find courage for you, if you are so afraid of the world. And that's so certain, dear, that I mean never to marry, nor to change, until you do—and then only on the same day."

"Oh," said Rosamond, quickly, "I never mean to be married. I know all about marriage. It wouldn't suit me at all. And, of course, Sophy will feel the same as me. But, of course, *you* can do as you like."

"Can I?" asked Oswald, a little ruefully: for he had been flattering himself that he had at last reached the point of plain speaking. "However—we'll see about that. Of course, I know how young you are now——"

"I am fifteen!" said Rosamond.

" And—well, I'm afraid I can't make you see all in a minute what I mean. Would you mind changing Crossmarsh for Windgates? After all, that wouldn't be so very much of a change."

" Oh, Oswald!" she suddenly exclaimed, " are you asking ME to marry YOU?"

" Of course I am. I'm asking you to wait for me—and to know that everything I think of, and everything I ever do, is all to make the time come nearer. So, dear, you needn't be afraid that a single thing in your life shall not be just as you will. You don't know all about marriage: nobody knows anything about such a marriage as I will try to make ours. I'll begin to make Windgates exactly what you would like to find it—I'll begin five minutes after I get home : it will take five minutes to put my horse up, or else I'd begin still sooner. *Will* you wait?"

He was speaking eagerly and warmly, now that the plunge, which had at one time appeared so impossible, had been made. And, therefore he was beginning to forget his intention of only asking Rosamond to wait in order that he might not spend the next few years in anxious doubting. He came close to her, and took both her hands in one of his own. But he tried in vain to read her eyes, which met his as if she had been utterly wrong in her boast, and, instead of knowing all about marriage knew nothing of it at all, preface, or chapter, from title-page to end.

" O course I will—wait," said she. " It is easy enough to do that; but, indeed, Oswald, I don't want to marry anybody at all."

" Ah, but you will—and if that anybody is not me——You said, just now, you liked me 'all That.' Do you want anybody you like to be miserable for years? I must know *now* whether I am to win you or lose you in time to come. I suppose I have told you all I meant to tell you—now. Only from this hour think of me in only one way—as one who means to live for you whether you ever let him or no, and who is always living and waiting for you, till you find out all that—that—*my* love for *you* means. And——"

He was speaking very quietly and slowly, but something in his voice or in his eyes made her withdraw her hands. She did not understand; but something in all this felt like the shadow of—Change.

3 A

"Promise me this now," said he, "and—that isn't much, dear! I won't ask anything else, till I know what you'll say. It's a great thing to give a man Hope, that will last him for years—for months, anyway. Promise that you will remember all this, and will wait till I ask you again. Will you? You can promise all with just one word!"

It was certainly little that he was asking—no more than any man might ask of any girl whose fancy was free. But his eyes hung upon her lips as if they were about to speak his doom for good and all. If the love he had for her was too deeply rooted for passion, it was therefore all the more part and parcel of himself, and it was for the first time spreading visibly open the blossoms, upon the fruit whereof hung all the hopes he had formed for all his life long. The delicate lips parted, and the word of answer—might it be of hope!—seemed trembling into life, when——

"Rosamond! Rosamond!" cried Sophy, bounding in, "where *have* you been all this while? And Oswald, too! I don't know what has happened, but I just happened to be on the lawn when a man on horseback, and in a uniform, rode up, for Uncle Æneas, to the front door. I've been looking for you, to tell you, everywhere, and look; there he goes!"

Oswald was very fond of Rosamond's sister, but he had never till that moment fully realised Sophy's peculiarities in the way of seeing everything, and of telling, as though it were a matter of life and death, everything that she saw, without regard to place or time. But there was no help for it now—the coming word had been startled away, and could not now be recalled. Courting Rosamond was surely only to be compared with chasing a butterfly, with films of gossamer for fences stronger than oak and iron, and with a chance at any moment of finding the hunt thrown out by the interference of a gnat or bee. However, the heart must be faint indeed that will yield even to lions and eagles. Another time would make itself or else be made. So, instead of amazing poor unwelcome Sophy with a sharp word, Oswald looked from the greenhouse door at the man on horseback, in uniform. And Rosamond, more grateful to her sister than she could tell, was only too glad to look also.

"By Jove, if it isn't Brown, from Lowmoor!" exclaimed Oswald, who had long ago forgotten the boom of the distant gun, which might have reminded him that the world contains other stories besides his own. "What's up, Brown? What brings *you* here?"

"Ah, Mr. Hargrave, I'm not sorry to see *you*," said the warder, touching his cap to the two girls, as Sophy ran forward and took Oswald's hand, while Rosamond shrank back on finding herself face to face with Lowmoor in flesh and blood, human and real, and unmistakably branded even with a coat, cap, belt, and buttons of its own. "It's nothing very particular, but if you'll walk on a step or two I'll tell you what I've told Mr. Fane."

"All right. Go back to the house with—with Rosamond, Sophy," said Oswald, gathering that the warder did not wish to speak before the girls. "I sha'n't be long. There—now I'm at your service, Brown. It's about that escaped convict, I suppose?"

"Yes, Mr. Hargrave. And a more desperate——"

His voice sunk, and became mixed with the crunch of his horse's shoes upon the gravel, so that not even Sophy, though she pricked her ears to their utmost reach, could gather a word more.

"Rosamond," said Sophy, as the two sisters turned slowly towards the house, "I don't know what it all means, but Mr. and Mrs. Pitcairn went off as fast as if their house was on fire, and you and Oswald have been talking in the greenhouse for hours, as if *he* was in your great secret instead of me, and now he's gone off with that man in uniform. There *is* something—and I'm left out of it all. I believe it all began with that gun. What *was* Oswald saying to you in the greenhouse all that while?"

Rosamond had never had a secret from her sister in her life. But things were even already, if ever so little, changed since the boom of that gun. Rosamond had received her first offer, and she had found it so hard to understand that how could Sophy be expected to understand it at all. She had to put it all into thoughts before she could try to translate it into words.

"Please, Sophy," she pleaded, "don't ask me any questions now! I'll tell you all about everything to-morrow, the first thing, between waking and getting up."

"Oh, dear! that will never do. I shall be kept awake all night with thinking—you know I always am whenever I think, and then when it's time to wake I shall be too sleepy to listen. Tell me now—please!"

"Indeed I can't, Sophy."

"Is it anything about—me?"

"Nothing in the world."

"And you won't tell?   Oh, Rosamond, I never knew you unkind before!"

"I can't.   I wish—but never mind."

"No—never mind!   I suppose you're sworn to secrecy—but I'm not; and as that man in uniform is at the bottom of it all, *he* can't complain if I just—just happen to be behind the laurels while he and Oswald are crawling along the drive."

And off Sophy ran, with feet as quick as her ears.

CHAPTER V.

Such tricks
Our own minds play us, that we, oftentimes
Taking false phantoms for the truth of flesh,
And winds for voices, are betrayed thereby
To taking truths for dreams phantastical.
All is not gold that glitters, preach the wise;
And naught that gleams is golden, prates the fool.

PART, at least, of the latest news turned out to be true enough —the Pitcairns had gone home. On ordinary occasions, Rosamond would have been rather sorry, for she would have wanted to hear the rest of that story about the undiscovered island. She was a world-wide traveller in fancy, in spite of her feelings against actual change. Uncle Æneas, as he usually did in the evening, had shut himself up with his bones from the skeleton of dead Time; and Oswald did not return. So Rosamond, at the open bay window, read a book, upside down, until Sophy returned, looking as important as if she had just been made a cabinet minister. She also brought a book to the bay window; and it is quite possible that she also may have read the wrong side upwards, for she had a wonderful knack of reflecting her sister in outward actions, so that the few people who had ever had an opportunity of observing them used to call the two girls as like as two peas. Only it so happened that Sophy also had her original side, and in that matter the observant people were, naturally enough, as wrong as they always are.

Rosamond was silent, while the summer twilight deepened, and so was Sophy. But there are as many sorts of silence as there are tongues to break it. Rosamond was silent because she did not want to speak—Sophy because she wanted to be spoken to. However, since the mountain would not come to Mahomet——

"You needn't trouble to wake me early to-morrow morning, Rosamond!" said she. "If you were in your castle I should give the signal for important news."

"Important news!" echoed Rosamond, waking up from what was neither sleep, nor thought, nor dream, nor voyage of fancy but from some mental mood known neither to men, nor women, nor children, but to girls alone—unrecognised when they come, and forgotten when they go. "Why, Sophy, I declare I had forgotten you were there!"

"Don't you want to know?"

"Of course I do."

"I don't know what Oswald was saying to you, but I *do* know why the Pitcairns hurried off, and why the man came from Lowmoor, and why, instead of coming back to the house, Oswald had Nancy out of the stable and saddled her himself, and galloped off with the man. I happened to be just behind the laurels at first, and afterwards, Rosamond, I just chanced to be in the loose box while Oswald was saddling Nancy. And—oh! Rosamond, do you know—the gaoler and Oswald have galloped off to hunt a man!"

"A man?" A slow flash of summer lightning played over the far line of the sea, and, dumb as it was, brought back the signal gun to mind. "Oh, Sophy—the man who has escaped from the gaol?"

Sophy nodded. "They don't know what has become of him, or where he may be, or what he may do. He might rob, or perhaps murder somebody before he is taken again. It's like as if a lion or tiger had broken out of a show. But don't you think we'd better have lights? Isn't it getting rather dark to read?"

"I'm not reading Sophy. Do you want to read?"

"Well, perhaps not exactly to read. But we might want, presently, to do something else, you know; it's still an hour to bed time, and——"

"Does Uncle Æneas know?"

"He knows, and the Pitcairns know, and that's why they went off home, to put everything safe there. I didn't hear that, but I suppose that's why. But *you* mustn't know anything, because we weren't to be told, for fear we might be afraid—as if that was a likely thing! What was that, Rosamond?"

"What was what?" asked Rosamond, herself a little startled by Sophy's sudden whisper which, in anybody possessing less courage, might certainly have been mistaken for fear.

"That rustling sort of noise. It *is* getting dark, Rosamond—really dark : and the lightning looks so blue and odd ; and I do really want to read. Let's shut the window and ring for candles."

" And Oswald ? "

" I told you. He knows all the places and the ways about, and he's gone to help catch the robber—if they can."

" Sophy, I'm afraid it's very dreadful, but——"

" But what ? " What's dreadful ? " asked Sophy, whose chair had been all the while walking nearer to Rosamond's until now it could come no nearer.

" I *can't* help it. I hope they won't catch that man."

" Not catch a man who robs and kills ? "

" But suppose he's innocent—suppose he's been in prison by mistake. Think of that other man who fell over Furnace Point, Sophy ! I can't get it out of my mind. And then, if Oswald finds him, and if they fight. Did you hear why the man was in prison ?—what he has done ? "

" Only that it was something very dreadful indeed."

New things so seldom happen in Crossmarsh or, rather, so seldom used to happen there, that when they did they assumed a size and a shape inconceivable by most of us, who are brought every hour with things the least of which would have been there the lasting landmark of a year's history. A man had escaped from Lowmoor, and the warders were after him. What then ? He will presently be caught : and in five minutes there will be a fire, or a war, or a libel that will wash such a trifle clean off our minds. And this we call living. But it was in Crossmarsh that people really lived, making much of little things and giving themselves up to the influence of what they called great ones. Rosamond was not frightened in the vulgar sense—that is to say, lest a ruffian at large should be lying in wait to spring upon her from behind a hedge in one of her walks, or should even now be watching for an opportunity to make a dash through the bay window. She was not infected by Sophy's half-triumphant trembling over the terrible news she had been the first to gather. But she felt that Crossmarsh, with one of the lost souls of Lowmoor wandering over it like a condemned demon at large, was not the Crossmarsh that she had chosen for her whole life's abode— the one point of peace and safety between the world beyond the hills and the world beyond the sea. The intrusive element had even made itself outwardly perceptible in the sort of panic reported by Sophy, and in the complete silence and solitude which had followed upon a more than commonly social afternoon. But it also seemed to Rosamond as if there were something beyond the common course of nature in the dark, moonless, starless, windless twilight of a cloudy midsummer night, and more than coincidence in the chance that the gun which had set the new influence free had also been the preface for Oswald's strange and still but dimly comprehended words:

Cliff Cottage was early resting and early rising. Uncle Æneas, indeed, would sometimes sit up half-way through the night over some new find of Silver Moldwarp's, but on such occasions he would rise all the earlier, in order to return the sooner to a fresh study of the treasure which had meanwhile delighted his dreams. To-night he departed, a little from the established routine. He sent off the girls to bed a full half-hour before the usual time, and the rest of his proceedings would have remained unknown had not Sophy, half undressed, just happened to be taking the air at the head of the stairs when he went round and locked, doubled locked, and wherever practicable, bolted every door : no easy task, for such precautions, though customary in theory, had fallen into abeyance at the cottage for years. Then he went out and Sophy heard him unfastening old Rover's chain. Finally, she skipped into a dark corner just in time, unseen herself, to see Uncle Æneas carrying the plate, the butler's charge, into his own room.

"I sha'n't sleep a single wink, Rosamond!" said she. And, so saying, she fell asleep soundly.

It was Rosamond who, well-nigh for the first time in her life, found sleep impossible. She did not even close her eyes, and not being provided with a stock of night-thoughts, such as may either conjure sleep into coming or enable the more perverse insomniac to kill the crawling hours, she found wakefulness intolerable. Half a dozen times she went to the window, and looked out seaward, while Sophy—who evidently neither woke nor slept by halves—never stirred. Yet she was tired, and, though she was so broad awake, Oswald's courtship itself became as unreal as if the day had been the night, and she had dreamed therein. Then imagination fairly woke up, and claimed to be exorcised.

"Yes ; I will!" said she, half aloud. "Sophy won't wake till I come back, and if she does, she'll know where I am."

So she dressed herself, lighted one candle and supplied herself

with a second, and went out into the passage, and closed the
door softly behind her. The cottage was built far too well
to contain creaking boards, and her footsteps were unheard
even by herself until she reached that bare lumber room, with
, the one table, the one chair, and the heap of straw in the corner,
where she had been interrupted that morning in the middle of her
spells. Placing the candle on the table she turned the key in the
door, and arranged her magical properties—an ink-bottle without
a stand, a thin heap of paper, and a quill pen.

Never had she felt in better form for the prosecution of that
great secret which was, as yet, only known to herself and Sophy,
and which interested Sophy mainly, if not entirely, because it was
a secret in which she alone was permitted to share. Her body was
fired, her mind confused, and her spirit broad awake: the place,
the solitude, and the feeble light which left the corners of the loft
in gloom suggested all sorts of capricious shadows and wild
images: and everybody knows how the small hours of the four
and twenty are a kind of inspiration in themselves. The nonsense
which filters through thought into a semblance of sense when the
sun shines, seems all superior to sense in those midnight hours,
and floods itself out wholesale. Rosamond Fane having no
foolish fear of critics and readers before her, filled her pen at once,
and lost not a moment in finishing the sentence into which Sophy's
ill-timed summons had broken :

". . . . when there rose before their wondering gaze that
terrible form. The gleam of the torches first turned blue and
was then lost in the glow that gleamed from the cavernous eyes
of the phantom. Even in that moment of terror Callista noticed
a blood-red cross in the centre of its brow, and remembered how
the mysterious Montalvan had told her by that brand the whole
mystery would become clear. She threw herself on her knees
beside the priest, and grasped his sable robe. 'Speak! phantom!'
said the priest. 'Who art thou?—and whence comest thou?—
and why?' A strange groan made the walls of the chamber
quake and tremble. To the ears of the priest it meant naught;
but it said to Callista, "Lady, behold in me the spirit of the
miserable Demetrius—branded with the brand of Cain!" It
seemed to her that a powerful sentence, she knew not how, had
slipped from her pen, and she paused to listen to the melancholy
music that it seemed to her, under the glamour of night, excitement, and solitude, to contain. The ring of it felt, indeed, almost

too good to be her own. Yet she was sure she had never met
with it in any of her books, and was conscious of the poet's glow
when the poorest bit of work is glorified to the workman's eyes
by the flying sparks of the forge at work and the roar of the
labouring wind.

But, after such a stroke as that, to continue the description of
the murderer's ghost was much less easy than it had been to begin.
She re-read her morning's work, dwelling upon the fine points, and
here and there mending them. But somehow her written words
no longer realised her conception of the scene. It all came before
her so much better when she looked away from her paper, and
leaned back in her chair, and allowed the priest and Lady Callista,
and the murderous apparition to act before her. There was
something wanting in all that she had written heretofore, with
the single-minded purpose of indulging an instinct, and of some
day seeing how the work of her pen could make Sophy's blood
run cold, for every author must needs write for some public, and
Sophy was Rosamond's. Now, however, either Oswald had
proved himself the most unheroic of lovers, or else her own great
love-scene between the beautiful Callista and the mysterious
Montalvan was all wrong. And then—since the morning there
was a real murderer abroad. Her miserable Demetrius lacked
the *cachet* of a lost soul from Lowmoor, whose very existence,
invisibly ghost-like as it was, had been enough to charge the
air of Crossmarsh with sudden and pervading thunder.

How much better, could she find the words, would she raise her
ghost now! She began the half of another sentence, and then a
few words of another; but the inspiration, which had seemed ready
to last all night, refused any longer to come at her bidding. Her
fancies seemed to take upon them the visible form in which such
things appear to ghost-seers, looking with contempt on the feeble
efforts of words to follow them. The old loft expanded easily into
the vast and ancient hall of her story, with gallery and daïs, just
as she had seen in the illustrated county history. The air was
heavy enough with heat, and the one candle was burning dimly
enough to represent to the life the impotent light of the torches.
She was herself a flesh and blood Callista, with a real lover, who
had set out on a desperate life and death chase, and impressed with
an actual atmosphere of crime and mystery. Indeed, she was in
worse plight than Callista with her priest. She was alone—all
alone. She never thought of returning to her bed: it is of the

nature of such moods to hold us where we are till we have exhausted all the influence that holds our minds not unwilling prisoners.

But where was the spectre? That, at least, she had no desire to raise. All the rest, though made up of the most intangible fancies, was quite real enough for one who was keeping a vigil of candle-light in such a place, and at such an hour. Yet Fancy is not one of those creatures who can be fixed to its place, and forbidden to wander beyond a given line. . . . She could swear that the air was growing thicker and closer in one corner of the room; she could almost swear that she saw the motion in that more compact and darker air that suggested the presence of an unsubstantial form.

Then her heart misgave her. It was not for this that she had come to use the magic of her pen. She gave herself a mental shake, passed her hands quickly and roughly over her eyes and forehead, plunged her pen into the ink, and again sat down to the table. She even wrote a whole sentence. But it was incoherent, and was written really as a sort of charm against the visible appearance of the unseen. She was ashamed to run away from a freak of fancy, and yet she could not, for the life of her, but feel that the air in that corner was growing thicker and darker, and the presence concentrating itself there more and more. She could not write, and she dared not look round.

The strain was growing terrible. Who is strong enough to battle against causeless fear, or to stir hand or foot when bound with invisible chains? "They would not hurt us if they could; they could not if they would," she forced herself to remember; and found that old jingling charm of daylight reason against midnight spectres as unavailing as thousands of wiser people have found it before her. She might certainly have said her prayers and the hymn which begs protection against all powers of darkness; but she had a natural shame of turning prayer into a talisman against childish terrors. So she sat spell-bound, pen in hand, listening, and hearing nothing—not looking, for fear of what she might see. "Branded with the brand of Cain!" Suppose she should look up, and those caverns of eyes, and between them the cross of crimson, and——

Her shoulder was grasped by a heavy hand.

CHAPTER VI.

Gil Elrich till that ladie came,
And ran before her knee—
"Now help and hide me soon, fair Dame,
Out of thy great pitie."
But she forth spake, "And though I would
And had withal the power,
How will they deem of maidenhood
Who find thee here in bower?"
"Then out," quoth he, "on Hope and all—
On maid be bale and ban
Who'll chide her Hawk when finches fall,
But hound a hunted Man!"

"HUSH!" breathed a voice in her ear. "Don't scream—don't faint: I shall do you no harm."

There was not the least chance of her doing either. One must have a voice to scream with, and one's heart must be alive and going before it faints—and Rosamond's breath was paralysed and her heart standing still. She was too petrified even to be called afraid: for fear, like pain, has a limit beyond which it cannot go. And, for another thing, she had never fainted in her life, and so did not know how.

"Of course she could not help looking: and was almost reassured to find that the eyes were not cavernous and that there was no crimson cross between them. Her nerves had been strung to such a point of tension, that she would have been amazed at nothing: and it was a loosening of the cords to find that the owner of the voice and the grasp was of real flesh and blood, after all. But, as exaltation died down, fear arose. Though but mortal like herself, he was no very attractive object upon whom her eyes were riveted. Perhaps he might not have been ill-looking under more favourable circumstances; but what she saw was a tall man, obviously a good many years older than Oswald, with a closely shaven face, closely cropped hair, and a strange bundle of clothes upon him that had evidently been made for a man of at most half his size. His legs were bare below the knees, and his arms nearly to the elbows—and, singularly enough, the garments, if such they could be called, did not seem entirely unfamiliar to her. But the man himself was an utter stranger: so she must have been mistaken about his clothes.

"Indeed you need not be in the least alarmed," said he, rather quickly and eagerly, "though it is likely enough you should be." His voice was pleasant enough, and had the accent of a gentleman. "I am neither a burglar, nor—anything of that kind. You are a woman—or you will be one, some day. I don't suppose you have yet learned that it is the right thing to betray the hunted beast to the hounds; of course, if you have, I am in your hands."

Rosamond was trembling all over: but all her knowledge of life was innocent, and she was therefore spared the extremity of fear. A boy might have been frightened enough, but Rosamond was at any rate unconscious of having any more cause for fear than if she had been a boy. Her heart was sound, and her health perfect—and those things mean courage, in whatever chance humour the nerves may be.

"Who are you?" she asked, in a voice that was at least decently firm.

"First of all—are you a Miss Fane? Then, did you ever hear of a place called Lowmoor? But of course you have—you know all about it, I dare say; but you never yet heard of a man escaping from it. Very well—I have escaped from Lowmoor."

So this was the very being whose freedom that gun had proclaimed! And yet, startling as it was to learn that she was alone, almost in the dark, with the creature which had spread fear and confusion around, Rosamond was scarcely any longer surprised. Indeed, it seemed to her now as if his presence in her own citadel in Cliff Cottage were the most natural thing in the world—in short, as if she had stumbled unwittingly upon an actual spell, and had really raised the spectre of which she had only dreamed.

"*Are* you?" gasped she.

"Ah—that is better! I see you are a brave girl. For that matter, I expect you were a good bit less afraid, even when you first felt my hand, than I was when I first saw you. I suppose you think it's a strange place to find an escaped convict—in the house of a justice. Well, it was the last place where anybody was likely to look for me, that's all. There's the whole story of my escape from beginning to end—doing precisely what would occur to nobody in his senses. And now the same question comes in—what's the most unlikely thing for anybody in his senses to do?"

As he spoke, rather to himself than to her, as if to give her time for the recovery of startled nerves, a sense of reaction—of disappointment—I hardly know the right word, began to come over Rosamond. His language was too much like that to which she had been accustomed, differing only in greater readiness and fluency: in spite of his extraordinary costume, the man was far too much like any mere ordinary man. He even seemed, instead of being mysterious and terrible, composed, subdued—even heedfully gentle in his bearing. Had she been better acquainted with convicts, these very qualities would have seemed remarkable even to the point of mystery. But, in her ignorance, she began to be almost annoyed with herself that she could not contrive to be appropriately afraid.

Wherefore it must be concluded that the convict, whatever else he may have been, understood the indescribable and unteachable art of depriving those with whom he had to deal of at least one set of defensive weapons—their fears. Rosamond became able to distinguish the man himself from the effect given him by his clothes, and—being with no prejudices, save of her own making—felt that his breadth of chest and shoulders, his length of limb, and his Roman cast of features ought to be formidable, not to the weak, but only to the strong. Being what she was, it was hardly possible that she should fear strength, especially when strength spoke gently. She began at last actually to think—and, thinking, wondered how she might best and soonest ensure the man's escape by the way he came, and hurry back to her bed, never to return to her castle after nightfall again.

But his next words—though spoken as gently as by a woman—were these:

" A man in his senses—he would begin by strangling you, and hiding the body where it would take long to find, because dead tongues tell no tales. I know how that would double my chances —and if I was taken in spite of them, I should, at any rate, be better off than at Lowmoor, because I should be hanged—and, therefore, I'll do nothing of the kind. What would a man in his senses *not* do ? "

He seated himself on the table, and absently began to turn over the loose leaves of Rosamond's manuscript, but without reading them.

" I will tell you," said he; " it's my one chance: I'll do it, because it is the maddest thing in the world—I'll trust a woman and a strange woman, not with life, that's nothing, but with liberty. I'm just run to earth here; and needs must, when the devil drives. Miss Fane, you are young; that is to say, you are still too wise to take for granted that when a gaol-bird says he is innocent of all real crime, except that of gaol-breaking, he must needs be lying. You must judge for yourself whether I'm the kind of man, apart from these clothes, to have robbed, forged, burnt hay ricks, or done anything else to fit myself for an idiot asylum. The truth is, Miss Fane, that I am one of those poor devils, more common than people, who are old and foolish, think for, who am punished for nothing at all. I tell you that, on the honour of a gentleman, which is a thing that a lady is bound to believe. And now for my plan: I mean to stay here, in this room, till one of two things happen; till either you give me up to injustice, or till the hunt has run by. I put myself into your hands, even as Sisera did into Jael's."

" Here ? " faltered Rosamond.

" Here. When you leave the room, you need only lock the door and pocket the key. When you came in—some half hour, or whatever it was, ago—you locked the door and then sat down to your story. Of course that means that this out-of-the-way corner of a rambling house is your own particular bower, where you can rely upon being alone and undisturbed. Aye, and I found the door locked from the outside when I squeezed myself through the window. In short, this is your own citadel of which you alone keep the key. Very good—then nobody need know of my presence in the house, save you and this most fortunate heap of straw. If I am taken, I shall not envy you your conscience, which has allowed you to betray an innocent man, who trusts you because he has none else to trust to in the whole wide world. If I starve—but no, Jael did not starve Sisera— you might hang a dog, but you'd hardly starve him. There, that is my plan. And now you'd better go back to bed; and I hope you'll sleep half as well as I, who am going, on that straw, to dream for the first time that I am free without its being only a dream. Good night, Miss Fane, and take my thanks for the brave, kind thing you are going to do for one who has put life, liberty, faith, hope, all that he has, into your hands."

" I cannot! " cried Rosamond, not in the least disbelieving his assertions of innocence, but feeling, all in a moment, and with no need of help from thought, all that the attempt to carry out such a plan would mean; "don't ask me; I'm sorry if you are in trouble that you don't deserve. I will help you out of the house——"

" As you will," said the convict, yawning and rubbing his eyes. " I have told you the circumstances. It is for you to decide —not me. Only, I won't leave the house. If I am to be taken it shall be here, and it shall be by you. Sleep over it; sleep is counsel, you know. Permit me, Miss Fane, if you will trust me with your key for a moment, I will unlock the door."

It is not good to feel that another's will is making itself the master of one's own. But it was not strange that the will of this exceedingly singular convict was mastering one so ill-tried as Rosamond's, fighting, as it was, upon such unfamiliar ground. Had he commanded or threatened, she might have found courage to escape: had he gone upon his knees and implored her to save him, his object must have been injured by the contempt with which weakness regards weakness. But he had simply trusted to the honour which forbids treachery, assuming that such an appeal cannot possibly be made from one human creature to another in vain, and he had expressed his trust with a cool decision of manner which was in itself a power, and with a dignity that even his grotesque costume could not lessen, nay, rather increased by force of contrast, and by giving the man's own personality an air of essential superiority to all outward and accidental conditions. She gave him the key. He unlocked and opened the door for her to pass out, and returned her the key with a bow, neither too low to seem theatrical, nor too slight for reverence and courtesy, and gravely significant of present trust and future gratitude.

"Now you will kindly lock me in," said he; " and for to-morrow, you will, I hope, remember that you have a prisoner who has not eaten anything but a handful of wheat-ears since breakfast-time at Lowmoor. Good night, Miss Fane. You are a brave young lady, and nobody can be brave without being true."

There was no need to bid her lock and double lock the door. She listened for a moment, with beating heart, until she heard the faint rustle of straw, and crept back into her bedroom and her bed, as miserable as a girl could be, save for a lingering hope that, when morning came, the whole of that night's work would prove to be but the nightmare which its beginning had seemed.

And indeed, when the night with all its mysteries was freely blotted out, and the sun, already high in the sky, called all the world to begin a new summer day, such an adventure could not have seemed otherwise than a dream to man or woman, boy or girl. From the very heaviest and most dreamless sleep she had ever known, Rosamond was aroused by Sophy singing—as a rule, it was Rosamond's morning toilette that waked Sophy. For a whole long minute her mind was a clean blank; she only knew

4

that sho was awake and alive. And when the first memory of her
midnight watch came back, it was at first indeed with a shudder,
but then with a feeling of joyful relief that it had been but a bad
dream after all.

"Oh, Sophy!" she began, "I have had such a strange——"
But she was fairly awake now, and her mind grasped reality.
What was to be done? That escaped prisoner was actually and
absolutely in the house ; and it depended upon her whether he was
straightway to be returned to all the vague terrors of Lowmoor,
or whether she was to burden herself with such a secret, and her
life with attempting to hide that which could not be hidden for
long. She turned round upon her pillow, affecting to have fallen
asleep again, until she might imagine what she ought to do. Of
course, she could go straight to Uncle Æneas, and tell him all.
It would not take long to send for a constable, or to Lowmoor, for
help, and her mind would once more be open and free. But no—
it would be no such thing. If the man was in truth guiltless of
crime, how could she bring herself to be the means of re-setting
the world—that world beyond the hills—upon its work of cruelty,
injustice and wrong? She felt that she would never know a single
happy moment again. And even if a real wolf, rightly pursued
by the hunters, had crawled into her castle, and, licking her hands,
had thrown himself upon her mercy, how could she find the heart
to betray the miserable wretch to its foes ?

Perhaps there are girls of her age—perhaps even in Crossmarsh
—who know how to distinguish between the opposing claims of
justice and honour, and would not feel called upon to sacrifice their
own peace of mind to Quixotic notions of loyalty to trusts im-
posed on them against their wills. Nevertheless, I hope and I
believe their good sense to be so rare, and I admire it so little, that,
were it shared by Rosamond, I should hold her at once too exceptional,
and too contemptible for her fortunes to be worth the following
let others take what view they please. Guilty or innocent of unknown crimes, the man had spoken the simple truth in telling her
that his liberty—his life it may be—lay in the hands of a girl of
fifteen. How far an instinctive knowledge of the material he had
to work upon had suggested his scheme she was not to know, and
even had she owned more prudence, the man's readiness to trust to
the honour of a stranger might have fairly argued honour in him.

"When *are* you going to get up ?" asked Sophy, long before
Rosamond had found a clue to the maze in which she was wander-

ing. "I'm nearly dressed, and in less than five minutes there'll be the breakfast bell."

Well, there was no help for it. Rosamond must face her day, all undecided and unprepared. She was not sorry to be late, however, since that would give her the reprieve of dressing alone. She said nothing while crawling out of bed, and Sophy was herself in too much of a scramble, in order to make up for the consequences of an over-long sleep, to take notice of her sister's silence. Before the five minutes could have passed the bell rang, and Sophy scampered downstairs.

How Rosamond envied Sophy! It was the first time in her life that she had woke to a single care—and, for a first, what a care. In spite of her lateness she did not hurry. But she was ready at last to face her troubles, and went down with a sense of weight dragging upon her—and a weight was in truth dragging her, though it was only the weight of a key. Even during the length of the staircase she found time to ask herself a hundred questions a hundred times—Have they found that man in that room? Have they not found him? Will they think that I look strangely, and ask me questions to find out why? And, above all, oh! *what* ought I to do?

Nothing, however, is less likely to happen than what we hope, except what we fear. Rosamond looked to find everything as usual—her uncle in his place, devouring his toast and some newly found flint in alternate mouthfuls, and Sophy doing her best to delay the tea-making, so as to give her sister time to avoid the charge of late rising. So much was she usually the first to be up and down that her appearing last would have been a family event on ordinary occasions, and have drawn the eyes of Uncle Æneas as if to the sudden entrance of the Phœnician sun-dial. As it proved, she heard voices in full talk, and recognised one of them as Oswald's. So she crept in quietly under the cover of the conversation, and avoided all but a general and including nod of good morning. Oswald recognised her entrance, but the others were intent upon what he was saying—so intent that he could not stop speaking :

"No, Mr. Fane—I believe I know every inch of the cliffs and every hole; and we didn't miss a point where a man could have gone over. And then——"

"Is it possible," asked Uncle Æneas, "that he has gone over where a man *can't* go over? That——"

"Ah, you're thinking of that old business of Furnace Point? No, it's impossible. He couldn't have reached the cliffs, reckon it as we may, till the tide had turned, and if he had walked over the edge his body must have been found on the shore. Besides, men don't escape in order to kill themselves—at least, not to kill themselves till there's nothing left to do. This fellow is young, Brown says, and healthy and strong, and couldn't have escaped from a place like Lowmoor without miracles of courage and skill. They can't find out how it was done, even now, and he had been a gentleman, they say, though a desperate sort of one. Brown, who's a sharp fellow, tracked him close to Pix-Knoll—that he can swear to. But there's no hiding place within a mile of that, and if he'd taken to any road, high or bye, in the prison dress, he'd be safe in Lowmoor now."

"I needn't ask *you*, Oswald, if you've left no corner unexplored?"

"We could ride, between sunset and breakfast-time, over more ground than a man could run. And a prisoner from Lowmoor isn't likely to know the ropes of the country—let alone when he's being tracked by one who's hunted, and shot, and fished and birds'-nested over it ever since he was born. Let me alone for that, Uncle Æneas; barring your own house, there isn't a spot in Crossmarsh we haven't been over, high or low, land or shore."

"And you conclude he is alive, and at large? But where?"

"He couldn't have got out of Crossmarsh, for we must have had news of him. So, after all I've said, it's my firm belief that he's still in this very neighbourhood; though where in the name of miracles he can have chanced on a hiding place I don't know."

Oswald's idle mention of a place so impossible as her own house for the convict's refuge drove all the colour from the cheek of Rosamond. But, lest her confusion should be noticed, she spoke: and—

"Is it certain he has done—is guilty—of anything?" asked she.

"Bless the girl! a convict—an escaped convict—from Lowmoor!" exclaimed Uncle Æneas, in some surprise. "I must give you some elementary readings in the law of England, my dear. Well, Oswald, and what do you propose to do?"

"He *must* be caught. We can't have an escaped convict wandering about at large. The houses won't be safe, nor a woman, nor a child, nor a man who has got to go out alone with anything on him worth losing. Of course, everybody about the place has been

warned, and the police will see that there's no getting out of the
circle within which he must be. Of course there'll be a reward
out, to make the people look alive. As for me—well, I'm not
going to throw away my night's ride; I'm going to have that
scoundrel—dead or alive. I'm not going to give in when once I've
put my hand to anything; no, whatever it may be."

As he spoke, he looked straightly at Rosamond : and her conscious blush made him believe that she had comprehended what
lay at the root of his words. For his "whatever it may be" meant
the hand and heart of Rosamond herself, and not the body of any
felon, dead or alive. Not that it was Oswald's way to boast, but
he meant the whole world to know that he was not to be turned
from the purpose of his life; while, in his present mood, manly
action commended itself to him both as an outlet for his energy, a
salve for his suspense, and, in some indirect fashion, a way of
proving his devotion. Even so, in certain good old times, the way
to a lady's favour was identical with the path that led to enchanters'
caves, giants' castles, and dragons' dens. So long as love lasts will
that same knighthood last; and here were knight to do, deed to be
done, and lady's eyes to see.

Could Oswald only have guessed that she whose steps abroad he
was preparing—in the name of public safety—to secure from peril:
could he have guessed that she was hiding the wizard, the dragon,
the giant, the evil knight, secret in her own bower ! For a
moment, seeing what the hunter, and not the quarry, thought of
the hunt, she was inclined to make a clean breast of it all. But
then it felt such a horrible thing to betray a fellow creature, bird,
beast, or man, to its pursuers—it could not be done. Had Oswald
been less bent upon the man-hunt, it is possible she might have
made a confidant of her old playfellow, and all have ended well:
for it is not good that even the guiltless should be able to escape
unlawfully from the hands of the law. She could trust Oswald,
even as this hunted convict had trusted her; but, alas, she had
watchfully read in his eyes and heard in the tones of his voice that
she could only trust him to do what he thought right, and that he
would never think it right to let this man go free. When would
breakfast be over, so that she might be free to think these things
out alone ?

Oh, if only they would search the house, and break down the
door of her castle, so long as that were done of their own motion,
and without treacherous hint or help from her ! That would be

a way out of the difficulty indeed—so complete that it was something to pray for. But even as she had been ashamed last night to pray against imaginary fears, so now it would be like taking a mean advantage to ask the power of Heaven to do what would soil her own hands ; to ask, as it were, an angel to do dirty work for her. If she had ever thought of betraying the convict, her lips were sealed now.

"By the Lord Harry," suddenly exclaimed Uncle Æneas. "I have it. I have *him!* Aye, Oswald, by the heels! There's something in having an old brain, after all."

"Indeed," said Oswald: "Is there any place in Crossmarsh where——"

"Aye, my lad, there's sure to be. Don't worry yourself: after your night's hunt you must be dog-tired. I'll—I'll set Silver Moldwarp on him: there! There's nothing in Crossmarsh that Silver Moldwarp won't smell out. I'll have him round in half-an-hour."

Alas—there was no thought among them all of looking under their feet, none. Why should there be? the houses of justices are not chosen by escaped criminals to hide in. Uncle Æneas swallowed his last mouthful of tea, pocketed his flint, and went out to give orders for the immediate appearance of the man who could find everything—even Phœnician sun-dials.

Sophy vanished altogether.

Oswald lingered about for another word with Rosamond : but she dared not listen to a word, lest she should betray what had now grown into a secret that she must guard, or be a dishonoured traitor. He could only misread her coldness, and ride off, either back to Windgates, with his errand undone, or else further on his search, to see if he, though unable to catch a girl, might at least catch a man.

Rosamond seized the first chance of cutting off half the breakfast loaf and carrying it to her castle door—just when vanished Sophy, by the merest chance, happened to have her in full sight from the top of the stairs.

CHAPTER VII.

And when they won to the walls of brick
    That had tossed back battle with lightsome scorn
The builded bulwark and rampart thick
    Were melt to the mist of a summer morn :

And when to the midmost keep they won
    That a thousand knights might not hope to win,
Each gate of steel and each girth of stone,
    As carven of cobweb, hath let them in.

A S she approached the door of her castle, Rosamond was
seized with an awful hope that the man who had shown
himself such an adept at imprisoning himself might have
disappeared again, either through the window, or the wall, or the
floor, or the roof, or by whatever path it was that he had entered.
It would be so much more than a relief—it would be so simple and
natural to find that nothing had really happened after all. For
there are things so impossible that it is easier to disbelieve in the
memory of our own eyes and our own ears than to believe. What
a delight it would be to draw a free breath on finding her room
empty, and to feel herself without a secret once more!

Everything was so silent as she listened at the door, with a
beating heart, that the wish it could be so almost grew up into the
hope that it might be so. The fear that it might not be so swallowed up all the remains of meaner fear. She opened the door as
gently as possible. It was never really light there, owing to the
height of the windows, the badness of the glass, and the small-
ness of the panes. It was not immediately, therefore, that all
hope died away. But alas, the death of hope's last whisper had
to come. There, on the straw heap, sat the Man.

"Good morning, Miss Fane," said he, courteously and even
pleasantly, as she closed the door. "Ah—and bread! I was getting so famished that I almost fancied you meant to get rid of me
by starvation. Give me the loaf, if you please. Did you ever
see a wolf killed, Miss Fane?"

"A wolf?" the word did not come agreeably from the lips of
this strong and wild-looking scare-crow. For the long night, and
the cold daybreak, and unbroken hunger, had done their work
upon him, and he was really looking, in broad daylight, the
desperate criminal that he professed not to be.

"Never? Then you shall see me kill one now. But—pray sit
down. It won't take long."

She did not obey the invitation to make herself at home in her
own room but 'woodst, ondering how all this was to end, while

the convict tore the bread into huge fragments and devoured them
greedily. Not for five good minutes did he speak a single word.
At last he paused in his work, drew a strong sigh, and said,
"Do you bake at home?"

"Yes," said Rosamond, with a start from her hopeless thought:
for, under the circumstances, so homely a question was surely the
most startling that could have been devised.

"So do we—at Lowmoor: but nothing like this. 'Liberty and
a crust,' indeed! this is liberty and Ambrosia. There—the wolf is
pretty near dead now: at any rate asleep till dinner time. And
now to business. The rest of the bread won't hinder talking. But—
while we talk, Miss Fane—pray oblige me by taking a chair.
You would rather stand? Then so will I. In the first place,
Miss Fane"—another bite, and an almost simultaneous swallow—
"I mustn't forget manners. I must thank you for being kind—
no, that would be nothing to you; I mean I must thank you for
being brave. It wanted a little courage to come all alone with
that loaf to a hunted, heaven-forsaken man like me, when you
could have got rid of him in a moment, with a word or a scream.
Women are not often brave, Miss Fane, and men, poor creatures,
more seldom still. I was driven to trust you with more than my
life last night, because it was my one last desperate chance; but
I hardly half-believed that I *could* trust you. I heard a mouse
scrambling once, outside the door; and so sure was I that I had
fallen into a trap, that I thought you had brought the police or
the gaolers upon me: and if you had I wouldn't have blamed you.
A mouse wouldn't frighten you, Miss Fane—but it frightened me.
Do you know what made me trust you through thick and "—
another bite and swallow—"thin? This was it—not a triumph
of literature, but written with a pen dipped into a heart for an
inkstand, and a good big heart too. I knew the hand that wrote
this," said he, bringing down his fist upon her pile of scrawl,
"wouldn't deprive even a real wolf of bread and water and open
air."

Something like the maternal instinct—the only thing that fears
nothing—arose in Rosamond at seeing her brood of fancies covered
by a strange hand, and at hearing that they had already been pro-
faned by sacrilegious eyes. In any case, perhaps, no shame, in
point of heat and sharpness, equals the shame of being detected
in a first act of authorship, where the fancy is concerned. If
Uncle Æneas had been the criminal, she would have wished for

the floor to open and cover her—even Sophy, her intended public, was not to set eyes on a word until the moment, if it should ever come, when the last word was written and copied; and even then she might lack the courage, even if she should retain the desire. This had been written only for the writing's sake, as children write: and it may be that she held to it all the more closely, as half conscious that she was too quickly out-growing its inspiration, just as a girl may make a younger girl an excuse for playing with her doll, or as a boy who has become half a man may still hide away his old make-believes in a dark corner of his heart, to take them out and play with them when he is quite sure that he is quite alone.

" Give me my papers ! " she said, feeling like a detected criminal but speaking like a real Queen. " You have no right—those are my papers, and this is my room ! "

" And therefore my place of refuge," said he. " Of course I hadn't a shadow of a right to read this romance of yours. Of course I haven't a ghost of a right to be here at all. But I don't beg pardon for either. I've read *you* in your romance, Miss Fane; and I feel as safe here as if I had your wizard's invisible ring. You can no more betray a man to whom you have given bread than Flora Macdonald could have given up Prince Charley. Could you—yes or no ? "

But there was no need to read her writings—in which, after all, an author is mostly prone to paint himself as he is not—to feel that Rosamond Fane could no more betray a trust than she could give up her worst enemy to his pursuers. With all his masterful ease of manner, this condemned soul (according to her theories of Lowmoor) was inspiring her with a dread which felt, to her innocence, almost like what she fancied must be hate: and his having read the secret of her life gave him the kind of awful influence that comes of knowing all the mysteries of one's mind and soul.

" I have done all I can," said she. " This is not my house, though it is my room. You—if you were my own sister, I could do nothing for you; nothing in the world."

" In fact, you are as anxious to be clear of me as I assuredly am —or rather assuredly was—to be clear of you. Well ? "

" Perhaps—if you are not found—I can manage to bring you something to eat: just once more before you go. But you *will* be found. Mr. Fane, my uncle, is a magistrate; Silver Moldwarp has been sent for, who finds out everything ; Oswald—Mr. Hargrave—who knows every inch of all the land, is riding after you everywhere——"

"And therefore the only place for me is the only place where Silver Moldwarp, who finds everything, and Oswald—Mr. Hargrave —who rides everywhere,—will neither look nor ride." He spoke in a tone she had not yet heard from him, and she did not understand it, for she had never yet, so strange a place was Crossmarsh, seen or heard a sneer. "Who is Oswald—Mr. Hargrave? And what has he to do with the affair?"

"Mr. Hargrave, of Windgates," said she, stiffly. "He is not likely to let go anything that he once takes up—till it is done."

The convict growled something to himself, in which more accustomed ears might have recognised words hardly suited to a girl's ears. "I never counted on *that* wind!" said he. "Well—if one trusts a man, one tells some woman ; if one trusts a woman, one tells some man. Of course, *he* has read this romance of yours, this Mr. Hargrave, of Windgates? *He* may find me here, without riding?"

Not even the faded remembrance of what had passed yesterday in the greenhouse rendered Rosamond conscious that her mention of a man by his Christian name had at once suggested the conclusion that he must needs be her lover to her most unwelcome guest. There are girls, scarcely older in years, who would have read in the words, in the passing sneer, and in the suppressed eagerness of the half-question, something deeper than an escaped convict's dread of discovery—that is to say, jealousy. He had, beyond question, too much to think of to have a thought for love-making at first or second sight, even were such a thing under any conditions outrageously absurd: but danger, and hunger, and loneliness, and weariness, and watching will make their victim melt at the faintest touch of long unknown kindness, and a girl's voice had become a new sight, a girl's voice a new sound, to the ex-inmate of Lowmoor. The girl who was not Rosamond would have felt, at least, one thrill of fearful pride before leaving the room and closing the door upon this gaunt, perhaps desperate, certain evilly handsome scarecrow for good and all. Even Rosamond herself could not help feeling indignant, though she knew not wholly why.

"Nobody *ever* comes into this room but myself," she exclaimed imprudently, forgetting that the opposite belief would be the most efficient means of scaring him away—"Nobody in the world!"

Three taps on the door—count one, two, three, four—two taps —count three—one blow.

The convict, as well he might, started and turned pale. It was clearly a signal of some sort—and, to a man with only himself to think of, what thing could it mean but one ? Rosamond could almost hear the clench of his teeth, as he threw upon her a look of upbraiding—no; she could never betray him now. That reproachful glance, thrown by a strong man, who believed himself betrayed, and by her, would have been past her bearing if it had been deserved. In fancy, before there was time for the next count, she felt the remorse of a traitor: come now what might, her course was sealed.

" Quick, quick ! " she could only whisper, " hide yourself under the straw—and don't rustle or move." How Rosamond, even Rosamond, who had never before had a secret in her life, should be suddenly inspired with the sole shift for keeping so great an one, belongs to the chapter of mysteries—and of common things.

She was as long as possible in opening the door, since for a long man to hide himself under a straw heap is by no means so easy as it sounds. But it was done as quickly as it might; and Rosamond, having thrown a glance round the room to make sure that there was nothing in sight that might tell tales to Sophy's sharp eyes, answered the signal.

" What is the news now ? " she asked, trying to fill the doorway. " Am I wanted, again ? Oh, Sophy, so busy as I am, I only wish the world would leave me alone ! "

" Silver Moldwarp's come—and of course, I thought," said Sophy, while her eyes tried to look over Rosamond's head into the farther twilight, " I thought you would like to know."

" Does he guess anything ? Does he think he can find―― "

" I don't know. He's with Uncle Æneas now. But you ought to come down and see him—he's such a figure of fun ! He always did wear the strangest sort of clothes ; but he must have bought of a beggar those he's got now. Do go and look at him, Rosamond; *I'll* guard your castle while you're gone."

Rosamond's secret felt as if it were choking her—she would as soon have left Sophy alone with it as a cat with a basin of cream. "No, no," she gasped, " I don't want to see Silver Moldwarp—and certainly not his old clothes. Anyhow that—that man, he isn't found ? "

" I only wish he were ! Please don't shut yourself up to-day; I don't like to go about the house alone. *We* don't believe in ghosts, of course—not in real ones: but I've been fancying myself seeing things ever since breakfast, and hearing things, too; and I don't like it at all."

" Hearing things! What things ? "

"Strange voices, and things like those. I wouldn't go back through the lumber room and along the passage alone for the world. It seemed as if people were talking in your castle—not out loud, nor whispering, but between. I thought you never *would* open the door ! "

Rosamond's heart was sinking deeper and deeper—she had forgotten that stone walls have voices, and that Sophy had ears as well as eyes. " Voices ? " she asked in a faint voice, that harmonised well with the touch of panic in her sister's humour. " What did they say ? "

" That was the worst of it," said Sophy. "I couldn't make out a single word. Do you think the house *is* haunted ? I should lose my senses if I was to sit all alone in a dark empty room like you. I *must* come in, till you're ready to go. I feel as if that horrible wretch they're trying to find was coming down the passage after me. Do come into the garden, Rosamond—it's sunshine there."

It would have been easy enough for Rosamond to lock the door and go back at once to the living rooms or the garden ; but she was still but a tyro in plotting, and she fancied it would look suspicious if she refused admission into her castle-tower. It is true she had done so fifty times before, out of nothing but whim ; but now she had become afraid to move a finger, lest that finger itself should prove a traitor. As for looking so much as the hall clock straight in the face, she felt that she would never have the courage to do such a thing again. So she made way for Sophy to enter, and followed in an agony, from which the only attainable relief was to press her finger-nails hard into her palms.

" No," said Sophy, "I can *not* make out what makes you so fond of sitting here. But what a lot you have written, to be sure. What have you been doing with dry bread ? I saw you with the rest of the loaf after breakfast, and there's nothing left of it but crumbs, and not many of them."

" Bread ? Oh, I often get hungry when I'm working," faltered Rosamond—a reason as true to the letter as was ever made by a hungry girl who grew in sea air. " Yes, the story is nearly done now. I—I wish it had never been begun. I know what we'll do, Sophy! We'll take it out into the garden, now, this minute, and I'll read it you as far as it's gone.".

"But there are ghosts in it, aren't there—and murderers?"

"Yes, plenty!"

"Then, Rosamond, I think I'd rather wait till it's *quite* finished. I want to get all that sort of people out of my eyes and ears. Not that I mind them so much, any more, now that I'm here with you. After all, it's snug to have a castle all to one's self, and all one's own. When you're married to Oswald—oh, yes, *I* know!—I'll take this for myself, only I won't keep it just like it is now. I'd have company—I'll have a big cage for canaries, and two or three dogs, and a kitten, and perhaps an owl. And—good gracious, Rosamond! what *is* the matter with that straw?"

Poor Rosamond felt that she was indeed bearing the very last straw.

"What straw?" she gasped, as well as her throat would let her.

"I saw it—it moved!"

"And you heard voices! and you saw ghosts!" cried Rosamond, who had almost foreknown what must come. But she also knew that she must hold out to the last, for honour's sake, and let herself be torn in quarters by wild horses, if need'were, rather than let so contemptible a thing as cowardice betray the man who had trusted his all to her courage. "Come, Sophy, I will see Silver Moldwarp after all."

"One minute, Rosamond; I *must* see if there's anything under that straw!"

Rosamond contrived to place herself between Sophy and the far from easy bed where the convict lay.

"No, Sophy, what nonsense! What should there be?"

"It might be a mouse, or a bat, or a cat with kittens. It might be something that would do for my room, you know."

It was too late to repent the over-cleverness which had let this irrepressible detective into the room. That Sophy would dive into the straw-heap, unless very speedily prevented by some extraordinary means, was as certain as that the convict was hidden there. And then? Then either Rosamond must either have to bear the life-long remorse of feeling herself responsible for the return to Lowmoor of a condemned soul, or else—the thought was not too horrible to rise up before her like the apparition she had

conjured up last night—this desperate man might prefer the doing
of murder to the loss of liberty. She could be almost willing, for
her own part, to lose life if that were the only means of getting
rid of her secret—but, if Sophy, groping among the straw for a
kitten or a mouse, were suddenly to be grasped round the throat by
the hand of a murderer? Rosamond turned faint, and for a
moment the light of day turned to a chaos of sparks, and the air
seemed filled with the buzzing of bees. Only by a desperate effort
she gathered herself together.

"Sophy," said she, "do me a real favour—please; pray don't
look under that straw."

"Oh, Rosamond! Why?" asked Sophy. "What *can* you have
hidden that I'm not to see?"

The sisters were really very like boy and girl, or Rosamond
would surely have known better than to think that the way to
keep a secret is to implore that it shall not be unlocked, so long as
the key is in the door.

"Nothing; you'll know some day; at least perhaps you will."

It was a challenge to a game of hide and find: for how could
Sophy dream that Rosamond was not making up some new play?
Rosamond's one real secret was her story; and even that was
shared with Sophy, as were all other things.

"Oswald says you are a real witch," said she, "and that you
come here to work real spells. Do you keep your—what is it they
call it—your Familiar under that straw?"

"Perhaps," said Rosamond. "But please, pray, never mind
what it is now. I want to go out. Please don't tease me now."

Even Sophy, struck by something in her voice, and perhaps in
her face, began to think that all this mystery was something more
than play.

"I'll tell you what it is," said she, with her best grown-up-
woman-of-the-world air; "you've been seeing things, and hearing
whispers and strange talking, as well as me. They all came from
your castle: and, now we're in the castle, it all seems to belong to
the straw. "I'm not going to be frightened by bogeys, nor shall
you. Ghosts *are* nonsense, you know—and there's nothing in the
house that could hurt us, if it's alive. And so—here goes!"

"Sophy!" cried Rosamond, holding out both her arms to bar
the way.

But Sophy, though not famous for courage before known and
intelligible dangers, would have charged a regiment of soldiers i

they barred her way to the ghost of a secret, and have opened Pandora's box or Bluebeard's chamber, as surely as if she had been christened Eve. In an instant she had dived under Rosamond's right arm, and was scattering the straw.

Rosamond fancied she heard a scream, but could not tell whether the cry was Sophy's or her own. In truth it was her own: but it was audible only to herself—voice and limbs were paralysed as by nightmare. Had the moment been less terrible, she must have swooned. And then——

"There!" cried Sophy, in triumph. "As if I didn't know there was nothing at all, all the time!"

Had Rosamond indeed lost her senses?—or had the convict indeed been but a monstrous apparition, created of overwrought fancies and dreams. There stood Sophy, waist deep in the scattered straw. But there was neither cat nor convict, murderer nor man.

CHAPTER VIII.

SIR MIDAS.
    If you had seen, sir, half that I have *known !*
    Spirits from space in flesh-and-blood-like form—
    (Materialised, we term it)—if you'd seen
    Twice two make five, and chairs with tables dance,
    And great Lord Bacon taught in other worlds,
    Come back to jabber like the parish fool,
    And harps, unfingered, twang themselves, and all
    The laws of Newton topsy-turvy-wise —
    You'd surely, sir, have faith ?
COLONEL HOTWELL.
            I would indeed—
    In Doctor Bolus : and I'd send for him.`

"OF course," said Silver Moldwarp, with a slightly superior smile, of course they'll find neither nothing nor nobody if they go to work that way. That's the fault of all the regular detectives, sir. They think to find a thing by looking. But that aren't *my* way."

"I know you're a clever fellow, Moldwarp," said Uncle Æneas, who was giving his prime minister a private audience in the library; "that's why I sent for you. But what is your way ?"

"That's their mistake, sir—to think they'll find things by looking. And whether it's a Flint or whether it's an Eleflint, the principle's the same. The way to find a thing's by *not* looking."

"By not looking? Bless my soul!"

"That's right, sir. What's the way, if you're lost a-horseback, to find the high road, but to give the animal his head and leave him to instinc', sir? That's my way. When I want to find anything, I get on the back of instinc', and straight I go: but I could never tell you how I got there for a hundred pounds. The others can always tell you the way they went, but 'tis always to nowhere. Now, sir, do you think it likely a desperate character, and as cunning as an old fox, would go where any mortal soul would think of looking for him? No, sir; you don't think anything of the kind. And you're right, sir—just as you always *are* right, and as I never know'd you wrong. Ah, Mr. Fane, begging your pardon, you've that eye for an axe as'd puzzle old Harry to take in *you*."

"Well, Moldwarp," said Uncle Æneas, "I certainly do think Mr. Hargrave over confident in supposing that the rascal could be discovered by means of mere topographical knowledge. What you say only confirms my own original view. But you understand the gravity of the occasion? Here is a desperate character from Lowmoor at large in Crossmarsh, if he's anywhere. If he is finally to make good his escape, he must manage to supply himself with food, money, and clothes. Not a house in the parish is safe as long as he is at large. Not a man can safely go out after dark, nor a woman at all. As you say, the authorities have lamentably broken down. You suppose he *is* in Crossmarsh, Moldwarp?"

"Yes, sir, I do. He couldn't have cleared the parish in his prison clothes; and if he had changed 'em, by force or trick, we'd have heard tell of it long afore now."

"Of course there'll be a reward issued for his apprehension. But, whatever it is, I, on my own account, as the principal resident in this parish, will add fifty pounds to whoever gives such information as will lead to the apprehension of this Lawrence Derwent —yes, fifty pounds. Great Heaven! To think there's an escaped convict about, in the same parish with a house like this, Moldwarp—with a museum of flints worth their weight in gold!"

"Aye, sir—to think of that indeed!"

"This house is a national responsibility, Moldwarp. Suppose the man were to break in some night and carry off some priceless link in the history of the aboriginal Phœnicians—the labour of a life, and the intentions of Providence, might be destroyed. While that man is at large and exposed to such temptations in the shape of flints, I shall not be able to sleep in my bed, and be unfit for my work all next day. It is worth paying fifty pounds for peace of mind."

"I'll give you that, sir—leastways, a piece of *my* mind. And that's not to trust overmuch to a young gentleman like Mr. Hargrave. He's young, you see; and if he goes scouring all over the country, he'll find nothing himself, and he'll only spoil the game of them that can. A young gentleman, galloping that gait, would scare away that Fenian Sun-Dyle. If I'm to earn that fifty pound I must earn it my own way. And I can't if you don't put in a word to hinder Mr. Hargrave."

"Well, Moldwarp—there is sense in what you say. But—you said something about a sun-dial, a Phœnician sun-dial; how do *you* know that if there's one thing wanting to be found—what do you know of such things? What put the idea into *your* mind?"

For a moment, Mr. Moldwarp looked a little disconcerted. But it was only a moment before he scratched his head and smiled again his superior smile. "There it is, sir! I couldn't tell you how! You might as well ask a bee how he knows there's honey in a flower. He'd cnly buzz—and that buzz would mean natural instinc', Mr. Fane. That's how I find things, and no other way."

"Aye, Moldwarp, but I don't understand how a man hits on things by chance, without knowing what's wanted."

"As you say, sir, 'tis just beyond mortal understanding; nobody that understands things is ever able to do anything any more. Why don't you find the axes and the flints ?—because you understand 'em. What comes of my not knowing one from t'other?—why I find 'em. If you, sir, was to understand the works of my mind 'twould be all the same as if I was to understand yours, and then we'd be of no more use than if we understood why we was both born."

"Well, well," said Uncle Æneas, hastily, not wholly convinced, but not caring to follow farther in the direction of so unwelcome a conclusion as that Silver Moldwarp might not be so complete an ignoramus as his patron choose to believe him. "Well, well: I dare say that's all very true. I'll speak to Hargrave; the lad's reasonable—at least, in most things—and he'll see the need of your setting to work in your own way. And about this Lawrence Derwent—how are you going to begin?"

"That's instinc', sir!"

"But bless my soul, instinct isn't dumb, I suppose? What does it say?"

Uncle Æneas would far sooner have lost confidence in himself
than in Silver Moldwarp ; but impatience to justify his own faith
in the man who could find everything rendered him impatient, and
the impatience expressing itself somewhat testily, may have seemed
to Moldwarp in the slightest degree flavoured with suspicion. At
any rate, he thought it advisable to satisfy his patron's desire for
something definite by suggesting something in the shape of practical course of action.

"Instinc' says, sir, says she, that I'll take the boat out of the
boat-house, and course along under the cliffs, and overhaul the
holes and caves. If that scoundrel's neither drowned nor dry he
must be between the two. And if he's in a hole, sir, I'll spot him
with half an eye. He must have scrambled up, or scrambled down,
and if there's a scratch on the rock, or pebble out of place,
or a tuft of grass awry, I'll know if it's been done by man or
cony—and there's none else to leave a mark except myself,
and I know my own marks as sure as sure. That's the voice
of instinc', Mr. Fane."

"Aye, Moldwarp, and of reason too. I said from the beginning that the man would make for the caves, but you'll want
help ?"

"No, thank you, sir. Helping's hindering, all over the world.
I'll just go along with the tide, and the pair of sculls. Another
man would be interfering with instinc', and may be asking why
I did this ? and, why I didn't do that ? or went here, or didn't
go along there, till I didn't know sense from reason. I'll have
him, if he's alive. And if he's not alive, why he's drowned. And
you won't say a word to Mr. Hargrave, sir, if you please—except
to tell him not to go scattering my flints, and, maybe breaking
to bits things you'd like to have found whole."

"Bless my soul, Moldwarp—that's true. I never thought of
what might come of riding about the country off the roads.
Why that confounded mare's shoe might strike on a Phœnician
sun—Better let fifty convicts loose than have *that* happen. I'll
tell him !—Come in !"

"Uncle," said Sophy, opening the door without coming in.

"Well, what is it ? Don't you see I'm busy with Moldwarp ?"

"I want you to come to Rosamond, if you please, uncle. I'm
afraid she's ill."

  *   *   *   *   *

Rosamond was not ill. But it was not strange that she seemed so : it would not have been wonderful if she were. Not only had she been living under the burden of an intolerable secret, but the unaccountable disappearance of the convict from his hiding place and from the room itself made havoc of her whole mind. Unless she had been dreaming, he had been there. The straw heap had moved before her own eyes as well as before Sophy's; he could not have left it without being seen by her, as well as by the quickest eyes in the world; there was no other hiding place in that empty room, and the window was too high for a tall man to reach without using either the chair or table. And yet he had vanished, as completely as if he had never been there at all.

When Sophy first plunged into the straw, she had half covered her eyes with her hands; when she removed them, all sense of relief was lost in incredulous wonder. Were magic and witchcraft real—had she, while engaged in the creation of apparitions, been playing with edged tools and fire? Was the occupation, or the crime, of the condemned souls in Lowmoor truly of a sort that defied and over-turned the laws of nature? Mr. Pitcairn had told her tales of Indian conjurers—of the great basket trick, and how a man can throw a rope's end into the air, and climb up the rope, coiling it after him till he and it are out of sight, and seemingly lost midway to the sky. But this feat was to the full as wonderful as these; it was the work rather of a wizard, who can control nature for great ends, than of a conjurer who is hired only to surprise and amuse. With awe of Lowmoor deepened in her, she was in the mood to give way to a belief in magic and in all maddening things.

"Into the air !" was all she could say to Sophy, who, wondering at her sudden paleness, and change of voice, took her sister's hand and led her from the chamber of mystery. Then, safely away at last from an atmosphere that seemed charged with a necromancer's fumes, she lay down upon the sofa in the parlour, with flowers within, and the window open to the sunshine and birds, and closed her eyes. She neither fainted nor slept; but yet, for some needful instants of rest, her mind and memory became closed. It was the instinct of health and strength to preserve themselves ; and health and strength were Rosamond's fairy godmothers, who had promised never to fail her whatever might betide.

But Sophy, who had never seen sickness except in a labourer's cottage, was alarmed ; and Rosamond's next living sensation was the sight of her uncle's anxious face, who bent over her and held

5 A

her hand. He was as sparing as his favourite flints of the signs of affection; and Rosamond's heart, touched to its depth, felt like a criminal's. The need of confession healthily possessed her, and confession no longer meant so much as the imagination of treachery. If the human-seeming creature had ever been there, he was gone now, and safe, no doubt, in some region where nature has no laws, and where such things as this can be.

Her uncle listened in silence as she contrived, incoherently enough, to deliver the story of her nightmare, while Sophy sat at her feet in fascinated amaze. She was not interrupted by a word : and even when she had finished, Uncle Æneas did not ask her a single question. He only shook his head gloomily.

"Yes, yes, my dear," he said, "I daresay—I've no doubt—it all happened just exactly as you say. We oughtn't to have let you hear about such things. Justice work, and men like that and their doings, aren't fit things to fill little girls' brains. I think you'd better go to bed and go to sleep. I don't wonder at your lying awake, with all my coins and flints in the house; I must buy a safe and put everything into it every night at bedtime. See your sister upstairs to her room, Sophy, and when you've seen her in bed come back to me."

"Bed, uncle!" exclaimed Rosamond. "No; why half the day hasn't gone, and I'm as well——"

"Yes, yes, my dear. No doubt you're perfectly well, but you'll go to bed all the same. Sophy, take your sister to her room."

Uncle Æneas did not often interfere with his nieces' liberty, but old-fashioned obedience to lawful authority was one of the laws of their life, and Rosamond did not dream of rebellion—and, for that matter, she was growing hungry for rest and solitude. The companionship of Sophy would only be a burden to her for some hours to come.

"Then uncle," she asked, as she rose from the sofa, "then—you don't think all I saw was true?"

"God bless my soul, no—bless my soul, yes, I mean. But don't worry over it any more, there's a good girl ; don't be afraid of the man any more. He's gone, and Moldwarp will find him, and then he'll be kept safe enough, you may be sure, for the rest of his days—for he's in for life, I'm told. There, go to sleep like a good girl, and forget it all."

"And—and—you don't think I did wrong?"

"No, no: don't worry, that's all. Be off with you, and don't let me hear about it any more."

"Oh, Rosamond," said Sophy, on their way upstairs, "and have you really been hiding that prisoner, all alone? I wonder you aren't dead of fear! Why didn't you scream, and call up the house? Why didn't you call me?"

"Indeed, Sophy, I can't tell you all about it now, I must think it all out, for I'm sure there must be something about it all that can't be really true. Sophy, forgive me. I'll never try to hide anything from you any more. It's the first time, and the last too, so forgive me—please do. But how could I give up that poor runaway? You'd have done just like I did, indeed."

"Indeed, I wouldn't though," said Sophy, "I should have run away back to bed, and hid under the clothes. I don't pretend to be brave, like you," she added, for Rosamond was still her heroine and her chief, and she felt that her heroine had somehow risen to the occasion, though she hardly comprehended how.

"*Will* you forgive me, dear?" asked Rosamond, humbly, the larger nature bowing before the smaller, as is the way of larger natures, always and everywhere.

"Of course I do. And—and—I think—I'll never try to find things out again, only I do wonder how he got away. I must find out that, or else I shall never be able to rest in my grave."

"I'm afraid, Sophy, there are a great many things that we'd much better not try to understand. I don't want anything to happen any more. I want things to go on just as they are for ever. Promise me you'll never marry anybody, Sophy. If you won't I never will."

"What—not Oswald?"

"No—nobody."

"Then, neither will I. But you're quite sure you'll never have any secrets from me any more?"

Rosamond laid down upon her bed without undressing. Sophy brought her book and then returned to Uncle Æneas in the library.

"Ah, there you are," he said, stopping in the middle of an impatient walk up and down the room. "Have you seen her safe upstairs?"

"Yes, uncle. But *how* did he get away?"

"Then say nothing to the other servants, but go into the yard or up the long garden, and find Pritchard, and tell him to ride over to the village, and give this note at once to Dr. Hawker, and to trot fast all the way."

"Dr. Hawker, uncle?"

"Bless my soul, yes—who else, when Rosamond's got the fever on the brain? But don't say a word about that to Pritchard, or to another soul about the place till Hawker's been. They might think it catching——"

ꞁ "Then you don't believe, uncle——"

"Bless the child, no! As if an escaped convict would hide in the house of a justice—as if he could get in, and, being in, as if he could get out again—absurd! And, on her own showing, there was no convict—convicts at Lowmoor don't treat young ladies, and a houseful with throats to cut, and of priceless arch-æological treasures to steal, in that fine gentlemanly sort of way. She's been reading too many story-books, and has been patching up a *réchauffé* of Claude Duval, or some such lady-killing scoundrel. I shall overhaul that lumber room, not for convicts, but for books; and if I find what I expect, I'll take a leaf out of old Don Quixote, and have a bonfire without waiting for November. That straw will come in well. And *do* I believe that a man of flesh and blood can vanish, like a hobgoblin on a broomstick, through solid walls!"

"Oh, uncle? Is she ill?"

"She's been scared about that convict being at large, and it's got to her brain. But she mayn't be seriously ill—if Hawker gets here pretty soon."

Off ran Sophy. Illness had never yet come to the cottage, and she scarcely knew how to feel towards it when it did come. Could it mean that Rosamond might die? But nothing like that could happen—that would mean the end of the world. Of course her uncle was right, and Rosamond could really have seen nothing; but Sophy remembered how she herself had been tricked by phantom voices along the passage, and how she herself had seen the straw-heap move. Had she also received a touch of fever on the brain? But, with this appalling shadow hanging over Rosamond, she had reason enough for feeling fevered now. Having delivered her message to Pritchard, the groom and gardener, with an attempt at prudence and reticence that suggested nothing less than a sudden outbreak of plague, and with an evasion of questions that amounted to exaggerated answers, she crept back to the house, and, not daring to disturb her sister, gave herself up to tears until she was tired.

Rosamond, alone at last, and free from the burden of her secret, closed her eyes, and wished and wished so strongly that the wish almost persuaded her that her night and morning had been a dream, and nothing but a dream, or, at any rate, a visitation from that unknown and lawless world beyond the hills. People who are unused to wonders, believe in them when they come more easily than those who live in an atmosphere of strange things. At last, however, the sense of infinite relief possessed her; and, after her sleepless night, set her sleeping. She slept so sound and so long that she knew nothing, towards the end of the afternoon, of the visit of Dr. Hawker, who, having heard her story, came and shook his head over her, and very properly ordered that on no account should she be disturbed. " She's called in Dr. Nature," said he, " and I won't interfere till he goes. When he gives up the case, call me again. It's a case of cerebral excitement; but I hope that inflammation may be averted with proper care. Miss Rosamond is of a peculiar type, of the nervous temperament, I should say. Strange things, those morbid fancies ; but we may look for plenty of them, with an escaped convict roaming over the country. Mrs. Hawker, when she heard of it, went off into hysterics; she's a highly organised type of the nervous temperament, too. Miss Sophy had better not sleep in the same room to-night, for fear the patient should be disturbed ; every minute's sleep is worth a pound of medicine. But she can be somewhere within call : patients like these are liable to have bad dreams. Die, did you ask, Miss Sophy ? Nonsense—or perhaps when she's a great grandmother of eighty years old. Only keep her quiet and let her sleep : that's all. Her being woke up before her time is just the one chance—and there's always one—of things going wrong."

The counsel was wise, and it made Sophy happy again : for, though her heart had not yet grown to be very large, it was all Rosamond's. She even rose to the occasion, and took infinite precautions to ensure her sister's slumber from being disturbed by the remotest of accidents. She shut every window in the house, and stood sentry, without any shoes, on the landing outside the bedroom door, so as to compel silence on all who went up or down. At tea-time, she poured out the milk drop by drop, and would not stir her sugar for fear the spoon should rattle. And her going to bed—among the creepy sensations belonging to the first experience of a solitary room—was as much a miracle of swiftness and

silence as her sleep was of soundness so soon as the pillow
was touched by her golden hair.

It was dark when Rosamond woke: but she was not ignorant
of the hour, because the hall clock, which Sophy had unaccounta-
ably forgotten to stop, struck eleven immediately afterwards.
"I *have* slept!" thought she. "What can it mean? And I am
not undressed—yes, I was sent to bed: I remember now. Sophy,
—are you there?" she whispered; but no answer came, nor, when
she listened, could she hear the faintest breathing. "They're very
late in coming to bed," thought she. She rose, groped her way to
the door, and looked out upon the landing. All was dark; the
hall lamp was out, and the tick of the hall clock was the only sound.

She worked her way back to Sophy's bed, and found it empty.
It all seemed very odd; and of course Sophy ought to have slept
lightly enough, in the next room, to hear her moving. However, Rosamond could find a match, and lighted a candle, and
presently discovered that Sophy's room had been changed. "Am
I going to be ill?" thought she. "And yet I don't feel different
from usual. But perhaps I do feel different without knowing it;
and surely people don't sleep all day and half through the night
when they're well. I wish Sophy was awake, but I can't wake
her; she looks a great deal too happy. Oh, I hope I am not going
to fall ill—and oh, if I am, there's my story: nobody must find
that; nobody must ever see that now. I must get hold of that,
and tear it to bits, before I ever go into that horrible castle again."

After the part it had played in her terrible adventure, the
creature of her mere fancy had been blighted out of life and soul.
She would never be able, herself, to bear the sight of it again;
and the vision of herself laid up helplessly ill, while her uncle, and
perhaps Oswald Hargrave, were exploring her bower and rifling
her past of its mysteries, was not to be borne. That must be
averted at any cost, even at that of another, one more, one last
visit to the castle, where she had formerly spent so many happy
and busily idle hours. She might find herself ill to-morrow, the
deed must be done now. Yet she shuddered as she thought of a
repetition of last night's journey. It was like courting fresh disaster, and she fore-knew that, as she followed the passages to her
citadel, the echo of her feet would become visible phantoms.
Still they would be but empty phantoms, this time, after all;
the manuscript must be seized and forthwith destroyed, as if it
were some evil charm. She need not linger a moment in the

room, she need but snatch the papers from the table, lock the door behind, fly back to bed and safety, and let herself fall ill, if so she must, with a clear mind. Sophy might wake at any instant. The deed must be done, and now.

She had expected so much from the terror that flieth by darkness that the reality fell infinitely short of her fears. It was true that the boards would creak, and that the failure of the ticking clock to rouse the household was scarcely short of a miracle. But for the rest, the powers of darkness did not molest her on the road. For the last time—for the very last time—she entered that dreary room, which the light of her one bedroom candle rendered more dreary and dismal still. Her hand was on the papers, the deed was well-nigh done. But at that moment another hand was laid upon her shoulder.

" You are come at last!" said—He.

Let those picture the poor girl's misery who have the power. It passes mine.

" I am half dead with hunger, half mad with waiting," said he. " But never mind now. After all, you could have chosen no better time. For heaven's sake, don't look so scared; bring your wits together. Don't you want to be rid of me for good and all? Won't you understand that I've found the way to escape clean off never to see you again, if you'll only be half as brave, for a short ten minutes, as you were, God bless you, last night and this morning? Come—you must be; you shall. Do you think I want to stay here? And do you want me to stay? Listen—be yourself. Don't you understand that you are to rid yourself of me; to help me to go?"

" I can do nothing more," said she, faintly.

" Yes—you can. And you have no time to loose. I know, better than you, that any minute may bring somebody to this room. The very stupidest of them all can't go on without looking in the right place for ever. Their stupidity—even theirs—has reached its last limit by now. There's a boat-house, isn't there, where you keep a boat, with sculls?"

" Yes," said she, without in the least wondering how he had come to know.

" Is it locked or open?"

" Not locked." His former mesmeric force over her was returning rapidly.

" Then—you must let me out of the house, and show me the way. I'm sailor enough to pull a boat in a calm, and I shall know where to make for. If I can get off at once, I shall have as many dark hours as I need. Come."

" No!" she managed to bring out, with what seemed to be the last remnant of strength that was left in her.

" Then—Miss Fane—there is only one thing to be done. I can't stay here and starve ; and I won't be taken back to Lowmoor for nothing. Do you understand ? "

She did not understand ; at least not wholly. But she could guess his drift, and began to be conscious that only her courage stood between a desperate man and some desperate deed. His voice and his manner, for all their quiet ease, and their unfailing courtesy, were for that very reason more significant than threats could have been. Whatever it might cost her, the man must go, and in his own way.

" Are you ready now ? " asked he. " You have only to guide me to the boat-house, and then to return as quietly as you please. You can wake in the morning, certain of there not being a sign left to show that I have been here for a single hour. When the boat's missed, that will be nothing to you. You will never be troubled by me again. I shall be either on the other side of the world, and alive, or dead at the bottom of the sea. If you pause one moment longer, you are a fool, and on your own head be whatever comes of your folly."

" Anything to be sure he is gone for ever ! " thought Rosamond. And, somehow, she felt as if the convict read her thoughts as he followed her from the room.

CHAPTER IX.

Even thus he fares who, on the hill
    Where toward the sunset wandered she,
Feels, at one stroke, his heart turn chill—
By paths her feet have blest, what ill
        Should make him start to see ?
Only a glove, or ring, you'll say,
    That she had lost the while she stood
To watch the war of gold and grey
His ear hath caught from love's estray
        A whisper—as of Blood.

' WELL, Moldwarp," asked Uncle Æneas next morning before breakfast, " what have you found ? You took the boat out yesterday—eh ? "

"I did that, sir—aye, and this morning again too. I'm on my way up from the boat-house now."

" Well ? "

" I can't say I've found much to speak of—not as yet. But——"

" Then it seems," said Oswald, who had ridden over on chance of hearing news, " that your instinct hasn't turned out so much better than mine ? "

" I beg your pardon, Mr. Hargrave. I didn't say I'd found nothing. Not much to speak of don't mean nothing at all. Only so sure as you begin to ask questions of instinc', off she goes."

" Oswald," said Uncle Æneas, a little sharp, " don't bother the man. He has ways of his own. You can't expect even Silver Moldwarp to find everything in a day."

" All right," said Oswald. " Of course genius had nothing to do with reason, as all the world knows. My belief is that the man has got out of this country altogether in spite of everyone. Still, every notion's good for something, and I won't own myself beat till I've tried everything. My horse wants a rest, and I want to change my limbs. I'll take a pull along shore myself, and see what instinct will do for me."

" Well, what do you say to that, Moldwarp ? " asked Uncle Æneas.

" Well, sir, nothing but what, if Mr. Hargrave likes the job, it's all one to me."

" All right," said Oswald. " Then, Mr. Fane, if you'll let me, I'll breakfast here."

" And you'd better get some breakfast yourself, Moldwarp," said Uncle Æneas, thus taking occasion to save his 'prime minister' from the cross examination that he seemed to see gathering in Oswald's eyes. " You don't understand Moldwarp," he said, as the latter, no less ready to take advantage of the occasion for escape, left the library. " If that man, Derwent, is to be found, Moldwarp will find him—only he must do it in his own way. You may wager what you like he wouldn't have given up the boat to you if he hadn't put himself on a track that he's going to follow up ashore. That's Moldwarp all over; he never understands anything, and he never can explain anything, but he'll go for whatever's wanted as straight as a hound."

Oswald did not affect Silver Moldwarp, but he had no call to interfere with any man's hobby, so he said nothing, but went for a stroll in the garden till breakfast time. Of Rosamond's illness

he had heard nothing, for he had spoken to nobody about the
place but Mr. Fane, who had slept off all anxiety on that score,
and scarcely cared to enter upon the topic of his niece with her
unreasonable lover without real occasion.

Meanwhile Moldwarp carried his own reflections with him.
"Confound that Oswald Hargrave!" thought he. " If they find
that murdering thief they'll find my jacket pocket, and if they
find my jacket pocket, I may live to Methuselah before I get hold
of such another green-handed pump as Squire Fane. I know what
Master Oswald thinks—he don't believe I ever went out in that
boat at all, and he wants to spy. Ah, my lad, you may be one
too many for Silver Moldwarp, but Silver Moldwarp's a baker's
dozen too many for you! You expect to find a dry old tub fit for
firewood, so you may say, ' Holloa, this hasn't felt the touch of
salt water since 'twas last painted, whenever that may be!' "

Moldwarp was, as has been said, exceedingly prone to talk half,
or even quite aloud to himself, for he was his only companion
during the daytime, and his own only friend and confidant always.
Thus soliloquy, which in most cases is but a convenient makeshift,
was in his case a reality. Only it was one of his many instincts
that he never thus suffered his tongue to take its needful exercise
at times or places where it could be overheard.

Of these places the boat-house was not one. Indeed, it was the
least frequented spot in all the ground belonging to the cottage, for
it was difficult to get at, and the boat itself was never used—it
fulfilled the purpose of its existence by being there to be used some
time next summer that never came, and meanwhile by being one of
the orthodox properties of a house by the sea. Still, like a grand
piano, there was a household tradition that it was not an idler, and
that Moldwarp should have had it out was assumed to be quite in
the natural course of things. He was therefore no little taken
back when he found that, despite the confident assertions he had
made not a minute ago of his having not only used the boat but of
having left the boat in safety, that no boat was there.

" If I haven't let my confounded instinc' run me into a fix now!'
exclaimed he, in his half-thought, half-speech. " It looks uncommon like as if some of the fishers had been making free with what
nobody was likely to miss from year's end to year's end—and I
can't go back from it now, that I had her out all yesterday, and all
this morning up to breakfast time. Things aren't looking quite so
pleasant all round that I can afford to be bothered with lies. I've

had that confounded boat, that I must stick to—my truth's my character; and as I said 'twas here ten minutes ago, why, here it must have been. But then, what must have become of the brute within ten minutes ago ? Devil take the tub, if this isn't a tougher job than chipping out that Fenian Dyle ! And if there isn't that Paul Pry of a Hargrave coming down ! "

But there again Silver Moldwarp's celebrated instinct had contrived to lead its owner wrong. It may be that the fear was father to the thought, for it would certainly have been an awkward business for Silver Moldwarp, while unprepared with a story that would hold together, to have the boat-house found empty by Oswald Hargrave. The right conclusion would be the only one open—that the boat had been absent, nobody could guess how long, at the time when Silver Moldwarp had professed to be using her, and that, for a man who made simplicity and straightforwardness his principal stock in trade, would never do. Moreover, perhaps because Oswald Hargrave somewhat mistrusted Silver Moldwarp, Silver Moldwarp had an especial objection to being caught in a common-place, bungling, utterly inartistic lie by Oswald Hargrave. For the man was a real artist in his way, and was really ashamed of a lie that lacked even a respectable amount of ingenuity. The merest tyro, he felt, would, before saying he had been using the boat, have made sure that the boat was there to be used. However, there was not the immediate call upon his readiness of wit that he feared.

Oswald, on reaching the steep cliff path that led to the cove, turned aside, and lounged along the edge of the cliff itself, just outside the low wall of the kitchen garden. This particular part of the path, originally made for the coast-guard, was not without a certain promise of possible danger for weak heads, and was therefore the fuller of pleasure for strong ones. The young man, to Silver Moldwarp's infinite relief, seated himself upon the wall, and enjoyed the sheer down-look into the ebbing tide, and its angry battle as it retreated from the steep shelves of the shingle. The tide there rose high and fell low; when high it covered the narrow beach and met the cliffs, and was never, at its lowest, other than deep water, leaving nothing in the way of flotsam and jetsam behind. It need not be said that Rosamond, as always, was deep down in the mind of the man whose fixed purpose was to become her husband in due time and her lover for all time; but her mental presence was so constant and so deep that he had plenty of mind to spare for daily things, and the seizure of the escaped convict, if only for the reason that he had undertaken it, was fixed in his mind also. " Moldwarp is a conceited ass," thought he. " He's bound to do something, but doesn't know what—and pottering about with a boat is the best way of wasting time till everything's forgotten, and till Uncle Æneas gets into a hurry for him to be at the flints again. However, if I take a boat too, and prove there's nothing to be found that way, I shall stop a false scent—and that helps to find the true one. And it may bring the fox out of his hole, wherever it is, if he's let think that the hunt's called off. If he isn't starved out or tempted out by this time to-morrow, I shall begin to think he's walked over this precipice in the dark, and been washed out into the deep sea. By Jove, if he's done that, he wouldn't have left even his body behind him. It wouldn't be a bad place even to dive over, for a man who knew how to swim at high tide. It isn't like Furnace Point, where the rocks wouldn't give him even so much chance as that of being drowned. What in the name of——"

His eye had been suddenly caught by something which, though it had nothing to do with Lawrence Derwent, seemed to require looking into. It was not the way of straw hats at Crossmarsh, any more than in more civilised quarters of the globe, to grow on gorse bushes ready made. But that was what Oswald Hargrave, craning the edge of the precipice, and speculating on the fate of one who should slip or spring over, very distinctly saw. The bush was not on the narrow path itself, but hung out a few inches below the edge, an advanced guard, or sentinel, of vegetation ; and held tightly among the thorns was a brown straw hat, with a narrow brim and blue ribbon—a small hat, such as a girl might wear for playing at sailors, and, though like thousands of others, perfectly familiar to Oswald's eyes. It did not require a second glance to recognise the hat which Rosamond had worn the day before yesterday in the garden, and a hundred times before.

There was no reason for suspecting mystery or evil in a very natural trick of the wind. Rosamond had, no doubt, been walking on the safe side of the wall, when some playfully-minded breeze had teased her by blowing her hat out of the reach of her hands. It was a fine opportunity for a lover with the least touch of the knight about him. Oswald laid himself flat on the path, and pushed himself forward, holding the stem of the bush with his left hand, till, with almost half his body extended beyond the brink of the precipice, his right fingers reached the straw brim. It was less easy to draw himself back again, but he succeeded at last in standing with the recovered hat in his smarting and bleeding fingers. But it was Rosamond's very own hat, and well worth a good many scratches.

"I must get Sophy to help me play her a trick about this," thought he. "The witch mustn't think there's no magic in the world but her own."

Clearly Oswald Hargrave was no despairing lover, who took his repulse of yesterday for the loss of a pitched battle. And, for that matter, it would be difficult for any man to feel very hopeless on so bright and fair a morning. Pleased at having begun the day by doing something for Rosamond, and something which was ennobled by the element of just possible peril, he touched with his lips what had touched her hair, vaulted over the wall, and went towards the house in search of Sophy. Before reaching the front door he heard himself accosted from behind with a hearty

"Holloa, Hargrave—you here? You've come to ask after Miss Rosamond, I suppose? How is she to-day?"

"What—haven't you heard she isn't well? But you've just arrived, I suppose. This is my day out your way, so I've come over early, before starting on my regular round."

"Miss Fane—ill?" asked Oswald, in surprise and dismay.

"Yes," said the Doctor, who knew nothing of the nature of Oswald's interest in Rosamond, and therefore thought himself free to talk openly: "I didn't like to frighten old Fane and Miss Sophy when I was called in yesterday, but it's lucky if she's been able to sleep off a threat of brain fever. The heat, I suppose, and an intensely excited condition of nerves. She was asleep when I saw her, but she had been delirious—and one knows what that means."

"Good God!" exclaimed Oswald, "and I have heard nothing—not a word! What——"

"Yes. She fancied, and told her uncle and her sister, that she had been helping to hide that man from Lowmoor—that he had come out of a heap of straw in some room where she was at night, and that she had been obliged to give him food and shelter, and—but here's Mr. Fane. Well, Mr. Fane, has she slept out yet? She hasn't been disturbed?"

But Oswald broke in before Uncle Æneas, who, grown hungry, had come out to gather his breakfast flock, could answer. "And what makes you think that fever, Doctor?" asked he, a little roughly. "Why should it not be *true?*"

"Because, my dear Hargrave," said the Doctor, "Fane here will tell you that certain portions of her story could not possibly be true. The end of the man was that he disappeared—no, vanished—into air. It could not be true, because it was a hallucination, a strange one, but nothing more. Perhaps Miss Sophy will see if her sister is awake, Mr. Fane?"

But before Uncle Æneas could find room for a word, and before Oswald could realise that Rosamond either had lost her senses or had gone through some terrible adventure incredible to archæologists and physicians, Sophy herself darted out of the house all scared and breathless, as if the man from Lowmoor himself was at her heels. She did not pause to notice Oswald or the Doctor, but seized Uncle Æneas by the hand, and cried out,

"She—is—Gone!"

"Rosamond? Miss Fane? Why what is the matter with her?"

There was no need to ask whom Sophy meant by She. But "gone" could have only one meaning; nor was there one there, save Dr. Hawker, who dared to give that meaning its name.

"Dead!" he exclaimed, most unprofessionally aghast, "I will go at once to her room."

"She is not in her room," cried poor Sophy; "she is not anywhere. I've hunted everywhere, high and low. She is gone, and, oh! her hat's gone too."

"Was this her—the hat, Sophy?" asked Oswald, in a strange, hollow voice, and deadly pale.

"Yes, yes," said Sophy with hope springing up in her eyes, "where did you find her? Where is she, after all?"

It was no time to spare the hearts or respect the hopes of others when it was he that had to deal the blow who himself felt the stroke the most keenly. "Where I found this?—on a furze bush, over the cliff," Oswald groaned, "and——"

Dr. Hawker looked at Uncle Æneas, who had collapsed, all bewildered. "If *that* has happened—if she woke too soon—if the worst has happened to her brain——"

"Speak out, man!" Uncle Æneas cried out, suddenly starting from his stupor. "You believe that—she—has gone out in a fit of fever-madness, and thrown herself from the cliff into the sea— is *that* what you believe?"

"Pray, Mr. Fane, calm yourself—be a man! Perhaps——"
"Moldwarp ahoy!" sung out Uncle Æneas. "Get out the boat—and, Oswald——"

But Oswald was already at the boathouse, and Sophy half way after him. So long as something, anything, could be done, though only to prove the worst to be the very worst, he would not realise the terrible fate that the Doctor's words implied—a young girl sent mad by a summer sun, and self-slain in a fit of delirious frenzy. But even while he hurried to the boat there came before his mind the only too clear picture of the pitch-dark midnight, the narrow path, the sheer cliff, the hungry tide, and the frenzied girl. He burst open the boat-house door. "The boat—at once!" he cried to Moldwarp, who stood within, staring out to sea.

"And that's the very thing I'm looking round the offing for," said Moldwarp. "Only half an hour ago I made her fast by the painter to that post—and I suppose it broke with rottedness, for anyhow 'tis broke and off, that blessed tub has gone all alone with the ebb—you may see her pitching out there this minute, if you've got your eyes. 'Twas no fault of mine, sir—maybe she'll be picked up yet; but anyhow we must stay ashore for to-day."

Silver Moldwarp spoke so straightly, and with such abstinence from all superfluous details and flourishes, that Oswald, much less Uncle Æneas, who had now overtaken the others, would not, even under less all-absorbing conditions, have dreamed of doubting him. To connect the absence of the boat with the absence of Rosamond, or either with the convict, was a process which could not possibly occur to any man's mind. Oswald could only feel faint with despair—Uncle Æneas was already grown older by ten years. Dr. Hawker must be right. And then there was Sophy——

"I have killed her!" the poor child cried. "I fell asleep. I did not hear her go——"

"No, Sophy!" said Oswald, coming to his senses. "For God's sake don't get that into your mind—it was not you——"

Moldwarp, knowing nothing of what had happened, looked from one to the other. So he did not perceive that Sophy, her ruling passion intensified, or at least turned into instinct by despair, or perhaps in the forlorn hope that any trifle might give light, had picked up from a dark corner a tattered old jacket from some hole in which fell a chisel and a cheap note-book, bound in frayed leather. With miserably passive face she placed the book and

6

chisel in Oswald's unnerved and passive fingers. But Moldwarp, his attention called by the movement, caught sight of the garment, though not of the note-book, made a pounce at the former as it lay on Sophy's arm, and recovered it somewhat rudely.

"Begging your pardon, miss—but that's my old coat," said he.

Oswald, catching one last ray of Sophy's struggling hope, glanced at the book, and then at the tool, first slightly, but then more sharply. And then he looked straight at Moldwarp, and openly held out chisel and book towards Uncle Æneas.

"I believe," said he, firmly enough out of his heavy and desperate heart, "that she was not mad—that her story was true. I believe it, because I believe that the man who stands there, being a liar by trade, has lied about the boat: that it was there yesterday, and not there this morning. I believe Her story, because it is hers, and because it contradicts his lie. For his lie and her truth mean that the man out of Lowmoor is even now at sea—if this means Murder—I will *not* give way, nor sit down and mourn—no, not for a single hour. If I never find Her, I will never rest till I find *Him*."

None longer noticed Sophy, who had broken down into passionate and remorseful tears. To the Doctor his words were those of one whom desperate grief and horror had turned into a madman. But little did Oswald to whom flints were but flints, reckon on the effect of the chisel and note-book upon a collector's soul. Uncle Æneas loved his niece dearly: I have said that the shock of her horrible fate had aged him by ten years. But his nieces had never, like the flints of Pix-Knoll, grasped the foundations of his nature. He, also, saw in the note-book, among a score of like things, the working notes of the Phœnician Dial, precisely as it existed in his own mind; he also took note of the chisel—then, seeing the guilt-brazened face of the detected impostor who had been trading on his heart's desire, he turned away, aged ten, nay twenty years more. What, after all, was the death of a girl? She had been spared this—she was better off than he.

But Oswald, misreading him, placed his hand on the old man's shoulder. "Love is over," said he, sternly. "But, since hell has proved stronger than heaven—therefore vengeance remains."

CHAPTER X.

Use Fortune for a slave, she'll cheat your will:
Dare her as foe dares foe, she'll conquer still ;
Deny her force, and swift her force shall fall—
But he who trusts her blindly, gaineth all.

"MISS FANE," said Lawrence Derwent, the convict, "I must most humbly apologise. But necessity knows no law."

So, in the gentlest of voices, he addressed the girl who was alone with him, far out at sea. He had rowed hard, the night had been dark, and the morning grey ; and even now, though the hour of sunrise was long past, the nearer of the two steep shores of the sea looked but a bank of clouds—the farther was unseen. Rosamond—for it was she—could only imagine that she was herself one of those lost souls, whose doom, ever since she could remember, had hung over her like an awe. Or rather, she could only feel this—imagination could not grasp the truth of a situation that defied the reach of dreams. Had she been but a year older in heart, she must have been prostrate with physical fear. But a soul suddenly whirled away out of life, as she seemed to herself to be, and into the region of doom, has nothing left to fear —the worst has come. Only a few days ago alive, and happy, and at unbroken peace, and never dreaming of change, but as of something too infinitely dreadful to concern her and hers—now, alone with this man, who seemed something far else than man, and on the sea, which stood to her for the border-land of all outer mystery ; it was enough to make her despair. It might have been natural to cast about for the chances of human help from human peril. But she had been driven to believe, in spite of herself, that he who had borne her off belonged to a world whose creatures are gifted, or cursed, with super-human powers —that he could read her thoughts, and command nature herself to obey his will. Moreover, it might surely have been natural to be overwhelmed with desperate wonder, if wonder, however desperate, were not all too weak a word. But Rosamond had long learned to regard the whole outer world, with Lowmoor in it, from a point of belief that would not have regarded the adventures of Sindbad himself as wonderful, had she been told that they were true. For Rosamond's fancy, at any rate, was as bold and uncompromising at fifteen years old as it had been at five.

6 A

She had not yet learned to look upon the sunrise as not surpassing all imaginable wonders, or upon the flights of the wildest dreams as approaching the wonder of the rising of the sun. She had given one startled scream, when her companion had lifted her into the boat before pushing off from the shore, but she had no hope that it could have been heard in the sleeping cottage. through the roar of the sea; or that, had it been heard through sleep, it would have suggested anything but a sea-bird out fishing at an untimely hour. Since then, she had only remained passive —and, indeed, the bravest could have done no more. It was not that she felt herself at a desperate man's mercy. Derwent was no mere man to her.

"I must apologise most humbly," said he, again, resting on his by no means energetic oars, and wiping his brow. "I assure you I had to conquer myself, and, after a hard battle, to put you to all this—well, say trouble. And it pains me all the more—for you are a brave girl. Come, have you nothing to ask? Nothing to say?"

"What is to happen to me?"

"On my life, I could not have believed in a girl who would not have torn out at least one of my eyes. I assure you that I was prepared to pay one, as the lowest price I could expect to pay for liberty. You have been my guardian angel—all through. If I knew how to find speech for such dumb things as thanks—but I can't do that. Nobody ever can. Only for this night's work sake I am your slave, for ever and a day."

It was not the first time that something in his voice though certainly not in his words, had made the girl almost hate herself for feeling herself so much a slave, or rather, for not being able to comprehend the confusion of fancy and faith, error and honour, that had brought her here. If she could only be sure that, in helping this creature, she had been following the clear light of plain duty, and of her own free will, she might have dared the unknown worst of her doom. It was too late for this assurance now, for all freedom of will had passed out of her hands. But her very helplessness inspired her to rebel.

"Then," said she, as if taking him at his word, "put me ashore again, anywhere; I will find my own way home, even from Furnace Point."

"You ask me the one impossible thing. No, Miss Fane; that I cannot do. If I could have done that, I would not have

carried you off: I did not bring you out to sea to put you on
shore. Pray don't look at me like that. On my honour, Miss
Fane, I mean you no harm, no possible avoidable harm. There,
we can let the tide take care of us now. Ah, it's a comfort to
be able to drift again. Whether I'm to be henceforth gaol-bird
or free-bird, luck must decide it now. I've done my all; the rest
is a matter of heads and tails. Just think of it, Miss Fane,
at this moment all the thousand chances that go to make an hour
of the world's life are being shaken over me, and will soon be
thrown. I can't even cog the dice, and yet something tells me
that I shall win the game. Since I won eight thousand in one
night, without a break in the luck, I never felt like this before.
It's true that I never before felt half so hungry, and, maybe,
hunger helps a man to feel hopeful."

Rosamond's had been but the poorest pretence of rebellion,
after all. His apparently meaningless words, spoken like the
commonplaces of a morning call, ceased to touch her ears. She
could only crouch in the stern, dead to the fresh breeze that
followed them, and blind to the sunlight that was now beginning to
make a golden path for the boat upon the waves. The glory of
yesterday was returning to the sky and the sea. But that same
glory of light revealed something more. At first she sat, with
her elbows on her knees, and her chin upon her hands, in a state
of absolute blindness, only wondering if God knew what He was
doing with her, and with Sophy, and with all at home. But, as
the breeze blew fresher, and as the waves began to dance to its
more lively tune, she saw the cliffs receding on either side, and, in
front, a line of white that she knew, by instinct, to be the edge
of the open sea. She felt herself turn pale and her heart sink.
She was drifting out of the last sight of the world to the threshold
of doom; nay, being danced thither to the music of sunlight
and wind.

"How soon will it be," she asked the wind, "before I die?"
Despair was deepening into awe.

"No man on earth knows that," said Derwent, less lightly.
"What makes you think death an inch nearer here than in the
safest place on earth, which is a gaol? Listen to me, Miss Fane,
and when you have listened, think of me as you please, but not
till then. Whatever has happened, we are in the same boat now
—truly enough; and, till we are out of it, for both our sakes we
must be comrades and friends; are you listening?"

"I hear," said Rosamond, answering him with her lips, but not with her eyes, which were alive only to the vanishing shores and the nearing line of foam. For she was as one who, in the midst of life and strength, is called upon to watch the parting of the shores of life and the nearing of the ocean of death, and yet is not allowed to leave behind a word of comfort or of farewell. She thought of Sophy, and of the uncle who had hitherto seemed of such small account in her life, and of Oswald, her old playfellow, from whom she had scarcely parted friends. How had she treasured so little the mere daisies that grew on Pix-Knoll? She would never see them again—and in their place only the terrible smile of the sea.

"Think," said Derwent, torturing with his voice the last hours in which she might make at least her thoughts her own; "think of what is ten thousand times more horrible than the most hideous of deaths—the life of a man, young, strong, able, who knows how to think, and how to live, condemned to a prison cell until he is old! No, *you* can't think of it; only such a man himself can conceive what it means, nor then truly until he has tried. I have tried it: and, if I could, I would not dare tell you all it means. You needn't know half to answer this—is there any imaginable thing a human being would not do to escape from hell? Having escaped, is there anything he would not do to remain free? Have I escaped—as some would say by miracle—to throw my last chance away for the sake of a child of whom I know nothing, scarcely so much as her name? When I said there is nothing I would not do for you if I could, I was not thinking of impossible things. I would cut off my right hand, Miss Fane, because I am grateful, but I could not go back to Lowmoor, because, though I am grateful, I am a man."

"Yes," said Rosamond, compelled to answer, " I *can* understand how a man would do anything to be free. But "—she dared to look round once more, and in the matter of daring all things for freedom, she was very far indeed from being gifted with a man's soul; he saw her shudder, as she added bitterly—"what need had you of me?"

"My dear young lady," said Derwent, "you are rashly inquiring into the great mystery of creation. Why must the weak always suffer for the strong? Why, that some may live must others die? I presume you would welcome my return to Lowmoor, in order that you might be at home again. If you

wish to know what need I had of you—simply, I dared not leave
you behind. I have learned not to trust you, Miss Fane. Your
heart is as true as steel, and you have the honour of a man ; but
you have a woman's tongue—you would betray me against your
will : you have done so already, ten to one. I tell you that I
would have killed you, without scruple, if that had been the only
way of silencing the only tongue that could tell the story of how
I left the land, and what there was between your boat and me.
The boat will be missed—perhaps it has been missed now : and
your conscious silence would have put them on the track more
surely than your open speech would have done. Leaving you
on shore would have been the same as sending the bellman round.
There is an Oswald, I remember—and, as I said before, what one
woman knows in the morning, at least one man knows in the
afternoon. No—if I had strangled you I should have been less a
fool than if I had left you on shore alive. That was one reason
why ; another was that your loss would throw people off my trail ;
they won't connect you with me, and your vanishing will put out
of people's minds the unprofitable search for one for whom nobody
cares but the law—that's reason number two. Another was that,
if we fall in with the help I'm looking for, your presence will
account for a good many things—that's reason number three.
Reason number four is—well, because carrying you off is
cogging the dice, and getting the whip-hand of fortune, after
all."

He paused, as if waiting for her to question him. But he had
to take her silence for questioning.

"Yes," he went on, "it's all matter of chance with me. But
it's different with you. I take you with me in the capacity of
guardian angel, Miss Fane. With you on board, this boat, cockle
shell as it is, will come to no harm ; and though we may reach
starvation point, we shall not starve. I mean what I say—though
it may sound as superstitious as faith always sounds to fools.
Till he or she has lived his—or her—life out, nobody dies : else
the universe would be a sheer bungle from beginning to
end. I may have lived my own life out, for aught I know. But
yours has not begun. You have the health of a mountain
nymph ; you are brave : you are wise, in your own way : you are
of the stuff of which nature makes heroes—your time is not
come. As to myself, it may be that your life's work is to save
mine ; for it may be my life that has got to be lived out, after all.

But, if not so long as you are in this boat, the boat dares not sink, and therefore I cannot drown; you will not starve, which means that help will come to me in coming to you. If Heaven lets you suffer for my deeds, then Heaven is ruled by fiends. And, as Heaven can't protect you without protecting me, or drown me without drowning you—you have reason number four: maybe the best and wisest of them all. Have you heard of the sword, the edge of which is the bridge to Mahomet's Paradise? The saints pass it—the sinners fall into the flames. This is the bridge to life and freedom. You *must* pass it—I cling to your skirts so tightly that you also must perish if I fall. Since you cannot be lost for my sake, I must be saved for yours."

The picture called up by his words was certainly not likely to lessen any of the fear that awe had left her. Nor was his catalogue of reasons, for all its frankness, of a nature to reassure any creature that found itself to be helplessly in this man's hands, and held to be of use in them. A very real earnestness had been increasingly revealing itself through his habitual, perhaps partly affected, lightness and indifference of tone; whether his professed belief in her protection, as if innocence were magic, was honest or no, his other reasons for complicating his escape with the apparent encumbrance of a girl were sound enough, and argued deliberately an unscrupulous heart no less than a singularly ready brain. No doubt he had found plenty of time to lay out his plans in detail while imprisoned in what had once been Rosamond's castle; but actual details seldom shape themselves so exactly in accordance with the best laid plans. Rosamond felt herself falling more and more helplessly into his grasp at every word. After all, the serpent, despite his fame, is a frank and honest creature, and the bird who comes to him has not, like the antelope or the lion, to complain of ambush and treachery.

"Oh," cried Rosamond's heart to her, "if Oswald could see me now!" The cry found no voice, but her companion's next words came as if in answer—

"And if you want a last reason, it is," said he, "that I, knowing what you are now, and what you will be, need you as no other man needs you, or will ever know how. I am staking more on this than liberty. Well: we shall know the end soon, now."

Truly it seemed to Rosamond that they would indeed very soon know the end. What was his plan of saving himself in mid sea, and how far at her cost, were matters far too practical for her to gather. He was apparently drifting, and leaving everything to the caprice of the waves, which still, whether by the effect of a constant current, or of a still ebbing tide, carried the boat, though very slowly, still perceptibly farther from the lands. Small crafts were occasionally in sight, but Derwent appeared neither to seek nor to avoid them. For themselves, they were as unnoticeable as if they had been Moldwarp and Oswald—the hunters instead of the hunted. And with the passing of each sail, another hold upon life appeared to pass away; in truth, Rosamond hardly knew whether she was dead or alive.

Want of sleep and food were also telling, not the less because it was not thought of—at least by her, any more than was the passage of time, during which, since her companion's last words, silence remained unbroken.

" You had better pull your skirt over your head," said he at last, " the sun is getting strong; though I can't be sorry you lost your hat—that was a lucky chance on the whole, and promises well for the end. But it won't be lucky if you get a sunstroke——"

" What does that matter? " asked she, faintly.

" Everything—to me; so do as you are told. And I think we may eat a mouthful, now, without being wasteful. Here is the loaf that we—stole. After all, you have a right to your own bread, any way : and I will take my share as a gift, as I did before. Help may be long in coming, and we must eke out our supplies— but all the same, it's time to break into them now. I wish there had been more time to lay in supplies. Break the loaf yourself, if you please—you have the cleaner hands."

Rosamond ate, forced by the now conscious hunger that proclaimed her spirit to be not even as yet wholly subdued. Then, to escape from further speech, she turned away her face, affecting to sleep, and indeed hoping that she might sleep, so that, if the approaching ocean was to devour her, she might perish before waking. She prayed silently as she best could, but scarcely with full faith—for she had to pray for miracles. Derwent's faith, in whatever it lay, must have been ten thousand times stronger than hers. He ate his bread slowly, as if to get all possible good out of its last crumb, and then giving himself up to complete inaction, sat stolidly with folded arms, as if he were a good Mussulman with the most supreme trust in destiny. Whatever he might be, even Rosamond could not but feel that there was something in his power of patience that, in a good sense, was more than human. She had found him capable of calculating and combining every chance, and at the same time of daring all things when there was anything to dare—and now she found him no less capable of the hardest thing of all: of doing nothing when there was nothing to be done. If she could only read one fragment of his mind as she believed him able to read, through and through, the whole of hers! Meanwhile she could only credit him with some plan of action of which this absolute inaction was but a part, instead of its being the whole of his plan, and in truth the blind waiting upon fortune which it appeared to be. He had calculated the least impossible out of a thousand chances without one that was not desperate among them and that was all. It must have been true that he had faith—and he had said that it was in Her.

She no longer watched the vanishing of the shore, or the nearing of the sea. Her heart had grown too faint and too dull for that as well as her eyes. But at last the darkening of that long afternoon warned her that the night was at hand—the terror of darkness: the only new terror that remained. Death, if it were coming, had not even the mercy to come quickly. For the first time she buried her face in her hands, and moaned.

"Sit still and steady, Miss Fane, for life's sake!" cried Derwent, "I knew it—there was the one chance, *your* chance, and it has come. Only don't speak—and for heaven's sake, don't stir!"

Had Rosamond forthwith beheld an open miracle, she would have thought it nothing strange. Indeed, the more it was of a miracle, the less strange it would have been. However, there was nothing strange to see—only her companion in peril hastily stripping from his body Silver Moldwarp's ragged shirt and tying it flagwise to the end of an oar. It was a signal that there was still light enough to be seen over a good breadth of water: but to what, and to whom? Were they the hunters, with Oswald at their head, and had the hunted man given in? Alas! his voice was far too full of hope, or rather of hope changed into joy. She dared not look round, to see what he had seen. Her heat beat violently with the dread that her flash of hope would die out all too soon.

Nothing happened. Was nothing ever to happen—was it her doom to drift in this wise through an eternity of nights and days? It was not as if she could call to mind a single sin that deserved the name. She tried to lift her eyes now, but failed—she was too weak even to see, and even the extemporised signal of distress, though but just over her head, was only visible through the mist that makes eyes blind. Even her perfect strength, worn out as she was both in body and mind, could no longer bear the strain, and the merest flash of hope was only enough, not to renew it, but to make it give way. She felt rather than saw, that Derwent's eyes were upon her, as if bidding her to become deaf and blind. Presently she saw nothing, not even the flag, and the last thing she heard was a dull rhythm as of phantom oars; then followed a rush of waters, as she threw up her arms, and felt herself sinking into the depth of the sea. Yet even to the utmost depth the over-mastering gaze of the demon who had usurped the rule of her life followed her. "Sophy!" she cried, faintly; "Oswald!" she tried to cry out, more faintly still. It was her last thought, that Oswald could not hear.

Faint, however, as the cry was, it had been heard. And he who heard it smiled with a sort of triumph—for he knew that they were no phantoms who pulled the approaching oars.

"Anyhow—exit Oswald!" said he. "I have seen a new thing under the sun : a girl who faints—at the right time."

CHAPTER XI.

And if the Queen herself would give
    Her crown to buy from me
My homely weeds, and bid me live
    As royally as she—
Yet if she won, full well I ween,
    The things I lost thereby,
She still would be the crowned Queen,
    The beggar still were I.

IT will have been gathered that the escape from Lowmoor of the man called Lawrence Derwent had not been wholly due to any extraordinary amount of what is commonly considered skill. He had been marvellously favoured by fortune ; but then on the other hand he had earned her favours by trusting her boldly. Every chance had been against him from first to last, and yet he had won every throw. No doubt he had shown wisdom in his first choice of a hiding place—that is to say, the very house where he was the least likely to be looked for : but then the houses are few which contain a room where a man may lie hid for whole days together, and a daughter of the house upon whom he might rely as upon Rosamond. And even with her he would not have been safe had it not been for a combination of chances that the best skilled of players could not have prepared. Uncle Æneas, Sophy, Oswald Hargrave, Silver Moldwarp, nay, even such indirect agents of fortune `as Mr. Pitcairn and the Doctor, had joined · together to aid him, and, as if all this had not been enough, his reliance upon the guardianship of Rosamond's presence had been justified.

Even, as he had said, Rosamond's fit of weakness had been marvellously well timed. When she came to herself, with what seemed to her an agonising death-struggle out of death, she for an instant had lost memory, and believed herself to be on land. But she soon realised that her terrible adventure had only entered upon a new and even more inexplicable phase. She was no longer in the boat indeed, but its light dance had been exchanged for a steady swiftness, soon to be accounted for by the swelling of canvas and the lapping of divided waves. She lay upon the deck of a schooner, near the wheel, and, while she opened her eyes, she heard a sharp order roughly shouted in a shrill foreign tongue. What had happened now? Only yesterday she had been at home, and more safely and surely there, anyone would think, than a prisoner in Lowmoor. This evening she was out at sea, among dark-skinned and bearded sailors, dressed in outlandish colours, and, to her eyes, like a crew of savages. She could never have dreamed it possible that she would live to look round for Derwent for some assurance of safety. Yet the face of one's worst enemy may be the most welcome sight—and so it was then to her. At any rate, it was known.

At that moment he, bare-headed, was talking fluently in that same foreign tongue with one who was presumably in authority· The latter was a heavily-built man, with a sallow skin, a bristling black beard over half his face, quick black eyes, and bushy hair dressed in a blue cloth shirt open at the throat, and with a large knife hanging from his leather belt by a cord. Of their talk she could not of course comprehend a single word : she only noticed that while the sailor frequently shrugged his shoulders and scowled, Derwent maintained his fluent ease, and was as elaborately courteous as when he had first entered her castle from the heap of straw. Unscrupulous scoundrel Derwent might be ; but, even in his beggar's rags, with his cropped hair, and with the rough stubble with which three days had covered lip, cheeks, and chin, he could not lose the air of a gentleman—or at least of having been so, once upon a time.

He was beside her so soon as her eyes opened, and in a moment she became the centre of a group whose curiosity appeared but little restrained by discipline. She tried to rise, but fell back feebly. Derwent spoke a few words to the skipper, if such he were, and then—and though not without more confusion than would have sufficed to clear a frigate's deck for action—the space round her was left free, and a half negro, more than half naked, and grinning like an ape, lurched up with a tin pan of something steaming in his hand.

"I told you," said Derwent, more solemnly than she had thought him able to speak, "I told you that I was safe with you, and that you were safe everywhere. The last chance—the chance I played for but hardly dared hope for—has come. I am a free man, thanks to you—free as air. You must take a little of this; whatever it's made of it's food, and you are half starved."

"Where am I now?" She could hardly hear her own whisper; but he heard.

"Don't talk—eat. You see where you are. Don't fear these fellows; I daresay they look rough enough to you, but you won't be with them long. I've settled everything."

"I only want to know one thing," said Rosamond, her eyes searching in vain for the land. "I only want to know if I am ever to see Sophy, ever to be home again?"

"Hark!" said Derwent, as if he had not heard her question, 'if I haven't forgotten all my sea-craft, we're in for a breeze, and as good a one as I could choose with the whole compass before me. You must learn to wait Miss Fane. Judge what the need of freedom means to me, when, for its sake, I must make you second to it, with all my gratitude, and though knowing all you feel. You must submit to be lost for a little while. Hearts of sisters and uncles don't break, and they'll hear you're safe quite soon enough: you shall write at once from wherever we land."

She could not help starting to her feet, her faintness had gone. "From wherever we land? From where?"

"Have patience! By such luck as I never dared dream, we are on a foreign schooner, outward bound. Who we are, except that we are sea-waifs, worn out and starving, they neither know nor care. I shall work our passage, and they won't find they've made a bad bargain. We are on board the *Mercedes*, of St. Sebastian, from Blaiseborough to——"

"Where?"

" Well, Miss Fane—with some sort of cargo—to the South
'Seas. Spain has possessions, you know, in that part of the world:
perhaps the Philippines, but I don't exactly know yet, nor why
she should have taken Blaiseborough in her course. However, so
far as I can judge she's a sound craft, not overloaded, and the
Basques are good sailors, and not a bad lot take them all round."

" To the South Seas ! "

" So I hear. I'm afraid you'll have to rough it a little, perhaps
a good deal ; and for some reasons of course it's unlucky that
you're the only woman on board. But I read you very wrongly if
you're not born to be a sailor, Miss Fane. It will be something
to have made a voyage to the Philippines in a Spanish trader."

i "As if I cared for that!" she cried, clasping her hands.
"Sophy, they will all think me dead, and I shall be at the other
side of the world; God knows where. . . . God forgive you,
whatever you are. I shall not die, I suppose, and some day I shall
be at home again ; though Heaven knows when. No ; I am not
afraid of the sea, nor of these men, among whom you have brought
me. What could happen to me more than this ? I am not afraid,
not even of *you !*"

" Nor need you," said he humbly. " And of nothing else, so
long as I am here."

In one important respect, at any rate, the man whose name
Rosamond knew not even yet proved to be right. Indescribably
rough as were the quarters into which a delicately reared English
girl had fallen, she was made to feel herself treated with kindness, at any rate with goodwill. Nor was this entirely a matter
of course, as some who have been thrown by the sea upon the
charity of such crews as that of the *Mercedes* can tell. It need
not be said that nothing short of the profound sleep of exhaustion
into which she fell before midnight could abate Rosamond's
terrible distress of mind ; indeed, to attempt to picture it, save
by unwritten thought, must be in vain. It was too great to miss
any comfort, and yet not too great to notice that what could be
done for her comfort, where her mere presence was an encumbrance, had been done. The *Mercedes* had certainly not been
built to carry passengers ; she was by no means over clean, and
the sailors themselves were sacrificed so far as possible to the
merchandise, so that they had but scant opportunity of making
further sacrifice for others. Yet, in some manner, room was

found or made. Too ignorant to fear what other women would
have feared, too familiar with phantoms and wonders to fear
them longer, too helpless and hopeless for the active thoughts
that banish sleep, she did sleep in some corner that had been
cleared for her below deck, and did not even dream.

Only a few days ago, she had been as safe as any English girl
may feel herself to be in the heart of home. There was no girl in
England so little likely to find herself plunged into the midst of
such an adventure as this was like to prove; but yesterday left
safe on her own bed, now sailing before the wind for the South
Seas; believed dead, and vanished alive. And all this, because a
convict had broken gaol; as though Lowmoor and the cottage at
Crossmarsh were, in anything but distance, nearer to one another
than the poles; or, absolutely nearer than wealth and the poverty
that starves next door. Accident had, indeed, made her utterly dependent upon Derwent, even in the matter of language; she had
no way of knowing so much as the story he had manufactured to
account for the presence of a young man and young woman in an
open boat out at sea. In the concoction of such a story he was
the last man in the world who was likely to be found at a loss;
and, indeed, for that matter, there were a hundred equally
plausible and open to him. It will happen, now and then, that
those who have set out for pleasure have lost their oars, or otherwise broken down, and found themselves unable to make for home
again. Or, again, the story of a love-flight, well told, commends
itself at once to Southern ears, especially if the heroine be sufficiently young and fair. Or, even the bold confession of a desperate
crime, and a flight for life, may, to such a crew as that of the
Mercedes seemed, enlist the deepest sympathies of all. How things
might have gone, with the pilot from Blaiseborough still on board,
is not so easy to say; but even in this matter, the chance of which
had, happily for his complete confidence in Rosamond's star, failed
to occur to him, Derwent had been befriended by fortune. A man
so amazingly befriended had the right to trust his own star for
evermore; and, if he had failed to find a fitting story, must have
proved himself no better than a fool. But, beyond this, he could
prove his ability to be that prize of prizes, a man who will do two
men's work for the pay of none. Nor was Rosamond herself one
of those waifs who are supposed to bring a ship the ill luck of the
prophet Jonah, unless, indeed, the fine weather should chance to
fall foul.

But all these things were beyond her knowing or guessing. She could only return upon deck when she awoke, at last, to fold her hands, and look blankly round the unbroken horizon of the open sea. One of the crew, passing her about his work, said something to her in his unknown tongue, and, with a friendly smile that might pass for a good morning, in the place of the general scowl that seemed to be part and parcel of the cargo of the *Mercedes;* but the smile was as useless as the words. Every sailor on board might be her zealous friend, if he could know her story; but her story was not one that could be told by signs. She did not see Derwent. It was a relief; and yet the absence of her enemy made her feel yet more without a friend.

That day, and for the next, and for the next, until the days grew past counting, the fine weather and the favouring breeze held on. It was a golden year; and the year's monotony of colour was reflected by the life of Rosamond on board her prison. The most passionate lover of the sea would have found the voyage dull, and Rosamond was assuredly in no mood to give her interest in the thousand daily things that should have fed her fancy with fresh interest all day long. Yet it was impossible that any human mind could pass through such a period of suspense and solitude without either losing its balance, and going mad, once for all, or else adapting itself in some measure, to the most maddening condition; so it was well for Rosamond that she was young. After all, every day, though it carried her farther away from Crossmarsh, in point of distance, carried her nearer in point of time. At any rate, in a strange country, she would be able to throw off the tyranny from which she could not escape, while at sea, without wings; and meanwhile, until the need for action came, she was safe from having to put herself face to face with the question of how she should return.

Were it seen through the eyes of the Spanish skipper, or, perhaps, through those of Lawrence Derwent, the voyage of the *Mercedes* would, no doubt, be a history itself, and not a page well-nigh as blank as was the sea itself, for the greater part of the time. But few, or rather none, would care to read the journal of a voyage in a slaver kept by a slave, at least beyond the first page. By the time that custom had dulled her first despair, it had also dulled her senses to the mere discomforts of such a voyage; and, it was surely something, even though it seemed shameful to regard such lesser evils, that she had been carried off without a change of clothes, that all the conditions of her life were not only hard and rough but repulsive, and that even such kindness as she received was rough and outlandish to the last extreme. She had to accustom herself to strange food strangely prepared and uncleanly served, and to strange sounds that she could not understand. Her whole communication with some fragment of the outer world as the *Mercedes* contained was only obtained through the man who had brought her here, and who might tell her just as much or as little as he pleased. Seen through Rosamond's eyes, a sailing voyage half round the world was a blank, or rather such a voyage as some of us have made in a dream between two dreams. Climate followed climate; sail after sail came into sight and disappeared, latitude after latitude was passed, but the days remained the same, as undistinguishable as shroud from shroud by a landswoman's eyes. And yet there were times when the uncertainty of strange shores made her almost dread to think of the day when the *Mercedes* would at last cast anchor, and when, without even an enemy's aid she would have to find her way back home alone; and how that was to be done was a prospect as blank as the sea.

One day—in what month or even in what season of the year she knew not, for she had lost count of time at the outset, and left it to Derwent to guess at the questions that she never put to him— Derwent being idle for the moment, or in a mood for talk, came to where she was standing, and leant beside her over the low stern. Though, during so dull a fair-weather voyage, his idle hours must have been many, he had not often made use of them in this way, but on the whole, except when there was occasion, had shown his gratitude by avoiding her; sometimes two days would pass together without his making an opportunity for speaking to her.

" We ought to be near an end of our voyage by now," said he, " if this wonderful wind but half holds. Do you know why it is that they have treated you as nearly like a princess as this vile old hulk will allow ? It's because you've brought them a passage the like of which the best and fastest craft doesn't make once in a lifetime. That's their notion—that you're a sort of sea-angel that the *Mercedes* had the luck to find; and upon my soul I believe it's true. You are a mystery to them, but the wind vouches for you. If you had picked up any of their language, you would have heard the wildest things said of you—and yet none so very wild. There's a Basque fellow here who's going to give a silver heart to Saint Rosamunda. I tell him there's none in the calendar, but he

7

says he knows better; and, after all, what should a heretic like me know of such things?"

This was speaking in yet a new vein. With nothing to answer, she turned her face to a distant cloud, the only dark spot visible on earth or in heaven, as being the thing that was farthest away from him, and perhaps the thing that was nearest to home of all that she could see.

"Miss Fane," said he, more gravely, "there is at least one thing I must talk to you about before this voyage ends. You do not know all you have done in saving me from that English gaol. If you did know, you would think all that you have gone through a cheap price to have paid—or at any rate well worth the paying. I have been obliged to make you pay it against your will— to rob you of it, as it were; but you would be glad, if I know you, and if you knew all. The work is done. We shall soon be at anchor now, and I shall be beyond the reach of friend or foe. Tho man that I have been will have died—so utterly that I will not even tell you his name. I shall be a new man with a new name. Miss Fane, hate the dead man as much as you will since you cannot know all; but, for God's sake, don't hate the new."

There was such real earnestness in his speech that, for the first time she could not help feeling that what the man was now saying was simple and true.

"I have not blamed you for doing the best you could for yourself," said she. "As you said to me, long ago, what were I or mine to you? And what should they be?"

"They should be everything—and they are. But I am not free till we are ashore. It will be my duty to guard you then; not against my will, as you have saved me, but with all my heart and soul."

"You will send me—home?"

"I am coming to that matter, Miss Fane. What are they thinking at Crossmarsh? That you are dead, drowned, or lost over the cliffs. They will have given up the search by now and time has turned you into a memory. I tell you there is no power on earth that can henceforth, by searching, find me or you. You are dead, and so am I. You have a sister, I believe?——"

"And you have broken her heart."

"Indeed, I have done nothing of the kind. Why, she can't have grown a heart at her age; and if she has, it will mend. Miss Fane, it is your duty not to throw away on a country parish a life such as yours was made to be. Recognise the road that has opened for you through me—the road that will lead you to those high places for which you are made. I have watched you from hour to hour every day, and have learned to know you through and through. You believe yourself to be in the apathy of despair. You are nothing of the kind. You will find yourself a woman by the time you land; you have not once lost courage, nor broken down under what would have killed nine girls out of ten—but what am I saying? It all comes to this—I have escaped from gaol, and you from a home that was worse than a gaol for such as you. You no more dare go back again than I. You are free. You dare not throw your freedom away."

"I do not understand—not one word!" said Rosamond, startled at last, by his growing earnestness, into listening as she had never listened before. "As if I am not breaking my own heart over Sophy—as if it were not like dying every minute till I see them all again!"

"So you think—now. But how will you think when you have grown old in some Crossmarsh or other, and think how you once had the chance given you of living your life, with which Heaven trusted you, and how you let it go? Chances like this are inspirations; they are commands, and they never come again. Every creature has its one grand chance, and this is yours. Do you suppose it is for nothing that this has come to you, before you have lost a year? I will tell you my whole story, and when you know that you shall decide whether you and I together are not made to do with the world what we will."

Her spirit, so long deadened into an unnatural sleep, was touched into waking life, and there flashed across her mind an old engraving she had once seen of the Temptation on the Pinnacle of the Temple. Who was this man who could make himself invisible at will, and was now, in so many plain words, offering her the kingdoms of the earth and the glory of them in exchange for her home?

Again she looked towards the black spot of cloud in the distance, but not in such a manner as to see that while she had been listening it had grown till nearly half the sky was clouded astern.

"I cannot—I *will* not understand!" she exclaimed, again. "If I were a queen—like what these men think I am—I would sooner never reach the shore alive, than understand one word."

"You mean you would call up a storm? As if anything you

could do would change what is to be! You were glued to Crossmarsh like a limpet to a rock—and here you are in the Pacific,
and the same power which has forced you so far will force you to
the end, you may be sure. If you are to be a queen, a queen you
will be. Miss Fane—you *cannot* go home!"

"Cannot!" she said, aghast—for what, after all, had her will
yet been able to prove against this man's power ? "Do you mean
that I shall die ?" For surely no power less strong than death
had the right to deny her all that life meant to her, or could ever
mean.

"I mean——But, good God! what is this ?" he cried, suddenly
starting from her and looking round in dismay. For suddenly
as if she who had appealed to the elements to aid her had been
taken at her word, the darkness of the sky had overtaken them
and the fresh breeze was lost in a thunder of wind. "Below at
once with you, Rosamond—Miss Fane!" cried Derwent, raising
her as best he could, for both had been thrown over, and had rolled
half across the deck, as the *Mercedes* was sent well-nigh flat upon
the waves with the blow of the wind.

Counting over a thousand chances, so as not to miss the least of
them, he had yet forgotten to include in his reckoning a tropical
storm. There was nothing that thousands have not encountered
in the sudden fury that suddenly, one may say in a moment, maddened the whole air without warning or seeming cause. It is true
that while Derwent had been endeavouring to whisper the teach-
ings of the serpent into Rosamond's ears, the Spanish skipper's
eyes had been less idle, and that some good minutes before the
outbreak had sufficed to take in every inch of sail. But, for the
rest, the *Mercedes* was at the mercy of the hurricane, as it lashed
and tore the sea into a madness to rival its own. The wind itself
seemed black, and to be the cause of the heavy darkness that thick-
ened around. It was no British crew ; and shouts, oaths, and yells
battled with the wind—prayers, also, which some of the sailors of
the *Mercedes* seemed to hold more efficacious than praying with
the strength of their hands. It is true that to keep his legs was
as much as the most active could do ; and Derwent did not repeat
his perfectly impracticable order to Rosamond to take refuge below.
The world had become a chaos of darkness and wind.

A sailor could doubtless give a better account. To Rosamond,
it was chaos indeed—but yet, with this supreme peril, her fears,
her constant companions, were swept away as if they had never

been born. The sight of the hand of God cast out all the fear of man. She could pray now, faithfully and without shame; for she seemed to see and feel the presence to which she prayed. "Sophy thinks me dead—let her think true!" thought she.

Suddenly, in the midst of it all, she heard a crash as if the ship were breaking; then the *Mercedes* fell over, and, when she recovered herself, lay like a log that the waves themselves could no longer move.

"Miss Fane!" shouted Derwent, above the yells of the skipper and the crew, "*you* can be brave—show it now, by not moving foot or hand."

The *Mercedes* had become unnaturally steady; but also lay unnaturally low in the waves, which were breaking over her bows as she pitched forward heavily, as if with the intention of plunging below. Taking advantage of her log-like state, Derwent made his way to where the crew were gathered in confusion. Rosamond, seeing the group, as if it were of shadows through the black wind, heard for some minutes the sounds of a noisy consultation, which, after awhile, ended in silence, Derwent's voice being the last that was heard. Then, looking beyond the group, she seemed to be conscious of a yet larger and darker shadow looming full in the course of the *Mercedes*, and out of the direction of the pursuing clouds. How long the storm had lasted, she could not tell; but though no sailor, she knew it had been long enough to drive the schooner out of her path before leaving her with a shifted cargo and broken down.

In another minute Derwent was again by her side. "Do what I tell you," said he, "without a word. There is real danger—you are one who are best told—the confounded cargo is rolling, and there's no sort of doubt has knocked its way through the hold; and nothing can be done in such a sea, and we pitching in the dark dead towards a lee shore, that may be anywhere in the world for all these imbeciles can tell."

"Is it a wreck?" asked Rosamond in a voice more quiet than his own.

"We may go to pieces any moment. And *I* have brought *you* —but I'm not going to trouble you now. We shall get what we deserve, no doubt at last—I and you. But there's one chance yet. Come! Yes for the sake of all you hope to see again, you must hold to my arm now—even mine."

The chance appeared to be that, with a shore in sight and reach, the boats carried by the *Mercedes* might save her crew before the waves rolled over and through her; for that she was sinking bodily there was no doubt at all, literally beaten to pieces by the loosened cargo, whatever it was, and the tornado's fury. Derwent brought her, not without difficulty, into the midst of the desperate crew, who now regarded their former guardian angel with threatening gestures and evil eyes. She had but mocked them with fair breezes the more surely to destroy them with a storm—this witch who had come among them straight from the sea.

But she understood the full meaning neither of their gestures, nor their words. She only knew what the whirl of the next instants left her the sense to feel and see. The boat was speedily on the waves, that now came nearly deck high, and was held by a single rope to prevent her, till she was filled and could be cast off, from being carried away.

" The lady first !" cried Derwent; and she found herself, she knew not how, thrust into the boat that seemed to strain at the rope for freedom. She clambered as best she could over the thwarts, to make all the room she could, but none followed her. What was being done ? Some desperate quarrel seemed to be raging on board, even at that awful time. Where was Derwent ? He, surely, did not mean to drown. Suddenly she felt the rope strain, while the clamour on board grew fiercer than ever. It was as if none would enter the boat, which the presence of the storm-witch had doomed. Then she heard a heavy splash, as if some part of the ship had given away: and then all became as silent as the grave. What did it all mean, she cried out ?—but only the wind answered her.

It was horrible. She cried out again; but her cry was silenced by a shock of the boat against the side of the *Mercedes*. A great wave heaved up between them : she could feel the cable strain to its utmost—and then, like a sea-bird set free, the boat gave an upward leap, and bounded forward through the black air and over the black water, as if it were a living thing, bearing her on—Heaven knew whither !—and, at last, utterly alone.

What followed must surely have been a dream—only that dreams are ten thousand times less strange.

She was lying on a beach of white sand, too weak to move, and with the sensation of a horrible aching in all her limbs. She still heard the beat of the sea, but the wind was dead, and the sky was heavenly blue. A fragrance more soft and mystical than that of the sea filled the air, and trees of a strange growth, such as she had seen in books of travels, climbed half-way up a cliff at the further end of the bay. And she was being stared at, as though they were made of eyes, by a boy and a girl, of perhaps some eight years old, as beautiful as Cupid and Psyche, as brown as coffee berries, and as naked as they had been born.

She tried to speak; but, so soon as they saw her eyes, they took to their heels.

CHAPTER XII.

When misers make their florins fly,
And gamesters bid the dice good-bye—
Is't you, madame, who ask them why?
But if the answer still be far,
Ask why the toper breaks his jar,
And hind with tiger wageth war:
Or why (if still the lesson's lost)
Should calmest pools grow tempest tost,
Or what unfreezeth hearts of frost—
Why I, struck through the heart by thee,
Yet bless the hand that slayeth me—
'Tis Love, madame, or Lunacy.

IT is quite possible to pass through a long life without finding occasion to make personal acquaintance with the name of Derwent. On the other hand, it is not altogether so uncommon as to make it inevitable that any respectable people who happened to bear it should feel disgraced by learning that their distinction is shared by an inmate of one of Her Majesty's gaols. At any rate, the Derwents of Longwood and of Wilton Square were the last people in the world likely to be troubled by more or less kind enquiries behind their backs, if anything happened to a namesake in Lowmoor. No such enquiries would be conducted in Town and in the season, when and where the world has a short memory, whatever might be the case round their country seat, where memories are too often uncomfortably long; and never forget if there has been a hanging matter in any family, even a century ago.

The Derwents—at least such of them as were in town for a season of no ancient date—were four: Horace Derwent, his mother, and his two sisters, Catherine and Anne. Horace was the only son of his mother, and she was a widow. Such a description, however, though absolutely true, only shows how misleading truth may be. Pity would be entirely wasted on an only son with some eight thousand a year of his own and with his sisters well provided for, or upon a rich widow, whose loss—according to those who had known the late Colonel Derwent best—had been in every respect clear gain. Liberty for oneself, power over others, plenty of money, and the removal of a husband whom one regrets, three hundred and sixty-five times a year, ever having married, are not matters that call for any excessive sympathy.

No doubt the Derwents kept their family skeleton, being human. But, whatever he was, he was an exceptionally accommodating and unobtrusive skeleton, and gave marvellously little trouble, keeping himself well out of the way. He was certainly not visibly present in the morning-room where Kate and Anne Derwent were busily engaged together over some all-absorbing and mysterious, but laughter-provoking occupation—his place was occupied by the sunshine, who knows how to make himself at home in a big house in Wilton Square quite as well as in a poor man's country cottage. Despite romantic belief, all the good things of this life are not engrossed by the poor, comparatively well off though they un-questionably are. Kate and Anne were fine, fair girls of a good and healthy sort—girls who, at first sight, obviously knew how to ride, walk, dance, talk, laugh, and to suit themselves comfortably and gracefully to their position in life, whatever it might be. Kate was the elder, livelier, and smaller: Anne the younger, graver, and statelier. But their difference was much more apparent to their relations and their intimate friends than to the outside world.

"I don't believe," said Kate, " there ever was such a muddle of a visiting list like ours. Every year we hoe up the weeds and sow salt, and roll the grass, and every year the weeds come up worse than ever. Oh, dear ! "

" Come," said Anne, in her more placid manner, " I don't think it's quite so bad as that after all. There are some very amusing people, I'm sure——"

" Oh, yes—amusing. But it's such a mixture, that's what I mean. Cabbages are useful, and green peas are delicious, but one doesn't plant them among the geraniums——"

" Nor geraniums among the cabbages—that's true. But because we don't, that's no reason why we shouldn't, is it, dear ? I'll have my garden mixed, if ever I have one of my own. I'll put all my seeds and bulbs and things into one basket and have it shaken out all over the ground anyhow——"

" Do let's stick to work," said Kate, " or it'll be lunch time before we've half done. The question is, *shall* we send cards to the Coles?"

" Well—*they're* not amusing, certainly. They're neither geraniums nor green peas, neither delicious nor beautiful. But they may be cabbages. I wonder if they are?"

" Cabbages, Anne?"

" Yes—useful, you know; and some people are passionately fond of cabbages. How did we come to know the Coles?"

" Let me see—I didn't pick them up: nor you. It must have been Horace——"

" Oh, no, Kate—they're not at all in his line. The girls are rich, and are not pretty; and Horace never looks at a girl unless she's very pretty and very poor. It must have been mamma."

" Ah—that's just the worst of it; we all go on making our own friends, and then nobody ever knows who belongs to who. It's my firm belief, Anne, that people come here that none of us know, because they've found out that each of us will think they belong to the other. Horace is bad enough that way, but mamma's the worst of us all. She has no criterion at all. Something must really be done to restrain mamma. Some day we shall find ourselves introducing a bishop to his own tailor. or some other terrible thing. My dear Anne—who *are* the Coles?"

" Well, put a big M against the Coles—meaning, ask mamma. Who comes next?"

" The Pitcairns."

" Good gracious—P doesn't come next to C?"

" Well, it didn't use to; but I said this list is a muddle. Perhaps the name's Cairn, not Pitcairn, and Pit's the Christian name."

" My dear, dear, dear Kate, have we come to this then, that we don't know of our friends so much as even their names?"

" Yes, Anne, that *is* what it is coming to indeed—thanks to Horace, and mamma, and a little bit to you. But as to the Cairns, or the Pitcairns, or the Pits, things aren't quite so far gone—*I* know *them*."

"So it seems, dear—name and all! Who are they? Did we know them last year?"

" I think so; anyhow, we knew them very well the year before —very intimately indeed. They were here three afternoons. I met them at the—somebody or other's. He's a clergyman, in the country—an Irishman; and she was a Miss Somebody, who had money. Have you ever noticed, Anne, that the wives of Irish clergymen were mostly Miss Somebodys with money? She isn't very nice, but he is, and they're all right, in every way. Yes, we'll have the Pits—I mean the Cairns. Write them a card. After all, I dare say they're not in town this year, and won't come."

"There. I've made it Pitcairn or Pit Cairn—they may read it just as they please. Craven—Carrington—Deane : they're all right. Dash—good gracious, Kate, what human being of our acquaintance answers to the name of Dash ?"

"I'm sure I don't know. I shall go off my head, if this sort of thing goes on much longer. We've got to get to the Z's, and we've only just begun the D's—oh, dear ! No—I can't remember one single, solitary Dash. By the way, isn't there a Countess Dash, or somebody ? "

"Not that I know of. Well—mark Dash with H,for ask Horace. It doesn't sound like one of mamma's people."

"And what do you want to ask Horace, if you please ? " asked a good-looking, easy-going young man as he lounged in, with his hands deep down in the pockets of his shooting coat. " Here he stands to answer for himself, if he can."

" Oh, Horace ! " cried Kate the impulsive, " I was never half so glad to see you before ! Who is Dash ! If you can't tell us I shall go wild."

"Dash ? *Horatius sum—non Œdipus*, my dear child. Why do you want to know ? "

"Because we're going to be ' at home,' you know, for the season, and are letting the world know. *The* world ! Four worlds —mamma's, Anne's, yours, and mine. *Do* the Dashes belong to yours ? "

" The Dashes? Then there's more than one Dash, is there ? "

" I suppose so. There's only one Dash down, but when nobody knows people there's sure to be any number of them. Do you know Dash, Horace ? "

"No, Kate. On second thoughts—well: no, again."

"Then there is nothing left me but to go wild."

" She thinks we are getting rather mixed," said Anne.

" Rather, indeed ! " said Kate, tossing back her curls.

" Perhaps I can help you," said the head of the house, the squire of Longwood, with his pleasant smile. He was quite a young man, coming between Kate and Anne, in point of age, unmistakably their brother, but without either Kate's briskness or Anne's dignity. He was big, but of the lazy, good-humoured type—at home in the fields and on the moors, where he showed plenty of staying power if little energy, but when at home scarcely taking the trouble to hold himself upright, and contriving to do rather less than any other living man of his age, weight and size.

"*You* help, Horace?" asked Anne, calmly. "Do you know what you would have to do? No, dear. This is work for strong women, not for weak men."

"All the better, Nan. I'm always glad to hear of woman's work—it means a good time coming for the likes of me. So you're at that old visiting list, are you? I suppose you've got everybody down?"

"Everybody, Horace," said Kate. "That wouldn't so much matter, only that we've got nobody too—and which is which——"

"I bet you," said Horace Derwent, with a little extra laziness of manner, " that you haven't got everybody down."

"Horace," said Kate, solemnly, "if you will kindly take the Post Office Directory—no, not the Court Guide, but the Post Office Directory—and find me out of it one single, solitary name that isn't in our visiting list, I'll——"

"Have you sent a card to the Fanes?"

"No. We're only in the D's. We've been pulled up by Dash Who are the Fanes? Do I know them?"

"Well, Kate," said Horace, colouring ever so little, "I don't know that you do—indeed, if it comes to that, I'm sure you don't. Fact is, I didn't know them myself till the other day. But you'd like them, awfully—you and Anne, I mean. Yes—send him a card by all manner of means."

"Oh—*him?*"

" Yes; we certainly do want young men," said Anne, reflectively. "There are always girls; but young men are becoming an extinct species, it seems to me. Any of your friends, Horace, are sure to be useful, if it's only to let themselves be seen in the doorway. Yes—I vote decidedly for Mr. Fane."

" H'm—not that he's exactly young."

"Well, middle-aged will do. What is he—captain—colonel? What's his address? I must enter him properly, you know."

"Oh—Mr. Not that he's exactly middle-aged——"

" It seems to me," said Anne, with the air of a judge, and holding her pen suspended over the place for entry, " it seems to me that this begins to call for further enquiry, sir. What claims has an unknown Mr. Fane, who cannot even be called exactly elderly, to a place in our doorway, which is already too narrow for half our friends?"

"I tell you what it is, young woman," said Horace, beginning a tour of the room, and examining every article it contained as if it were new to him: "our fault is that we have everybody through that doorway—which means nobody. Fane is neither everybody nor nobody—he's somebody, which is quite another pair of shoes. He's old enough to be my father—but we've got a taste in common——"

"Oh, Horace! Horses?" asked Kate.

"Cigars?" asked Anne.

"No. Books—*old* books!" said Horace, without the ghost of a smile.

There are some assertions which, however ludicrous from their associations, are so outrageous, so utterly monstrous, as to deprive the quickest-witted hearers of the faculty of laughter—nay, of faculties, save that of an amazed stare. So it was with Catherine and Anne Derwent, who were quick enough at laughter, as a rule, but who knew their brother, and fancied they knew how far a taste for books could prove a bond of sympathy between him and his fellow creatures. For, so far as they were aware, Horace had never read a real book in his life, and that he should recognise the distinction between old books and new books was, in itself, an incomprehensible marvel. The girls looked at one another to read the jest, if they could, in each other's eyes; but failed.

"Good gracious! *Books*, Horace!" exclaimed Kate.

"Heavenly powers, Horace! *Books!*" cried Anne.

"Yes," said their brother, coolly, as he let himself fall into a chair. "They really are most interesting things—especially first editions, and tall copies, and all that sort of thing. Fane could show you some books that would make you stare. I'm going to make a library myself, all of black letter, and Fane can give me hints at starting. The only thing I'm sorry about is that I've lost so much time; but Fane must have been double my age when he began. Yes—book-hunting's just the finest sport in the world: and you must send a card to Fane."

It was as if a bishop had suddenly launched out in praise of cock-fighting. Neither at school, nor at college, nor since he entered the world, had Horace Derwent shown the faintest tendency towards the most compulsory kinds of scholarship. Nobody had expected it from him, and indeed his attitude towards bookishness had been too indifferent even to amount to contempt—it had been identical with that of a Polynesian cannibal towards the music of the future : that is to say, no attitude at all. Saul among the prophets was nothing to Horace Derwent among the folios. His sisters were tinged with as much literature as the rulers of the novel-market considered necessary for young ladies, and on the strength of this took credit for being as well read as the majority of their fellow creatures, as indeed they were : but such terms as first editions and tall copies made them feel that their brother, their unlettered brother, had passed beyond them at a single flight and—well, they stared once more.

"No," said Kate, emphatically, after a long pause. "N , Horace. Those sort of people belong to mamma. We don't want elderly book-worms. I know the kind. I saw one once at the Cravens. He was introduced to me ; and the only thing he said was to ask me if I didn't think the room was very warm. I sai' nr : and that finished him, poor man. I can see Mr, Fane in my min "s eye—a little old gentleman, with his clothes put on nohow, and a wig, and a snuff-box ; and, oh, Horace ! to think of your being some day like that—buying books that you can't read, and that nobody else wants to. Horace—I put down my slipper. I'll have nothing of the kind. You shall not take snuff. You shall not wear a wig. I am your elder sister ; and I'll have nothing of the kind—so there ! "

"Nonsense, Kate," said her brother, stretching out his legs, thrusting his hands deeper into his pockets, and languidly contemplating his toes ; book-hunters are the jolliest fellows going. Besides, it's intellectual, and all that sort of thing. I'm tired of being stupid—I am indeed. I must have a rational pursuit ; and it's time I began. It isn't as if one had to read the books, you know. I don't believe Fane ever reads—he hasn't the time. The great thing is to get hold of something that nobody else ever had, and for which all the other fellows would give their ears. I'm beginning to make the Derwent collection ; and I've found a fellow who's a wonderful hand at finding bargains—for, you see, it's a point of honour to get things as cheaply as one can, so that ruining oneself's impossible. You can get a dozen big things in books for the rent of a moor."

"Where did you pick up this Mr. Fane ? " asked Anne. "If he

has converted you to books, even their outsides—well, he must be a very extraordinary man."

"He is," said Horace. "Don't be afraid—he's a gentleman. As my guide, philosopher and friend, you must send him a card."

"Must?" asked Kate. "Well—see what slaves we sisters are. His initial, if you please?"

"A—E—diphthong, you know."

"Good gracious, Horace! I hardly know how to write such a thing! Hasn't the man got even an honest Christian name? Well. There: Mr. A—E. diphthong Fane. Address?"

"Oh, let me see—28, Richmond Place. That's enough. And by the way——"

"Well?"

"You may as well put in Miss Fane, too. There's a Miss Fane. There—I suppose it's about lunch time: I feel so, anyhow."

He rose. But the uncomprehending look had, before he left his chair, already passed out of both his sisters' eyes. Those two pair of eyes met, and the lips below them shared the same smile.

"Yes, Horace," said Anne, demurely, "Mr.—and Miss—Fane shall receive a card."

Horace nodded, and lounged out of the room, whistling as if nothing had happened.

"Anne, dear?" asked Kate.

"Kate, dear?" answered Anne.

"Is this number thirty-one or thirty-two?"

"Miss Fane? Let me see—I think it's number thirty-three."

"All very pretty, and all very poor. Yes, Anne—book-hunting is a delightful sport, after all. I wonder how the book will be bound."

"Yes, Kate—and what there'll be to read inside. With most of Horace's books it's been, I'm afraid, Longwood—written on the heart. Oh, what geese we were not to guess what Horace's taste for books means! And the great Derwent collection! And to think that he thinks that *we* don't understand!"

"Well, Anne—anyhow a weight's *off* my mind. I was afraid Horace was going mad; but I'm not now. If ever he takes to conchology, or tatting, or the use of the globes, I sha'n't be troubled any more. If it's conchology, I shall remember that there's a lady in the lobster-shell, and understand."

"Hush," whispered Kate. "Here's mamma."

CHAPTER XIII.

What means such talk to me? My wings, I trow
Are over-wide and strong for peddling trips
That sparrows practise on the housetops—mine
Are as the eagle's, sir, that toward the sun
Take flight: and mine the eagle's cosmic eyes
That take the parish for a paddock: prove
The shire as but a blot of random ink,
And all your England but a bank of wool.
My eyes are all too large to see in small,
Yea, to perceive aught meaner than the world:
And e'en the world is petty—for I need
A mirror vast and deep enough to hold
Mine own pervading image. Bring me straight
The solar disc—'tis broad enough to serve.

EVERY family has its own peculiar forms of humour, unless indeed it is so unfortunate as to have no sort of humour at all. The Derwents were, in reality, very amiable people, who, being conscious that they were a trifle commonplace and too much like their neighbours, habitually, and unconsciously, developed certain harmless eccentricities, which the ill-natured might call affectations. Herein I speak of the ladies of the household: for Horace was as absolutely unaffected and as content with his commonplaceness as an able-bodied young man can be in these self-conscious and self contemplating days.

These characteristics of her son were completely acceptable to Mrs. Derwent, who, having been allowed no will of her own during the colonel's life, was, since his death, all the more bent upon making up for lost time. She loved management, and her easy-tempered son was only too willing to be managed—it saved him all the trouble of life, and left him all the pleasure, for his mother's despotism was entirely of the indulgent and benevolent order. That he was not without a will of his own Mrs. Derwent had occasionally suspected: but there had never been the least occasion as yet for a collision, and possibly an instinctive prudence warned her to postpone the occasion as long as possible. Of course, she, as a woman and a mother, did not know that ready and habitual submission on the part of a man is the worst possible security for his subjection, because it only shows him to be too strong-minded to waste his self-assertion upon trifles, while occasions that are not trifles are necessarily few and far between. Nothing as yet had seemed to Horace Derwent important enough to demand the infinite discomfort and worry of a domestic battle—

not even the most temporarily exciting of those thirty-two or
thirty-three love affairs that his sisters had ascribed to him.
Still his mother, being his mother, foresaw that, though it might
be the three hundred and thirty-third, his fate must come at last;
and she also had observed his remarkable preference for poverty
as an element in a woman's attraction. Nor had she any the
more sympathy with her son's taste for having herself been both
pretty and poor before the colonel came.

She was still a good-looking woman of her years—partly perhaps because she had been no longer poor. In this, her later
middle age, she had exchanged gracefulness for graciousness,
brilliancy for dignity, and represented what her Anne might hope
to become. It is sometimes dangerous for a mother to be very
like a daughter, by thus setting present beauty side by side with
the picture of its doom. This was not the case here. Rather,
seeing the mother and daughter together, a man meditating
marriage would feel assured that the girl came of a good, staying
stock, and that she would only cease to be pretty in order to
become handsome. And, as to that matter, Mrs. Derwent, looking scarcely more than forty, with her fine features, her gracious
presence, her fresh complexion, her bright eyes, her amiable
smile, and her exceedingly handsome life interest in her son's
estate, enjoyed without any sort of restriction, was not unlikely
in some quarters to prove even her daughter's rival. She had not
the faintest thought of marrying again—liberty, sprung from the
colonel's grave, was too precious a plant to be thrown away. But,
during the more recent years of her widowhood, she had received
more than one offer, though she had kept that fact from her
children: and, not only so, she had so contrived to refuse her
offers as in every case to retain the would-be lover as a firm and
devoted friend. Indeed, Mrs. Derwent had an altogether extraordinary faculty for making many friends, and keeping them all.
She was certainly not a brilliant woman, either in thought or in
speech: but, just as certainly, she was no fool.

"Well, dears," she said, as she made her first appearance
that day—for she was a very late riser, not out of laziness,
but as a believer in plenty of sleep and ease as the most effectual
of youth-preservers—"how are you getting on with our friends?"

"Not much better than the hare," said Kate. "I'm afraid—he,
couldn't have had many more than we; or more like the tortoise
in the other fable. We haven't finished C."

"Then I must help you I suppose."

"If you can't, mamma, nobody can. Are we to send cards to the Coles?"

"*Are* you, Kate? Why, good gracious, child—why who should you send them to if you were to leave out the Coles? Why, they're among the very best people we know. I don't exactly know who they are, but they're always at the best houses, and—why don't you remember their garden party last year? No —I remember now we weren't able to go: I was thinking of the Deanes. The Coles, let me see, I think old Cole has something to do with business, in a very big way, or else he's a Royal Academician, or an Indian judge—I'm not quite sure, but he's certainly one of the three, or anyhow something of the same kind. At any rate he's a very great man: and his daughters are most charming girls—not pretty, of course, but just as good as gold."

"And Dash. Who's Dash, mamma?" asked Anne.

"Dash, my dear?"

"Yes—Dash. I asked Horace: but he didn't know."

"Give me the book. Yes—there's Dash, to be sure; and at the same address as the Deanes'. It must be Mrs. Deane's sister: she has a sister very often with her, I know. You had better send a card to Miss Dash, as she's down—it can't do any harm, and might give offence: and I wouldn't hurt Lady Deane's feelings for the world. The book seems all right," said Mrs. Derwent, as she turned over the pages, and read a name at random here and there. "Fane—let me see: who are the Fanes?"

"Some of Horace's people," said Anne. "He made us enter them just before you came down."

"Indeed? Horace doesn't often trouble himself about such things—or indeed much about anything, indoors. I don't know any Fanes: but it's a good name. The Marchioness of Horchester was a Fane. Richmond Place. . . . Did he tell you who they are?"

"Oh, yes," said Anne. "Horace has turned book-worm, it seems—and Mr. Fane is a very big book-worm, indeed. They're kindred souls."

"Horace—Book-worm! My dear what *do* you mean?"

"He says book-hunting is better than fox-hunting; and he is going to make a Derwent collection, all in black letter——"

"My dear!" exclaimed her mother, "do you know what you're saying? Of course it's quite right to have Mr. Fane at our

8

_ouse, if he's a distinguished man. A great many people do take
an interest in books, I know—but Horace! It doesn't seem
natural—why, he was over seven years old before he could read.
And his father never read anything either, except the *Times*,
and the *Army and Navy Gazette*, and *Hoyle's Games*, and now
and then the cookery book when his liver was particularly
troublesome. I hope Horace isn't going to be crotchety. I must
see to this—I must indeed. If he begins with books, he may go
on to pictures, and then to diamonds: and it's not as if he were a
rich man."

Mrs. Derwent fell into a brown study: for this new departure
on the part of her son was fully as inexplicable to her as to
Kate and Anne. Indeed it was more so, for she had studied
Horace through and through, and believed that she knew him by
heart, with no more than that slight, concealed misgiving that
he was capable of a certain obstinacy, hitherto unexercised and
ever invisible. Kate and Anne, having their suspicions of how
the land lay, nevertheless felt bound in honour not to spoil sport,
and, besides, were caught by a very natural and wholesome spirit
of curiosity to see and judge this Miss Fane for themselves, before
deciding whether she was to be suppressed or no. So they went
on with their work, or rather with their chat about their work,
until they had spent long enough over doing nothing to feel
their consciences at ease, and to be justified in considering that
something attempted, something done, had earned the right to
spend the afternoon as they pleased.

On this occasion, their pleasure was to order the carriage, to
make some calls, while that of Mrs. Derwent was to stay at
home. Indeed it had been at her own suggestion that she and
her daughters parted company, on the score that she had some
letters to write, and also wanted a long day's rest before beginning
the evening's dissipation. But, when left alone in the morning-
room, she did not begin to write letters: indeed, she did not
attempt to occupy herself in any way, beyond strolling leisurely
up and down the room, and taking an occasional glance at the
mirror in passing. She had every reason to be satisfied with
what she saw there: and when a loud double knock at the street
door was followed by the announcement of "Dr. Rackstraw,"
she was as ready for the reception of a visitor as if she had been
expecting a duke for hours.

"Tell Dr. Rackstraw that I will see him here," said she.

Dr. Rackstraw was a striking and even interesting-looking man, and not the less so for not being stamped with any of the conventional signs of the English gentleman, such as might be expected on the part of anybody admitted as a matter of course into the room where the ladies of Longwood received only their most intimate and particular friends. It is the reverse of disrespectful to the British colonies to say that their gentlemen are not of any conventional pattern: and there was in this sense a decidedly colonial cut about Dr. Rackstraw. But there was something more: or rather colonialism intensified. He was nearly, if not fully, six feet high, and lean to gauntness, something after the accepted model of a North-Western trapper—all steel and whip-cord. His face was completely and carefully shaved, and his complexion had been tanned into what, both in colour and texture, resembled leather, so that it was not easy to tell his age. As to that matter, he had obviously done and seen too much to be young; but, on the other hand, any point beyond the first stage of middle age was inconsistent with the almost child-like curve of his singularly handsome lips, his clear blue eyes and his perfectly unwrinkled skin. His hair, also, worn rather affectedly long, was still thick and soft. But, despite these almost feminine attributes, emphasised by the Greek style of his features generally, Dr. Rackstraw's prevalent expression was that of alertness and thoroughly masculine vigour and energy. Yet, he was grave, even melancholy, in his expression and bearing, so that altogether a physiognomist would have found him a singularly interesting, because inconsistent and even self-contradictory, study. He was dressed in the deepest of black and the whitest of linen—a bad choice, because his long black frock coat besides being too new and too glossy, emphasised the lean angularity of his six feet of stature, and somehow seemed to bring out the points of manner and carriage least consistent with the position of being perfectly at home in Mrs. Derwent's morning-room that he appeared to assume.

On the whole, what with his long brown hair, his long black coat, the cherubic curl of his lips, and the frosty steel of his deep-set blue eyes, he was not a man to whom his fellow men were likely all at once to take kindly. Women, however, judge men by a very different code of signals, and, above all, are indifferent, or rather blind, to those details which classify a man as Gentleman, or as the contrary, or as of merely neutral colour. Men are often amazed at the paste that women take for diamond—but then, to be sure, there is no certainty that they are always right about one another and women always wrong. As may have been always gathered, Mrs. Derwent was an exceedingly large-minded woman in the matter of acquaintances—her heart was as wide as her doors, and admitted more than the laws of mechanics allow.

"You got my note, then, dear Mrs. Derwent?" asked Doctor Rackstraw, in a hard, rather high, but clear and not unmusical voice, with a slight twang about it—not American, or Continental, but still not wholly English: a voice that would alone suffice to call attention to its owner, so inspired was it with marked individuality. "It was good of you to remain in this beautiful afternoon."

"Oh, no—there was no goodness about it at all," said she. "Indeed, I am in want of your advice about a hundred things—but they'll keep. In fact, now, when I come to think of them, I hardly remember what they are. I got so into the way of coming to you for advice in poor Colonel Derwent's time that whenever any little thing troubles me I want to send for you—and then they're really so small that, when you do come, they're gone. Not that it's altogether like that, to-day."

"There would be no trouble at all, dear Mrs. Derwent, dear friend," said he, "if you would only see things in their proper light : if you could only see how it is a law of nature that man is nothing without woman, and woman nothing, nay, less than nothing, without man——"

"Hush! No more of that, if you please," said Mrs. Derwent, hastily, and colouring quickly. But she found means to glance in the mirror as she blushed, and the sight of her own colour made her smile. "We are to be friends, you know, like we've always been. How shall I ever be able to ask your advice again, if you *will* forget that I'm an old lady with a grown-up son?"

"I can't forget what I never knew," said he solemnly. "There are some women—and some men too—that never grow old; you are one of those women—I am one of those men. Do you know that I am younger now than I was at twenty-one? The secret's easy—it comes of merging my own existence in that of others. There are times, my dear friend, when I forget the very existence of Hermon Rackstraw, almost his very name, so absorbed am I in the realisation of myself as a mere atom in the progress of the universe and of humanity. That is a terrible thought at times."

"It must be!" said Mrs. Derwent: for one of her charms was her readiness and completeness of sympathy, quite independently of her comprehenson. She could at the same moment sympathise, quite honestly, with the artist and with his rival, with the fox and with the hounds; a point to which the loftiest intelligence can never hope to attain, so much more catholic are hearts than minds. "It must be terrible indeed?"

"Yes, dear friend. But it is not so terrible as when the atom wakes to discover that it also is an entity, and—Alone! Dear friend, have you realised what it means to be alone?"

"I'm not sure I have, since the colonel died. You see, I have Kate, and Anne, and Horace now: and you and all my friends."

"True. You are a happy woman. And I have—my fellow creatures. I ought not to complain. Only there is so much to be done, and so little time to do it in : so much and so little means. However, I didn't come to talk of my own troubles. And you said you have some of your own."

"Well, I have. At least, not exactly troubles, but——But you have something to say to me?"

"Something—but, whatever it is, it can wait for what *you* have to say to *me*. My something is only a request for a very small favour. What is yours?"

"Oh, I'm afraid it will seem very small to a man like you, with the business of all the world on your hands——"

He looked quickly at her for a moment, as if to see whether her words were not a trifle tainted with sarcasm. But finding no sign of such a thing, he corrected her. "No, not the business— the welfare," said he. "The welfare of those dark regions where the torch of civilisation has never yet beamed. As Agassiz said, when a thing begins to pay, it has nothing more to do with me. I am a pioneer."

"It's about Horace—my son."

"Yes, my dear friend?"

"You know what a boy he is—not exactly learned, or clever, but still the best of boys. I thought, till to-day, there wasn't a thought in his heart that I didn't know——"

"Yes: mothers always think that, well?—"

"And to-day, the girls tell me, he has set up a crotchet for collecting books. If it had been horses, or dogs, or guns, or postage stamps—but books ! What *can* it mean ? "

Dr. Rackstraw considered. " Certainly," said he, " I should not have said, off-hand, that books were much in my young friend's line. And it's an awkward sort of a craze, too : books are costly things."

" Indeed they are ! Why the girl's novels cost a guinea and a half, I believe, when they're new."

" A guinea and a half ! Do you know that old books have often cost a thousand guineas and more ? Why a man, dear Mrs. Derwent, had better take to gambling, right away. And there's no use in them—none. The time is coming when every book that wasn't written last week will be treated as a relic of the dark ages —as it ought to be. Old books are the petrifactions of old, that is to say false, ideas. The newspaper is the literature of the future—the book that a man buys, and reads, and throws away, and that leaves his mind as open as it found it. Whenever I open up any of this world's dark corners—whether in Africa or in Polynesia —I set up a printing press the first thing, for the press is the great engine of civilisation, next to steam, and the press means the newspaper. Mr. Derwent's fancy is distinctly reactionary, and diverts money backwards, which is distinctly unnatural and wrong. Is this the first time he has been troubled with such dangerous ideas ? "

" Then it *is* dangerous ? Good gracious—a thousand guineas for one book—how big it must have been ! You alarm me, Doctor Rackstraw. I'm glad I sent for you, indeed. Will you speak to him ? "

Dr. Rackstraw shook his head. " I'm afraid it would be of little use," said he. " I don't know why, but Mr. Horace Derwent distrusts me, though I am the most devoted of his friends, Perhaps he thinks me a little too near the throne— though I'm far enough from it, God knows . . . . But I mustn't speak of that. Is this the first time he has had such a craze ? "

" You agree with me that it must be stopped, then ? "

" Surely I do."

" And what do you suppose can be the cause ? "

" I cannot venture to suppose, my dear friend. I have reason to believe, I know. Here is a young man, full of health, life, and energy—and blessed with a mother such as—such as—you,

dear Mrs. Derwent, dear friend : but he has no occupation—none
worthy of such privileges as his are. If I had half his means, I
would by this time have civilised the half of Africa; I would
have dressed every negro in clothes like my own, and have
embraced them in the railway system of the world. It can be
done—and I know how. At this very moment I have three
schemes of the kind on hand. I am but a pioneer—Mr. Horace
might be a field-marshal of civilisation, if he pleased. Don't be
afraid : he needn't go out anywhere : he needn't leave your apron
—his home, for a single day. All he need do would be to give his
name to one of my—those—three companions, and serve on the
board. He wouldn't be running after old books then! Speak to
him seriously, dear Mrs. Derwent. Dear friend, I don't want to
revive unpleasant memories, but Lawrence Derwent—his half-
brother, the colonel's eldest son— he, too, was a young man with
nothing to do. And see to what *he* came ! "

Whether Dr. Hermon Rackstraw intended the result or not,
Mrs. Derwent flushed up in another sort of fashion than when he
was giving the widow to understand that, with or without hope,
she was the one woman in the world to him.

" Dr. Rackstraw ! " she exclaimed, with a sharpness in her voice
which spoke more plainly of departed youth than all the other
effects of all her years, " what, in the name of Heaven, has
a forger, a convict, to do with *my* son ? "

" Except that they were the sons of one father—nothing :
thank God, nothing, dear friend. I never knew the colonel's
first wife, Lawrence's mother ; but the colonel must have had
strangely contradictory tastes. She must have been as unlike you
as an alligator from a damask rose. But these skeletons—what
household has them not ?—are not meant to be forgotten. They
have their use, and there use is to warn. Mr. Horace, though
he don't like me, is not likely to do anything ungentlemanly,
that I am the first to allow. But the same fatal idleness, which
leads one man into crime will lead another into book collecting,
or some other folly which, under all the circumstances of life, is
also criminal in its own way. Mr. Horace has, I believe, eight
thousand a year, and will have more. But what is eight thousand
a year to a book-hunter? A drop in the ocean. He'll be through
his capital in no time, as sure as my name's Hermon Rackstraw.
And all for what ?—a shelf full of lumber that he can't even
read. It's not forgery, but it's ruin. And, under all the circum-

stances, I'm hanged, dear friend, if I know which is the worst of the two. Lawrence Derwent lost Longwood by his fault; see that Mr. Horace don't lose it by his folly, that's all. There, I speak my mind, as a pioneer; but I love that boy as if he were mine as well as yours—and I wish he were!"

The case was too urgent to admit of Mrs. Derwent's noticing certain vulgarities in her adviser-general's way of putting things; and, indeed, his picture had fairly frightened her. She had not been able, without masculine help, to see things from so panoramic a point of view. He saw the state of mind into which his zeal had thrown her, and struck again.

"When I first became acquainted with Colonel Derwent," said he, "his son Lawrence was as fine a lad as you'd wish to see. But he had nothing to do, except what he fancied. Now it was yachting, now it was dicing, now it was stage-playing; but the paramount claims of humanity upon every human atom he could never be made to see. I don't believe he cared a cent whether the women of the Cactus Islands got their stuffs from Lancashire, or whether they had no stuffs at all. His father cut him off without a shilling—I will say for the colonel that he was a just man in money matters—and very properly made Mr. Horace his heir. You know what happened—the young man, having no fixed principles, tried to set things straight by producing a later will—forged—and Lowmoor was *his* end. But what's sauce for the—the one, is sauce for the other, my dear friend. Mr. Horace couldn't do anything unbecoming an honest man and a gentleman—no, no. But he can lose Longwood as surely as his brother. Cards, my dear friend, have been called the devil's books. But no less surely, Books—*old* Books—are the devil's cards."

"You frighten me out of my wits!" said Horace's mother, rising and pacing the room. "I never thought of all this—it is dreadful! We must think what is to be done. . . . But I mustn't be selfish. What did *you* want to say to *me!*"

"Oh—I was half forgetting. After the sad business you have told me, it seems so small. No, I'm wrong. After all, nothing's small. And, in a way, this is really a great thing, though it won't take five minutes to tell."

"I'm thinking of my boy! But I can listen. Well?"

"It's rather a curious circumstance—if it wasn't that too many curious circumstances happen to me to be noticeable one more than the other. I needn't tell you of my old connection with the

Goblin Islands; you know all about that—that's where Port Rack-straw is, which is now bidding fair to be a centre of civilisation in one of the most neglected corners of the world. I am Agent-General for the Goblin Islands, and in that capacity I have received notice that I shall shortly be called upon to do the honours to a most illustrious personage — in short to a Real Queen!"

" Good gracious !—a Queen ? "

" Yes : a Real Queen. The Queen of an unknown island— think of there being an unknown island on the world's map in these days ? Even I, who have reason to know how behind-hand the geographers even still are, was surprised. But there's no question about it, dear friend. It must, however, have become known to some extent, since I was in those seas, and since the last maps were made, became obviously, if the Queen of that Island has discovered the rest of the world, some portion of the world must have discovered the Island. However, that may be, my correspondent, who is my agent at Port Rackstraw, or rather whose agent-general I am in Great Britain, writes me that Her Majesty landed recently from a large canoe at the largest of the Goblins, not far from Port Rackstraw, and managed to convey to my agent-correspondent her desire to visit this country. I don't know how she ever came to hear of this country—I hope, if it was from shipwrecked sailors, that the process of cooking them was not too painfully long——"

" Good gracious !" exclaimed Mrs. Derwent, starting.

" There are notorious cannibals in those seas," said Dr. Rack-straw, quietly. " I have been nearly eaten myself, more than a dozen times : no doubt if I fattened better, I shouldn't be now sit-ing here. Anyhow, the desire to break through her barbaric limits shows remarkable enlightenment in a queen of unheard-of savages whether they be cannibals or no. It is an occasion of stupendous interest—a supreme opportunity, dear friend! We have had African princes, Indian princes, kings from the Sandwich Islands, Japanese embassies— but never a queen from an island absolutely unknown. Think what she will see and learn, and what a responsibility rests upon us, who will have the making or marring of that island to the end of time! I shall lose no time—she is due at Southampton the day after to-morrow. I shall lose not a day in taking her to Birmingham and Manchester, and the Black Country, and all our really civilised districts, and make her give

orders for cotton goods and hardware, and machinery, and everything that an enlightened community can want to buy, or that an
enlightened Empire can want to sell.   But even British commerce
isn't everything.   Her Majesty must learn British culture too.
Would you, in the sacred name of civilisation, dear friend, send
one of these cards of yours to this Real Queen?"
   "A Queen!"
   Mrs. Derwent was impressed by the title, though borne by a
savage, who probably would not have known the meaning of the
word.   But after a full minute's rumination, her thoughts took
another turn.
   "Of course as you put it like that."
   "In the sacred name of civilisation?"
   "Yes—like that—I don't like to refuse.   But a black woman—
perhaps a cannibal!   And, oh, Dr. Rackstraw —are you sure they
wear enough clothes?"
   "Oh—the colour's nothing, it gives distinction to a room, and
excites conversation.   As for cannibalism—I don't know how Her
Majesty may live at home, but if she is one, all the better; there's
a delight in civilising a good, right down square barbarian that
one never gets out of your milk-and-water savage.   Mark my
words—she'll be converted from that by her first ice cream.   As
for dress—she will of course conform to the custom of the
country.   If you'll give me the address of your dressmaker, I'll
put Her Majesty into her hands the day after she arrives.   Dear
friend—next to steam, and above the printing press, the foremost
of all civilising agents is a dressmaker, like yours."
   "She is certainly an artist in her way. . . .   Well, I suppose I must consent—though really the idea, it is so strange and
eccentric, makes me almost afraid.   And how in the world shall I
direct the card?"
   "Ah—my correspondent writes that she wishes to be incognita: at first, at any rate.   As far as I can make out, her proper
title is Queen — Queen Ngahoung Qhlawu, of the Island of
Apahu.   But that won't do at all.   There are reasons, good
reasons, for her going about as a private person: queens never
learn, and only see what they're shown.   We must have a name
and style that won't look odd in a hotel book, and that won't
be out of keeping with a lady of colour.   Let me see—you'd
better .make out your card to Senhora Miranda.   That sounds
Portuguese, and euphonius, and perfectly vague—distinguished,

pronounceable, and telling nothing at all. She shall be Senhora Miranda while she's here."

"Perhaps you would kindly write the name on the card," said Mrs. Derwent, seeking among the chaos of cards, filled and un-filled, that had been left unsorted by her daughters for one that would serve : " I'm not good at foreign names." Evidently Dr. Rackstraw's recommendation of a new acquaintance was all-sufficient for her, though to everybody who knew him less inti-mately his account of the real queen whom he professed to have caught in the interests of civilisation might seem to require a little judicious sifting before his faith in the report of his corres-pondent in the Goblin Islands could be cordially shared. " Here is a card," said Mrs. Derwent, at last, taking one from the heap. "No— that is for Mr. Fane. What's this ? Mr. *and Miss* Fane ! "

A light seemed all at once to break upon her—a ray of the same light that had broken upon the girls when they first heard of a Miss Fane. "Dr. Rackstraw !" said she.

" Yes, dear friend ? "

" Do you know any people of the name of Fane ? "

" No. I never knew anybody named Fane."

" They live at 28, Richmond Place. And——"

" Well ?—"

" I want you to find out for me who they are."

CHAPTER XIV.

> While wearily I wandered round,
>   I heard a whispered song—
> " In seven years are all things found,
>   If they be lost so long.
> There's magic on that number set :
>   And they that part in tears,
> Yet cannot in one hour forget.
>   May meet—in Seven years."

HERMON RACKSTRAW, the self-appointed agent-general for the civilisation of savages, and reported by those who did not like him to make a very fair commercial profit out of his calling, might easily have executed the behest of the well-looking and well-left widow if, instead of conversing with the mother, he had followed the son. Sure enough, Horace Derwent's newly awakened passion for old black letter, which had sown such a harvest of dismay in the family bosom, carried him straight to the house in Richmond Place, where it was to be indulged.

Not many such houses are to be seen: though probably this
city of all things has never been at any time without one or two.
For the thing or creature that is not to be found in London is not
to be found in the world.

Horace, at the street door, asked for Mr. Fane, and was admitted. But the admission apparently amounted merely to a per-
mission to attack a series of barricades. The entrance passage was
piled with books, presumably, from their exposure to all comers,
of but little value; even less must have been the worth of those
which served for stumbling-blocks upon the stairs. It was rather
the entrance to the cave of a slovenly student than of a careful
collector; and Horace, in the earlier days of his hobby, had wondered what sort of servant would consent to stay in a place where
not a tray could be carried upstairs or down without imminent
risk to the neck of bearer. But he had long ceased to wonder
at such impersonal questions. He found his own way into
what had no doubt been intended for the drawing-room, to find
confusion ten times confounded. It was a fairly large room,
but how it was furnished no mortal eyes could tell, seeing
that it was the headquarters of the army of volumes whereof
the landing, the staircase, and the passage, were but the out-
posts of the advanced guard. But, straight as an arrow, his
eyes went straight to a certain corner between the fire-place and
one of the windows. They lighted up by the road, and he moved
eagerly forward, but at the same moment, from the side of the
girl who had brought the brightness into his eyes, there rose,
as if from a cave of books, the figure of a grave young man,
without a coat, and with the sleeves rolled back as for labour.
Horace looked vexed, and he lounged forward after his normal
fashion, as if he were merely making an ordinary morning call.

"You seem busy, Miss Fane," said he, holding out his hand.

"Oh, don't touch me!" cried the girl. "Look at my hands,
and touch me if you dare," she said, holding up two palms that
were certainly strangely black for those of a young lady — his
sisters had never dreamed of hands like these.

It is a long long time since we have seen or thought of Sophy.
Indeed, she has grown out of all knowing; for since we knew her
when she was that high—and "that" was very little—it is going
on for nine years. And yet she has neither grown so much nor
changed so much as might be warranted by the difference between
one-and-twenty and thirteen; for she is still small and vivacious,

and her eyes are as much like soft lightning as ever they were. The spirit of curiosity had not, it is to be feared, been exorcised by the incantations of time, and a sprite of mischief seemed to have had a finger in the twisting of every brown curl. That no woman would have called her pretty, I am sure. That nine men out of ten would have sworn that she was pretty, I am equally sure : at, any rate, Horace Derwent swore it, as he looked, lazily, indeed, but with looks of little favour, towards the strange young man without a coat and with turned up sleeves. He was evidently not a carpenter or a man from the pantechnicon—so what the devil was his business there?

"Mr. Hargrave—Mr. Derwent," said Sophy, bringing two volumes together with a bang, and making their dust fly. "Mr. Hargrave is helping me re-arrange the library. A new folio has come in, and that obliges all the shelves to be arranged over again. Mr. Derwent, will you take off your coat, and roll up your sleeves, and help, too?"

Horace bowed his acknowledgment of the introduction, and was a little surprised to notice that this Mr. Hargrave, for no apparent reason, started and changed colour on hearing his name—perhaps the fellow was shy. Altogether he was not, so Horace thought, a prepossessing person, with his set, almost sullen look, his general awkwardness, the atmosphere of dust which he appeared to exhale, and, above all, his close proximity to Sophy Fane. Horace would have given much to know how long he had been there.

"If I could help you I'd take off twenty coats," said Horace, "but I don't see why you shouldn't rest a minute. So your uncle has been getting a new treasure, has he? Is he better to-day?"

"Yes, a little. But you won't see him," said Sophy, between a smile and a sigh. "He has a new treasure, as you say—and he's carried it off into his den, so that nobody may come between it and him. We're turning the house out of windows to make a place for it, Oswald—Mr. Hargrave—and I."

That "Oswald and I" almost made Horace hate Mr. Hargrave. But he was much too true a young Briton to show his feelings; and only protested against the occupation of his silent rival by clearing a dozen volumes off the corner of the sofa, and sitting down.

"You are sadly lazy!" said she.

"Lazy—yes! Sadly—no. The fact is, I only came to let your

uncle know that I've been searching everywhere, all over London for an uncut what's-his-name—Hunsden's *Flora*, you know, that he said he'd give his ears for; and that at last I've run her down. At least, I hope so; and I thought he might be glad to know."

"Glad? Glad isn't the word! But don't tell him so to-day—you'll spoil his present pleasure. Wait till that's in its place, which, from the look of things I should think would be in about ten years, and then let him know that there's something still left to live for. Thank you indeed, Mr. Derwent; not that I *can* thank you for so much kindness, so much trouble—*do* you mind taking a *very* dusty hand?"

He did not mind; he not only took the very dusty hand, but, regardless of the coatless rival among the book-heaps, touched it with his lips, and held it for an instant more. Strange to say, when this was over, and he looked up, the coatless rival had vanished from the room.

"Miss Fane," said he, "you really oughtn't to work like this. Why should one new book cause chaos to come again?"

"Oh, I don't mind. It's something to do. And you know my uncle. If it wasn't for the books, arranging, and the disarranging, and the re-arranging—but no; nobody could quite know, but Oswald and me."

"Oswald?" asked Horace, his lips, just now made warm by the dusty little hand, all at once struck cold again.

"Yes, Mr. Hargrave, the gentleman who was here just now."

"And who is Mr. Hargrave? I didn't know you had any friends I hadn't seen. Is he a *great* friend of yours?"

"Only the oldest friend we have in the world. We don't see much of him, I wish we saw more, but he's a good deal abroad. He—he wanted to marry my poor sister, Rosamond, who died. He's never forgotten her, and he never will—no, though he's a man."

"*Though* he's a man! Because he's a man, you mean. As if I could forget—a woman I loved," said Horace, unmindful of numbers one to thirty-two, but feeling that his prejudice against Oswald Hargrave had been at any rate hasty and premature. "Poor fellow! I can understand it, though, if she was anything like you.'

"But she was not the least bit like me! She was the most beautiful, the cleverest, the very best girl that ever was born, or that ever will be. Talk of me beside Rosamond—me! She would have died for me, and I would have died for her; and when she did die—well, there was the end of life, of everything but old books, for us all. Everytning broke to pieces after that; poor Oswald's heart, and uncle's antiquities, that turned out to be frauds, and our old country life—and—but, well, I can't do in a stress what she would have done, but I do what I can. I can dust books; so—here goes again."

The bang of the two dusty volumes went hard to Horace Derwent's heart this time.

"Sophy," began he, unconscious that for the first time he had spoken her Christian name aloud.

But she was, or seemed to be, intent upon other things. She was punishing the books heavily, and her eyes were filling with tears. Horace knew something about the story of the Fanes, and had guessed, wrongly enough, a great deal more than he could possibly know; but at this moment he felt that all his guessing had all been wrong. But he had long guessed that he loved her; and he knew it now.

"I *will* help you with those books," said he, looking at the tears in her eyes.

But his very look must have dried them. "You help?" she asked, with a bright little laugh, as natural as the sunshine in the heart of an April shower. "Why, I don't believe you could work if you tried. But I forgot—to have got that *Flora* you must have worked and walked indeed——"

"And you gave me your fingers for it. Will you give them again?"

But, alas for his hope to keep those blackened fingers for at least one instant longer than before; at that most promising of moments Oswald Hargrave came back into the room, clothed this time, and like a common Christian man; and two more easy mannered people than Horace and Sophy no interrupter of a *téte-à-téte* could possibly have found.

"Then shall I bring the *Flora?*" asked Horace, carelessly enough, "the next time I call?"

"Please—if you can. I needn't give it him all at once——"

"Then I will go now," he said, almost with a sigh: for there was little pleasure in remaining with this silent Oswald to make a third.

That visit had not been what he had hoped—nay, it had been much less, for nine times out of ten, except when her uncle was present he had found her alone, and her uncle was deep in some

new old book every tenth time. Still he had fallen more deeply
in love, and that was something to make his few minutes in Richmond Place not wholly in vain. For it is the loving (I speak
subject to correction) that is the great thing in love after all.
Sophy had not said much, but what she had said about her
dead sister had seemed to him full of heart, and her readiness to
laugh through her tears and to cry through her laughter had
touched him with the whole secret of the spring. It was a real
disappointment to him, however, when, being inclined to go home
in company with his own thoughts the longest way, for the sake
of such solitude as the streets alone can give a man, he was overtaken by Oswald Hargrave a very few yards from the door.

So Hargrave had been delaying to obtain the priceless privilege of
last words ; and Horace might have finished his visit in peace if he
had only had the patience to stay on. Unquestionably Hargrave
was a bore. But still the man who had broken his heart for the
dead sister was to be pitied and borne with, for Horace was a good-
natured fellow, even when crossed, and he fancied he knew how
he would feel if Sophy should suddenly walk over a cliff into the
sea, as poor Rosamond had done. Thank God that it had been
Rosamond and not Sophy! So he thrust his hands into his
pockets, and asked, quite good-humouredly :

"Are you going my way ? I'm after that *Flora*. Are you a
book-worm too ? "

" Not I," said Oswald : and, for the first time heard to speak, it
was wonderful how the whole manner and expression of this grave
young man seemed to improve; " but I'll help you angle for the
Flora, if you don't mind." Horace felt as if the eyes of his companion were seeking to penetrate him—it was an odd feeling and
not an agreeable one, callous as Horace was to the fancies with
which sensitive people are troubled.

If he could only have guessed what his name, the name of Derwent, meant to Oswald Hargrave ; but what need is there to specu-
late on what might have happened had he known what he could
not know ? For Oswald, and Oswald alone, had clung to the hope,
so passionate as to amount to the faith which scorns reason, that
Rosamond might not have perished ; that her incredible romance
was no dream of fever, but simply and literally true, and that
Derwent, the escaped forger from Lowmoor, might be forced to
unravel the mystery could he be found anywhere within the circle
of the world. He knew how to keep his faith to himself, as sane

men know how to keep a secret what others would take for a craze. But he had changed the life of a farmer for that of a man as devoted to a craze as if he had been named Æneas Fane. Derwent is at any rate uncommon enough to serve for a way-mark to a pursuer who had hitherto sought for the slightest sign of a trail in vain.

Assuredly this frank-looking, easy-going young gentleman was no escaped convict: that was too absurd a notion even to serve as a straw for a drowning man. But, according to all accounts, the convict himself had been a gentleman, or at least in the position of one : he must therefore have had connections in the same condition of life, and this casual meeting with one Derwent might possibly lead to the discovery of another. Men with fixed ideas are prone to see the finger of fate in all things. So he strove to unbend, not unsuccessfully, while the two young men strolled on, talking of this thing and that, first of books, of which neither knew anything; then of the same thing in relation to Æneas Fane; then a little, but not much, of Sophy; then of more masculine matters, and at last drifting into horses and guns, where they found a common ground.

"He isn't half a bad fellow after all," thought Horace, after a while. "And if he's almost Sophy's brother, I must cultivate him; but if I had been he, and Sophy had been Rosamond, *I* shouldn't have had the heart to talk of such things as he can. I don't half believe the fellow's as heart-broken as Sophy thinks, after all. Here's the place where I'm told the *Flora* hangs out,' said he. "A queer enough shop, by Jove! but then these places where they breed book-worms mostly are. Do you mind comin g'i i ?"

"Not a bit," said Oswald, who had not yet contrived to get in e question that could bear upon so awkward a business as the discovery whether a Derwent like this had ever had the most distant cousin in Lowmoor.

Horace, who, as a collector, was studying the fine art of bargaining, did not announce his errand at once, but chose to put the raw lad, who kept the dark, out-of-the-way shop, or rather cross between a shop and stall, off the scent by taking down volumes at random from the shelves, chaffing a little meanwhile in a very unbookworm like way. Oswald lounged farther into the premises, also looking at volumes in the same random manner, until he nearly reached a desk separated from the shop by a ground glass door. And, while standing here, he distinctly heard these words spoken,

9

n a certain north-country accent which he had not heard since
Silver Moldwarp had been detected in forging Phœnician dials nine
years ago—

" I'm never mistook, Mister.   Instinc's a sure guide.   And if the
villain that nigh did for me in Pix-Knoll's named Lawrence Der-
·went, then Lawrence Derwent, with these very eyes I saw Tuesday
morning, as plain as I see——"

"Shop!" cried the lad. "Here's a gentleman 'quiring after
that there *Floorer*——"

It was Silver Moldwarp, with his ragged jacket exchanged for an
almost professional suit of black, and with gilt spectacles on nose,
who emerged from the den behind the glass door.   Oswald rapidly
turned his back, and affected to be absorbed in the nearest shelves.
His companion had evidently heard nothing.   But, though thus
quick-witted enough to conceal himself from the rascal who seemed
to know so much, Oswald's heart was literally standing still.
After nine long years of search to light upon this accident after
all!   The finger of fate, indeed?—Say rather fate's open hand.
" To him who waits, all things come."

CHAPTER XV.

Light up the hall—throw wide the door:
The house is white, without, within
Each secret nook is swept and clean,
With greenest rushes on the floor.

The spirit of infinite unrest
Who till to-night possessed my gate
Hath flown before the hour's too late
To welcome in a better guest.
      *   *   *   *   *
Who needs to knock when doors are wide?
Welcome ! For none would seek to pass
These portals save the pure. Alas !
'Tis He—'tis He, with seven beside !

THAT terrible discovery—that his niece was dead, and that
Silver Moldwarp was an impostor—had fallen with
crushing force upon Æneas Fane.   Up to that moment
there was not a more perfectly happy elderly gentleman in exis·
tence; he had no anxieties, no troubles, no cares.   As a justice of
the peace, and as otherwise the most important person in the
parish, he could feel himself of use in the world, and, since his
actual duties amounted to nothing, he might lie down to sleep
every night of his life in the happy consciousness that all had
been well done and none omitted.   But, above all, he possessed

the one, true, infallible secret of human happiness—he had a hobby. Not only so, but he possessed in Pix-Knoll a treasure house of ever fresh antiquity to which Pompeii was a poor modern invention, only fit to amuse the vulgar, and the British Museum little more than a lumber room. Moreover, he rode his hobby with brains—with real brains, in their way. He was not a mere collector, but had staked his mind and his soul upon the belief that, from the historical fossils of Pix-Knoll he, a greater Cuvier, was restoring, not merely the skeletons of birds and beasts, but the very image of pre-historic Man—accounting for the unaccountable, and playing Œdipus to the arch Sphynx of the world. Nor as yet had his theories been put upon printed paper, and so exposed to that microscopic criticism of envious or jealous rivals which robs great discoveries of so much of their bloom. As yet he was in the happy state of being his own public, his own only critic, and the judge of his own present merits and future fame. Nor was he, like so many great collectors and other discoverers, troubled by his woman-kind: while at the same time he had the advantage over those no less many others who are without woman-kind to trouble them. His nieces, united, did not amount to a wife. A wife—a thousand to one—would have distracted his attention, made havoc of his flints, dusted his shelves, despised his hobby as stuff and nonsense, and sent Silver Moldwarp about his business pretty quickly. All this she would have done had she been a woman of tact: if she had been otherwise—but that supposition is too cruel. Rosamond and Sophy simply gave the house its home feeling, and kept the flints from turning too hard and cold. If he loved the work of Silver Moldwarp's rascally fingers like a poet and a lover, he would have given his second-best arrowhead to save either of the children from any real and lasting sorrow. Can many men say as much? Can any whole-hearted collecting man say more? Nay, I will go further—he would have given up all hope of obtaining a real Phœnician sun-dial to save Rosamond from dying. But when her horrible death was accompanied at the same moment by clear and open proof that Silver Moldwarp was an impostor, forger, cheat, that he himself, Æneas Fane, had been a dupe and an idiot, and that Pix-Knoll, instead of being a library of unwritten history, was merely a common chalk-pit— why then Rosamond's fate was only death, but Silver Moldwarp's exposure was the end of the world. Life had come down with a run, like a house of cards: and what is so hideous as to wake to

the consciousness of a fooled and wasted life when one is no longe
young enough to begin again?

For years afterwards Sophy could not bring herself to think of
the terrible time that followed; for months, she, child as she was,
feared to lie down in her bed, for fear it should haunt her dreams.
No very deep feelings were needed to make it seem as if, with the
loss of Rosamond, life had been roughly wrenched in two; while
to Oswald and the few neighbours it seemed as if her uncle would
never recover from the blow. Incapable of imagining that he was
half maddened, or rather half paralysed, with the murder of his
hobby-horse, and believing him to be somewhat dull and cold-
hearted, the apparent breaking of his heart over the loss of his
niece bewildered even the parish doctor; he seemed unable to lift
up his head, and kept his room in what was taken for an excess
of grief, but was in reality an agony of shame. He did grieve
for Rosamond—more, perhaps, than he himself knew. But the
greater passion must needs swallow up the less; and, while the
flints of Pix-Knoll were the ruins of a man's pride and vanity, the
loss of Rosamond was just the loss of Rosamond, and nothing more.
It was but a miserable part of an infinitely more miserable
whole.

Oswald, helped by the Pitcairns and the Doctor, thought his
best for Sophy—all that was left of Rosamond in the world. The
house whence her sister had been taken and where her uncle was
in this state of mind and body, was no place for a child to be left
in alone. But even this grave consideration had to be delayed;
for at the first suggestion of Sophy's going to stay for a little
while with the Pitcairns, Uncle Æneas broke into a fit of anger—
the first in which he had ever been seen. He never seemed to
want the child about him, and yet he was manifestly unable to
bear the thought that he was to be deprived of the last real thing,
however trifling, that had been left him of his exploded collection.
So Sophy had to be left alone for the present: and then the anger
fit was succeeded by one of brooding in absolute silence and solitude. "We must have another opinion," said the Doctor to
Oswald. "He'll be going melancholy mad: and I don't understand it at all. Of course it's bad to lose a niece in that way,
poor young thing, or in any other—but it's not a thing to go mad
for. Why the poor girl's lover, if she'd been old enough to have
one, couldn't have done more." But, at the end of many days,
Sophy herself was startled by the sudden appearance of Uncle

Æneas in the drawing-room; he had not made his appearance once among his shelves and drawers since their contents had been proved to be lies.

He did not say a word, or even seem to notice that she was there—though, indeed, that was Sophy's way, to be wherever anything was happening, and to see without being seen. Some change appeared to have come over the old gentleman, though the child was still too young to realise what it meant to him to come among the treasures which had turned to dust and rubbish like Fairy gold. After a moment or two he went out of the room, and presently returned, dragging in a large sack, which had once held potatoes. Then he pulled out all his shelves and his drawers, tossed and swept their contents into the sack, and rang the bell for the housemaid. "Send Pritchard here," said he.

The man came. " Pritchard," said Uncle Æneas, shortly, "put this sack of rubbish into a wheelbarrow, wheel it to the cliff, and turn it over into the sea. Sophy, my dear," he said, turning to his niece, " of all the idiotic crazes that a man can take up, archæology is the most idiotic and the most crazy. It was invented by rogues to cheat fools—or else by fools to give rogues a trade. What can it signify what men did before we were born ? Not a flint—not a flint, Sophy ! "

Sophy had now and then thought herself rather wicked for not being able to respect the flints sufficiently, or to see their beauties. But the loss of her sister, her heroine, almost her idol, had left her little heart very sore, and the tears ran to her eyes when she saw her uncle contemptuously discarding the household gods with his own hands. And to be thrown over that cliff—where Rosamond had gone to be swallowed by the sea which Sophy felt she would dread and hate for evermore !

But Uncle Æneas had become wonderfully calm. It was cl a · that the wholesale destruction of his idol, now it was proved but of common stone, did not cost him a single pang. " They want you to go to the Pitcairns," said he. " There's no need for that— and I rather fancy they want to put me into a madhouse : but there's no need for that either, my dear. I'm sane—for the first time since I picked up the first bit of trash on Pix-Knoll. But they'ie all right in one thing—Crossmarsh is no longer the place for me and you. Bless my soul it would be like living in a grave : and I can't meet the neighbours after what has happened: no, never

again. I can't sit on the bench while all the Court's saying,
'That's Fane of Crossmarsh: the old fool that was cheated by
Silver Moldwarp, and didn't know an ancient Phœnician's work
from a modern English knave's.' We'll travel: you shall see the
world before you cry your eyes and your heart out, little girl.
We won't stay here. But we won't part. Now She's gone, and
They're gone—there's not much but you and me left in the
world."

This was by no means in his old vein of talk, such as that in which
he had received Oswald's first offer for the hand of poor Rosamond.
But it was gentler, and kinder, and not without sense, and it made
Sophy cry all the more. Nor could Oswald, when he heard of
his old friend's plan, find it in his heart to persuade him to remain
in a place where every gorse-bush and every flint-stone would
henceforth be a monument of misery and, in Æneas Fane's case,
of morbid shame. Oswald Hargrave breathed no further word
of his faith, a faith beyond the reach of reason, that Rosamond,
whom he loved, was still either to be discovered or avenged. He
saw what Sophy could not see—that Æneas Fane was changed
and softened because broken down, and that a complete change of
place and life was in reality the wisest medicine that could be
prescribed. So, before long, Sophy had bidden Crossmarsh a half-
sorrowful, half-hopeful good-bye, and had crossed those limits of
the outer world which her dead sister's fancy had clothed with
such awe.

Well—Sophy was, after all, but a child. Twelve or thirteen
years are not enough for a soul to take root in life, and to be killed
or even much hurt, by the process of uprooting. She had loved
Rosamond with the love of sister for sister, of sister for brother,
of friend for friend, almost of daughter for mother, all in one: and
yet, at the end of a year's journeying to and fro, her need of Rosamond in her life was over, and, by the end of another, memory itself
had grown dim. Rosamond would always occupy the shrine of
a saint in her heart, not to be thought of without tears: but then
Sophy's tears were as near her eyes as her laugh was near her lips,
and such shrines are never left open all day long. It was a
pleasant, rambling life they led, unspoiled by definite plans or by
more lessons than her eager curiosity inspired her to learn; while
the languages of many lands came to her without any troublesome
sort of learning. Sometimes they would make a long stay of many
months at some place that pleased them: sometimes they would

make a long tour. By the time Sophy was eighteen she had become, in many respects, a citizeness of the world, and yet, by luck, or by instinct, or by quickness of wit, she, though an heiress and something of a beauty, had kept her heart as well as her hand as free as air. As for her uncle, though he had never recovered his old manner, he was, to all appearance, as sane as if he had never found Silver Moldwarp or lost poor half-forgotten Rosamond : and he was falling into the position of his niece's very humble and obedient slave more and more day by day. In short, Fate was doing her utmost to spoil Sophy : and the only wonder was that it took such a power as Fate so long to do.

But Fate had other views in store than the spoiling of a girl. *Naturam expellas*—Pitchfork Dame Nature out, yet back she'll crawl.

One day—it was at Venice—Uncle Æneas picked up from some dealer or other a fragment of lace that would please Sophy : or that he thought would please her. And so it did : but the acquisition pleased Uncle Æneas himself—though he knew nothing whatever about such things—still more. In a week he had read a book about lace : in a month he had as many specimens as would fill a large portmanteau : in another he had to increase the amount of his luggage to meet this new demand. "I intend to make a great collection of all the sorts of lace in the world," argued he, "old and new. It *ought* to be done. There's no archæology about it—no, no. It doesn't take one back more than three hundred years—a mere yesterday. And it is beautiful in itself, and the production still goes on." Sophy thought nothing of the matter, and, as she wrote to Oswald Hargrave (then, for reasons best known to himself, in the United States), it gave Uncle Æneas a new interest in life, and revived his energies. They began to travel with a purpose now ; and——

Yes—you may reform the criminal : you may cure the drunkard : you may make the camel pass through the needle's eye—such things have been done ; you may, perhaps, wean a smoker from his pipe—such a thing may once have been known : but a collector from his hobby, not without murder. He who had made a museum of used penny stamps and curiously marked oyster-shells in his childhood, and coins in his hot youth, and imaginary flint knives and arrow-heads in his middle age, could not escape from the law of his being. Why should he, indeed ? He had nothing else to do; and nothing wearies so utterly as travel without an aim. To be satisfied with doing nothing, one must sit still—and then people find it easy enough, considering how many such people there are. In short, Æneas Fane was himself again. The only difference in him now was that he had lost constancy—there had to be some effect from a disenchantment so great as to have unhinged his mind. You may mend a broken rope, but there will always be a knot in it: and in Æneas Fane's case the knot was a readiness to change from purpose to purpose, whenever some new temptation fell in his way. Even as the most inconstant of lovers is he whose heart, in spite of himself, remains true to the memory of a false first love, so did Æneas Fane, jilted by pre-historic archæology, fly from mistress to mistress—from lace to porcelain, from porcelain to butterflies. And then he no longer had the parish of Crossmarsh, but all Europe, for his hunting ground; and every city, old and new, had a fascination of its own. He became a very Don Juan of *vertu*, and made the acquaintance of a hundred new Moldwarps, both Jew and Gentile, though perhaps of few able so completely to meet his wishes half way as the old.

And so by swift and sure descent, he fell, in due course, into the hands spread open to receive him at the bottom of the slope of the collector's Avernus—into those of the Book Fiend. From those claws alone there is no return. He possessed the two grand qualifications for a veritable bibliomaniac; he knew nothing of books, and he never read them. There is no need to tell how the taste began. No doubt it began with a thousand accidents, all converging towards one point, as all the magnetic needles in the world converge to a common pole. But it had an unlooked-for effect upon the life of Sophy, who was strong enough to twist her mere uncle round her finger, but not to turn an inch from his path her uncle *plus* a craze. A man cannot carry about a library, even though he travel with half the luggage of an American *belle*. He and she had to settle down, so that the last new Fane collection might fix itself and grow. And thus it had come to pass that 23, Richmond Place, became a great literary lumber room, into which all the Moldwarps of that department of trade shot, with much profit to themselves, what would otherwise have been their bad bargains.

Of course all this cost money. But Sophy, who had never had occasion to learn what money means, took it all for granted, and never thought of asking—considering that Uncle Æneas scarcely had a penny of his own—whence all the money came. It was much more strange that, after her girlhood of travel and well-nigh daily excitement, she could settle down, in fair content, to a dull life of dust and mould, wherein the grand incidents were the perpetual shifting of the contents of the shelves; for Uncle Æneas arranged his library on system, and one new acquisition implied universal change. The best of girls would have ample excuse for fretting and beating her wings. Then why did not Sophy, who, if a good enough girl as girls go, was still very far from being the best of girls?

Perhaps, as yet, not even Sophy herself could have told why.

"Oswald has been here," said she, when, both her visitors having taken their leave, her uncle came in to see the result of her work, with a folio under his arm, and a duodecimo in his hand. He was certainly older than nine years ago, and had breathed the air of books long and deeply enough to have acquired the look and bearing of a scholar. Perhaps about this there was a certain amount of scarcely conscious affectation: but there was none in the less upright carriage of the shoulders, and the half-weary manner that he had never quite lost since his life had been snapped in two.

"I know it—he has been with me. And young—what's his name?—has been here, too."

"Yes, uncle," said Sophy, with scarcely the dream of a blush; "he came to say he had found that book, the *Flora.*"

"Aye? Bless my soul! He's a good lad, and has the making of a real man in him. Now Oswald, with all his merits, will never be a real man—I don't believe he knows one book from another. Ah, the *Flora!*—when do you think it will be here?"

"I think—I'm almost sure—Mr. Derwent is going to see about it to-day."

"That young Derwent, Sophy, is as fine a fellow as ever lived! How have you been getting on?"

"Famously—thanks to Oswald! He's had his coat off, working like ten. See there, uncle—nine shelves arranged."

Uncle Æneas looked critically from the nine shelves that were arranged to the chaos remaining on the floor, from which the new order had been growing so slowly, and with so much labour of hands, patience, method, and brains. "Well," said he, "then there's not so much harm done, after all. I was afraid you'd have done more."

"More ?—why I thought you'd have said we'd done wonders!" said she.

But then there's the *Flora* coming, you see! So, you must see for yourself, that arrangement we've been making will never do. It must be revised and recast, entirely. The *Flora* must go on that shelf: and it will have to be the point of a new section, which will alter all the others."

"Oh, Uncle! *Do* you mean all to-day's work is to be thrown away, and all those shelves emptied, and——"

"Not thrown away, Sophy. This is literary work, you know: you can't take too much trouble with that—the more you take, the better it's done. I'll spend this evening in drawing up a new arrangement, ready for the *Flora*, and then to-morrow you and Oswald can begin all over again. Just think, Sophy— the *Flora :* the only copy in the whole world!"

There must indeed have been some unseen element in Sophy's London life to make this sort of life endurable ; for this sort of labour in vain, and this sort of talk, had become the story of every day. Fortunately, for this afternoon at least, her work was over, and, until the new arrangement was ripe for discussion, she was free to take up a book—it was not one of her uncle's—in which she was interested enough to think her own thoughts over; and they were far from being unpleasant ones. Meanwhile, her uncle, catalogue and pencil in hand, inspected the shelves, with his mind full of the *Flora.* For the hundredth time since he had become a slave of the Book Demon he felt that he had not lived in vain; his shoulders straightened, his chest expanded, and he now and then paused to stroke the back of some once supreme treasure as fondly as if it were alive.

Sophy was sitting in the window : and—exactly as in old times —it was just while she happened to be sitting there that a stranger passed along the terrace whose appearance caught her attention. Nine years of varied scenes had cultivated and developed, instead of rendering callous and dull, her natural genius for seeing and hearing everything that went on around her ; and, without the least effort, she had become perfectly familiar, by sight, with every man, woman, child, dog, cat, and canary who made up the population of Richmond Place, and even with the friends and relations who came to see them. It was not the sign of a large mind, but, in her case at least, it was no sign of an ill-natured one. On the contrary, her faculty helped to keep her

heart fresh by turning an ordinary thoroughfare into a perpetual comedy, with its heroes and heroines, its mysteries and its
oddities; and it may be that, after all, watching one's neighbours
overmuch is the better fault than heeding them too little. Had
Rosamond been alive, she would no doubt have buried herself in
the back of the house with her fancies—she would have seen nothing but hats and bonnets from the front windows, while Sophy
would have seen nothing from the back but the cats, so differently
are such common things as human eyes made. There was nothing
out of the way, of course, in the fact that a strange man, tall and
lean, was walking along the pavement of Richmond Place. Strangers of all shapes and sizes are common in London, and Richmond
Place was open to them all. But Sophy's attention was caught by
the entirely individual manner in which he wore his hat well at the
back of his head, by a certain defiant and aggressive carriage of his
umbrella, and by his unfashionable length of stride. He pulled
up at the door of No. 30, and took a view of the door. Then he
turned back, and knocked at the door, the Fanes' own door, under
Sophy's very eyes. There must be something really strange about
this stranger, after all.

"Oh, uncle!" she exclaimed—unnecessarily enough—"there's
somebody at the door!"

"Oswald, I suppose? I'm glad of it—he can get down these
books again. Or—Bless my soul, if it should be the *Flora* and
that young man!"

"No, uncle—it's nobody we know."

"'Dr. Hermon Rackstraw?'" asked Uncle Æneas, reading
from the stranger's card that the maidservant contrived to carry
across the barricades. "Who's Doctor Hermon Rackstraw?
What does he want? Did he say? Wants to see me for a
minute on business? Well I'm very busy, as you see; but if it's
only for a minute, I suppose I must see him, though, in a library
like this, minutes are precious things. No—don't show him into
the study; show him in here. . . . It doesn't do to show a
complete stranger into the study, Sophy, there are things
there I'd think twice before letting my own brother, if I
had one, see. Things I'd scarcely trust my own self alone
with, if they belonged to somebody else, and I had my great
coat on. . . . Dr. Rackstraw?" he asked, a little more doubt-
fully, as the visitor's long legs took the barricades, two at a time.

"I am Dr. Rackstraw," said the other. "I hope you will forgive me, sir, for dispensing with forms and ceremonies, but, if you ever come to know me better, you will find that I am not a ceremonious man." He caught sight of Sophy in her corner, and bowed. "The truth is, I ventured to call in the hope that a great master, like yourself, would pardon the intrusion of a humble, sadly ignorant, but enthusiastic pilgrim. In short, I have heard that the Fane Collection is rapidly getting to be one of the wonders of the world: and, as a traveller, I hoped I might be permitted to inspect it, as one of the lions of London. I trust I was not wrong?"

"Bless my soul!" exclaimed Uncle Æneas, holding out his hand, and colouring like a girl with pleasure and pride, for this was his first word of sympathy—the first note blown for him upon the trumpet of Fame. Indeed—indeed, Dr.—Rackstraw, I had no idea—Of course a bibliophile like yourself—Not that my little collection is much to boast of as yet, though I have one or two things worth seeing—Pray sit down, if you can find a chair; we are hard at work arranging you see. Sophy—Dr. Rackstraw; Dr. Rackstraw—my niece, Miss Fane."

"I am deeply honoured, I'm sure," said Dr. Rackstraw, as Sophy was brought formally into view. "Travellers are always privileged, but to receive me at once so generously into a treasure-house like this is something more than kind."

"You are a traveller?" asked Uncle Æneas, struck by something in the general appearance and manner of his visitor. "Are you an American? I have met many Americans on the Continent, and some of them are terrible rivals to us poor European bibliophiles——"

"No, sir—I have been in America, but I am not an American; and I have been in Australia, but am not an Australian: and among the Cannibals, but am not a Cannibal. And I was born in England but am not exactly an Englishman. I am a citizen of no mean city—that is to say, of the World. My position in London is that of Agent-General for the Goblin Islands: so I am a man of the future. But I am a man of the past too, when I get a whiff of the calf-skin and leather—sweeter to us book hunters, Miss Fane, than *eau de cologne.*"

"Do you mean that my modest collection has been heard of in the Goblin Islands?" asked Uncle Æneas. "That is very wonderful to hear! I can't guess how it happened—I thought I was quite unknown!"

" Ah, Mr. Fane—don't you remember what the poet says of
Glory : how she ' shuns those who chase her—those who shun,
pursues ' ?   I'm afraid that literature isn't very highly developed
in the Goblin Islands as yet, but I'm doing what I can,
and it is one of my visions to found a library—a real
library, such as you and I understand the word—at Port
Rackstraw——"

But Uncle Æneas did not want to talk about the Goblin Islands
of which until this moment he had never heard the name. I have
said he had blushed like a girl—and well he might, for he was in
the position of a girl who, after waiting long for her first lover
receives at last her first offer when she was least of all dreaming
of such a thing.   A sort of glory, not his own, appeared to radiate
from Dr. Hermon Rackstraw, and the whole air took the colours of
the rose.

" Yes, yes," said Uncle Æneas, hastily.   " But you want to see
my books—such as they are.   I'm sorry their present temporary
disarrangment on the floors and landings makes the catalogue useless until I have made a new one, but I can get without trouble at
the best things.   Ah—here's something you'll enjoy; a first edition of
the complete poetical works of Anon, 1617, printed by—let me see;
ah, of course, Nemo.   Or wait—before you look at that, here's a
black letter copy of the famous treatise of the Dutch Jesuit, Van
Daft, on the sixth angle of the pentagon—I bought it for no more
than two hundred florins at Frankfort, in the Judengasse.   Three
leaves are missing, I'm sorry to say—but then I don't believe there's
another copy of that book in existence that has lost three leaves
. . . . And here's a binding——"

And so he mounted his hobby, and made it gallop.   Dr. Rackstraw, though he had given the impression of a talkative person,
said but little, and generally played the part of a wise man who,
for his own purposes, has to play an intelligent part in respect of
a subject which he does not understand.   Uncle Æneas, once set
going, could have enjoyed going on till the end of time : and ye
presently, without any apparent check, the talk ceased to be quite
so one-sided, and to include not only the books themselves, but
the people and the incidents connected with their acquisition
It was the *Flora*, still uppermost in the heart of Uncle Æneas,
which touched this fuller key.   " What's the name of the young
fellow who's taking so much trouble about it, Sophy ? asked he,

" Mr. Derwent, uncle, do you mean ? "

" Yes—Derwent; it's so difficult to fix names that one never sees in a catalogue——"

" Indeed," asked Dr. Rackstraw. " I know some Derwents very well. I wonder if it's any of those."

" Not unlikely," said Uncle Æneas. " Under my guidance he's getting to know something about books, too.   It isn't everybody who could go straight, by instinct, to a book like the *Flora*, as he's done.   It reminds me of another man, that——No : Bless my soul what am I saying ?· I mean—he's a young man that my niece "and I came across somewhere abroad.   Where was it, Sophy ? "

It was when we were last in Switzerland," said she.

" Ah, yes—Switzerland : the most uninteresting country in the world.   You might stay there for a year, and not find a thing worth looking at—much less buying——"

" I know—Horace Derwent; I know him well.   A fine young fellow, and with a most extraordinary love of—books, as you say.   I've known the whole family for years.   What a curious family history theirs has been, to be sure ! "

" Indeed ? " asked Uncle Æneas, carelessly, while feeling that his first disciple was beginning to slip from his clutch, he searched for some other wonder.   Sophy's ears began to prick; so she turned her eyes upon her book, and unostentatiously turned over a page.   What could Horace Derwent's family history signify to her ?

" Yes," said Dr. Rackstraw, while he also turned over the pages of the last volume that had been given him to examine.   " It isn't every man in his position, you see, who has a convict for a half-brother, or who comes into a fine estate without being his father's eldest son.   But of course you know all that——"

" No," said Uncle Æneas, " I never heard.   Confound that *Mother Goose*—I *must* find it though——"

" The old colonel's heir, you see—son by a first marriage—was a wild lot; a bad lot, I'm afraid I must say.   He did his best to get himself cut off with a shilling, and, when he succeeded, he had no right to complain.   He was the Lawrence Derwent, you know, who was sentenced to penal servitude, or transportation— I forget which—for destroying the will that made his little half-brother, Horace, the heir.   It was a bad case—he stole the will from where it was kept in the very room where his father lay dying, and destroyed it under his dying father's very eyes. Luckily—providentially, I should say—there was plenty of proof .

of what the contents of the will were; or else our friend Horace, and his sisters, and his mother, would have been beggars, and— but, as I said before, there's a providence about these things, and justice was done. Perhaps you remember the trial, Mr. Fane? It made some noise in its time. . . . Yes—this is a curious book indeed; quite unique, I should say."

Sophy, though she continued to turn over her own pages, felt that the eyes of Dr. Rackstraw were resting upon her in a manner that made her feel fidgety and uncomfortable—as if either he could read in her the precise amount of the interest she took in Horace Derwent, and was making her conscious of it also, or as if he were venturing to admire her, on his own account, in a manner to which her long course of foreign travel had, while giving her considerable experience of it, failed to accustom her. She did not choose to let herself be driven from the room, but she could not help feeling relieved when all her uncle's efforts to detain him were exhausted, and the long legs, the long frock coat, and the uncomfortable eyes were gone at last.

" I don't like Dr. Rackstraw!" said she, closing her book, and tossing it aside. "Do you?"

"Not *like* him? Bless my soul, child! Why he's the most intellectual man I ever met. He really does understand books; he doesn't only talk about them——"

" He certainly did not say much—about books," said Sophy.

" Of course not. He came to learn, and very naturally listened to me. But what he did say was to the purpose. I only hope he'll come again. It has always been one of my great sorrows, Sophy—of course it isn't your fault—that I shall leave nobody behind me to take a properly intelligent interest in my work, and to carry it on when I am gone. I'm not collecting for the nation, you know, to have the collection of a life-time swamped and scattered. You heard, didn't you, what Dr. Rackstraw said of the Fane Collection—even so far as it has gone? I've been waiting to meet with some such man all my life. Who knows but this Dr. Rackstraw—with his learning, his vast experience, his evident ability, and his modesty—may be the very man?"

Sophy, until this hour, would have said that she knew her uncle, her constant companion of years, better than she knew herself. But now she felt as if all her experience had been thrown away. Never till now had his secret vanity been touched and exposed, and the hunger for sympathy in his pursuits, which no human being had ever dreamed of giving him, received the promise of being satisfied. One who had seen less of him than she might have perceived symptoms of something far more dangerous than mere hobby-riding in the change which all these years had wrought in the Squire of Crossmarsh; a hundred things would have struck comparative strangers as strange which appeared perfectly natural to her, who had only really known him (or thought so) since Silver Moldwarp's time. It needed some such incident as this afternoon's visit to make her realise that the eccentricities of Uncle Æneas were something deeper than an idle elderly gentleman's way of killing time.

"No," said she, "I do *not* like Dr. Rackstraw. And why did he make such a point of telling us that scandal about the Derwents. What was it to us, or to him?"

"Scandal—the Derwents? Why you must have been asleep over our book-talk, my dear, and dreaming! I never heard a word of anything of the kind. Well—I suppose it is natural for a child like you to find men's talk dull—Dr. Rackstraw's—or young Derwent's—or mine! Never mind, my dear; Nature knew what she was about when she made men and women with different minds. There never was yet a book huntress. I know what I'm about—and you can't possibly dislike Dr. Rackstraw, when I tell you that I have never met a man who gave me such a complete sense of intellectual power."

Sophy had been unable to see any signs of the intellect; but she had to confess to herself that the man's very impudence had served as evidence of some sort of power. He had not said a single word worth the saying, and she was convinced in her heart that he cared as little about old books as he knew of them, and that he knew about them rather less than nothing—so why had he called? Surely, not merely to rake up for the benefit of strangers old scandals about their friends. She wished he had never called, and yet could not have given the ghost of a reason why,

CHAPTER XVI.

I come from where night falls clearer
  Than your morning sun can rise—
From an earth that to heaven draws nearer
  Than your vision of paradise :
For the things that your dreamers dream, we behold them with open eyes.

From the heart of an ancient garden
  Girt fast with four walls of peace,
Where he who is set for warden
  From his vigil shall never cease
Nor quench the flame of his sword till the trumpet shall sound Release.

"YOU need not trouble yourself about the Fanes," said Dr. Rackstraw to Mrs. Derwent. "I have done your bidding, you see, and have surveyed the whole land. The old gentleman is the most hopeless old idiot to be found out of an asylum. I enquired about him of a man in the trade with whom I have some acquaintance and who would be likely to know : and he told me what I afterwards saw for myself—that the poor old fellow is on the high road to Bedlam, or to the workhouse, or both together. He'll give the most enormous prices for any trash in the shape of a book that nobody else would give a straw for, and fancies he's gathering a library that's to be the wonder of the world. That's his form of monomania, it seems. He got acquainted with Mr. Horace abroad—as for leading him into any extravagant or disreputable courses, the notion is absurd. He is simply a ridiculous old idiot—that's all."

"Not quite all," said Mrs. Derwent. "Thank you very much for your trouble, but it wasn't the father I wanted to hear about —it was the girl. As if I thought for a moment that Horace was likely to get entangled with a bookworm! London isn't the Goblin Islands, you know——"

"And girls have a great deal to do with what happens in London? True, dear friend—and in the Goblin Islands also. Still, in this case, I don't know we need trouble ourselves about Miss Sophia Fane. I saw her. She's a poor, washed out little thing, without a good feature or a word to say for herself—one goose, who wouldn't be able to say 'Bo' to another——"

"Which means, that she is sly. But—are they well off, should you say? What Fanes are they? Do they live in good style— or how? Who knows them—whom do they know? Really you have told me nothing at all. And surely you see the importance—Horace is so young, and so much depends on his making no mistake that will hang about him all his days."

10

" Oh—as to that—my bookselling friend knows all about them;
at least all there's any need to know. They're Fanes of somewhere—County people, who've been abroad for some years.
They know nobody in particular, and nobody in particular knows
them. Their house is good enough, but they evidently have no
establishment, and it's all a litter of books—you tumble over
them even on the stairs."

" Thank you," said Mrs. Derwent. " I think we women see
things the quickest, after all. County people who live abroad for
years, and then hide themselves away in town without establishment or friends—I think we know what that means; and indeed
I guessed as much all along. Of course I must let that card go,
but I shall know where I am."

" And that other card—to Senhora Miranda, I mean ? "

" To the Queen of —— ? Yes: it's gone."

" I thank you, dear Mrs. Derwent. I assure you that she'll
be the lioness of the season—a Real Queen. I must see about
meeting and preparing for her; but I sha'n't be absent many
days."

Lest there should be any suspicion of mystery attaching to
the proceedings of Dr. Hermon Rackstraw in relation to Horace
Derwent's suspected love affair, let it be understood at once that
he had, simply in obedience to the desire of that careful mother,
Mrs. Derwent, betaken himself to the authority from whom he
was likely to learn most of the manners and customs of any
particular connoisseur in Mr. Fane's reputed line—an elderly
dealer in curiosities of all kinds, literary and otherwise, who
traded within a narrow. but profitable connection under the name
of Crake & Co. " Fane ? what—old Fane of Crossmarsh ? I should
think I did, too! " was the answer of the representative of the
firm. " A regular old ass—but as rich as a mine, if that's what
you want to know. I never see him—for reasons; and if he knew
my name was Moldwarp, I should lose my best customer! like I
once lost him before, in another line, before I turned respectable.
I was in his service—what we call professional flinting—when
young Lawrence Derwent got out o' Lowmoor; and then dis-
agreeables happened that made me and him not part the best o'
friends. But somehow I'd an instinc' that him and me was made
for one another—why, Doctor, that old addle-pate could no more
live without a Moldwarp round than he can see through a mill-
ston'. Either me or Miss Sophy will be well off when he goes.

But, Doctor, begging your pardon, what do you want of old Fane?
That old ignoramus is a perquisite of my own."

" I. don't want to meddle with you—I'm glad to hear you've got
hold of a good thing. I wanted to know who he was, that's all.
So your old gentleman's well off—eh? Responsible in business,
and all that kind of thing?"

" I wish I was half as 'sponsible—that's all. Why, he owns half
Crossmarsh—and he'll spend more on a maggot than most men
will on their living. Why, if he was to get sick of books, I'd only
have to change the name of my firm, and make him rise to auto-
scraps—old boots—anything old in art or nature, so long as it was
new. But he'll be no good to *you*, Mister—none in the world.
He aren't *your* sort of fool."

" All right, Moldwarp. I'm glad you've got such a good connection. Good-day."

" Oh, no—I don't mind telling you whatever you please. If I
found a gold mine under the water-butt in my back-yard—and
I've found more unlikely things than that—I'd tell *you*. If you're
thinking of working on old Fane, I've no call to be afraid. I saw
a more unlikely thing, only Tuesday. If I was to tell you how I've
seen somebody back in England, and in London for all that—but
there's no need, seeing how you mean to leave my customers alone."

" What!" cried Hermon Rackstraw, with a start; " stuff and
nonsense, man, He'll no more dare show his face this side of the
Atlantic, if he's alive, than, if he's dead, he'd show it this side the
grave. You've made a mistake, that's all."

" I'm never mistook, Mister. Instinc's a sure guide. And if the
villain that nigh did for me in Pix-Knoll's named Lawrence Derwent, with these very eyes I saw Tuesday morning as plain as I
see——"

But at this moment the bookseller was summoned to the shop,
and Dr. Rackstraw, who knew the premises, chose to leave by way
of a side door before his friend became again disengaged. Indeed
he fancied he caught the voice of Mrs. Derwent's son, and there
was no reason why he should give himself the trouble of explain-
ing how he also came to be found in a shop that could have no
possible attractions for one who looked upon all relics of a benighted past with a civilised scorn. If the announcement of the
re-appearance in London of Lawrence Derwent the convict had
been intended as a threat of some kind from the book broker to
the Agent-General, it must have miscarried, for there was no

additional cloud upon the brow of the latter when he arrived in Richmond Place. After all, a man who is immersed in the affairs of a territory like the Goblin Islands can hardly condescend to trouble himself over long about private affairs—especially when they are merely those of his friends.

But *paullô majora canemus*—what were the affairs of the Goblin Islands themselves, and of all the Goblin Islanders, and all the trade of that rising emporium, Port Rackstraw, to the first public proof, for that season, that the Derwents of Wilton Square were at home?

Nothing of any note had happened meanwhile, so far as Mrs. Derwent was aware. The girls had gone on in their own pleasant way: Horace had developed no new signs of bibliomania: Dr. Rackstraw had been prevented by certain country engagements from returning direct from Southampton, and had only written to say that Senhora Miranda was to arrive, after all, by a later ship than the *Polynesia*, and could not be in town till a very few days before her introduction to the manners and customs of a civilised land. Mrs. Derwent still had her anxieties—pleasant ones, so far as they referred to the reception of barbarian royalty ; less pleasant so far as regarded Horace, of whose safety from the toils of the daughter of an obviously decayed house Dr. Rackstraw's report had failed to reassure her—men are so blind about girls, and plain girls are always the most dangerous of all. However, that card had gone, and Miss Fane would make a point of coming, and then the mother would see with her own eyes.

Kate had not exaggerated when she declared her family to be like the hare in the matter of many friends. At a fairly early hour of the evening the rooms of reception were nearly as full of flesh and blood as was Æneas Fane's drawing-room of books, and talk ran high and loud. Each member of the family had a set, more or less independent of the others ; but not opposed : and about Mrs. Derwent's especial circle was a quality of lionism which in some sort gave these crushes an air of distinction. She took pride in her numbers ; but not in mere numbers—she liked to be a social prism dealing only in coloured rays.

But to Horace Derwent, all the chattering crowd was but a legion of ghosts, and its talk but an echo of Babel. He was looking in vain for the guest who would bring the evening into life as a single digit placed before a row of ciphers gives them at once force and meaning. And he was full of faith as well as of hope and love, for he believed, as firmly as in his own existence, that his mother would exclaim, so soon as she set eyes on Sophy Fane, " There, of all women, is the wife for my boy." What man, nay, what woman, could fail to see all the charms and all the virtues incarnate in Sophy Fane ? This evening was to be the turning point in his life, when her foot would first cross the threshold of her future home. He was desperately hard hit—no doubt of that : and he had gone down before Sophy's finger tips as cleanly as if he had not been in love those three-and-thirty times before—and perhaps oftener, for sisters do not know everything. But why did she not come ? Life is too short to waste minutes in which seem like hours. Besides, he had hoped that she would be there before the crowd, so that she might be introduced to his mother with some sort of special distinction as became the future lady of Long-wood on first coming to her own. It was a new mood for a young man who had cultivated easy indifference as one of the fine arts, and who had been inclined to jest at scars because he had found wounds mere trifles, easier to heal even than to deal.

At last he caught sight, at the head of the stairs, if not of the goddess herself, yet an earthly sign of her.

" Ah, Hargrave ! I'm glad you've managed to find your way here at last," he said, but with his eyes further down the stairs. " I suppose you're with the Fanes ? I didn't think, though, that you foreigners would have outdone us in late hours—I hoped you'd have been here before the crowd, so that I might have introduced you to my people quietly. There's my mother only six yards off, if we could only get at her."

" Isn't Miss Fane here ? " asked Oswald, looking round. " Her uncle isn't coming, of course ; but I thought she'd have been here an hour ago. I couldn't bring her—I had business that I couldn't leave. I suppose getting out has been hard work for her, poor girl."

" You don't think there can be anything wrong ? "

" Wrong ? No. What should there be wrong ? " asked Oswald, rather wondering at such signs of needless anxiety on the part of his new friend—or rather acquaintance, for Oswald never made friends. It was Horace Derwent's name, not Horace Derwent himself, that had led him to cultivate a certain amount of com-radeship with the only visitor besides himself who ever came to the Fanes. An acquaintance with Horace was not much of a help towards a meeting with Lawrence; but combined with the hint he had overheard from an audible though invisible Moldwarp, it really seemed as if fortune or providence were gradually leading him to the point which he only lived to attain —the heart of the mystery of Rosamond, were she dead or living. Unhappily for him, he had been rich enough to devote his life to the pursuit of a phantom : and he had followed it with all the stubborn energy that, had she lived, would have won her. The quarry he was chasing was no phantom, to his eyes. He could not out-grow the faith that, after all, she to whom he had given his heart for ever could die.

As Horace Derwent had told him, he was within a very few paces of the step-mother of the man for whom he was still search-ing the world. Under the best of conditions an immediate intro-duction was out of the question ; for at that moment the lady was saying :

" Yes, Lady Deane—it is perfectly true. She is a Real Queen— —but she is supposed to be *incognita* for the present; and indeed her real name is not to be pronounced by civilised tongues. This will be her first appearance in civilised society. I expect she will feel a little surprised—I suppose she will have an interpreter, or I sha'n't exactly know what to do. However, Dr. Rackstraw will be here."

" Surprised ? " answered Lady Deane—a plain little old lady, with a brusque manner and bright eyes. " Yes—the manners of us natives must strike an intelligent traveller as curious indeed. For she is intelligent of course—travellers always are ; and igno-rance of a language is an advantage, because it doesn't disturb the impressions we came out with and intend to carry home again. But, by the way, what on earth made you send a card to poor Dash ? "

" *Poor* Dash ? Poor *Dash?* Why what have we done ? "

" Sent an invitation to my Skye terrier, my dear—the little creature would have come, of course, but she is ailing, and I per-suaded her to stay at home. Of course, though, it was very kind —so I've taken the liberty of bringing with me another young friend, neither so clever, nor so good, nor so amusing, but still worth knowing well enough to speak to. Mr. Richard Harding— Mrs. Derwent : and Miss Anne Derwent too. Mr Harding is another traveller of the usual intelligent kind. Poor Dash ! She has charged me with all manner of regrets and regards."

"It is a great pleasure for me to be here, Mrs. Derwent," said Mr. Richard Harding, in slow, languid, carefully modulated monotone, "and a great pride, besides. I have been so long abroad that I assure you the sight of a gathering like this has become almost as strange to me as it will be to your Queen. The only difference is, that thanks to Lady Deane and you, I feel like coming home."

There was something about Richard Harding that attracted Oswald's attention, trained for so many years to observe all things and all men. He was in the prime of middle age, tall and well built, and with something of the exaggeratedly easy air which some soldiers affect in order to hide the results of drill and pipeclay. His features were good and regular, the forehead being displayed the more by the desertion of the hair's advanced guard—desertion, however, more than balanced by the fulness of a brown moustache that completely covered the mouth, and of a beard that reached half way down the breast. One cheek was disfigured by a long scar, which somehow seemed to emphasise a certain peculiar glow in the eyes. The expression of the face was curiously complicated—one instinctively felt that its nonchalance, to correspond with its owner's carriage, covered sullenness, and that this in its turn covered passion. But he knew how to smite with grace as well as self-possession and dignity. Oswald was no theoretical physiognomist, but constant observation had sharpened his first impressions, and he felt that this Richard Harding might as an enemy prove dangerous, as a friend more dangerous still, as a lover most dangerous of all.

Poor Mrs. Derwent, confused and abashed by the discovery that a Skye terrier had somehow trotted into her visiting list, could only say that she was glad to see him, and turn towards some new comers, who, fortunately for her, just then happened to enter.

"Ah! Mr. Pitcairn—dear Mrs. Pitcairn! How fortunate! I am every moment expecting—who should you imagine? A Queen from the South Seas. I must introduce Mr. Pitcairn to her the very first of all—perhaps he will convert her on the spot, who knows?"

"Mr. Derwent—Mr. Harding," said Lady Deane, looking through Oswald, as if to say, What lion are you? What is *your* particular roar?

Horace Derwent, however, heard merely his own name; for his impatience was beginning to grow desperate, and he scarcely cared whether he was not behaving like a boor. He had looked for so much from this evening, and now the evening was more than half spent. Could anything have happened beyond the unpunctuality of a dressmaker, or a cabman's loss of his way ? The knocker had been at rest for a good half hour, and everybody had fallen into his or her circle of affinity nay, there were even noticeable signals of departing. He looked at Oswald, and could not comprehend how the latter could be content to look round the room instead of persistently in the direction of the front door.

Mr. Richard Harding, like Oswald, let himself fall back into the position of a looker on. Oswald took his position in silence ; but his fellow stranger did not seem disposed to be alone in a crowd.

"Warm, isn't it ? " he asked Oswald. "It's so long since I've seen more than a score of people in one room that it seems to me as if Mrs. Derwent had gathered together the population of the globe. So this is what you call being at home ? "

" I suppose so," said Oswald. "I have certainly been where this would represent all the men and women within a hundred mile circle."

" More like two hundred, as my experience goes ! were you ever in Nevada ? "

" I had business in Nevada," said Oswald, " some years ago."

" The deuce you had ! Fancy my tumbling over a man who knows Nevada ! But you'd find changes, even there, if you haven't been so far west for years. What was your business ? Silver, I suppose ? "

Oswald would never have suspected Mr. Harding of being from America, and much less from the wild west. His accent was peculiar and artificial, but certainly not in the least American, and his manner, though rather off-hand and perfectly unembarrassed, was that of a man who belonged to the precise circle in which he declared himself to be so complete a stranger. "No," said Oswald, " It wasn't on business—at least of that kind. Are you in Europe for the first time ? "

"Only for the second. I suppose you know the Derwents well ? Young Derwent is a good fellow, I hear from my friends the Deanes. I'm sorry you're not interested in silver, for it's the only thing I know how to talk about—I believe it's mostly to get silver out of my blood that I'm over here. Hollca—what's up now ? "

Horace Derwent's heart beat quickly in answer to a tremendous peal of the knocker. It was not the sort of flourish that was likely to announce the arrival of Sophy, but then she was not answerable for what her cabman might consider due to the dignity of his fare, and Horace, driven to despair of Sophy's coming, leaped at any last hope that the very latest of knocks might throw him. Some instinct, however, seemed to draw a closer crush round his mother, who brought herself full in front of the door Oswald and his new acquaintance from Nevada, standing where they had a full view of the stairs, saw a tall, cleanly shaven gentle man ascending with a lady upon his arm.

"Senhora Miranda!" announced the footman, who seemed to have been stationed in exactly the right place, and in exactly the right time, to do this particular guest the most impressive honour.

Mrs. Derwent curtseyed deeply. And then all knew that they were in the presence of a Queen—no doubt a heathen, perhaps a cannibal, but still a Real Queen.

Ngahoung Qhlawu, Queen of Apahu, considerably surprised the company. She was not black. She was not ugly. She was not dressed so as to make anybody blush or stare. On the contrary —she was not so dark as many an English brunette; she was dressed like a duchess; and she was simply the most beautiful woman in the room.

She was of a woman's middle height, rather under than over —that is to say, for an islander of the far South, remarkably tall. Had she been English, one would have set her down at about five-and-twenty years old—a reckoning which, considering that she came from latitudes where people age fast, would argue her to be very much younger. Her figure was exquisitely perfect, and her taste in dress was a miracle. Strange to say, her beautiful, large, soft, kind eyes were not brown, but the darkest of grey, and there was a tinge of brightness in her crown of brown curls that is seldom given by a southern sun. Her features were worthy of her form— of the purest and most regular type, but a little grave and sad of look, while her mouth had to make up for its graciousness and royal beauty for being a little larger than completeness of harmony is supposed to require. Not only was she a Queen, but she looked the very ideal of a Queen in grace and dignity of bearing, as well as in face and form. She needed no golden crown; and, moreover she looked a Queen in a yet higher sense—in the sense of one who would rule her people by the love that casteth out fear.

"Great heaven! What a lovely creature!" exclaimed the man from Nevada, to himself, but more than half aloud—nor was there any harm in that, seeing that he said it in English, and not in the unknown language of Apahu.   "Why, she is Venus—straight from the waves, or the stars!"

Strange women were nothing to Oswald ; but had not his eyes said amen, he would have been more or less than mortal man. Nay, the sight of this beautiful savage from an undiscovered country gave him that indescribable feeling suggested by the perfume of certain flowers—that he had stood as he was standing now, in the presence of this Senhora Miranda, in some other life or some other dream.   Indeed for the moment he scarcely knew whether he was waking or sleeping, so strongly did this caprice lay hold of him.   But when in his turn he tried to lay hold of it, and to grasp what it could mean, it was gone.

"And oh!—what jewels!" breathed an admiring sigh at his elbow.

And truly her rubies were of themselves glorious enough to make their wearer the lode-star of all eyes.   She wore them in her ears, round her neck, and on her bosom, the finest being fine enough for Sultans to fight for.   Only their setting was, to say the best of it, barbaric, and they were one and all cut so roughly and set so unskilfully as to lose full half their splendour—though quite enough remained to show what they really were.   What with the rubies, and the beauty that outshone them, people quite forgot to be disappointed that she was so utterly unlike any pre-conceived ideas of a royal cannibal.   They had looked for the royalty of burlesque—they were met by the royalty of nature.   What sort of an island could be Apahu, to produce such women and such gems?

"Madame," said Dr. Rackstraw, with his long and awkward bow, "permit me the honour of presenting to you my friend Mrs. Derwent—Miss Derwent—Miss Anne Derwent."

"The honour is mine—and the pleasure too," said Senhora Miranda, in a voice so peculiarly sweet and gentle that everybody forgot to notice, for full half a minute, that she had spoken, *not* in the language of Apahu—in English as pure as from foreign lips it had any need to be.   True, it was foreign English, of a kind— English, so to speak, softened, mellowed, and sweetened by southern air.   Moreover, her words stood clearly apart from one another, with the slightest of pauses between each, and each vowel and consonant received its full value. That is to say, she spoke better than well. But that did not make it the less strange that a lady fresh from an undiscovered island should speak any language but her own.

"The Senhora speaks English like a native!" said Doctor Rackstraw, with enthusiasm, in answer to Mrs. Derwent's look of bewilderment. "She learnt it all at sea ! "

"I am so glad, your ma—madam," said Mrs. Derwent; "it will make your visit to us so much more interesting! May I ask what you think of England ? Are you going to make a long stay ? Anything I and my children can do to make it pleasant, or profitable, we shall be only too proud and happy to do, I am sure."

"You are very, very kind," said Her Majesty. "Indeed, I cannot yet tell you what I think of England—I have seen so little of it yet—and it is all so different from my own country. It makes me a little *maäbé* —dazzled—confused. Your houses are so close together : we have nothing like what you call a town, and what Dr. Rackstraw tells me of your ways I do not yet comprehend."

"Ah!" said Mrs. Pitcairn, who was in the inner circle of this informal *levée,* "but you will learn—and then you will have so much to teach your people on your return : so much indeed."

The Queen smiled radiantly. "You are a great people," she said ; "mine are very small; I doubt if what you find good, would be good for them. For example, they would not like to live close together; and they would never learn to buy and sell, which Dr. Rackstraw tells me makes you what you are."

"You don't buy—you don't sell!" exclaimed Lady Deane. "Then what is the use of money ? "

"We have no money," said Senhora Miranda. "You see how different we are."

"You proceed upon the primæval system of barter ?" asked one of Mrs. Derwent's political friends. "That is interesting——"

"No," answered she, "we give one another whatever is wanted, unless we can make it for ourselves. If I want something I have not got, I go to somebody who has, and take it; if nobody has it, I go to somebody who can make it, and he makes it for me."

"Then do you mean to say, Senhora," asked the man from Nevada, "that if I take a fancy to your ruby necklace, and ask you for it, you would take it off and give it me, without more ado ?"

"Not at all! If anybody has what he wants to keep, he has it marked by the *Idbash*—the priest—and he must not give it till he has got the mark taken off again in the same way. Nobody would take it, then. I must not give my necklace, even if I will."

"Most interesting!" said the guest, with the sociological turn. "It is the principle of the *Taboo*. But if somebody broke the custom, what then?"

"My people never break customs," said Senhora Miranda, with a deep, sad sigh. "Never. It has never been done—it has never come into their minds to do. I understand what you mean; but the very thought of it fills me with fear. Please do not speak of such a thing again."

"It would entail a religious penalty?" asked Mr. Pitcairn. "I have been in the Pacific myself, and worked there. No doubt the breach of the *Taboo* you speak of would be followed by divine vengeance in this or another world."

"I don't know," said she, turning strangely red and pale. "Nobody knows—not even the *Idbash-fonh*, the great priest of all. Nobody would do it—nobody has done it—nobody ever will do it. That is all; please speak of something else. We never speak of such a dreadful thing as doing wrong; I have learned how—but not one of my people would know what you mean."

"By Jupiter!" said the man of Nevada, aside to Oswald, "but Her Majesty will lead a life of misery, if she stays another week on this unsqueamish planet—I told you she must have come straight from the stars. My belief is that her kingdom is somewhere in the milky way—the milk and watery way. But how lovely she is, to be sure! And it's queer—she gives me the notion that I've seen her before, aye, and heard her voice before, impossible though that must be. I wonder if the poets are right, when they say that we come into this world innocent from some other, and that our evil thoughts are but the gradual decaying of our memory of the world where our souls, not our brains and bodies, were born—and preciously bad our memories mostly are!"

Oswald could not help starting at hearing his own vague, mystical impression put into words, and by so unlikely a man. Was it thus that everybody was being affected by this most unaccountable woman in the same unaccountable way? Had he been less accustomed to observe with a purpose, he might have been able to guess at a wonderful solution of the mystery. But when reason knocks at the door, truth is apt to fly out of the window, The subtle impression of a pre-existent contact with the que:n of a country unknown to geographers had died out of him even before the man from Nevada had put it into words: and the words, so far from reviving it, by their very definiteness had given it a final death-blow. Still, the mere coincidence of the impression was strange.

"No," answered he, "our memories are strong enough "— as none had better cause to say than he. "But we can't remem· ber what has never been."

"I see—you're a practical man; so am I. And, as a practical man, I must get to know something more of this cannibal Venus, before she falls into the hands of the book-makers—I don't mean the betting men: I mean the worse kind. For she's doomed. In a week there will be her photograph all down Regent Street— in a month there'll be an exhaustive book out on her island: and no sooner than that, she'll have become a common, vulgar, beef-eating, brandy-drinking lioness—she's been corrupted already by her dressmaker. Do you know old Rackstraw ? "

"No, who is old Rackstraw ? "

"That fellow with her—her guide, philosopher, and friend. A very nice old gentleman indeed, whose life's devoted to the great cause of progress and civilisation all over the world. Mark my words—he'll never rest till he's established a newspaper and a model gaol in that unknown island. Benighted heathens— not to know what money means, and to look upon wrong doing as a thing not even to be named among decent people ! Why, we're more civilised, even in Nevada—eh ? "

"May I ask," said Lady Deane, "if your country has a—king?"

"No, indeed ! " said Senhora Miranda. "We have no king."

"I've half a mind that you shall, though," muttered the man from Nevada, with a smile towards Oswald. "Richard the First, King of the Ruby Islands, Emperor of the Milky Way. What do you say, Mr. Derwent. How would that be for high ? "

"I beg your pardon ? " asked Horace, starting out of an absent fit; for he now had Sophy's absence on the brain. The non-appearance of this girl was the first real disappointment he had ever known, or had been allowed to know.

"Or perhaps," said the other, who certainly seemed to have no shyness towards the newest of acquaintances, " you are thinking that Horatius Primus, Lord of Venus, Emperor of the Zodiac, would sound higher st'll What's the name of her country ? Will you introduce me to Rackstraw? . . . Thanks. Will you tell me, Doctor Rackstraw, the name of the country of which this lady is Queen?"

Oswald noticed that the man from Nevada looked straight into Dr. Rackstraw's eyes with a peculiar long and steady gaze, and, for the first time, spoke with a slightly American twang.

"Pardon me, Mr. Harding," said the Doctor; "Senhora Miranda is *incognita* at present; a fiction, no doubt, but etiquette must be observed. I would tell you with pleasure, were she not, in a certain special sense, under my charge; and of course you understand——"

"Oh, certainly. Nothing could be clearer. If I were you, and you were I, I should do just the same. Madam—may I venture to ask you the name of the country whence you have come?"

"Excuse me, sir—I must not name it," said she, in a low tone —almost in a whisper, not to be heard farther off than his and Oswald's ears. "It is *busqd*—secret: holy—but you have no such word. Of course you understand?"

"Oh—certainly. Nothing *could* be clearer, Madam. Will you allow me to get you some refreshment?" he asked, offering his arm.

She placed her fingers within it as if she had been used to drawing-room manners for years instead of minutes. Mrs. Derwent looked almost angrily towards Dr. Rackstraw and then towards Lady Deane. Who was this impudent stranger that had presumed to usurp the honour she had intended to reserve for the most distinguished man in the room—or perhaps, in his capacity of host, for her own son? "Your friend Mr. Harding does not seem over diffident," said she. "By the way, who *is* Mr. Harding? Is he anybody whose name we ought to know?"

"Oh, my dear, you must excuse him; he is just rolling in gold —or in silver, I should say. He brought letters to us from Sir John's correspondents in New York—he's a millionaire; and yet he's a gentleman. With all his money, and all his push and assurance, he *is* a gentleman. If I had a daughter—and you, my dear, have two: if I were you, I should take quite a fancy to Mr. Harding; I should indeed."

"He is certainly good-looking—and he does seem a gentleman, as you say. I should never have taken him for an American."

"Oh, there are Americans of all sorts now. We musn't be too particular in these days. Why the Queen's — do look—the Queen's eating chicken, just as if she were a Christian! And she's holding her fork like you or me! My dear, I am disappointed in your Queen. But it's true that her rubies are just glorious. You are a fortunate woman, my dear; two daughters and a son. I have only Dash—poor dear little thing."

"Hargrave, will you look after my sister?" asked Horace.

"Mr. Hargrave—my sister Anne." And he wearily turned to the duty of looking after the nearest at hand of his lady guests, who happened to be a plain and elderly nobody, deaf, and with nothing to say.—one of the flies found in every specimen of social amber who could only wonder at the distinction.

Oswald had already offered his arm to Miss Anne, when the footman to whom he had given his name on arriving handed him a note, directed to him in pencil in a hurried hand, brought, so he was told, by a maidservant who was waiting for an answer.

"Pray read it," said Anne Derwent. "Dear me, Mr Hargrave," she added, seeing the look that came over his face as he opened it, " I hope it is no bad news?"

"Yes—no—I hope not, Miss Derwent; but—you will not think me rude if I leave you? I *must* go—at once. You will forgive me, I am sure."

"Of course; pray don't mind me. Good-night, Mr. Hargrave," said Miss Anne, who had not been particularly taken with her brother's silent, door-way haunting friend, and was in some haste to watch Senhora Miranda feed. She reached the supper table just as the man from Nevada was pouring out Her Majesty's first glass of champagne. Meanwhile the searcher for Lawrence Derwent and Rosamond Fane was half way down the staircase reading once more the pencil note that had summoned him away:

"DEAR OSWALD,—Come at once, wherever you are. Uncle has been taken *very* ill.—SOPHY."

CHAPTER XVII.

Caspa.—But if thou hast occasion of a lie, see that it be of good, honest black, and not of your brown, nor of your grey, nor of your white the least of all. For out of black, what can grow more than black-ness? But out of white groweth fruit of the fiend's own colour, which is to darkness even what the hue of Saturn of a midwinter midnight showeth beside the glory of the light of a midsummer noon. See thou to it—misstrust a white horse, a white hand, a white sepulchre, and a WHITE LIE.

OSWALD lost no time in driving to the Fanes'. Sophy's message had startled and alarmed, but had scarcely surprised, him: for he had, since his return from his latest

chapter of travel, formed his own opinion as to the mental and
bodily condition of his old friend. He had been dreading a break-
down, and, during his impatient drive, only trusted that it might
be but of the body, and not of the mind. Well—in any case it
was fortunate he was in London, for Sophy's sake, who was that
rarest of mortals: an heiress without friends. If she needed him,
he must even consent to let his life's search grow cold for a time,
hard as that would be.

So he passed the literary fortifications, outworks, citadel, and all.
But, before he had time to look round the barely lighted drawing-
room or to ask a question, he heard a sob, so eloquent of desolation
and despair as to make him feel that something must have happened
that was worse than the worst he had feared.

"Sophy?" he said, half aloud. "What has happened? I am
here."

"And—he is Dead!" said she.

And what is more right and natural than that a man should
die? Surely, when we consider it in the cold light of reason, there
is no mystery of life greater than the manner in which we regard
so simple and so common a thing. After all, it is infinitely more
wonderful that a man should live than that he should die: for he
spends his moments amid a flight of poisoned arrows, and every
instant that he escapes is a new miracle. Nor was there any especial
element of pathos in the fact or in the manner of Æneas Fane's
departure from a world wherein his part had been to prove that
one man who gives his whole mind to the work can waste more
time than any ordinary ten. Unless indeed there might be something like pathos in the wonder what occupation could be found
beyond the grave for a collector's disembodied soul. To discover
the vanity of its own nature would be the same thing as sheer an-
nihilation—yet one cannot suppose that it would be let loose
among such tempting specimens as comets and stars. Yet Oswald,
who had remained unimpressed by all the flood of life from which
he had freshly come, felt all the awe which, in a house of Death,
tells a man that the new Master of that house is the one reality
among a world of phantoms and stage-shadows. He had, in his
wanderings, met with Death often: but had never till now been
under the same roof, alone with Him and a girl.

Try as we will, where Death is concerned only common-place
are the things we can feel, and only most utterly common-place the

things we can say, if we are so foolish as to say anything at all. Oswald was not foolish—at least in this way. Something no doubt would have to be done presently, when the time should come for business, but nothing now, except to give Sophy the comfort of an old friend's sympathetic presence until her tears should change into articulate words.

It was not long before he heard, in fragments, the story of the end of Æneas Fane. Sophy had been dressing for Mrs. Derwent's reception, and had gone to her uncle's study, his inmost treasure-house, to bid him good-night, and to see that he had all he could possibly want for the next few hours, only to find him crushed, as it were, into his armchair, scarcely conscious, and apparently in an agony of pain. An open book, the *Flora*, was at his feet, just where it had fallen from his hand. The nearest doctor came without a moment's delay : but her uncle had never rallied, had never spoken, had never made a conscious sign, and had died before Sophy had realised that he was dying.

Oswald remained in Richmond Place that night, sitting in the room where his old friend's heart had broken down, and thinking over Sophy's affairs. As to these he foresaw some little trouble, for these had been entirely in her uncle's hands from the beginning, and it would probably prove difficult to discover precisely how they stood, with a view to arranging them. However, that would be merely a question of time and trouble, not to be grudged to Rosamond's sister by Rosamond's lover, even though it meant the robbery of precious days from the work he lived for. Even from that point of view matters might have been worse: it was not as if he had just found that there was a hint of a clue in Central Africa or at the Antipodes, which unless it were grasped immediately would slip from his fingers. For Silver Moldwarp was in London: and, for the moment, Silver Moldwarp represented the whole of the clue—not much indeed, but still all. As for Sophy herself, he could not feel that the death of her uncle, at a reasonable age, would prove by any means an irreparable misfortune. The old gentleman, with his books upon the brain, had been doing his unconscious best to ruin the poor girl's life and to cut her off from her kind, and it had become inexplicable to Oswald that she had never rebelled— perhaps that was a sign that the crushing process was being only too well done. She would now be able to take her place in the world, or better still, to go down to live at Crossmarsh and live there quietly and usefully among her own people and on her own land.

11

She would easily find some middle-aged companion of the right
sort, and Oswald, wherever he might be, would somehow manage
to look after her in a general brotherly way.   .

And so, having overleaped the immediate trouble of the inquest
and the lawyers, and having disposed of Sophy in that masculine
manner which leaves the chances of love and marriage out of
every question except one's own, Oswald's mind was free to fall
back upon itself and Rosamond.   Not Death under the same roof
could for long interfere with that long thought which had become a second nature—which had only become the stronger with
the decline of passion, or rather had itself become a passion,
devouring alike all other realities and dreams.   It never occurred
to him that his search for one whom reason could not doubt was
dead, had been practically proved as vain as had been Æneas
Fane's for the Phœnician sun-dial.   It never occurred to him that
it was almost as endless and worthless as another man's devotion
of a life to getting richer, or yet another's to the pursuit of
pleasure.   If he thought of the matter in this light at all, it
seemed to him at the very least as sane as theirs.   Every man
tries to get what he most wants.   Oswald did not want more
money.   He did not want pleasure.   He did not want to make a
name.   There was nobody who needed his help : nor was he one
of those people who feel impelled to work for the benefit of the
world at large.   The ruling motive of his life was to carry out to
the end what he had begun : and he must cease to be himself, as
he was made, before he could lay this search aside.   And no less
must he cease to be himself before he could tear away from him
the faith that Rosamond had not perished nine years ago, and
therefore might be living still.   He thought the chance of finding
her living better worth working for than the possession of pleasure for which he had no taste, or of money, for which he had no
need.   I suppose he was another case of the dog who snatched at
the shadow.   But who is not ?   And then there is another legend
about a mote and a beam.

And now it was less likely that he would cease to be himself
than ever : because he had obtained an actual thread of a possible
clue for the first time during nine years.   Silver Moldwarp professed to have seen Lawrence Derwent, and in London.   Moreover
there was evidently more in this profession than had met the ear.
It meant that Lawrence Derwent had succeeded in his escape, and
that his movements were of interest to exceeding unlikely people,

and in a way that had a significance of its own. Silver Mold-warp's peculiar connection with Rosamond's disappearance re-mained unforgotten, and his connection moreover with the simultaneous disappearance of Lawrence Derwent from Lowmoor. Of course there had been nothing definite in the connection. But he had played a conspicuous part in the search for the latter, and had signalised his paraded failure by turning out to be an extra-ordinary skilful rogue. If those who hide can find, it is no less true that those know where not to look who do not want to find. Oswald remembered how he had searched the neighbourhood of Crossmarsh and Windgates, inland and along the shore, well-nigh inch by inch, while the gaol people and the police had been scarcely less active. The man from Lowmoor must have been hidden somewhere all the time, and supplied with food until the coast was clear. He could not have been thus hidden and supplied without friendly or purchased aid. Though a prisoner, he might be in a position to promise a reward : and, as one scoundrel, he might find a friend in another. Since that conversation at the bookseller's, Oswald had become half convinced that Silver Mold-warp had aided Lawrence Derwent to escape, and that through him the secret of the yet greater mystery was to be discovered, if it was to be discovered at all.

But this strong belief, well founded as it was, obliged him to proceed with the utmost caution. He wanted to get at Lawrence Derwent himself; and so cunning a rogue as Moldwarp was not to be dealt with easily. If the bookseller and the escaped convict were still friends, a word of warning would spoil all. So, as yet, he scarcely knew what to do. It was unfortunate that the old rascal knew him, and knew, moreover, that he knew him to be a rogue. Possibly a heavy bribe might serve, made conditional on results. But then Oswald was troubled with one rare quality— a distrust of his own sharpness. He fancied himself capable of being taken in, and Silver Moldwarp to be capable of taking in cleverer men than he. For had he not taken in, for years, a learned scholar like poor Æneas Fane?

No inspiration came to him that night, as he sat among the ghosts of forgotten authors that had been gathered together by hands now nearly as dead as they. Had his mind been free, and had it been open to fancies, he might have seen a vision of wasted labour impressive enough to turn him away from his own search, and to dismiss even Rosamond herself to the region of her fellow

shadows. If wo were to think of why we work, what work
would ever be done? Happily for Oswald, he never thought
of the Why, but always and only of the How. So he saw no
visions and dreamed no dreams. And when the morning came
his only thought was, with a sigh, that he had brought himself
no nearer to a plan, and, that, for the moment, the actual Sophy
must come before the shadowy Rosamond. Well—he needed
time to think. The change of thoughts might not prove wholly
thrown away.

He saw Sophy for a few minutes before going out on her business, and found her, now that her first outburst of grief and
terror had spent itself, scarcely able to realise a blow that, in
effect, had swept the whole of her past life away. Her affection
for her uncle had not been that which comes of sympathy—he
was not the man to have inspired the deepest sort of filial love,
even in a child of his own. But nobody can ever bo missed like
a man of one dominant and aggressive idea, who makes that the
centre of the household circle until all about him learn to regard
it as an essential and indispensable part of their own lives. Uncle
Æneas, with his coins, his flints, his laces, or his books, had been
bound up with every association of her life from the beginning—
she could only feel herself left alone without chart or compass
on a strange sea. The cable of habit had broken, with a sharper
shock than belongs to the severing of any more delicate and precious cord. Such grief is not the less sharp at the time for being
so much inspired with self-pity—rather the more: especially when
that troublesome creature, conscience, enters and charges us with
feeling less sorrow for our dead than for our living selves.

Oswald's first visit was to the doctor, who had no doubt done
his best in a case where, as he told his visitor, there was simply
nothing to be done. "Heart? unquestionably," said he. "Of
course there will have to be an examination, and an inquest: but
it will all be arranged very quietly, and with no pain or trouble
to the young lady."

Thence Oswald went to make arrangements for the funeral, and
then returned to the house, and, shutting himself in the study,
set to work upon sorting the papers which, alas, require no taste
for collecting to bring together.

Æneas Fane's documents mostly consisted of letters referring
to his various dealings, of obsolete catalogues, and of bibliographi-
cal memoranda. There were also a journal or two, kept in a

fragmentary manner: the draft of an unfinished monograph on an unusual form of the letter M in some manuscript or other; the lease of the house in London, and the ordinary bills and receipts of a housekeeper. Of such old letters or other written relics as give a soul to a dead man's *escritoire* there were no signs. The man had lived an absolutely single life in more senses than one—there was more pathos in the want of one such touch than in a whole cart-load of memories. Can he be rightly even called dead, who leaves no signs that he has ever been alive?

Then followed a rather curious paper—a scheme neatly drawn out on foolscap, for the establishment, custody, and development of the Fane library—a wonderful institution, containing ancient books to the value of a fabulous number of thousands of pounds, all the property of Miss Sophia Fane and her heirs, but to be available to students and scholars under certain stringent conditions therein fully specified. There was something of child's play, or of the revelry of imagination, in this elaborate scheme which found no comprehension in Oswald's strictly practical mind. Why should a reasonable being amuse himself with building such castles in the air? He did not recognise in it the one poem that Æneas Fane had ever written, not the less a poem for being composed in the form of legal prose. Looking at it from a reasonable point of view, it was preposterous altogether. It priced books as if they were diamonds, and treated Miss Sophia Fane as if its imagined possession rendered her a queen of millionaires, and through its author, an arch-benefactress of the world. There, for example, was that precious *Flora*, set down in the schedule as representing five thousand pounds sterling. It could not be a joke, because Æneas Fane would have thought it sacrilege to jest about such things. Perhaps Oswald would have understood it better, had he been conscious that he had a yet more unreasonable dream of his own. But then to be a man of action is to dream without knowing that one dreams.

He had been something more than two hours over this monotonous work when he came upon a document that made him start and knit his brows together quickly before he had read half-a-dozen lines. But even when he had read it twice through, first at a gallop, then slowly and carefully, he was yet more bewildered than at the beginning. This, at any rate, was no jest, whatever the other thing might be. He was engaged in a third anxious reading when a knock at the front door was followed by the card

66   *A REAL QUEEN.*

of Mr. Horace Derwent, with a pencilled request for at least one minute's interview.

There could not have been a moment at which he was less ready to be disturbed; for the document, taken by itself and without further light, meant ruin to Sophy at the hands of a madman, so far as he could yet guess at its meaning. However, he could hardly deny himself to the only friend, besides himself, of the dead man.

"What is all this terrible business?" asked Horace. "Good God—when I called and saw all the blinds down I thought—but thank God, I thought wrong. How is she—Miss Fane?"

"A terrible business? Yes, indeed. He died suddenly, of heart disease. Of course it is a terrible blow to the poor girl."

"And at the very time when we were making fools of ourselves —I was sure, though, all the time, that there was something wrong. What can I do?"

"Nothing. I am doing all there is to be done. I am almost her brother——"

"Yes: I know. But still I might do something. You are full of business, I see: and there must be other things—Of course she couldn't see everybody. But she might see me. . . . Hargrave —I thought *she* was dead, when I saw all those blinds. And even now—I can't say just what I mean—I want to see with my own eyes that she's alive."

Something in the tone or manner of his acquaintance struck Oswald with a new light, though his mind happened to be at the moment anything but open to any ideas save those connected with the estate of Æneas Fane. And that something made him far from anxious to allow a meeting until he had learned a great deal that was still utterly dark to him.

"No," he said, "I don't think Miss Fane would care to see anybody to-day—not even you. She hasn't borne the blow worse than she needs must, but I've no doubt she would wish to be alone: and as for doing anything, there is nothing to be done, more than I am doing now."

"Of course I should not wish to trouble her. Let me see— you're not related to the Fanes?"

"No. I only hoped to have been, But why do you ask? I am their oldest friend, and have known them since I was a child."

"Well then, Hargrave—I asked because I wanted to know

just how much right you had to speak for Miss Fane : that's all I fancy that perhaps she would see me : anyhow I should like the choice to be hers."

He did not speak in a manner at which anybody could possibly take offence, though it rather surprised Oswald by its most uncharacteristic air of decision. Evidently this quiet young man, to whom self-assertion had always seemed too much trouble to be worth the taking, was not without a will of his own, when he had occasion for its exercise. And, as to control of Sophy, whatever duties Oswald might assume, of rights he had absolutely none. Assuredly Sophy was entitled to see whomsoever she pleased. And in this case, how could he be sure that she would not please? Between any two given young men, one of them always feels himself, and generally with good reason, to be master, whenever there comes a clash of wills. As between Horace Derwent and Oswald Hargrave, this position had hitherto been held by the latter : and now it seemed that there was at any rate one matter in which the former meant to hold his own And rebellion was the easier, seeing that Oswald was, in all things save one, an eminently reasonable man, and therefore fore-doomed to give way before one who was not reasonable, and therefore stronger than reason.

"After all," said Horace, "there's no reason why I shouldn't make a clean breast of it to an old friend of the house like you— and I hope a friend of my own besides. I meant last night to ask her to be my wife—and I mean to ask her as soon as I find her able to listen. I must, therefore, know something of her plans : and it is now, in her trouble, that she ought to feel that I am by her side."

" You wish to marry Sophy Fane ! "

"Of course I do. Is there anybody who wouldn't, if he had the chance? Of course I don't know yet whether she would marry me. But I must know it, and that soon, if I'm to be any sort of use to myself, or good for anything in the world. And I am not without hope—why should I be? Of course it isn't a time to be talking to her of myself to-day, or perhaps for many days—but——"

But Oswald's ears were growing deaf, for his mind was wandering far away. The brother of Lawrence Derwent was proposing to marry the sister of Rosamond Fane.

Believing as he believed, that, in some undiscovered but doubt-

less terrible way, Lawrence Derwent was connected with the
death of Rosamond, if she were dead, or with her disappearance,
if she were yet living, the thought suggested even hideous possi-
bilities. Had Rosamond been murdered ? For it was that solution which lay at the root of his master passion of vengeance:
and in that case what could be more hideous than that Sophy
should unwittingly give her hand to her sister's murderer—unless
indeed she gave him her heart, which would be something more
hideous still. The tragedy of nine years ago was coming home to him
in a new way. And yet, ignorant as he was of all that had really
happened, and hanging his faith to a belief that reason scorned,
what explicable right had he to interfere between a young man
who was but an acquaintance, and a girl over whom he could
only usurp authority ? In the nature of things there was no sort
of reason why Horace Derwent of Longwood should not marry
Sophia Fane of Crossmarsh. They were of suitable age, apparently of suitable character: their social position was sufficiently
equal, and there was enough fortune on both sides, and to spare.
Moreover Sophy was now in absolute need of a protector, and
she might well live to a good old age without finding another:
the marriage looked as if it had been made in Heaven, and destined
to be brought to pass at Heaven's best time. And yet Oswald
knew in his heart that, till the mystery was made clear, the
marriage must not be.

And if Horace Derwent saw Sophy now, in the first hours of
her desolation, and with her past life wholly swept away, it
might be very well on the lover's part to mean to speak no word of
love; but that was no reason why the words should not come to
themselves. Both, under the shadow of death, would be rapt
into an exalted mood, when men and women speak not as they
will but as they feel. He, Oswald, would have no right to forbid
the banns. But his mission must go on to the end; and then
what an end, if it should be discovered that Sophy was bound by
stronger ties than blood to the house at whose door the blood of
her sister lay ? Oswald had persistently fought away the thought
of Rosamond's death till now. But now it rose before him as a
terrible possibility, though still connected with him whose disappearance was so inextricably bound up with hers.

"I will see if she can see you," said he. "Well," he thought
within himself as he went upstairs not to Sophy's room, but to
his own, "I'm afraid one must sometimes do some evil that

worse evil mayn't come—and if all should end well for these two they'll have lost nothing by being kept from meeting for a day. A white lie will hurt nobody but myself: and this might turn so that I oughtn't to mind being hurt by a black one. They must not meet, if I had to perjure myself black and blue. So here goes . . . . Derwent," said he, returning, "it's no use your staying: she really can't see anybody to-day, not even you. She has a bad headache—no wonder; and she's trying to sleep. It's the best thing she can do. To-morrow——"

It was the first lie that Oswald had tried to tell in his life, and he felt that he was telling it badly. Am I the first who has ever been driven to admit that a man who in any sense or degree was supposed to be playing a hero's part told a lie deliberately and for a purpose, in order to keep two lovers apart, and so played the villain's proper *rôle?* At any rate, this liar had the grace to be ashamed, though he did not for a moment alter his opinion as to its being better to hurt his own conscience, which mattered to nobody but himself, than to risk ruining others' lives. The shame seemed punishment enough—so far.

Still he obtained one unfair advantage upon which he had not reckoned—however badly and awkwardly he might lie, nobody, not even the acquaintance of an hour, would suspect Oswald Hargrave of having tried to lie. Surely it would pay some villain to tell the truth for twenty years, by way of investing in honesty, for the sake of the grand *coup* that he might make at the end.

Horace believed him—why should he not? But the thought of Sophy in pain as well as in sorrow went to his heart, and his head throbbed in sympathy with hers. "I'm sorry—awfully," said he. "But of course she mustn't be disturbed. Only, is there *nothing* I can do for her—nothing in the world? Nowhere I could go? By Jove, Hargrave, I wish I could do her any good by setting off to the North Pole——"

"I wish you could," said Oswald; this time with unquestionable honesty. "I wish anything could do her good, poor girl."

"I will call to-morrow," said Horace. "Good-bye." And off he set, to think of what might help to cheat away a headache, and more than ever in a state of mind of which his mother would disapprove.

Oswald sighed with relief when he was gone; and again turned to the paper over which he had been interrupted, though with a sigh of a different kind.

"Good God ! Fane must have been fit for a madhouse ! " he exclaimed in thought. "There was neither jest nor child's play about that library scheme. He has really believed that he was making Sophy's fortune by turning her land into—waste paper. His book-shelves hold all her estate, if this paper is not a dream. The poor girl has had a mad trustee—worse than mad, because he made everybody think him sane. Let me see—who was his lawyer ? Corbet, of Laxham, I suppose. Yes—I *must* run down. . . . And then there'll be that confounded young fellow calling to-morrow when my back's turned ; to-morrow and every day. What's to be done ; there must be no love-making till I've mastered Moldwarp ; and even *that* must wait, now . . . Well, there's nothing for it but another lie, and a large one this time. I've begun, and I must go through."

He rang the bell. The Fane's parlour-maid was a sharp girl, who had for some weeks realised that Oswald's was *maire du palais*, and was not likely to disobey the orders of a somewhat masterful young man.

"I'm going down into the country," said he, "perhaps for some days. You know Mr. Horace Derwent ? "

"Of course, sir. He that's just gone."

"Well, your mistress is very unwell at present, and on no account to be disturbed. She must see nobody except the doctor, *nobody :* you understand ? If Mr. Derwent calls to-morrow, or any other day before I come back, your mistress is not at home. And if he asks when she will be at home you must not know. No —you must say that she has gone into the country for some time, and that you don't know when she will be back : and that will prevent his calling again. It is of the utmost importance that she should be quite quiet, and not disturbed. Here's something for yourself, Susan. I trust your mistress to you, you see—and it depends upon if Mr. Derwent sees her whether I trust you again."

"Yes, sir," said Susan, as she took her fee, and smiled. What was more natural than that one young man should do his best to keep another out of the field while he himself was away. Oswald had not thought of that reading : but then, if he had thought of it, he would not have cared.

It was treachery, no doubt. But better treachery which could —as it seemed—cause no irreparable wrong than the risk of letting the brother of Lawrence Derwent whisper too closely in the ear of the sister of Rosamond Fane.

CHAPTER XVIII.

Alone!
Hath Music's self a sadder tone
Than lies in that one word—Alone?
Ah, if she hath, then let her speak
Her comfort unto hearts that break
For want of finding, mid the tares,
A weed more sorrowful than theirs—
For sorrow's deepest depths unknown
To all save those that mourn alone:
And half its bitterness is gone
Whene'er we find, 'neath moon or sun,
Some sadder heart to rest our burden on.

SOPHY was in truth so free from headache, and so little desirous of sleep, that she had heard the knock at the door, and her heart gave a little leap at its familiar sound. Whether she was actually in love with Horace, after the manner accepted in books and more or less in common conversation, she as yet hardly knew. But she would have thought it perfectly natural that he should be the first to call upon her in her trouble, and her very trouble itself made her miss him—Oswald was all very well; but then all he did was for the sake of her poor dead sister's memory, and nothing for her own. He could not save her from feeling alone and uncared for in the world.

She would assuredly have seen Horace. But, as the knock produced no result, and as she did not even hear of his having called, she could only suppose herself mistaken in the sound, while a shyness, very natural in her half-developed feeling towards him, kept her from showing any interest or betraying any disappointed expectation by enquiring. Since he had not seen her, it was not he; since he had not come, he had not cared to come. That was all perfectly right, of course, and she was not going to care—or at any rate to show Oswald or the servants that she cared.

Oswald had come up for the inquest and the funeral, but had only the scantiest and most unavoidable of talk with her, and had then left town again immediately. She scarcely noticed how full of gloom he had become—he was always grave and somewhat silent, and present circumstances were not of the sort to make any man otherwise. But he might have done something to give her cheer and comfort, and he brought her neither—he even put off everything in the shape of discussing her immediate plans. And, as the days went on, and brought nothing with them, the poor girl felt wofully in need of some excuse—to smile. She had cried enough; for her tears came easily and profusely, and when she wept she wept herself out, and required a change. One does not break one's heart over an elderly uncle whom one first knew as a collector of flints, among which his own heart appeared to be the arch specimen. Yet he was too lately gone for her to smile without an excuse, and none came. It seemed fourteen years since he had died, instead of fourteen days.

But long before that time, her pride had taken fire. Even if Horace Derwent did not care the value of a straw for her, common courtesy should have compelled the form of a visit from her uncle's professed friend. Her heart, at least, had never been party to the fiction that Horace was a veritable bookworm, who only called at Richmond Place out of a passion for first editions and worm-eaten bindings. Some instinct had told her that the book he came after was bound in another fashion, and was anything but a first edition of that wonderful volume called *Eve.* She had liked his visits—she had liked the visitor: and now it seemed as if his professed object in coming was the true one, and that she was humiliated by having been mistaken from the beginning. Her very error seemed to accuse her of conceit, and of an offence against all that was maidenly. How could she have been so vain a goose as to suppose that a brilliant young hero like Horace would come and spend hours among the dust and litter of dead men's brains for the sake of her voice and eyes? His real taste had no doubt been strange—but so were the tastes of young men in general. And after all, was it more strange than if he had really cared for so common-place a girl as Sophy Fane? If Rosamond had lived—then there *would* have been a reason for his coming, besides the books, thought she. "Well—I shall know better another time. There are old women in Crossmarsh—and I will be one of them. Yes: I will go—Home."

Of course she would not give another thought to Horace who, had treated her in a manner that really amounted to downright contempt. It is quite possible that if he did call now he would find the door closed to him by genuine orders given at first hand. But this question was not put to the test: and the only visitor who succeeded in passing Susan's sentry box, was the very last person whom she either expected or cared to see. It was Dr. Rackstraw. Perhaps the sentry remembered that she was to make an exception in favour of doctors; perhaps she too rashly assumed that the order was given for the sake of excluding a single visitor. Or perhaps Dr. Rackstraw, being accustomed to diplomacy, had

methods of his own for overcoming all ordinary forms of opposition. At any rate he made his appearance : and Sophy was
not ill pleased to see some sort of fellow creature, though she had
no liking for this particular specimen.

"I would have called long ago," he said, taking and holding her
hand as if he did not mean easily to let it go. "But I was away
from town when I heard the sad news. What can I say ? He was
a great and good man : one of the choice spirits of the world—and
I say it, though the past belonged to him, as the future to me. I
want to be of some use to you. What can I do ? "

"You are very kind," she said, managing to slip her hand away,
and rather wondering at such enthusiasm about her uncle—so true
it is that a man cannot be a prophet in his own country and
in his own house. She was the quicker to withdraw her hand for
feeling that the man she disliked was saying and doing what
Horace ought to have said and done a full fortnight ago, and she
was angry with herself for caring. "But there is nothing you can
do, thank you. I am not left without the best of friends."

"Ah—you mean my young friend, Horace Derwent ? " asked
Dr. Rackstraw, looking round at the untouched piles of books
that lay about just as their owner had left them. "Yes: he is a
good sort of young man, as young men go. Not that I should have
thought him exactly fitted to advise a girl in matters of business
a woman wants the help of an older head, and the grip of a harder
hand." He looked at her as she spoke with that long, penetrated
gaze that had made her feel so uncomfortable during his first
visit to her uncle : and his words had angered her.

"No," said she, sharply. "I do not mean Mr. Derwent. I have
not even seen him since—I mean Mr. Hargrave."

"What ! You mean to tell me—you mean to say you have not
seen Horace Derwent since my dear old friend and master went
where he is now conversing with those great spirits who on earth
conversed with him ? That is strange ! "

As before, she could not rid herself of the belief that he was
conscious of her thoughts : and heart, having been hurt, wished
to hide. "Why is it strange ? " she asked, with what she meant
for sublime indifference. He has nothing to do with my affairs.
such as they are. Now that my poor uncle is gone, it is not likely
that he would come."

Dr. Rackstraw was really for a moment surprised. He knew
Horace, and could not account for the fact that a lover, too far

gone to keep the whole world out of his secret, wearing his devotion, so to speak, written on his forehead, should not have been
near the house all this time. There was no engagement, he knew,
for in that case Horace would have told his mother at once, and
his mother would have told Dr. Rackstraw. As it happened, the
matter touched him very closely indeed. For the truth of the
matter is that the Agent-General for the Goblin Islands, having
called in Richmond Place to spy out the nakedness of the land,
had found a beauty and an heiress—a discovery not to be lightly
thrown away. Although Mrs. Derwent's sworn knight and
servant, he had a warm admiration for female beauty at large, of
a younger kind than his liege lady's: indeed so catholic was he
that the yellow skins, flat noses, tattooed cheeks, and lips turned
inside out of the *belles* of Port Rackstraw itself had more than
once led their Agent-General astray. But the apostle of civilisation preferred, on the whole, a civilised type of beauty, especially when it represented funds and lands. A philanthropist
is never too rich, and the Goblin Islands had not yet wholly de-
developed their trade.

"They must have quarrelled," thought he. "I always thought
the young man was a fool. It runs in the blood, I suppose. Not that
he would have been much discouraged even if he had found Horace
and Sophy actually engaged: for it was not likely that so weak a
vessel as Horace would endure against the will of Hermon Rackstraw, who had made a good thing out of the father, whose path
had been cleared of the elder son, and who had the control of the
mother's purse strings. There was certainly no reason why any
Derwent should for long prove troublesome to a Rackstraw. The
only point in the situation he did not like was Sophy's affectation
of indifference to cover real pique and anger. He knew Horace's
state of heart well enough, but had not supposed that Sophy's
heart had as yet spoken. Nor indeed had it, except to Dr. Rackstraw's ears—not by more than the faintest of whispers, even to
her own.

"No," he said, "of course it isn't likely he would come, unless
he cared to come. What I meant by strange was, that he hadn't
cared. However, I'm glad you're not without a real friend. What
are your plans?"

"Oh—I don't know. It doesn't much matter. I suppose I shall
go home to Crossmarsh, and stay there. It's a quiet place : and I
want quiet——"

"Is that Mr. Hargrave's plan?"

"His and mine."

"Then I beg leave to protest against your doing such a thing Forgive me for telling you that I know you—probably I alone know you. Yours is not the life or the nature to be buried, dear Miss Fane. I don't know what sort of a place Crossmarsh is, but I can fancy. You, with your beauty, and your grand nature, have a place to fill in the great world."

Sophy opened her eyes widely. "I am sadly afraid that you know you are talking nonsense," said she. "I am bound to believe my looking-glass: and if I am grand, how very small the small must be!" So she answered, with what she believed to be perfect honesty. But, nevertheless, she did not dislike Dr. Rackstraw quite so much as ten minutes ago. Evidently he was a bad judge of features and character, but such blunders at any rate showed a generous enthusiasm, which is anxious to praise. Anyhow Dr. Rackstraw avoided making one blunder—he had not seemed to be paying a compliment, but to be merely stating an obvious fact, for the sole purpose of drawing a logical conclusion.

"No, dear Miss Fane: you are not bound to believe your looking-glass: and it is a part of grandeur to believe itself small. I can quite believe that nobody has yet told you what I can tell you now. To appreciate a character like yours calls for the insight of perfect sympathy. Your uncle was a great man—but not in a way that could possibly sympathise with yours. Mr. Hargrave is—forgive me if I seem a little blunt: bluntness is our colonial virtue—is a little hard and narrow: Horace Derwent is but a boy. I do not pretend to grandeur, except in ideas, and for the benefit of humanity, but I have eyes, and I have a heart, and I have sympathy. Probably I know you better than you know yourself. I know something about Queens—and, if I were founding a new empire (than which many things are less impossible) I should offer you the crown."

"Thank you, Dr. Rackstraw. But I shall be a queen—queen of Crossmarsh. And I shall not be without subjects either——"

"No. You will not be without subjects, Miss Fane."

Her visitor was not so very awkward after all. For a moment she was vexed with herself, for she caught herself smiling, and it was for the first time during fourteen dreary days. But then she had been hungry for an excuse for smiling: and she was presently pleased to have shown somebody that at any rate she was not fretting after a faithless lover. Dr. Rackstraw never smiled. But he triumphed gravely, for he felt that the ice was begining to thaw. "She is but a child," thought he, though the prettiest that ever was made." He might not have fallen in love unless Crossmarsh had been in the bargain : but he was not thinking of Crossmarsh now. He could love for love's sake, and had done it often—in his own way.

Weariness, solitude, the sense of desertion on Sophy's past were combining to render any human being welcome, even if it had been the King himself instead of the Agent of the Goblin Islands. By the time that the postman's knock sounded at the end of half an hour, she had become really interested in her visitor. He had ceased to pay her compliments, but had not ceased to talk over her future plans, and somehow managed to make her feel that she was the centre of interest however far away the talk might wander for a time. Now and then, moreover, he used a touch of the art wherewith Othello won Desdemona's heart through her ears. The seas in which he had laboured were far enough away to baffle her somewhat vague ideas of Antipodean geography, and to permit of decidedly romantic episodes. Perhaps it might be found that even at the Round Table itself some of the knights were long and cadaverous, with unmusical voices and awkward limbs—such unquestionably was the Manchegan knight, the very flower and crown of chivalry. Dr. Hermon Rackstraw had not only fed the hungry with the fruits of the press and clothed the naked in Manchester cotton print, but he had fought actual battles, by sea and land, and had always won. Nay, there were indications that Venus as well as Mars and Jupiter had a hand in the horoscope of Dr. Hermon Rackstraw : and, in short, he was interesting her, although, had she been asked whether she liked him, she would still have answered no.

"Will you excuse me for a moment ? " she asked, when, at the end of that half hour the postman's knock was followed by a letter addressed in the hand of Oswald Hargave. "It will be on business ; and Mr. Hargrave would not write unless he had something important to say." He bowed submission : and she read —

"MY DEAR SOPHY,—I would have come to see you instead of writing, but your poor uncle's affairs must keep me here every day till they are settled. And in any case if I did not write to you, Corbet, of Laxham, your uncle's lawyer, would—and it is better you should hear bad news from me. There is no doubt that your uncle, acting with the best intentions in the world, has made use of his large powers as your trustee to invest as much of your property as he could in what he thought the best form of security from time to time—first in old lace, which he afterwards sold at a ruinous loss, then in similar things with the same result, and lastly in books, believing them for the time to be the best security of all. Unfortunately, he was mistaken; the last and fullest catalogue has been submitted to an expert, who says that the collection would sell for little more than as waste paper. Of course you used to sign and execute whatever documents he asked you—it was one of these which originally alarmed me—and of course he fully believed that he was acting in your interest, and was more than doubling your fortune. I will come to the worst at once: so that I may sooner get to a practical proposal. Your property at Crossmarsh is mortgaged to its full value. The rents will not be more than enough to pay the interest of the mortgages, and if the estate is sold, it will do no more than pay off the principal. Under all the circumstances, both Corbet and I think that the best way will be for you to sell Crossmarsh. That can be done, with the consent of the Court of Chancery, on your giving security that your sister or her representatives should sustain no loss by the sale, in case that question should ever arise. For her sake and for yours, you will look to me to supply the security : you know that I represent her interests and that they are my own. Next comes the question of how you are to live meanwhile. My dear Sophy, I never wished before that I was richer than is enough for one purpose, so that I might advance what is needed to save Crossmarsh, and to purchase your uncle's library at its value on paper. But that idea is hopeless : and I must ask you in plain terms to look on me as the brother that I once was to have been. Do not let her loss come between me and the right to help you. You will not blame your uncle, I know. He was an enthusiast, and did all things for what he believed to be the best : and only acted secretly because he believed in his own opinions too firmly to wish to be troubled with those of others. You will have to live quietly, of course, and in a different manner from that which I had planned for you. But you may be entirely free from anxiety, whether I live or die. That is the chief thing that I want you to understand; and you need only let me have a line, before I see you, to tell me that you

12

will be guided by me, who am always, dear Sophy, your most
affectionate friend and brother, OSWALD.

" Direct to me, to the care of E. Corbet, Esq., Solicitor, Laxham."

Dr. Rackstraw was no longer looking at her as if reading her.
On the contrary, he was looking as if he were reading one of the
books, which he had taken from the floor to occupy his time while
Sophy was reading her letter.

" You asked me just now if I had any plans," said she, " and
what they are."

She spoke with almost exaggerated quietness. But its exaggeration was just the quality of it that struck Dr. Rackstraw,
and, glancing towards her quickly from his book, he saw that
her cheeks were flushing and her eyes sparkling. " She is something much more than pretty!" thought he. " Yes," he said.
" Are they made ? I almost hope not—for it would be my am-
bition to advise. That is my mission, you know—to advise."

" Then I will take you at your word," said Sophy with unin-
tended eagerness in her tone. " I want you to tell me how I am
to earn my own living. *That* is my plan—and I don't know
how."

" To earn your living ? *You ?* "

" Yes—I. This letter tells me I have not a penny in the world.
I'm not sure whether it isn't really good news. Why should I be
rich when so many better people are poor ? And why should I
be idle when other women have to work so hard ? Poor uncle !—
it never came into my head that everything was not his, to do with
as he pleased. Money, for once, made one man perfectly happy—
I wouldn't have it back again. And the letter *is* good news—for
it tells me that I have a real friend—only he must think me a
wretch, when he thinks that the sister of the girl who has ruined
his life would be a burden on him to the weight of another straw.
If it's shameful to be idle and rich, it must be twice the shame to
be idle and poor."

" You bewilder and amaze me ! " said Dr. Rackstraw. " What
has happened ? I would advise you —I would help you, Heaven
knows. But perhaps you have read the letter wrong : it is so
easy to read a business letter wrong. Is it a question of a will ? "

" But you *will* put me in the way of earning a living ? You
can ? "

" No doubt; if there is need."

" There *is* need. As you will help me—you had better read

the letter. There is nothing in it that all the world may not know : and you will see if I have misread it. Don't think I'm crying over myself—I'm crying because Oswald is so kind. Oh, I wish Rosamond had lived instead of me! Everything would have been right for everybody, then."

Dr. Rackstraw took the letter, and read it carefully through. "It comes to this," thought he. "I was wrong in calling old Fane an old fool. I should have called him as mad as a March hare, with enough wit to hide it; mad as to the end, sane as to the means. And this young man wants Crossmarsh sold out and out either that he may throw a kindly veil over the eccentricities of Sophy's uncle or that he may buy Crossmarsh cheap—which it is depends on the character of that young man. But the advice is good, all the same. I don't want to be bothered with amateur brothers. They're a nuisance always, and mostly want, before they've done, to become something more. No: the girl mustn't take his money. That would never do. He'll think he's bought her, and expect gratitude. . . . The miserable young hound ! " he exclaimed, in an audible aside, as if his thoughts were too much for him, and had slipped out unawares.

"Dr. Rackstraw ! " cried Sophy, in a tone as if he had struck her.

"I beg your pardon," said he. "I didn't mean to think aloud. But I can't deny my own beliefs. I had been wondering why Horace Derwent hadn't been to see you. I don't wonder any more. He is a—well, an exceedingly prudent young man. As a trusted friend of your uncle, and an acquaintance of that really fine and generous fellow, Hargrave, he would find out, no man sooner, how you were likely to be left and—these things run in families, my dear child. His elder brother stole and destroyed his own father's will—and though that was a venial offence, by comparison it shows the sort of thing that's bred in the Derwent bone. That's what I meant by a 'miserable hound.' The expression was strong—but that it was too strong, or even strong enough, I cannot allow."

Sophy had thought he was speaking of Oswald. It hurt her hardly less to find he had been speaking of Horace, but in another way—everything had combined to embitter her against Horace, and she was angry with him more than she could have been with any man who had not made her care for him. For she was angry with herself. But, though she could not charge Dr. Rackstraw with injustice, it was one thing to feel that Horace Derwent

deserved hard words, quite another thing to hear him receive
what he deserved.

" But it was much too strong," said she. " He had no duty
towards me—not the least in the world. I never even expected
him to come. He was my uncle's friend—not mine. He had no
more reason for coming than you. I would have thanked him,
as I thank you. But I should have no more blamed you for not
coming than I blame him."

" That is because you are a dear, generous, unselfish girl. No
—I can *not* sit and hear black called white—it is just as dishonest
as the other thing. I happen to know that Mrs. Derwent was
afraid of you. She believed you poor before it was generally
known——"

Sophy flushed crimson, and her eyes sparkled tenfold.

" I know what you mean, Dr. Rackstraw—as if I would enter a
house where I was not received by all—by mothers and sisters—
with open arms! What business had these Derwents to suppose
that I was laying traps and snares for their precious son ? Since
you know them so well, you may tell them that I would not speak
to him henceforth, if he called a hundred times a day. I am poor,
and they are rich, but I am as well born, and as proud. There—
I have done with them all. Tell me what I shall do ? "

" Mr. Hargrave generously asks you to be his pensioner," said
he. " It is a handsome offer. A brother could do no more."

" And—and you advise me to become a burden on one who has
been spending life and fortune on—but you know nothing of all
that. Did you not hear me say I am proud ? "

" I understand you ! You are the true kinswoman of the great,
misunderstood spirit which is gone. . . . No : the Derwents,
one and all, are only dust to be shaken from your shoes. And it is
not for you, as you say, to be a pensioner on any man."

" Then tell me how to earn my bread. All these things belong
to my creditors, you see. I want to begin."

It has been said that, but for Crossmarsh, Dr. Rackstraw would
never have dreamed of making love to Sophy. But he was in
love with her now, after his manner, and, though marriage had
certainly ceased to be a prime object, he did not feel disposed to
lose the sense of ownership. He had never thought her so pretty,
and so piquante as now, when he had seen her in her varied moods
of grief, anger, and pride : and he certainly did not intend to lose
her until she was won. Poor, and alone, he could become every-

thing to her for just as long as he pleased ; and, to judge from his present feelings, he saw no reason why it should not please him to keep her his for ever. Horace, he felt, was struck out of the field : if she could be taken from the stronger and colder grasp of Oswald, she was won.

" I honour you, my dear child," said he. " Were I as rich as I am not, I would not insult your independence by offering you help that you could not take without loss of self respect. My feelings are identical with yours. Fortunately, you might have asked ninety-nine men in a hundred for advice, and they could have told you nothing but to wait and work till your chance came—if it came. I am the hundredth man. A lady in whom I am deeply interested—a Queen in her own country—indeed that very lady of whom I was speaking to your uncle not three weeks ago—requires the companionship of a young English lady to act as her secretary and fellow traveller, or rather her philosopher and friend. She is wonderfully like a European, considering all her disadvantages of education, and is miraculously intelligent, but of course there are little things that only a woman can learn from a woman and a girl—for she is little more—only from a girl of about her own age. I have been searching high and low for such a young lady—of course, imagining you to be in good circumstances, I did not presume to think of you. There is nothing you would not like in such a position. You would be the friend and maid of honour to a Real Queen, though of a barbarous kingdom : and—above all— you would be engaged in the great and glorious mission of civilising the benighted, forgotten corners of the human world. Think it over : and, as soon as you can, send me your decision. A word will do."

Sophy felt and looked a little alarmed. " I—I don't know," said she. " Yes, I remember your speaking of that Savage Queen. But mustn't one know her language ? And the responsibility——"

" She speaks English nearly as well as you. She learned it on the voyage—in the most wonderful way. As for the responsibility, that is mine. She is under my charge : and if I could feel that you were her friend I should be a happy man, and be able to attend to larger things."

Sophy cast down her eyes, and considered. In truth, when she had spoken so bravely about fighting her way through the world by the strength of her own hands, she had not supposed that a weapon would be put into her hands quite so soon. But the

impulse was on her, and she could not draw back without yet
further humiliation.   Besides, it would be so great a thing if she
could take her life into her own hands before writing to Oswald, and
could say, " Thank you with all my heart—but, you see, I can
stand alone." For in truth her pride had been sorely wounded on
all sides, and she needed to regain self-respect, and to revindicate
herself in her own eyes.

" You will need no recommendation," said Dr. Rackstraw, " but
mine.   Perhaps you might think it advisable to take another name
—a sort of *nom de guerre.*   No doubt you will see all sorts of
people, and you might not care to have yourself discussed in relation
to your own family affairs.   It would be best for you, no doubt, to
merge yourself in your position as secretary to the Queen.   But of
course that is for yourself to decide. . . . I mustn't venture yet
upon advertising her place of refuge to Master Horace," thought
he.   " He'll find it out, of course—but with three days' start a
man who doesn't win a race deserves to lose."

" My name?   I shall certainly take a new name.   I can't have
the Pitcairns and all the people in Crossmarsh talking about my
uncle—I want to begin my life, and to begin it free.   Of course
I will take a new name : I feel—I don't know why—as if I want
to hide."   She did not say, " From Horace "—but though she had
said that she did not know why, she did know why particularly
well.   " Will you wait for me five minutes ?   I shall not be more."

" I certainly have the art of managing women," said Dr. Rackstraw to himself, as soon as he was left alone.   " She adopts every
hint I make, as if it were her own.   Well—she's worth a little
trouble : or for that matter, a good deal : and the Queen will take
care of her, and she'll take care of the Queen. . . . Why—are you
going out, Miss Fane? " he asked, as Sophy returned, dressed for
walking.

" Are you not going to take me to the Queen ?   I have sent for
a cab—I *want* to go : and if I don't go at once—I'm afraid I shall
change my mind."

" It is the hand of Fate," said Dr. Rackstraw, solemnly, " that
sent me here to-day.   At once, then.   Come."

Sophy, in her exalted mood of decision and energy, heightened
by the fear of being afraid, did not see Horace Derwent, who, in
the exercise of some lover's folly, was without a shadow of reason
passing along the terrace on the opposite side.

"Then she is *not* out of town—and I *am* a fool!" thought he. "Well—it is never too late to mend. Women—they're all the same." And he strode off, wondering why it had been worth Sophy's while to play with him and then throw him away, while his feet seemed to beat the pavement to the old tune,

> "La donna e mobile qual piuma al vento—
>   Muta d'accento, e di pensier."

CHAPTER XIX.

> Not welcoming shores, though kissed by native seas,
> Not English daisies, nor ancestral trees
> Make home, save in a dream—though far we roam
> Name but one name, and magic leads us home.

SOPHY wondered, as she and her newly developed friend drove along in silence, where she was leaping to. Now that the plunge had been made, she realised that she had been leaping before thinking, and that her impulse had, in some inexplicable way, been directed from without rather than excited from within. But it was too late to withdraw now—she could only indulge a sort of hope that she might not satisfy this barbarian Queen, or that some other accident might keep the arrangement from being made. But, on the other hand, she could not possibly mistrust the good faith of Dr. Rackstraw, or repent having decided to act for herself without the aid or advice of Oswald, to whom she could only prove a burden. "I wish I had slept on it!" thought she, "only then, if I had, I should never have made up my mind—and if I had lost this chance I should not have deserved another. Since I am to earn my own bread somehow, the sooner I begin anyhow. I suppose I am as fit for an etiquette mistress, as I am for anything—and after all, if I do make a mistake or two, it won't matter much with a savage Queen. And if I don't suit, or if I can't get on, I can always go: and, as I shall have another name, no particular harm can be done. What *will* Oswald say ! But I shall have done right—and I sha'n't have to argue about doing it : it will be done."

Meanwhile the Senhora had made an unquestionable sensation. No doubt, when the first glamour of her beauty had spent itself, the general feeling was one of disappointment. As a savage, she was an impostor. But in other respects there was no doubt about her being a very charming and fascinating woman, and with an unconscious natural dignity without the least self-consciousness that added to her charm to an infinite extent, and she was talked over with something of the interest due to a Queen who wore one of the recognised crowns of the world.

And yet, who was she, after all?

Her jewels were undoubtedly real; and they spoke in her favour with an eloquence beyond the reach of all words. They were no impostors: and if she were an adventuress, as was hinted at by two most notorious crotcheteers, who did not like Dr. Rackstraw, her adventures must have been of a royal kind. It had become known that she was living very quietly and unostentatiously in expensive apartments taken for her by Dr. Rackstraw in Mayfair, where she had no fellow lodgers. On the morning after Mrs. Derwent's reception, that quiet house in Holford Street was a quiet house no more, and the door remained chronically open. But to the visitors, one and all—philanthropic, commercial, religious; tradesmen, speculators, and lion-hunters, the same answer was returned by the foreign servant in plain clothes—"Madam did not receive that day, and was fatigued." The visitors only had for their pains the view of an ordinary London entrance passage, and the power to say that they had left a card on royalty.

But Dr. Rackstraw had evidently the *petite* as well as the *grande entrée*: and he was instantly admitted, without even the trouble of enquiring if Madam received. Sophy's heart beat: for though the Doctor had by main force, as it were, taken possession of her faith, she felt as if she were entering a lion's den. She followed him up the rather dark stairs, and presently found herself in a rather gaudily but not uncomfortably furnished drawing-room, evidently arranged for tenants of wealth or rank, but without any special sort of character.

"You had better sit down," said Dr. Rackstraw, "and when the Senhora enters, don't try to pay her royal honour. She is *incognita,* you know—but of course if you bring in your Majesty once or twice, as if by accident, you will do yourself no harm. Don't be afraid, dear Miss Fane. . . . Ah—here she comes."

Sophy's heart could not help beating a little as she became aware of the entrance of a wonderfully graceful woman, exquisitely dressed, into the room. "Madam," said Dr. Rackstraw, "this young lady—the daughter of an old friend—is willing to take the post of your Majesty's secretary. You could not do better than accept her services, if I may venture to advise."

" Indeed ? " asked Her Majesty, with a gracious smile that made Sophy feel as if the sun had suddenly begun to shine. This a savage, indeed ? Sophy, always impressed by the nature of the moment, seemed to feel her heart drawn to the lady, scarcely older than herself, who had such a voice and such a smile. " She will be an admirable secretary, no doubt—but if she means to answer all my letters, she will have to work hard. Two hundred and seventeen letters, printed and written, all in one day ! Well—I shall have two secretaries : this young lady, and the fire : and I think the fire will have the most to do. How many wine merchants are there in London, Dr. Rackstraw ? I shall have an advertisement that I drink only lemonade. Pray sit down. Oh, what an evening last night ! I am tired."

" I thought you would be pleased."

" Pleased ? I was not pleased. In my country, we meet to rest, and to amuse ourselves : we sit down always, and all do just what we please. With you we had to stand and talk—talk—talk : my head aches still. How can one talk with nothing to say ? And you all had nothing to say, except ask stupid questions— which is rude. I am not going again to a company like that. I do not like my head to ache, or to breathe and smell—pah ! Would you mind leaving me a few minutes with this young lady alone ? "

Dr. Rackstraw bowed, and retired, with a glance towards Sophy to give her courage.

" What is your name ? " asked the Queen.

" My name ? " stammered Sophy. " Oh—Gray : Sophia Gray."

" Sophia—Sophy ? " asked the Queen, starting.

" Sophy is the short for Sophia, Madam."

" I know. I will call you Sophy, then, Miss Gray. I like the name," she said, with a deep sigh. " And I like you. You are not like those horrible women I saw last night. And mind, I don't engage you on Dr. Rackstraw's word. I engage you because —because I please. I shall not be a troublesome mistress, Miss Gray. Give me your hand."

Sophy touched the beautiful ,hand, and bent her lips over it, remembering that its beauty was a Queen's.

" No—not my hand ! " cried Her Majesty. " I like you- I want you to like me. Kiss my lips—"

And before Sophy could frame a wondering thought, the impulsive savage had thrown her arms round her neck, and her cheek was wet with tears that were not her own.

CHAPTER XX.

*" But of the Tree of the Knowledge of Good and Evil, thou shalt not eat of it :
for in the Day that thou eatest thereof thou shalt surely die."*

I HAVE not thought it worth while to insult my readers by
the formal information that Rosamond Fane had returned
to England Queen of Apahu. I only say so now because
the passing months have made it more than possible that some
among them may have forgotten the very existence of Rosamond
Fane. Indeed, who had not, save Oswald? For her uncle was
dead, and to her sister she belonged to an ancient dreamland : and
as to Crossmarsh, dozens of births, marriages, and deaths have
been written over the story of how Rosamond Fane had thrown
herself over the cliff in a brain fever. Nine days is the period
for wonder : and this was nine years.

Or rather it was nearer ten since the child of fifteen had been
taken up suddenly from such a home as Crossmarsh (whence she
had never been ten miles distant in her life) as it were up into the
clouds, and dropped straight therefrom upon an unknown shore
in the South Seas. That is perhaps the only adventure on record
for which the whole world and all time may be defied to furnish
a fellow—the one absolutely new thing that there has ever been
under the sun. She had just vanished without a trace from the
safest and quietest of English homes : and had woke out of a
nightmare—well, in Apahu : an island of which the most learned
geographer had never heard. Let that be matched in human
experience if it can. And yet the process had not a grain of
magic in it from first to last ; but, on the contrary, taken step by
step, contains no more unlikelihood than the things that are
always happening to us or around us, every day.

But to her, who till now had known no wonders greater than
sunrise and spring, the immediate pass had seemed such a chaos
of wonders that nothing could well seem wonderful any more It
was to her literally as if she had been lifted up into the sky by a
giant hand and dropped again at`random. She lay passively upon
the deliciously warm sand, upon which the caprice of the waves
had tossed her without hurt or pain. Perhaps, thought she, she
was dying or dead, and this was the threshold of the world of
souls. Perhaps Sophy and Uncle Æneas were standing round her
bed, watching the parting of spirit from clay—which is as likely

to be pleasant as not, if we only knew. Of course she felt weak, and her brain seemed to have done with thinking: but her languor felt like the presage of infinite rest, and her senses were bathed in an atmosphere of heavenly fragrant balm. And surely those two perfect children, unspoiled by a rag of mortal clothes, who stood gazing at her, hand in hand, with the eyes of fawns, must be the angels of the threshold—if only it were credible that the Cherubim have coffee-coloured skins.

Happily for this shuttlecock of destiny, it was not among the traditions of Apahu to treat a stranger in any of the methods accepted among the countries which Dr. Rackstraw counted civilised—the savages neither heaved bricks at her, nor mobbed her, nor invited her to dinner to see how she would feed. But they had their superstitions, for they were human : and the sight of a supremely beautiful girl, cast up as if by a miracle from the holy sea, speaking in unknown tongues, and of the complexion of sunshine, overcame the whole country with awe. She was a gift from the elements: and these islanders, in their ignorance, had no experience of any gifts straight from nature that were not divine. From the very beginning there was no doubt of Rosamond's social position in Apahu. Nature had written " Queen" upon her so that all eyes could read: and when the priests of an unknown God consecrated her to empire, they did but translate the language of nature into their own.

It was an ideal kingdom. There were no wars—no seditions— no parties—no crimes. There was not even poverty. A child of five years old could have ruled the island of Apahu. The people were as gentle as their climate, and not a philosopher among them dreamed of doubting that their complex and ancient system of ethics was as much a law of nature as life and death were. They were saturated with ceremonials and symbolisms, but they observed them as unconsciously as they breathed, or as children, who have no friends beyond their own nursery, take for granted the unwritten laws of their little world. Or rather as children, if civilised children were as childlike as the heathen savages of Apahu. Yet their minds were as quick as lightning to observe, and to reason after their manner, and their untainted health made life itself an all-sufficient pleasure, without the help of invention. They had their faults, as even their new Queen could see—they could not imagine that man has any higher mission than to take life as he finds it, to get the utmost good out of it, and to leave

it none the worse for his having been born. A brain with
centuries of Europe in it, could not fall into this view of things,
though that brain was but a girl's. In truth, the new Queen's was
the only burdened brain and sorrowful heart in Apahu. What
were the perfect climate, the fragrant air, even the human worship
and kindness, to her who was pining and wearying for the grey
skies and angry rocks of Crossmarsh, for the perfume of home, and
for those whose hearts she had left to break with suspense and
sorrow? She could not even get the utmost good out of evil—to
speak only in unknown tongues is to be deaf and dumb. However, she shared one grand quality with her subjects—Health, and
therefore Hope: and she could not tell that she was in a sea
whither no ship ever came. Sooner or later, release must come:
and with all her bodily needs amply supplied, she took to thinking.
And the first fruits of her thoughts were that, even at the worst,
she was the worst Christian in the island if she did not give
grateful thanks every day of her life for her wonderful preserva-
tion. The second, that she was almost the worst if she did not
take to heart the lesson that she was no less cared for than the
sparrows of the air and the lilies of the field. The third, that
thanks are to be rendered in deeds, not thoughts or words. She
had to choose between two things, and only two—rebellious
despair, and the acceptance of life on whatever conditions it had
been given: and the latter—so it seemed to a young woman whose
brains were English—meant the further acceptance of some sort
of duty. All her system of theology, such as it was, would be
overturned if all that had happened to her was without a reason
as well as a cause: for the logic of doubt had not reached Crossmarsh at that time. And what was the obvious work for a
Christian English girl in a heathen land? Clearly to bring these
forgotten sheep into her own fold.

The language came to her, at first slowly, then rapidly, as
a language always does when one is compelled to use it to escape
from being deaf and dumb. But it was unwritten, while the
young Queen was no grammarian: and, in addition to these
essential and accidental difficulties, she found it barren in words
to express even her elementary theology. So long as she talked
to the ladies of court out of the Sermon on the Mount, for
example, everything was plain sailing, until she was hopelessly
thrown out by the absolute incapacity of the Apahuic mind
to understand what was meant by doing wrong—not to speak

of sin. What was worse, she could not discover that anything was ever done that would have been called wrong in Apahu. The absence of words essential to all theology was due to the absence of the corresponding things. Once, indeed, a brilliant thought struck her. She imagined the case of a person who should slay a sea-bird, that being regarded as a consecrated creature, to serve for her first lesson in the difference between good and evil. The coffee-coloured Eve, upon whom she tried the experiment, hung down her head, said not a single word, and, at the end of the lesson, crept away with her face buried in her hands. The girl was a chatterbox: and yet, when Rosamond next met her, she maintained the same dead silence, and the next time, and the next, as if she had been suddenly struck dumb. Not only so, but none, even of her own kindred, spoke a word to the poor creature, who went about in melancholy plight as if she were impure. Rosamond addressed her; but in vain. She questioned others, equally in vain. Not till the first glimpse of the second new moon that followed did she recover her speech: nor till then was the too zealous missionary allowed to learn that the girl "had heard words not to be spoken: but she has forgotten them now."

" Then what should happen to the one who speaks such words?" asked the Queen of the old priest who had placed the sceptre in her hands, and was supposed to know—everything. "Surely it is the tongue, not the ear which is to blame."

, " The tongue would not speak if the ear did not listen," said the patriarch of Apahu. " The Queen's words are always wise, and may be spoken—but they must not be heard."

Such logic was unanswerable. She could not adopt Mr. Pitcairn's plan of converting her people with her fists: and yet there seemed no other means. She had to content herself with the practical theology of doing her duty in the state of life to which she had been called: and even this was difficult, seeing that there was so little to be done. Unconsciously to herself, the atmosphere of this island of innocence sank into her own spirit, and dulled even her memories of other times. She also began to forget that there was another world beyond the sea in which human life was a battle, and in sin and sorrow were something much more than names. Her very soul fell asleep, and even forgot to wonder whether it were dead or alive.

But one day, while wandering with two of her maids of honour along the sands, she saw what seemed to set her whole heart on fire. It was what looked at first like a purple cloud. But her eyes soon made out that it was—land. Now air and light will play such tricks now and then, and reveal across deserts of sea or sand the phantoms of invisible hills and streams. Fata Morgana was doubtless playing one of her tricks now. Never had the Queen of Apahu seen the sign of a distant shore or heard of such a sight having been given to the oldest or farthest reaching eyes. And yet this could be no fancy—so complete was the mirage that she could make out the shape of the cliffs, and even the masses of foliage above them and the white foam at their feet. She reached out both her arms, and, as her ladies' eyes followed hers, there came into view a nest of white huts with whiter sails slowly passing them. There was nobody in Apahu to scatter her vision by a lecture on the laws of light: and presently she was surrounded by what was called a crowd in that country, all more full of wonder than she. As she stood with outstretched arms towards the revelation of her own world, she looked as if spreading out her wings to fly—and ah, why had nature denied her wings? Nor did the vision pass till the sun went down with tropical swiftness: and then it remained in her dreams. For she dreamed she was at home, and fifteen years old.

There was nothing contrary to the laws of Apahu—since the case was without precedent—in this summons to their Queen to return for a season to the unknown world whence she had come. Where there was no tradition to the contrary, the royal will was law: and, moreover she had the privileges belonging to a mystery. The matter was laid before the sacred college (I must manage with English terms as best I can) and Rosamond's old priest, her especial counsellor, found himself in a minority of one. It was with sorrow that he brought her the tidings that, since she willed it, she must go. "I am an old man," said he, "I, also, am on the eve of my voyage back to that other world whence we all came. But old as I am, I, nor my father before me, though he lived to six score years, ever saw what you have shown us, even in a dream. It fills me with dread that we, with living eyes, have seen the land that lies beyond the grave. We have seen things not to be seen. What should this forbode to living souls?" It was thus that the Queen learned, for the first time, that Apahu regarded itself as the entire world, bounded by an infinite sea; and that her subjects believed her about to pass that ocean while still alive. And why not, when she had already crossed it full-grown.

"It is not for the old to teach the young," said her priest, sadly and humbly. "You are fresh from where you are going—I came from it as a child, and have long ago forgotten its ways. But I heard from my father, who heard it from his, and he from his fathers, that Apahu is blessed because its name has never been named to the evil spirits who live beyond the sea. Who they are I know not: only I tremble. I have guessed there is evil, for I have learned there is pain. I dread to think what ruler next may be sent us from the sea."

"But I shall learn all that the other world has to teach," said the Queen, "and all that I learn I shall be able to teach again. Do you think I will not return? Do I not love my people—the gentlest, kindest, best, that ever were known? Do I not owe you all more than I can ever repay? God has made me your Queen —God forbid that I should give up my crown to one who must needs love you all less than I! Only now I *must* go. In that other world I have a sister—kindred—friends. I shall find those who will teach me what I am hungering and thirsting to teach my people, and know not how. I shall come back—and it will not be long."

She was burning to start for those white huts and white sails which, though now become invisible, could not possibly be unattainable, since they had been seen. But she had passed those years of growth in her island during which a child becomes a woman: and this under influences which had made her one with the people among whom she had been thrown. Crossmarsh, with its blank life of solitary fancies, had left a clear page whereon Apahu might be written large, with nothing to erase or to confuse the letters. For all those years she had not been brought in contact with an English thought, or heard an English word. She had learned to dream even with a new tongue: and the silent power of Goodness had enveloped her till, though unknowingly, she was spoiled for this common life of ours—which indeed, save in her own fancies, she had never known. She hungered for home, but it never entered her head to become an escaped prisoner, and to throw off the duties which belonged to her as a Queen. She had made friends—she had imperceptibly learned to think their thoughts, and to make their ways hers. Of course she would return, and in such wise as to reward her people for their love a thousand-fold.

She belived that Rosamond Fane of Crossmarsh, and Queen Ngahoung of Apahu, were still one and the same: and that while she had been changing from a child into a woman, all her old world had been standing still.

She was longing for the return of her childhood; to see again the same flowers in the old garden, and to amaze Sophy with her reappearance from the grave. Nevertheless it was a sad as well as a solemn moment, when, the centre of a great, incomprehensible mystery, herself the mystery of mysteries, she stepped from the shore, in the sight of all her people into the great canoe which was to bear her across the world-encircling sea. She wore the consecrated jewels, rubies, and emeralds, and the circle out of which she stepped was formed of chief priests and judges in their robes of white, yellow, or crimson silk, of jewelled nobles, and of the ladies of the land. There were neither applauding shouts, nor tears. It was the will of the Queen, whose words were the oracle of fate, and awe silenced the voice of sorrow. She was about, without dying, to pass over the waters of life and death, which she alone had already passed without having been born. Twelve men, chosen by lot from the best mariners of the country, were to carry the royal canoe to the invisible shore. Not one, though bound upon so marvellous an adventure, betrayed a sign of doubt or of fear. Indeed no Apahuic was ever troubled with doubt of any kind; and they trusted their Queen as their mother, children that they were. Indeed, there was no visible sentiment among them all but pride, that this adventure had been trusted by destiny to their hands; and envy must have been found on the shore if such a serpent had been known in Apahu.

The voyage of the ship *Argo*—the first voyage of Columbus— the voyage of Queen Ngahoung: these three, each in its way, are the wonder voyages of the world. Faith was the grand element in the third. When the next sun rose, and the horizon was still as clear of land as it was of clouds, the Queen's heart sank a little; but her sailors' hearts were as stout as at starting. One does not travel from this world to the other in a day. They had seen the vision of the shore, and therefore knew which way to sail, and the wind seemed to know it too, for it set steadily to the same path, though not so strongly as to quarrel with the sea. Their unflinching faith gave their Queen hope: and on the morning of the fifth day they saw land—no mirage: and in the evening ran ashore. The Queen landed: her sailors kissed her hands and her feet, and sailed back for Apahu, to tell how they had touched the shore of the world of Souls and had returned alive.

But the country did not go into mourning for its Queen. She had said she would return: and words, even when promises, were sacred in Apahu. Only the Queen's old priest fell into a lethargy, wherein he spoke no words but these—"It is the End."

CHAPTER XXI.

I thought me free as thoughts are free,
   Or dreams of love that's past and o'er,
Nor feared I e'er again should see
   That shadow on the floor.

Yet who may hide his days so deep
   For foes to find? When dread was slain,
And memory's self had fall'n asleep,
   The shadow came again.

OSWALD HARGRAVE'S business at Laxham proved to be more complicated even than he had feared. His letter to Sophy but poorly represented the state into which a mad trustee, of reputed and unquestioned sanity, had contrived to bring them. With the aid of the lawyer, however, he contrived to clear up the business so far as to learn that Uncle Æneas had, with the aid of Sophy's signature whenever it was required, been investing her whole capital, and even whatever could be raised on mortgage or otherwise, in a mass of worthless and unsaleable rubbish— all for her benefit of course, but not the less to her ruin. With a cunning that must have grown with the growth of his craze, he had from time to time employed at least a dozen lawyers, so as to avoid the disagreeable necessity of having to hear good advice: while his own estate, which his mismanagement had rendered liable to his ward's, was simply *nil.*

There was certainly no reason why Oswald should consider himself answerable to one of two sisters simply because nine or ten years ago he had wished to marry the other. But his conscience had always been a jealous tyrant; and it told him that if he had not been spending all those years upon the pursuit of what he alone would not call a Phantom, he would have seen what was going on, and Rosamond's sister would have been an heiress still. "After all, dare *I* call Æneas Fane a madman?" he thought. "It is what men would call me—if they knew. If I could only be sure she is dead!—but then I know that Lawrence Derwent

13

lives: it is too late for thinking now.   After ten years, one *must* go on to the end. If I am mad—well, mad I must be."

But it did not strike him as a sign of madness that he should impoverish himself for Rosamond's sister's sake, though she had no more claim upon him than what he chose to imagine. And indeed there was a time—at least so we teach ourselves to believe —when nobody would have called him mad: when a knight who devoted his life to find or avenge a lady, and to punish a villian, would have had poems made in his honour. And after all, when I come to think of it, I cannot bring myself to decide that Oswald Hargrave's purpose was much less foolish, or even much more barren, than the ordinary purposes of life which are accepted as sane. No doubt he might have made a fortune, or written a book or whatever else it might be, with half the labour: but then to his mind Rosamond was better worth seeking than a fortune which she could not share, and as for books—well, living a book is as good as writing one, any day, and moreover he had no vanity, except in what consisted in finishing whatever he had happened to begin. As it was, there was only one book wanting to the world—the only book that he needed; the book that should have told him of Apahu.

Having, so far as was possible at present, arranged preliminaries with the lawyers at Laxham, subject to Sophy's approval which no doubt would be given, he was able, on his way back to town to return to the subject of Silver Moldwarp, in connection with Lawrence Derwent, and to the means by which he might render available that shadow of a clue. That still baffled him, and for the same reasons which had before raised up a fatal objection to every course he had been able to think of. He went out of his way to pass the book-shop on his way to his hotel—it was still there, but as unsuggestive as ever. If only he had a friend to whom he could give his whole confidence, and who had both the time and the craft, to act for him as a detective, much might be done: but if Moldwarp was in the interest of the escaped convict, Oswald's personal enquiries would only serve to put the rascal on his guard. And he had no desire for the help of law or police in hunting down Lawrence Derwent, though it would have been at service, seeing that the man was a felon who had broken gaol. But, if Rosamond were to be found, live or dead, Oswald must get the felon under his own personal power—the law might have him when he had been used and thrown away. So far as the purpose of his life was concerned, the time spent over Sophy's business had been clean thrown away.

He was just about starting for Richmond Place, when he received a letter from the lawyer at Laxham, enclosing another letter which had been addressed to him there and had arrived immediately after his departure. The address was in Sophy's hand-writing. "An answer to mine, I suppose—but there was no occasion for that," thought he. But when he had read it—" What in the name of all perverse folly is the meaning of this? Rackstraw—Miss Gray—companion and secretary to an outlandish Queen? What is Rackstraw, that he should meddle with her affairs and mine? This will never do."

So, instead of walking at his leisure to Richmond Place, in order to think out the great complication, he drove straight to Mayfair, and arrived just as another visitor had knocked and was waiting at the door. He recognised the man from Nevada: and he was also recognised, for his fellow visitor gave him a careless nod of half acquaintance, accompanied by a smile which seemed to convey some special meaning. "So you have found your way here, too?" asked he. "Oh, I remember—you are a traveller—Is the Senhora at home? Does she receive?" he asked, as the door was opened.

"Is Miss Fane here?" asked Oswald.

"The Senhora is at home, Mr. Harding," said the groom of the chambers respectfully, to the first enquiry. "Miss Fane? No Miss Fane lives here."

" I beg pardon—I mean Miss Gray," said Oswald, as the man from Nevada entered before him.

"Oh, yes—Miss Gray! She is with Madam."

And so Oswald, dimly groping for such clue as Silver Moldwarp's fingers might just possibly hold, all unconsciously entered the very centre of the maze.

" What you have seen of the world!" Rosamond was saying to her secretary. "It is wonderful—and you so young. Why, you must know everthing. You ought to be the queen of my poor people, instead of me. And—do you know England as well as you know all those places abroad? "

" I know very little of England, Madam," said Sophy. "Very little indeed."

" Did I not tell you never to call me ' Madam' again? Well, we shall both know more of England very soon. I am going on

a journey—and indeed I shall be glad, for London is a horror; not
at all what I expected. I can hardly breathe. But still of course
it is London that I must look for what I want—all the goodness,
and the wisdom, and the science that I must carry back with me,
when I go. Do you like London?"

"No," said Sophy with a sigh. "It is the only place where I
have ever known sorrow—and—but that is ungrateful. I am glad
to be in your service. You don't seem like a mistress: you seem
like a friend."

"Seem? No. I am. The minute I knew your name, I knew
we should be friends. Oh, I wish you could see my country—I
had forgotten, I didn't know, I mean, that England was so dark
and so close, and the people so gloomy and grave. And then the
poor who suffer, and the rich who do not help the poor—my dear
child, I sometimes wonder if after all my people could get much
good from yours. There is religion, of course—but—I wonder if
it is wrong to think that people who live up to their own, and
never do wrong, are best left alone. Oh, it is a dreadful responsibility to be a Queen. I wish you could see my country—with its
earth-like paradise and its skies like heaven, and its people, all as
beautiful as angels, and as wise as little children are! You mustn't
judge of them by me. I am full of doubts, and wants, and sorrows:
I have thoughts for which they have no words. Do you think it
would be best for them if I were never to go back to them again?"

It was the lioness asking advice of the mouse. "I think, Madam,"
said Sophy timidly, " I think your people have a great and a good
queen. But oh, if they are heathens!" she exclaimed, forgetting
that the Senhora must needs be a heathen too—"Of course they
must be taught all that—you must find some clergyman who will
tell you what to do——"

"I have seen dozens," said Rosamond sadly. "After I was seen
at the Derwents', they used to come and advise me every day.
They all talked very well, but none of them seemed to understand.
And then they all wanted me to have my people converted to different things: and out of every dozen the twelfth said that the
eleven others were wrong——"

"But religion is religion," said Sophy. "Any sort if it was Christian, would be better than none."

"Dear child—do you know that my people have lived in faith,
hope, and charity for hundreds, perhaps thousands, of years?
Will they and their fathers and their children be condemned for

knowing no better than to be content with these—just because, being blind to the darkness, they have been blind to the light too? I dread to bring among them the doubt, the terror of death, the want of charity, that I find here—everywhere. Let it be *my* fault that they are left blind. *My* sin will not be visited on *them.* If I refuse to let them know the truth, it will be my sin—not theirs."

This was a flight far and far beyond Sophy, who had never until this moment been taken into confidence by a heroine, who had learned from her queendom to place the good of her people before even her own soul. It was a new experience for the girl to hear right and wrong, sin and duty, and the relations of sovereign, Church, and people, treated, not as matters for books and sermons, but as real, practical things—as real, and of more intense moment, than going to market even.

"But enough of that," said Rosamond, with a sudden smile— though rather sad for all its sweetness, as if it were a confession that she had rather wasted her confidence upon her new friend. "I retract my wish that you were a queen. Tell me about yourself rather. You are an orphan—like me?"

"Yes—my father and mother both died, when I was quite a child."

"So did mine—but I can just remember my mother, though not her dying. Have you brothers? Sisters?"

"I have no brother. I had a sister once—but she died."

"You are indeed alone! But how came you to know Dr. Rackstraw?"

"He has been a very kind friend—and in bringing me to you, more kind than I can say. Do you know, I can hardly believe that you come from an unknown country, so far away? And you are nearly as fair as I."

"And you don't think me very much like a heathen savage?"

"Oh, Madam! You know I think you the loveliest woman in the world!"

"I am glad of that, my child! I want to give a good impression of my people; for I love them and am proud of them—I never knew how much till I came away. Do you know, I am half glad you are so alone? For perhaps you will go back with me—when I go. I want also to give a good impression of your people to mine. All the others here are so ugly, and are not gentle, as mine are, at all. Of course, Dr. Rackstraw is a man of genius—but I should

hardly like to take him as a specimen: he is not exactly beautiful.
How would you like to come ? "

" Madam," said Sophy, " there is nothing I would like better in
the world ! I *hate* England. I should like to leave it, and never
see it again."

" Now what does that mean ?" asked Rosamond, smiling through
a mist in her eyes at Sophy's flushed cheeks and eager tone. " You
must neither bring hate with you, nor call me Madam, if you are
to come with me. I *love* England—love her, though her face is all
frown while my island's is all sunlight and smile. And I mean to
love this dear, old, ugly England yet more. But, though I love it
ever so much, my people are my people : they must always come
first with me—first of all! I shall have to go back, at least for a
while—and so—it is settled—you will come too. Ah, you will not
hate England when you have been away for a year. You will
hunger for the sight of her very ugliness——"

"But indeed I would not—I want to go to *your* country—where
people do not only pretend to be friends, until one is poor. . . .
But one would think *you* were English ! It is very——"

"Strange? Not at all. If you were only a little browner and
a little taller you would pass for one of my people very well. And
you shall be one, since you will. You shall wear this *Qahoung*—
Ruby : that means you are one of my people now ; and my friend.
Now, kiss the hand of your Queen."

Sophy pressed her lips to those forgotten fingers, and the forgotten
lips touched her brow.

" Mistare Harding for the Senhora!" announced the Swiss.
" And a gentleman to see Miss Gray."

Rosamond's eyes, close to Sophy's face, saw the girl's face colour
yet more quickly than before and a startled look in her eyes. In
love affairs, Rosamond was a nun. But nuns know how to read,
and the language of love was not among the things that were
unknown in Apahu. " Are you so sure you hate England?"
whispered she. " Are you sure I am not punished for my greedi-
ness in being glad you have no friends but me? . . . . Let
me see—I think Mr. Harding comes to talk business: I will see
him here. You had better see your friend in the parlour, Miss
Gray. He may have business too."

Poor Sophy felt stricken with shame. She knew that her tell-
tale colour, so terribly out of season, had betrayed the hope and
fear of her heart that her nameless visitor would prove to be her

false friend and lover, whom she had vowed [never to see again. Who else should seek her out, and find her, despite her change of name ? It might be that he would be able to explain—her pride and her suspicion might have wronged him, after all. So she put on an air of ice, and the man from Nevada, who passed her on the stairs with a bow, was experimented upon by a half curtsey charged with frozen dignity. But her heart was beating as it had never beaten before : and, when she entered the parlour, it turned to real, not make-belief, frost, at the sight of Oswald Hargrave—the best and truest friend that she had in the world: and that without knowing that it was he to whom the apparent desertion of Horace was wholly due.

"What in heaven's name is the meaning of all this, Sophy ?" asked he, for his first word. "I arrange the best of plans for you —I am doing everything that can be done—and I find you in this strange service, under a false name. Here is your letter. What in heaven's name does it mean?"

"I know you are very, very kind. . . . But only think, Oswald—what *could* I do ? I can't take your money. I can't in-deed. Of course Crossmarsh must be sold, and that is the only way for the debts to be paid. Just think, Oswald—you have been spending all you have for poor Rosamond's sake : the living must not join the dead in wasting all your means. I am proud—I will earn my own bread, since I can: yes, and with comfort and ease. Indeed I have done well—better than well."

"But you must not be proud, Sophy. A fine sort of fellow I should be, while seeking Her, to let her sister serve or starve. Why have you changed your name ?"

"That's because I am proud too. And it's because—because— well, because I thought it best : and Dr. Rackstraw thought so too. It was he, you know, who introduced me to the Queen—the Senhora, I should say."

"Dr. Rackstraw! What can a stranger know of what you ought to do ?"

"Poor uncle's most intimate friend?"

"My dear girl—don't think I mean to be cross with you. But I know the world—at least most of it ; and I have learned two things. One is to trust a woman's *first* impression of a man. The second is to distrust the man who flatters another's—craze You took an instinctive dislike to Dr. Rackstraw at first sight: lesson number one. Dr. Rackstraw flattered your uncle to the top of his bent, pretending to love books with which the result

shows he knew nothing. And for this he must have had a motive:
lesson number two. I distrust Dr. Rackstraw because you did,
and you must, Sophy, because I do."

"Oswald! I never knew you unjust before. Yes—you *are*
unjust. Is a man to be condemned for ever because some silly
girl thinks him awkward and without manners? Why, where
would you all be? What has Dr. Rackstraw to gain from me?
He understood my pride at once—he has warned me of my friends
and enemies—he has been my friend even when he knew I was
poor—he has found me a situation in a thousand——"

"As companion to a savage: to an adventuress, for aught you
know, though probably he knows——"

"As friend to the loveliest and noblest woman I ever knew—
yes, if you put it that way. Oh, Oswald, don't be ungenerous—
unjust: that is not like you. If you could only see her: if you
could only hear her speak—how she loves her people, and would
even sacrifice her immortal soul for their happiness: how gentle
she is, and how kind, and how wise——"

"My dear, dear Sophy—she may seem all that, and yet she
may be no fit companion for you. She comes, I understand
from the South Seas. Now a South Sea Islander, fresh from her
own home, does not talk English like a native, dress like a duchess,
and look a Venus from some Italian picture. If I must put it
plainly—I am your brother, Sophy—I believe her to be some half-
bred Portuguese, clever, beautiful, accomplished as so many of
them are, whom Dr. Rackstraw has brought to England for ends
of his own. An unknown island? Absurd! But a woman like
that would be a grand bait for a company to explore non-existent ruby mines—and—you are too innocent to tell tales."

He knew that he was talking sound sense: but Sophy was fresh
from the influence some women have—that of fascinating their
own sex no less, or rather more, than Oswald's. "You are saying
horrible things, Oswald," cried she. "She is my Queen: I will
not have her slandered, even by you. You shall see her; you
shall judge if she's not even lovelier and nobler than I can say.
I *know*. Oh, Oswald—believe that I am doing what is right—I
must not be a burden on you: I can be of use to her."

"And—when she returns to her Atlantis, her Utopia, or where-
ever her ruby mines may be?"

"I am alone, Oswald. I have said I will go too."

Oswald paced the room silently. Then, "It is like witchcraft!"

said he. "Why did Rackstraw force himself into your uncle's confidence? Why did he encourage him in his waste? Why did he seize the first chance of bringing you into this woman's service, under a false name ? I must get to the bottom of this— and I will: though my hands are overfull already, and my wits over-burdened, Heaven knows. I am not hard, Sophy, nor un-generous I hope, nor unjust I know. You are Her sister—and mine. A girl like you is the best of instruments in unscrupulous hands, when they are playing a deep game. What end have I but your good? Who is this Rackstraw?"

"Talk of the devil indeed!" said the Doctor himself, who at that moment opened the door. "Mr. Hargrave? An unex-pected pleasure. Perhaps I can answer that question better than Miss Gray. I have been in countries—ha ha!—where such a question, in such a tone, would have had to be settled at some dozen paces distance : but I am a missionary of civilisation, and duels, being a survival of barbarism, are out of my line. Besides, your question was perfectly natural, since you wanted to know. I am Hermon Rackstraw, Doctor of Philosophy, Agent-General for the Goblin Islands. You can see my credentials at my office, if you have any business in that rising group, where land is still to be had cheap with a moral certainty of being able to sell it at fifty times the value in a very few years."

"Thanks," said Oswald, shortly. "I will call at your office— if you will let me know where it is, and name a time."

"Here is my card, Mr. Hargrave. You will find me any day, this week, between two and four."

"Then—Sophy—good-bye for to-day. To-morrow, or next day I will see you again. By that time you will have heard from Laxham, about the sale. *And in that matter you will be guided by them and me.*"

And so he left her, as if in anger—for which indeed he was surely not without cause. Dr. Rackstraw stroked his smooth chin in silence, while Sophy, her eyes swimming, listened to Oswald's footsteps as they passed into distance with what she took for an angry ring.

"Oh!" said she, when she heard them no more. "What *shall* I do to make my brother believe in my Queen? If he had only seen her—and now he is gone."

"I am afraid—very much afraid," said Dr. Rackstraw, "that Mr. Hargrave does not approve of what you have done. Never mind, dear Miss Fane. *We* know that you have done wisely and well. After all, that is the grand difficulty of doing right—that we can't make other people understand. It has been so with me, hundreds of times. You don't repent having done as you have done?"

"Not for a moment. And yet—but you can't know what anything like a quarrel with Oswald means."

"Indeed but I can. Do you think *I* can't understand everything that concerns *you?* Of course you could not take his—charity. He will see that for himself, in time. And you have your place in the world. I heard quite enough, as I came in, and afterwards, to see how the land lies, there. He mistrusts me—God knows why. But you do not?"

"No indeed! But that was not what distressed me so much—.but he has got such dreadful ideas about the Senhora——"

"Ah—he thinks her an impostor, eh?"

"What—you heard?"

"Not a word. But I know what notions always come into those dull, narrow minds. They never believe what they cannot understand. They have no *Faith,* dear Miss Fane, like you—and me. I hope I have brought you into a wider and nobler life—a life worth the living. You must trouble your head about all these trifles no more. We must leave them to the Hargraves and the Derwents—the moles and the butterflies. *We* must soar."

"Ah—you and the Senhora," sighed Sophy. "But I have no wings."

"Then I have no eyes. By the way, I think I've cleared up the mystery about our other friend—young Derwent, you know. He had a good reason for not coming after all."

"Indeed? Then——!"

"Yes—the best of all reasons. Mrs. Derwent—his mother——"

"Is she ill?"

"No—tells me he is just engaged to a Miss Craven: that's all. So of course, under the circumstances, one couldn't very well expect a young man to go about making morning calls. He lives in a rapture, you know—however, I'm glad to think it was only that, and not what we supposed. No: one should never judge harshly—never. There's always some good, honest reason for everything, if we only knew."

"Oh—is that all?"

"That's all. It will be a good match, and will please his

mother: and I'm glad of it, for he's not a bad sort of a young man."

"So am *I* glad—very glad indeed! Do you know how soon the Senhora means to go home?"

"Oh, not yet awhile. You needn't be afraid——"

"I'm sorry you don't know, because I hoped it would be soon. I am going with her——"

"And you are impatient to see that wonderful island of hers? Just so—there, you see, grow your wings! But there's no hurry —why do you want to fly away?"

"Because I do!" said Sophy, keeping down a rising sob, to her pain. "And that *is* all."

Her lover had the sense to see nothing, and to let her go with no more than some common-place word. Indeed for that matter he had not really seen everything: for though he had hurt her heart with intent, he had no means of knowing the depth and breadth of the wound. Of course she believed him. It was not as if Horace were her betrothed, of whom it would be against her duty to believe what might by the remotest possibility be a lie. Dr. Rackstraw was the family confidant, she knew, and what he had said could not possibly be wrong: besides, he himself had been treated unjustly by Oswald, and her sympathy, and her sense of justice, as well as her gratitude, were all on his side. Why should not Horace have been all the time engaged to another girl? Some men cannot help flirting—idiot that she had been, to fancy that it was more than his way, and that his visits had meant anything more than an easy way of killing time! And a "good" match—that meant that his *fiancée* was rich while Sophy was poor: and not even the exaltation of a lover could excuse a gentleman for taking no notice of the death of a friend, and for shaking off, as if she were the dust that had gathered on his feet, the only creature whom that friend had left, ruined and alone. She did not even seek the solitude of her own room to let her last sob free, and to recover her lost pride once for all. Not even so much debt was due to a dead dream: nor would she give Horace the paltry triumph over her of causing a single tear. She went straight to her mistress, forgetting that the Queen was not alone.

This was not by any means the first visit of the man from Nevada to Senhora Miranda. Rosamond rather liked him: and the better the more she saw of him. He was agreeable, apparently unaffected, and, so far from wanting her portrait, or her subscription, or her materials for books and articles, he amused her by discussing her persecutors in a tone of semi-cynical humour. On what pretence he had given himself a place in her life she could not have told: he had stepped into it easily, and as a matter of course, and altogether in such a manner, that it never occurred to her to ask the question. Nor did it occur to her to notice that he generally timed his visits, now increasingly frequent, to such hours as gave him the least chance of coming into collision with Dr. Rackstraw. Not that the latter, even without the aid of a secretary of his own choosing, was likely to be in the dark as to any of the Senhora's doings, or who came to see her, and how often, and when.

But *à propos* of the secretary—"So you have set up a companion," he was saying, while Sophy was engaged with Oswald. "And a very pretty girl she is—though she swept past me as if *she* were the Queen. Some friend of Rackstraw's, I suppose?'

"No—of mine."

"Of course it's all right you should have a maid of honour. And I'm glad she's your own friend. Have you seen anything of the—what's their name—Derwents lately? Wonderful people they are to be sure. But England 'is altogether a wonderful place for people like you and me. If I'm not very wrong, you won't be particularly sorry to go home. I sha'n't, I know."

"As to that—yes, and no. But have you nothing to say—nothing to tell?" asked Rosamond—patient in manner, but impatient in tone.

"Well, yes. A good deal. The difficulty is to know where to begin. Perhaps the best way will be to begin at the beginning," said he, drawing his chair imperceptibly nearer, and laying his right hand upon the table so that it might be within magnetic distance of hers. "You will listen? Well—then I will go back to the very beginning of all, so far as I need. Lightly as I seem to take life, I am here in England to take vengeance for a great wrong, and to extort justice under the very eyes of the law—I know that I am talking what would be called treason in Apahu—but never mind. England is not Apahu. I was driven out of England by a cabal of scoundrels. I know them all: and I trust to have them in my power. I come back rich—richer a hundred times than if I had had my rights at home. But my riches are nothing to me until they have bought vengeance and justice : you have been long enough in England to understand what I mean."

" Indeed I have!" said Rosamond. " But what has all this to do with——"

" Everything." His voice commonly so dry and languid, fell into a deep monotone, yet so soft that his words could hardly have been followed farther off than Rosamond's ears. "For some fifteen years I have lived for this that I have told you : and a purpose grows into a man's life, and becomes himself, for half that time. Until what seems like yesterday, I have been ready for murder, if that should be the only means to my only end. You see what sort of man I am : and I wish you to see. I want you to imagine how great the strength must be that is greater than my life, and that makes me—even me—as if all I have told you of had never been : that makes me ready to forget it all. What kind of strength is that? Can you tell?"

Rosamond had drawn back.

" Repentance?" said she.

" Repentance—for having set myself to undo a vile wrong? And you say that—you, a woman? You know as well as I."

" Then I do not choose to know," said the Queen, rising.

" Which means that you do know, whether you choose or not," said the man from Nevada, rising too. "You know it means that I love you—and that I could not love you more if I had known you for years. One does not learn how to make love, in the mines. But one does learn that a man is a mate for a Queen, and a Woman for a King, I offer you a Man, heart, and body, and soul. Oh, how can one speak passion? Look at me— see if I do not love you : let crowns be only the ghosts that they are. Let *us* be real—you and I."

He held out both his hands towards her : and the action, and the tones of his voice, turned his rough words into living and passionate things. Rosamond did indeed, without bidding, forget that she was a Queen. But her womanhood did not wake to meet him : it only trembled with dismay. Passion like his she had never seen.

" It is terrible !" she breathed. "I do not love you—and yoy love me! What have I done?"

" Never mind what you have done. You do not love me? But you can—you will. Love like mine makes love—or hate : nothing

between. Do you wish me to turn back into my old path, and
live for revenge? But what is the good of words? I have
hidden myself from you all this while—now I am what I am.
And I more than love you—I want to save you, too. For God's
sake throw away that sham crown, that can only end in miserable
pain. Remember I love you without so much as knowing your
trust—your nation—your name. I love you like a madman. I
see a beautiful woman in league with a villain for some devilish
ends. And I only love her, for herself; and for her sake I
will let the villain go, and spare his dupes and his tools besides.
Do you understand what a man's love can mean—*now?*"

"No—no: I do not understand. What ruin? What villian?
What crown? Why do you say all this now? Have you ceased
to be my friend?"

"I say all this now, because it will be too late before long.
Before long—unless you bid me spare him—your accomplice will
be a ruined man. And, for yourself, the world is already
asking dangerous questions about Apahu, and its jewels, and its
Queen. Let me save you from evil—love will come. My country
is real—there you will be a Real Queen."

"Am I going mad?" she cried.

"Yes—if you refuse to be saved," he answered. "And there
is only one way—and that is mine. I can give you everything—
wealth, luxury, passionate love: everything the heart of woman
can desire. Think of what your life is now—think of what it
would be with me!"

"Are you buying me?" asked Rosamond—for his last words
had made her Queen again. "Wealth, luxury? I have them, and
to spare. And passionate love? No—not as a price to be paid.
For the rest, I am only amazed. Your words mean nothing
What have I to fear? Oh, I am sorry for this, with all my heart
and soul—and hate, and vengeance: I did not cross the sea for
these. I am sorry—for I meant to have told you who I am:
why I am here: for what and whom I am searching in vain, till
my heart breaks and will not let me rest: for you could have
helped me then, you and no other—I thought—but I cannot tell
you now. I have nothing to do with love—of that kind. And
now——"

"Help you. Is it not all I ask for?—"

"But in your way—not mine. Do you not see I am sorry?
Good-bye."

"No—by God!" cried he. "There cannot be good-bye between you and me. Love and vengeance—there is nothing between left for me to choose. But I will warn you: though I so risk all. . . Have you ever heard your friend speak of Lawrence Derwent?"

"Never. *Lawrence* Derwent? I have never heard the name!"

"Then—Heaven help you—you have chosen between him and me. But you *shall* have time. No—not good-bye, even now. I have risked all; I will even risk more."

"Good-bye," said she. But, even as she spoke, all bewildered as she was by the burst of passion without preface from one who had seemed the calmest of men, and by threats and warnings that she could not comprehend, there came back the memory of that fatal evening when she had first heard that passionate monotone, pleading for pity and liberty. The man had changed, purposely, past knowing—but the voice had been taken off its guard: that voice which she could never forget till her dying day. How much *she* must have changed! But had he spoken truth when he said, "There can be no good-bye between you and me?"

His presence turned her cold, in the old magical way. Was he to be her doom—and to what end? As a child she had half believed him a wizard—what was she to believe him now? She trembled to think how nearly she had been upon the verge of telling him all, that he might find for her those whom she could not find.

"Ah—but there are some good things, even in England!" she exclaimed, as Sophy, with set lips and dim eyes, crept into the room. "Kiss me, dear—I am glad there is something even for a savage heathen to understand! To-morrow—to-morrow—perhaps I shall know what to do."

"To go home?" whispered Sophy.

"Child—why, you are crying!" cried the Queen, bursting into tears.

CHAPTER XXII.

Julian—What saith the saw ?
      " Whate'er you'd learn, affect to know it all."
Caspar.—Aye, master, but at that game two can play. For
      how goeth the by-word ?
      " If I chase thee, and thou chase me,
      The third man saith, Two fools there be."

THE office of the Agent-General for the Goblin Islands was
not built or furnished in such a manner as to put Canada or
Australia to shame. Indeed, the business of that enterprising
colony, at present without colonists, was transacted on the highest
floor but one of a high staircase in Mildew Court, which hides in
so obscure a corner of the City as to be almost as undiscoverable
as Apahu. The offices consisted of an inner and outer room, both
inconveniently small : the latter being occupied by an exceedingly
smart lad of sixteen or seventeen, and the former by the Agent-
General, whenever he was there. The boy must have had a good
berth of it, for he was very much his own master during office
hours, except for a disagreeable irregularity on the part of his employer which made it unsafe to count upon an uninterrupted hour.
But on the other hand he might for hours and days together be as
idle as he pleased; from which it may be inferred that the Agency
was not the sole occupation of Dr. Rackstraw. And this was the
truth : for he had a really distinguished name as a promoter of
philanthropic enterprise in the interest of commerce, or rather
of commerce in the interest of philanthropy and civilisation. He
had a really marvellous instinct for discovering old nooks and
corners of the globe where a stroke of business could be done in
beads, or damaged prints, or old rifles—the stroke might merely
be a flash, but it would now and then take a firm hold, and then
the Doctor undertook the supply of true civilisation at large.
Socially, his pursuit had a magnificent ring, and as nobody knew
much of the Goblin Islands, nobody dared to confess to ignorance
on a subject which regarded the extent and integrity of this great
empire. There are greater colonies about which quite as little is
generally known—this island has so much to remember that she
may be forgiven for not being very ready to worry herself over
her great-great-grandchildren, who are always astonishing her by
having grown so tall.

It happened, however, that, on the day following Oswald's visit
to Sophy, the Agent-General was at his proper office: not only so,

but he had business there. His visitor was a respectable elderly man dressed in black, and wearing gilt spectacles, who was addressing him earnestly.

"No, Mister," he was saying, "you do *not* play fair. And them that don't play fair have no call to complain if others act according. That's my moral, and that's the way of the world."

"Nonsense, Moldwarp," said Dr. Rackstraw. "Just have done with your 'instinc'' for once, and listen to reason. You did me a service. I don't deny it was a big one. I paid you for it—and you can't deny I paid you a big price for a big thing——"

"Precious big—when in six months I had to be back at the flint trade again for bread and cheese!"

"I could find you the capital, Moldwarp, but I couldn't find you the qualities of industry, prudence, thrift, and sobriety. If you squandered what you had, what was that to me? And you forget. When you made the flint trade, as you call the forgery of antiquities, too hot to hold you, who was it that set you up in the old book trade, where your qualities so eminently fitted you to succeed? You are ungrateful, Moldwarp. That's what you are."

"Gratitude's all very well in its place, but it's not business. I can manufacture anything that's wanted—no man better, from an old MS. to a tenpenny nail. But my best customer's in his coffin and his effects are being overhauled: and I must make a new start, if it's only as a professor of leger-de-main. There's apparitions to be paid for, and bills."

"Well?"

"Well! That's a queer word for you to say!"

"Indeed? Why?"

"Because I don't see any call for make-believing 'twixt you and I. My instinc's to go straight wherever it may be. You just take a word in season, Mister. I gave it you once, and now I'll give it you again."

"Gammon, Moldwarp. You mean that cock-and-bull story about young Derwent being still somewhere in the world? What then?"

"What then! Why, it gives me the choice of a market—that's all. In the world! He's in England. He's in London. And if I like, I can lay my hand upon him in an hour. What you say to that, Mister—eh?"

"Silver Moldwarp. You are the cleverest rascal I ever knew.

14

Uneducated, you can puzzle a savant: and you can find whatever
you please to hide. But I'm not a savant, Silver Moldwarp. I'm
a practical man. If you take Lawrence Derwent into my confidence, he will simply find himself back again in Lowmoor, and
you will follow him. Do you suppose I couldn't prove up to the
hilt that you have been perpetrating a system of the grossest
frauds on my poor friend, Æneas Fane ? And, if that were not
enough—But never mind that. You will have to find a jury that will
believe a professional forger on his oath against my word. . . .
Simply, I can't be troubled with you any more. Why should I ?
Lawrence Derwent is a convicted felon, you are a notorious
rascal, and there's not a particle of evidence that Colonel Derwent
ever dreamed of a second will."

"Then you chuck me over like a rotten egg, Mr. Rackstraw ? "

"Bless the man! Does he think I employ a rascal to do dirty
work without reserving the power of chucking him over whenever
I please ? "

" I thought you said *I* was the cleverest rascal going—Eh ? "

" Of course I did : for you are——"

"Aye—and it's true, too: though there's ignorant folks might
be disposed to bar one. Ah, ingratitude—it's a wicked, shabby
thing. Well: give me natural instinc', after all. Instinc' !——"

"Take my advice, Moldwarp. Don't drink. Don't gamble.
Don't try to spend two pennies out of one. And then you'll find
rascality pay—and not till then. What's the good of being a
rascal, if you can't do better than an honest man ? And even at
the best, honesty pays best in the long run. Take pattern by me
—once poorer than you : I the dunce and you the genius."

" And you've beat genius by honesty ? And you call it honest
to suppress a dead man's last will ? "

"No, I do not, Silver Moldwarp. I never did such a thing.
since I was born."

" And who did then ? I should like to know."

" The world says it was Lawrence Derwent. I say it was *you.*
There—let it be which you please."

" Then all I can say is," cried the unfortunate bookseller, " give
me Instinc' before Honesty—that's all ! "

"Come in ! " cried Dr. Rackstraw, taking no notice of this outburst, in answer to a tap at the door.

" Mr. Hargrave, sir," said the smart boy.

"There—be off with you, Moldwarp," said Dr. Rackstraw, brusquely. "I'm always glad to see you; but business before pleasure, don't you know. Well, Mr. Hargrave—so you think of becoming a Goblin? If so, you are wise. But—why do you know one another, you two?"

"And do *you* know one another?" asked Oswald, face to face with Moldwarp, just within the doorway. "The world is small indeed." He was gaining time for thought how to act and what to say, for he could not help feeling that this accidental meeting might prove one of those chances which, once lost, never occur again. He was aware of Rackstraw's close connection with the Derwents: he had the best of reasons for knowing Moldwarp to be a rogue; and it required no detective skill to put together the fragments of a talk in the book-shop with the visit of the known rogue on a small scale to the suspected swindler on a large one. Suddenly there flashed into his mind a sentence which so struck to the centre of the matter that he could not tell whether it was an inspiration or a recollection—"Whate'er you'd learn, affect to know it all."

"No," said he. "Though I came on business, too—you were talking, I suppose, about the convict Lawrence Derwent, who escaped from Lowmoor. Am I wrong? It was about him I came."

As he spoke, he watched his friends. Moldwarp started, and looked hard at him: Dr. Rackstraw started, and glanced sharply at the door, as if to make sure that, though walls have ears, doors have no tongues.

"And what the devil made you think *that*, sir?" exclaimed he. "So you are a friend of Mr. Silver Moldwarp, eh? Then perhaps your friend will kindly tell you what I have said to him——"

"I suppose," said Oswald, quietly, "that you, as a friend of the family, would care to know where Lawrence Derwent is to be found—that's all."

"Oh! then I don't—and *that's* all. It seems to me, Mr. Hargrave, that you are rather fond of interfering in other people's concerns. No. I don't want to know what has become of a convicted felon. Nobody wants to know. I have had enough of this. If you don't come about land—I am busy. Perhaps you will allow me to wish you good-day."

"The man is a bully because he has something to hide," thought ald. I think I shall know how to deal with him. . . .

Good-day, then," said he. "Here is my card, if you wish to know anything after all." He made way for Moldwarp to pass before him, and then followed him downstairs. His intention was to keep the bookseller in sight, feeling sure that his pursuit would now lead him to the man he sought fairly straight and soon. But, as soon as he reached the street, Moldwarp turned round and faced him.

"I'm not fond of the sight of you, Mr. Hargrave," said he. "But I'll say for you that *you're* not one of them that tells lies. Do you know where this Lawrence Derwent is—aye or no?"

Oswald shrugged his shoulders. "It is no concern of yours," said he, and passed on, intending to turn and follow as soon as he could do so unobserved.

"No concern of mine, eh?" muttered Moldwarp. "Then I'll just be even with the three of ye!" And, waiting till the other was a convenient distance in advance, he sauntered out of Mildew Court and followed Oswald.

CHAPTER XXIII.

Round somewhere rolls the sun's red ball,
    The frozen poles sway round the sun:
Dame Earth spins round her poles, while all
    Round Her we mortals run.

So maze-wise whirls the race of feet,
    Of orbs, souls, planets, I, and You—
The marvel's not we never meet,
    But how we ever do.

OSWALD HARGRAVE thought that Silver Moldwarp would lead him to Lawrence Derwent.

Silver Moldwarp was sure that Oswald Hargrave would lead him circuitously to Lawrence Derwent.

The straight man believed that the crooked man would lead straight: the crooked man, that the straight man would lead crooked. But this was the only difference between them. Each believed himself to be tracking the other: and neither could guess that the other was tracking him.

Such misunderstandings happen often enough where, with the world for their hunting-ground, two lives go chasing one another up and down, and do not meet only because neither of them stands still. But when the game is played, in the most bald and matter-of-fact manner, in the streets of London, it must needs grow bewildering. Consider the problem. Oswald goes in advance, meaning to turn round presently and follow Moldwarp. But Moldwarp is following *him*. And so they are to all intents and purposes moving in a circle, wherein as a child may see, to speak of leading and following reduces the problem *ad absurdum*.

For Moldwarp of course it was the plainest sailing, because to all appearance Oswald was the guide, and he could not guess that the seeming guide was only shamming. But Oswald soon grew puzzled. He passed two or three turnings—there are any number of them in that part of London—and sauntered down the next. The chances were that Moldwarp would pass it: and he could then retrace his steps and put himself behind his pursuer. But Moldwarp took the same turning, too, still following.

That might, however, be accidental, his taking the identical turning down which Moldwarp had intended to go. However, the next experiment of the same kind could hardly fail. So he repeated the stratagem—only to find, on turning his head just enough to confirm the suspicion of his ears, that the other was after him still.

However, the theory of coincidence is not exhausted by two cases. Oswald tried a third, this time plunging into a court which forbade the idea of its being chosen without a motive. So quickly and so suddenly did he contrive to disappear, aided by the intervention of some men loading a cart between him and his pursuer, that this time Moldwarp actually shot past the entrance to the court, imagining that his guide was holding straight on. Oswald emerged again, at last having reversed the order. But presently Moldwarp began to waver, and then stopped.

Thought Oswald, " Has he lost himself or his way ? "

And it seemed as if he were right: for Moldwarp, after looking to the right and to the left, before and behind, up and down, retraced his steps and came back to the entrance of the court again. Moldwarp passed him so closely that the two men might almost have touched, had they pleased. Oswald counted ten, very slowly, and then stepped out of the dark entrance to follow once more.

" If he guessed I was following, and was trying to baffle me he has lost me at last," thought he. However, he took the precaution of crossing the street, so that his pursuing footsteps might tell no more tales.

But suddenly Moldwarp vanished : and was seen no more.

It was not down a turning : for just at that point there was none. Nor was it into air, for the man had no wings, nor under the earth, for his time was not yet come. Oswald could only clench his teeth, and his fists at having been so completely balked by this eel in gold spectacles. "He *did* know I was following him, confound him!" he swore, in somewhat stronger language, half aloud. "I'm no use at this sort of game. At this, only? No— at none: *I*, to think I can track the ghost of a girl over the world when I let a substantial knave like that vanish before my very eyes. Aye, and let him know that he has tricked me—that a common rogue like this should know what I would give the rest of my life to know, and that I cannot lay hands on him except to strangle the secret with the man. . . . I suppose I am beaten, now: beaten and shamed. I may as well go back and hoe my turnips: or if I find I'm not fit even for that, take to shying stones into the sea. Anyhow, that will be more useful than shying myself into Nowhere. Poor Sophy, though—we mustn't part bad friends. After all, it's not for me to see motes in eyes—a girl has a right to be foolish : but what business has a man to fail ? "

He walked on slowly till he found a cab: and then desperate at last of ever learning, much less of avenging, Rosamond's mysterious fate, he had himself driven straight to the very house in which she was dwelling, and where he had left her not much more than an hour ago. If he had only known—but If is If : that history whereto all the chronicles of all the ages are less than a grain of sand. Think of all that never has been, is not, cannot be, and never will be : what, beside such a boundless ocean, is all the history of the earth, past, present, and to come, but less than a grain of sand? Yet If contains it all—and more. Chaos itself was a universal If—Light the transmutation of If I be into I am.

It seemed as if Silver Moldwarp, on the contrary, had been transmuted from a very real I am into something less than If I be. But it was not so. As fully persuaded as Oswald that his attempt to follow had been discovered and that the other's leading was a deliberate misleading, he effaced himself by the simple means of vanishing, not into nothingness, but only into the warehouse in front of which the cart was loading. Why did not Oswald guess such an obvious cause for vanishing? As to that— *Tu quoque.* You, who ask the question, also saw those men and that warehouse but a minute ago, and had a better chance to remember it than a man whose whole life had been a training in the art of looking a long way off for things that lay close at hand. Besides, from his point of view, Moldwarp had no reason for such a method of disappearing; and it is not so easy to know what happens in the quietest of back streets unless one is told. Try your best to keep your eye upon any chosen passenger in any thoroughfare: and if he does not in ten minutes vanish in the manner of Moldwarp, you are a born detective, and should instantly apply for a place in Scotland Yard.

For such a place Silver Moldwarp should have applied: for, instead of falling out of the chase, he left the warehouse with a hasty apology for having intruded by mistake, and was in time to see Oswald hail the cab, though strain his ears as he might, he could not catch the address given to the driver. "Hanged if *I* aren't done!" thought he. But fortune favoured him: and before the cab was out of the street, another came into sight empty. "Follow that," said Moldwarp: "he knows where to go."

It was all plain sailing now: and Moldwarp had every reason to believe that he was being conducted straight to the man of whose whereabouts his guide knew as little as he. Or if not straight at any rate by a road that would lead to Lawrence Derwent in time. For in one thing the manufacturer of antiquities was no impostor. He had an honest, genuine faith in his own Instinct, which was his more modest word for genius: and, though he now and then took the name of Instinct in vain, it was always for cause, and not because he in the least confounded it with reason which he honestly despised, though he did not know it by name. It was instinct, he would have said, that led him to the conclusion, at first sight, that Æneas Fane was a bundle of golden feathers made for nimble fingers to pluck till not one remained. Instinct, in the matter of books or pebbles, had enabled those nimble fingers of his to work out hints that he had not learning enough to understand. Instinct, he would have said again, told him that a man like Oswald would not be engaged in trying to dodge and baffle him about the streets except to keep him from finding something or somebody that he wished to find and the other to conceal. Of course there was a dash of reason in this as there must be in all operations of even the least imperfect specimens of the human mind: but still there was little of the dash as might be: and only Instinct, barely diluted, could have told him that wherever Lawrence Derwent was to the knowledge of Oswald, there Oswald himself would be in no long time.

"Don't I mind how he tried to hunt the poor beggar down!" thought he, in his half audible way, as he drove along. "And all because he had been in gaol for breaking a law. If 'twas for breaking his own head, 'twould be cause enough: but what's a law? Even if 'tis broken, 'tis no more damaged than if you'd broke a stream of water out of a tap—on it goes. Young Hargrave's a bull-dog, and no mistake—wanting to get a poor devil that never hurt him nor his Lowmoor'd again after all these years. But fancy his going to old Rackstraw to join him in thief-catching—as a family matter! That's a game and a half—Never mind: 'twas a good instinc', that he came when I was by. Holloa— I suppose we're there. . . . Stop, I say! I'll get down here."

He had seen, from the window, the first cab stop at a certain door in a certain street in a very different neighbourhood from that in which the chase had begun. Moldwarp, while several doors behind, stopped the cab, and got out heavily and slowly, so as to give Oswald time to knock and enter before he exposed himself again to the public view. Oswald once within the house, he strolled towards the door to note the number. He had reached the first of its area railings, when the door opened, and a gentleman—not Oswald—emerged therefrom, came face to face with him for a moment, stared at him mechanically, and passed on: a tall, large built man, with a great brown beard.

"Now bless my mortal soul!" gasped Moldwarp. "Instinc"s an awful thing! That's the man!"

Instinct—if Silver Moldwarp was right now—had been justified indeed of her favourite child. He had followed Oswald, believing that Oswald knew. Oswald did not know: and yet he had led more straightly than he could have gone even if he had known. It was as if a lost wanderer had been guided by Will o' the Wisp straight home.

Moldwarp turned and brought himself abreast with the man from Nevada.

"Pardon, sir," said he. "Might I say a word?"

The rule for prudent conduct in the streets of London has been laid down thus—walk quick: and if anybody speaks to you, knock him down. There was, however, no apparent reason for committing sudden battery upon this elderly person in gold spectacles: and the man from Nevada, though he did not slacken his stride, only answered, in his most exotic twang,

"This is a free country, sir. Twenty if you please. Only to save time, don't ask for money——"

"Oh no, sir! I'm not one o' them sort. Silver Moldwarp's *my* name."

"Oh, a capital name, *too*—the first particularly."

"And I think we have a mutual friend—Rackstraw by name."

"Eh?"

"Hermon Rackstraw."

"I thank you, sir," said the man from Nevada, stiffly, with his twang intensified. "You wish to speak on some matter of business, I con—clude?"

"Yes, Mr. Lawrence Derwent, I do."

"I am afraid you are under some mistake," said the man from Nevada. "I am acquainted with Mr. Rackstraw: but my name is Harding: not—what name did you say?"

For a moment his coolness staggered Moldwarp. But—

"Lawrence Derwent is the name I said," said he. "And Lawrence Derwent is the name I say. Lawrence Derwent that was in Lowmoor goal for felony, and escaped nigh a dozen years ago."

"Oh—you are a detective, I suppose? All I can say is that I'm very sorry you've been wasting valuable time. Well—you're only doing your duty: and it doesn't matter. I'm in no sort of hurry. It will amuse me to prove that I am not an escaped convict, and I shall learn something about your police system over here. So, Mr. Moldwarp, till you learn your error, I am entirely in your hands."

"My Eye, Mister—but you *are* cool! If I didn't put faith in instinc'—But I do. You're Lawrence Derwent, out of Lowmoor: ten or twelve years older, and grown a beard. And bless you, if I was to hold up my hand to that peeler over there, into Lowmoor you'd be again. I'm no detective—I'm not one of them sort, not I."

"Policeman!" called the man from Nevada: not loudly, but quite loud enough to be heard. "Make this man scarce—he is annoying me. He insists upon it that I am somebody else—drunk, I suppose. Here is my card"—and he held out a half-crown.

"Come, sir," said the constable, "this won't do you know—

annoying a gentleman in this sort of way. You can go on, sir : I'll see to the other gent——"

"Now if here isn't a fuss over a mistake!" said Moldwarp. "I was only telling this gent that there were some friends asking after him he'd be pleased to meet, and have heard he's back from foreign parts—and he cuts up as rough as a bear. You mind your beat, my man, and let a pair of old friends have out their bit of a breeze in their own way."

The constable smiled, shook his head, and passed on, seeing no cause to interfere, in what seemed to be the mildest and most meaningless quarrel between respectable people in which he had ever been professionally engaged. He looked back once or twice, on the chance of a second summons : but only saw the two gentlemen walking side by side.

"I'd advise you not to do that again, Mr. Derwent," said Moldwarp, "that's all."

"Do what again? Show an intrusive blockhead who threatens me with the police that I mean to look to them for protection? Be off, whoever you are : or the next constable we meet shall take me on the charge of thrashing a blundering, meddlesome fellow whom I don't know from Adam half as much as he deserves."

"Eh—thrash *me?* You've done that, Squire : and once is enough o' that : my bones have been the same, to this day. As if I forget *you!* Lord, if I don't feel your knuckles in my wind-pipe still. Have you forgot Pix-Knoll, Crossmarsh, by Low-moor? Then so haven't I! Ah, you're older—and you're bigger —and you're hairier. But I go by the Eyes. Look into a man's eyes as I've looked into yours, and you'll never forget him. There's no two men's eyes alike : and they never change, don't eyes : leastwise the something in 'em don't, that differs man from man . . . . Ah, and I know you're here : and old Rackstraw knows you're here : and young Oswald Hargrave knows you're here : and here's the only friend you've got going to be thrashed for his pains . . . . Well, there. I scorn malice : it don't pay . . . . So what'll you stand if I put you up to doing old Rack-straw an ill-turn?"

The man from Nevada strode on in silence for one moment —no more. Then he said :

"Well, one mustn't be angry with a mistake. It's not very flattering to be mistaken for an escaped convict—however, out where I come from, I've known ex-gaolbirds who were very decent fellows indeed. It's a bit of an adventure : and adventures aren't too common in this dead-alive old London of yours not to be welcome. You're quite sure my name's Derwent, eh ? "

" Lawrence Derwent. Sure ? So are you."

" You've got pluck, old . gentleman, to recognise a man who would prefer to keep dark, I con—clude. Is he a desperate character—this Lawrence Derwent of yours ? Now look here, old gentleman. All this amuses me. I'm going to test your faith. You say your friend Derwent, who nearly throttled you, would like to do old Rackstraw an ill turn. I'm Harding, Rackstraw's friend, bound to report to him any plots I hear against his pocket, person, or good name. But if you have faith in your fancy more than in my word, you'll risk that, and tell me what bad turn you want to give me something to do."

" All right ! You tell me what Lawrence Derwent would give to know that old Rackstraw ought to be in Lowmoor instead of he ? The ungrateful old varmin——"

" I don't know. But I know I'd give five hundred dollars— a hundred pounds any day, to see the apostle of Christian civilisation on the wheel. He'd know what civilisation means then. By old Harry, 'twould be as good as a play."

" Now you tell me what Lawrence Derwent would give to the man whose instinc' tells him where to lay hand on the will old Rackstraw swore he never witnessed—eh ? "

" Good God! " exclaimed the man from Nevada, in a deep, full, English voice, suddenly stopping and facing the other full. " Speak out man—if this is a trap——"

" You've hit it now, Master Lawrence. Trap's the word," said the fox to the lion. " I've got you under my thumb—Instinc's a grand thing ! Because, you see, if you don't come down what's fitting, into gaol you go, and what I've said of a will have been but a bit of a lie like what any honest man may use to catch a thief : and there you are."

" I see. Then let me tell you, to begin with, that I am safer from gaol than you," said the man from Nevada, recovering his drawl. " All this was beginning to amuse me : but the best of comedies won't stand being too long. All the same I should like to hear the end of the story. I've a bit of business first : perhaps you won't mind coming round with me while I do it, and

then we can go somewhere and have the rest out comfortably
by ourselves ? "

" Mind. Not I. I mean sticking by you, governor, till this
job's done."

" You're not afraid of trusting yourself alone in a cab with an
escaped convict, who would probably prefer taking your life to
losing his own liberty, and maybe knows how ?   You say I
strangled you once before.   Are you game to run the risk
again ? "

" Oh, I aren't afraid this time.   If you strangle me, you'll
strangle what you'd be sorry for, if you ever came to know."

" So far so good then.   Hansom—Mildew Court, City.   In
with you, old gentleman.   Time's money you know."

" Mildew Court ! " stammered Moldwarp, for once taken aback,
and amazed.

" Why not ?   Now hold your tongue, please.   I can't talk in
cabs: and I've got a bit of business on my mind."

They reached Mildew Court: and the man from Nevada,
having dismissed the cab, went straight for the staircase of
the Agency General of the Goblin Islands.   Nor only so ;   he
went to the very landing of the same company, and knocked at
their very door.

" Bless your soul alive, man! " exclaimed Moldwarp, clutching
at his companion's arm while the knocker, having once fallen, was
in mid air—" Do you know who hangs out *here ?* "

" Is Dr. Rackstraw within ? "

Dr. Rackstraw was within ; and Moldwarp, cowed by such
courage into doubting even his own instinct, followed the man
from Nevada into the inner room.   Dr. Rackstraw, who was
engaged at his desk, unfolded his long legs and rose : seeing Moldwarp again, he stared.

" I've come to trouble you on a queer business, Doctor," said
the man from Nevada.   " But I won't apologise for bothering an
Apostle—I should say a—a—you know what I mean—of civilisation till I've done.   I am haunted by an elderly gentleman, who
claims acquaintance with you, and insists upon it that I am an
escaped convict from one of your gaols.   Will you kindly identify
me ?   For he talks of the police, and I don't know what all :
which is worrying to a quiet stranger.   Do tell this elderly person that he's an ass, and get him to go."

, Dr. Rackstraw spent a moment in transferring his attention to his visitors from the papers before him. "Mr. Harding—of Nevada?" said he. "An escaped convict, indeed! So this fellow has been bothering you, too, has he, as well as me? Yes: he has got a craze that an unfortunate relative of some dear friends of mine, who got himself into trouble, and whose sentence is not expired, is now in London, and at large. As if a convict who had once escaped, would be such a fool!"

"Of course he wouldn't—it would be going into the lion's den. Only I should like you to say whether there is much likeness between me and your friend's unfortunate relative—because if there is, it may be awkward you see. I knew a case where Judge Lynch hanged a man because he resembled a murderer in having a broken nose. Did you know the unfortunate relative well?" asked the man from Nevada, bringing his face into the strongest light he could find, while Moldwarp felt his faith in Instinct fading away—or rather being shattered under a crushing blow.

"A prince of the silver mines like a felon!" said Dr. Rackstraw: "Impossible—as soon would a civilised manufacturer, the heir of all the ages, resemble a savage whose custom he has not yet obtained. As soon——"

"There is *no* likeness then? None at all?"

"No. Not a ghost. None. As a skilled physiognomist—which as a student of ethnology I am bound to be—I assert there is none. . . . Moldwarp!" said he, "I told you this very afternoon that it is nothing to me, nothing whether Lawrence Derwent is dead or alive. I then thought you a rascal—now I can only, in charity, suppose you to be insane. You have Lawrence Derwent on the brain. Mr. Harding agrees with me that you are insane. Mr. Harding—if this uncivilised monomaniac annoys you again, I trust you will communicate with Me."

"Then," exclaimed Silver Moldwarp, "then all I say is—Damn instinc' for a liar and a fool!"

He was crawling out of the court with his tail between his legs, when he felt a heavy hand on his shoulder.

"I *am* Lawrence Derwent," said the man from Nevada. "The way to test if a thing is a trap is to walk in and see— Come in here. We'll have a quiet drink, and you shall say what you please. I suppose you're some worn out tool of Rackstraw's? Never mind, old gentleman. An ill tool's best for an ill turn."

CHAPTER XXIV.

The rarest weed that ever a wight
In ever a hedge might look to see ?
I cannot mind its name aright,
But I think they call it Honesty.
Yet some do name it Old Man's Beard,
And Virgin's Bower to some 'twill be:
And so by a-many names, I'm feared,
Is called what's called—is it Honesty ?
For as many as they that live by land,
And as many as they that sail the sea,
So few be the folk that will fail to stand
To a lie, for the sake of—Honesty.

THUS only two persons recognised Rosamond's nightmare —one by his voice, the other by his eyes.

" You wouldn't think it," began the fox to the lion, as soon as they were alone in that most complete of solitudes, a city cellar where men hurried in and out, and used their lips and their tongues, but never their eyes or ears ; " you wouldn't think it, but me and old Rackstraw was schoolmates together, once on a

" Indeed I would though," said Lawrence Derwent. "And I wouldn't send a son of mine to that school."

" And I were top-boy in grammar. But Rackstraw were bottom all round. And now, there be him, and here be I."

"Well ? I follow you so far. You called top what is called bottom in our schools. Well ? I suppose it isn't for murdering the Queen's English you want me to pay you for putting old Rackstraw in gaol ? "

" Wait a bit, Mister. I've got to tell my tale my own way ; and 'tis never the short cut that brings one first home.   'Twas an old country grammar school, where the head master was eighty-three years old, and stone blind, and the second was deaf, and eighty-four.   Rackstraw and me were the boys. There aren't no such schools now. So I used to spend the time practising conjuring and such like, and Rackstraw, he used to look on : and when the deaf master was keeping school, I used to study the violin."

" Well, Mister, when I done with education, I got into a scrape in our village, about a girl me and Rackstraw was both after : so I went into a booth that went round the fairs, and never clapped eyes on either of 'em for years.   When I did, 'twas at Halehurst, where Longwood's hard by."

" We're getting nearer. Well ?·"

" I was pretty low down and hard up, that day. In fact, I'd been sleeping under a haystack, and was trying to fiddle up a few coppers to get a bite of food. And as I was fiddling to the stones in the street—round things, and worse for naked feet than knives —who should come by, a-horseback, but old Rackstraw : and not like a beggar, neither, for he was dressed like you or me. And there was a young gentleman with him that was Lawrence Derwent by name, son and heir to Colonel Derwent of Longwood, as I came to know."

" Yes ; I remember once seeing in the High Street of Hale-hurst, the raggedest of fiddlers making his fiddle croak like a raven of ill omen, as I rode with that scoundrel to the house where my father lay dying. So it was you, who gave me that only wel-come home . . . . Well ? "

" You *were* in a hurry : but old Rackstraw knew me : for he nodded, and chucked me a sovereign. I thought at first 'twas a farthing, I hadn't seen one so long. I stared : for chucking sovereigns about, that was never old Rackstraw's way. Guess if instinc' didn't lead me into the first public near. I astonished the yokels a bit, with some tricks and tunes, and got the talk on Rackstraw—— "

" And I'll tell you what you ought to have heard. That my father had given me a stepmother. That Rackstraw, who had travelled with them from India, got hold of my stepmother, with his missionary jargon, and that between them they set my own father against his own son—even to getting him to make a will that left Rackstraw a small fortune, and put my young half brother Horace into the place of the heir. Is that what you heard ? "

" Somewhat like : but mostly that the heir, Mr. Lawrence, was a bad lot, and was bringing the old Colonel's grey hairs with sorrow to the grave. Never mind, Mister, I've been a bit wild myself, before I turned archæologer. I don't think a bit the worse of you for that ; not I."

Within the last few moments the whole manner, voice, it may almost be said the features, of Lawrence Derwent had undergone a change. Hitherto, it could only be by a marvellous effort of systematic self-control that the passionate and masterful lover of Queen Rosamond had, all in a moment, become the keen and bold fencer with Moldwarp and Rackstraw. Now, convinced that he might for once throw off his long disguise, he stretched himself out, morally speaking, with an infinite sense of relief, saddened, and for the moment softened by the memories of what had been before he became a hunted man. He had not heard his father named since he had been convicted of robbing his father's death-bed; Moldwarp's words were beginning to fall on wandering ears. Rosamond had only flashed across evil days : with his trained faculty for shifting almost at will from mood to mood, he could lay even her aside.

"Mister," said Moldwarp, "don't put your face a dozen years like that afore old Rackstraw. He'd *know* you now ! "

"Go on with your story," said Lawrence sharply. "Never mind my face. Get to the trial—when I was found guilty of— guilty, when, Rackstraw's lies and plots against me being exposed, my father sent for me and forgave me, nay, begged *my* forgiveness, and bade me, with my own hands, and before his dying eyes, destroy the will he had been induced to make by slander and lies——"

"So that you was left heir-at-law. Now, Mr. Lawrence, what did you do next after you, by the old Colonel's orders, burnt that there will ? "

"Rode into Halehurst for the doctor, as hard as I could go."

"And when you got back to Longwood—"

"My father had died. . . . Man, if you have nothing to say but all this thrice thrashed out stuff, why do you bring me here ? Can I send Rackstraw to the treadmill for lies ? "

"Well, Mister, you was a goodish time gone : for I was about the place—I'd took to run errands for old ¦Rackstraw ; and he sent for me : looking as pale and white as a ghost : and 'Moldwarp, my man,' says he, ' you're wanted to witness the Colonel's will. He's making one himself out of his own head, and I'm helping of him to write it down. And be quick, for the rattle's ᶴ coming on.'"

"What—another will ? When I was gone ? Go on, for God's sake——"

"True enough, there sat up the Colonel in bed, with paper before him and a pen in his hand. Going, but sensible. Nobody else in the room but Rackstraw and me. He signed: and then Rackstraw put his ugly name for witness : and then I put mine. Then Rackstraw sent me off to call the wife and childer to see the last gasp: but before they could get to the room, the old Colonel was gone. And it's my belief, Mister, old Rackstraw took care of that : it don't take much of a throttle to polish off a dying man : and them that's dying can tell tales, while them that's dead tell none."

"Now, by——"

"Don't get excited, Mister; leastways not here. That will said how the old one was revoked : and how you was to be heir to everything, money and land: and left something to the others and to old Rackstraw not a hang."

" And Rackstraw swore that the first will was the last made ? But a murderer—why should he strain at false witness? And you—*you*, knowing this, let a murderer swear away my liberty, my more than life—mine ? "

" A man must live, Mister. There had to be two witnesses— so Rackstraw chose *me*. I aren't ashamed. He knew if there's one thing I'm not capable for, it's being ungrateful—and to a old schoolmate, and all. One of you had to be lugged, you see. Why shouldn't it be you? If 1 hadn't been second witness, 'twould have been him."

" True. Moldwarp—How is it you know the contents of that second will ? "

" Because I read it. Because, being light fingered by trade, I took it out of old Rackstraw's pocket, and put in another as like outside as two peas, for him to burn."

"What!" cried Lawrence Derwent, forgetting where he was and trembling all over. " You have that will—now ? "

"Maybe no. Maybe aye. I want to do what's right, and I want to punish ingratitude. If, being a gentleman, you behave like one, the will's your own. If, not being a gentleman, you don't, why, 'tis but instinc' to act according. Old Rackstraw might turn grateful again if I told him what I told you."

" No, no! I am rich enough to buy back my rights twenty times. Do you suppose I came back to England for the pleasure of putting my head into a lion's den ? I came back to find means of ruining those who had ruined me : and it would not have proved hard to ruin a greedy adventurer and a fool of a boy. I am rich enough to ruin fifty Horace Derwents, and a hundred Hermon Rackstraws. But now—if you have told me the one good grain of truth in a bushel of lies—when that will is in my hands, Silver Moldwarp, you shall receive—let me see

15

Ten thousand pounds. That's high enough, I suppose, to make sure of you ? "

"Ten thousand!—Well, yes, Mr. Lawrence: I might manage to make it do—if I could make sure——"

"No Ifs, Mr. Moldwarp. And wait a bit: We must see how we stand. Suppose—suppose I produce this will, and Rackstraw and my half brother contest it as a forgery: you're clever at such things, you know. How then ? "

" Then I shall have to prove it aren't one—that's all."

"And in what position shall *you* be ? "

" Me ! What need I do but pocket your bit of gratitude, which is a thing I like to see? All you've got to do, seeing you've got to be so rich, is to buy a certain house that's just got into the market. I didn't like to carry a document like that about me, for fear of accidents; and owing to a misfortune, I hadn't the chance to bring it away when I had to leave. Nor for that matter was it any good to me while Rackstraw kept grateful and you was not to be found, or dead may be. I stowed it there because 'twas the last place where 'twould be looked for, the people of the house not knowing so much as how there were Derwents in the world. You buy that house, and when you've got settled, some morning you'll get a homonymous letter, telling you what corner's worth your looking to. Then you'll advertise for one Silver Moldwarp; and I shall answer it, and give all my evidence as innocent as a bird—all that's needful. Being witness of a will's no crime . . . . and after getting the will, and before me giving evidence, you can hand over that ten——"

" If I get my foot on old Rackstraw, we sha'n't quarrel about terms. By God, I'd give all the silver in Nevada to be master of Longwood, and of my rights, for a day. Moldwarp, you're not a man I'd trust alone with half a crown. But I'm going to trust you in this, because I believe that for ten thousand pounds you'd sell your soul; and I run no risk, whether this is trumps or no. What's the house I'm to buy ? "

" Crossmarsh. *You* know the neighbourhood, Mr. Lawrence— 'tis by Lowmoor. Belonged to an old deceased customer of mine, named Fane."

" Crossmarsh—Fane ! And my father's will is hidden *there ?* "

CHAPTER XXV.

Only a woman's whim—only the gleam
Of that faint lightning in an August sky,
Too subtle and too swift to question whence
It comes, or whither goes, or what portends:
Only the meteor—Nature's seeming whim,
But born of Law too deep for reason's reach:
Only the outcome of an inner life,
As when we dream the breath of flowers unknown:
Only the discord but for which the flow
Of song were else too passing sweet and smooth—
These are the voices of a secret soul
Where memories, hopes, and wonders blend and pant
For freedom and for language, still in vain.
And so we say, we who behold the sign
But not the soul—only a random note,
Only a worthless, idle, woman's whim.

HER discovery, in the voice of her friend Harding of Nevada. of the being, seemingly human, who had thrown her whole life into magical confusion, filled Rosamond with a vague terror. She recalled, with a shudder, the gospel of her people, that Apahu alone was the world of men and women, and that the ocean was visible death that parted them from the infinite abode of angels, demons, and disembodied souls. She had never realised till now how penetrated she had become with the atmosphere wherein she had grown a woman and had ceased to be a child. She remembered, with a trembling of the heart, how this seeming man had been able to become visible and invisible at will; how he had been able to read her thoughts; how he transformed her from an English country girl into a Barbarian Queen, so to speak, with a wave of his hand. Could it be that every human soul has a spirit ruler over its birth, its life, and its death : that this being was hers: that her recollection of her far-off girlhood was the reminiscence of a world where one lives before one is born: that her passage into Apahu, through fever and storm, was her true mortal birth ; and that her return to England was in truth (as her priest had taught her) the sacrilegious intrusion by a living soul before its time into the world beyond the ocean and the grave—that her spirit Lord was there waiting to receive her, and to claim his own?

And then she was hopelessly alone. There was none whom she could take into her confidence ; and her social experiences made her shrink from the talk that would follow were she to tell to strangers' ears a tale of adventure in which indeed she could not fairly expect any human being to believe. Her history had become herself, which she recoiled from the thought of laying bare. And

15 A

then the more she saw of England, the more she doubted the prudence of exporting its wisdom and its virtues to a land that was
already as wise as the fowls of the air and the lilics of the field.
She herself had ceased to be a wonder of the season, having long
ago fulfilled her nine days, and she shrank from calling fresh attention to herself in a new form.

If she could only meet her sister in this grim, grey, threatening
spirit world—then, indeed, might she cease to be homesick for the
Island of Apahu.

But of her old life, or, as it almost seemed now, of her old
dream, no trace had she yet found. First of all, her letter to
Sophy, addressed to Crossmarsh (for she dreaded to appear suddenly out of her grave) received no answer; and no wonder, seeing
that Sophy's latest address was some *Post Restante* abroad. Then,
dreading possible death or change, she had written to the firm of
solicitors who had transacted her uncle's business at the period of
his comparative sanity, signing herself as Senhora Miranda, and
enquiring if all was well at Crossmarsh, and, if not, what was ill.
For all answer, she learned that years ago Mr. Fane, of Crossmarsh,
had withdrawn his business and his papers from the firm, the
name of a firm in London being given to which she was referred:
that Mr. Fane and his niece were understood to be travelling on
the Continent, and that Crossmarsh was standing empty. The
second firm, being applied to, could only tell that they had transacted certain business for Mr. Fane, but retained none of his papers,
and could tell her nothing—with such subterranean cunning had
the lunatic trustee gone to work so that no one lawyer, or firm of
lawyers, might be in a position to control his breaches of trust, or
to interfere with the mad investment she was making for the
benefit of his country, his ward, and his craze. Oswald Hargrave,
with the best legal aid, had barely been able to trace them and
piece them together: no wonder that Rosamond, unaided, failed
—or at any rate had failed in twice the time.

A book will some day have to be written on the craft of madmen
—how it transcends that of a Moldwarp more than that of a Moldwarp transcends that of a Rackstraw, or of any other commoner,
and therefore more successful, rogue. For as a madman surpasses three sane men in strength, so he surpasses six sane men in
cunning; and when—as statistics tell us is to be--the mad come
to outnumber those who are otherwise, things will go hard for us
who consider ourselves sane. We outwit them by numbers, they

will then out<del>…</del> us by numbers, strength, craft, and all. Rosamond, remembering Unc'e Æneas as the sanest and wisest of men, lost the thread utterly: for her own adventures did not seem so marvellous, as that he and Sophy should have become wanderers over the face of the world.

At last, instead of at first (not having acquired the business sense in Apahu), she wrote to Oswald Hargrave. Her corespondence, on all sorts of uninteresting matters, wa3 large, and Dr. Rackstraw, being with her during some part of most days, often acted as her postman—more often than not, indeed, except in the case of those letters which concerned her old life, and which she had invariably posted with her own hands. But there was no more reason why she should not have a letter for a Hargrave, than for a Pitcairn, or a Rackstraw: he might be a missionary, or a spirit merchant, or a begging-letter writer, or a hundred other things.

But Dr. Rackstraw, assuming that a letter directed to Oswald Hargrave must needs have been written by Sophy, and not thinking it for the girl's advantage that she should be in correspondence with a bad adviser, forgot to post the letter: or rather he let it fall accidentally into the fire. And the accident gave him the keenest possible regret: because he might so easily have read it before burning. However, nobody can be always wise; even Hermon Rackstraw, being human, was bound to lapse into partial honesty now and then. Besides he was not a poor man, like Moldwarp, who cannot afford honesty unless he happen to find it a marketable commodity.

So Rosamond had no letter even from the man who loved her when she was a child: he had gone away too.

Then, getting rid both of her philosopher and of her secretary for the occasion, she asked Mr. Pitcairn, now in charge of a London parish, to take tea, ostensibly to consult him on certain theological difficulties: in reality to pump him about Crossmarsh, without appearing to have any purpose, or letting her hand appear —as every woman, however untaught, knows how to do. It was easy enough to get him to compare his experiences of an English country rectory with those which he had brought from the South Seas.

"If I was a young man again," said he, "I'd go out to *your* country. From what I can make out, they don't know right from wrong. Of course you'll take out a clergyman or two when you go? You might even get a bishop, if you go to the proper society and will guarantee the funds. Only mind he's one of the right sort—a tall man, with good broad shoulders who'll stand no non-sense and no back-sliding. Get the measure and girth of your biggest priest, and don't take a bishop who isn't half a head higher and six inches larger round : let him be broad church and high church too."

" I think you would make a good bishop, Mr. Pitcairn."

" So Mrs. Pitcairn says. But *nolo episcopari :* which means ' anything for a quiet life,' in the vulgar tongue. I'm sometimes sorry I left my quiet country parish for this London of ours : I had enough missionary work while I was young, and they won't allow conversion by battery here, though it's the only way."

" Ah, yes—I forgot : we were talking about your country parish —forgive me for interrupting you—and your neighbours, weren't we ? The Fanes. You were just telling me about them : and I was getting interested. What sort of people were the Fanes ? "

" Ah, poor people. Old Fane—Yes I liked old Fane. He had his whims, and was a bad listener ; but he was a good neighbour, and a gentleman every inch of him. He had a niece—a sad story. She drowned herself one night in a fit of brain fever. I remember it well, poor girl. Not that it wasn't for the best. She was one of those fantastical, dreamy things that are as like as not to go wrong, and are safe, any way, to lay hold of life by the wrong end."

" And the other ? " asked Rosamond, hastily. " What became of her ? "

"The other. Did I say there were two ? "

" I thought so——"

" No doubt, I did, then. There were two. Rosamond, I think —no : it was Rosamond that was drowned. I don't know any-thing about the other : haven't heard of her for years. I suppose she's still abroad : married most likely. It's the saddest part of life, the way one loses sight of one's old friends. It came on me like a shock, the other day, when I heard my old country neigh-bour, Fane, was gone."

" Gone ? What do you mean by—gone ? "

" Oh, it's only our English euphemism for Dead : and I like it best—Dead isn't a Christian word. Poor old Crossmarsh—it must be changed, without old Fane and without me."

Had Rosamond been less thunderstruck by a piece of news which everybody hears a hundred times and a hundred times again, as if it were always told for the first time, she must have betrayed herself. As it was, she made no attempt at concealment, and would have burst into frank, open tears had not her old acquaintance shown himself so much more freezing and repellant than an utter stranger—an indifferent and forgetful friend. It was that last "Me" which chilled her outburst and froze her tears. And indeed the blank feeling that of those whom she had come from the opposite end of the earth to seek one who had gone for ever was of itself inconsistent with any sudden burst of sorrow. The ache that such blows cause is dead and dull.

"When,"—she asked harshly and icily. "And where?"

"Oh, poor old fellow—I didn't hear when. Somewhere abroad, of course. He was always abroad. By the way, I think I can recommend you a capital young clergyman to take out as your court chaplain: he's a curate of my own—not much of a scholar, but with a biceps like a cannon ball, and not a fault except that he doesn't hit it off with Mrs. Pitcairn. Shall I tell him to call?"

So, for the present, ended Rosamond's coming home. What had been the use of it all—had she, by parting from her people, rebelled against Destiny and Providence? She had come back only to find all things changed: her guardian dead, her home empty, her friends lost or forgetful, her sister Heaven knew where. All things were so immutable in Apahu, and had been so immutable at Crossmarsh, that the laws of nature seemed to be outraged. Her faithful secretary saw no more of her for that day: nor her philosopher for two more. And, when he was at last admitted, he found the Queen dressed in mourning, such as Englishwomen wear for their nearest kin.

This philosopher of hers had made as yet but little progress in his love-making. He could not indeed complain of any lack of friendliness on the part of the girl whom he had succeeded in withdrawing from all her other associations, but he had succeeded only too well—Sophy had become as it were merely the echo and shadow of her mistress and queen. He seldom saw her alone, and, when he did, she avoided all his attempts to turn her talk upon herself and away from her heroine, so that, growing impatient, he began to detest the very name of the Senhora Miranda. His influence over Sophy, great as it assuredly had been,

and as ho had felt it to be, appeared to be paling before runt of
the Senhora, as the glow of fire pales and dies out under the beams
of the sun. However, he meant to win her, and he had plenty of
time: and he was a man who really understood the use of time—
not merely as something to be spent, but to be economised, and in-
vested, without any hurry to realise.

He, like the rest of her diminishing acquaintance, had long set
down the Queen as a very woman in the matter of caprice, and her
sudden appearance in the deepest of black was only one evidence
more of a quality that he hoped in time to turn to good account in
his designs upon the heart of Sophy. But, capricious and whimsi-
cal as he thought her, he was not prepared for the intention with
which she one morning favoured him.

"I am tired of London," said she, as she played with an open
newspaper. "I think I have learned all here that will be of any
good to my people—there was really very little to learn. But I
don't want to go back just yet . . . . and I want to be by myself
for a little while, in the country, and by the sea. Here is an ad-
vertisment in the newspaper, which suits me exactly: just as if it
were printed for my eyes to see."

"Oh, those advertisements," said Dr. Rackstraw. "Yes: *they*
are always just what everybody wants—what have you found?"

"A house, with lands, and grounds, and everything *I* want, to
be sold."

"Your Majesty thinks of buying an estate in England!"
exclaimed Dr. Rackstraw, immediately casting about in his mind
for the chance of turning this new caprice to the account of business,
for, though his irons were mostly abroad, he had a few at home.
"You think of settling among us for good and all?"

"I don't know what I think—I am just wearied out with thinking," said she, "and I want to go to sleep somewhere, where I
haven't got to choose between opening the windows for fear of
stifling and shutting them for fear of noise. But I don't understand
business. Go to these lawyers, or men of business, or whatever
they are, and buy this place for me, and then come back again as
soon as it is done."

"Oh!" sighed Sophy, "then you are going—you are not 'going
home,' after all?"

"Yes—no. Would you mind leaving me for five minutes, while
I talk business with Dr. Rackstraw? . . . . Doctor, before I talk
about this house, I'm glad you came: I want to thank you for

bringing me that child. She is made of starlight—or as you would say of gold."

" Yes, indeed. You cannot think better of her than I."

" She is good, like *my* people. How is it that being good means being unhappy."

"Unhappy! Do you mean that Sophy is unhappy, and with you?"

" She has become like a daughter to me. But in my country daughters tell their mothers all their sorrows: and I know no more of her than just her name, and that you are her friend. She reminds me of a girl in my country who listened to words that ought not to be spoken—about killing a holy bird. She was unholy till the second new moon. Has Miss Gray ever done anything wrong that she effaces herself so? You may tell me—I am her mother and her Queen, not her judge : and it will make no difference to me. She has been my daughter till past the second new moon, by a long ime."

Dr. Rackstraw pondered and frowned. It was of the utmost importance that Sophy, under the wing of the Queen, that is to say under his own watchful control, should be kept apart from her true lover and from the renewal of the influence of her old friend. If Senhora Miranda became acquainted with the real story of her maid of honour, her royal generosity would certainly not rest until the mists of his own devising were cleared away. So he looked at the ceiling, stroked his chin and said,

" Wrong, your Majesty, is a word that may mean almost anything—it often means right, just as right often means wrong. Of course there are reasons why Miss Gray should wish to forget the past, and to begin life all over again. Of course there was no reason why she should not enter into your service. I brought her to you, chiefly because I knew she would serve you well—but also because I knew that in your service she would be safe from that most cruel of all cruel things: idle curiosity. I felt secure that not a word would be said by you or yours to make her conscious of her past, or to make her dread her future . . . . I am glad for her sake that you think of a retirement into the country—"

If right and wrong have many meanings, Love has surely more. Love had inspired Dr. Rackstraw to keep this girl to himself by hinting away her good name albeit—a stroke of business that would have occurred to perhaps no other man in the world. But then he, ignoble himself, had brains enough to have discovered the lioness in the Queen of Apahu : and so,

"I thank you with all my heart," said she. "She is more than ever my daughter now: and not one word will I speak that may hinder her forgetting . . . . Yes: I know this world beyond th sea well enough now: I have read, and heard, and seen, how Christians, who call my people blind, savage heathens, deal with one another just when love and pardon are all in all. She shall go back with me. Ah—*I* know what it means to be alone—all alone. So thank you for understanding me: you are worthy to be a savage and a heathen . . . . Yes; London worse than wearies me. About this purchase. I am getting impatient to go."

"I'm afraid an estate can't, in this benighted, old-fashioned England of ours, be bought in a day. It isn't like the system I've introduced into the Goblins, where ten thousand acres can be transferred, and the purchase money paid down, by two strokes of the pen."

"At any rate as soon as you can. I don't understand business, or I wouldn't trouble you. Here is the advertisement. It will tell you the name of the estate, and where to go."

"*By order of the Court of Chancery,*" he began to read. "Crossmarsh? . . . . Your Majesty thinks of buying *Crossmarsh?*——"

"Why not? Do you know the place? Why should I not buy Crossmarsh if I please?"

If Dr. Rackstraw were sitting in the Palace of Truth, he would have found it easy enough to answer. He would have said: "Because she whom I chose to call Miss Gray will be the seller; because you and she cannot be kept in ignorance of it: because Crossmarsh is the very last place on earth where I would have her go: because Oswald Hargrave will be her neighbour: because, whatever happens, she will have escaped back to the very citadel of old associations out of my hands, before their grasp has become secure." He was so taken aback by the extraordinary accident of this capricious princess having taken a fancy to Crossmarsh that the fates seemed to have joined in league against his passion, and for once, he scarcely knew what to say.

"Crossmarsh—let me see: oh, the very worst part of the coast of all England for scenery: not a civilised town within miles; not even a railway: all swamps and malaria: and—ah—I remember: next door to a convict prison. Dear Madam, you would die of typhoid fever in a month, if you weren't murdered before——"

"You seem prejudiced against the neighbourhood?" asked

Rosamond, a little surprised. "Have you ever been there ? Never mind I have set my mind on this particular estate: and, if I don't like it, I can sell it again, and come away. Please go and buy it——"

"It is my duty to protest, Madam!" exclaimed Dr. Rackstraw. "There are dozens of lovely places in England—hundreds : scores. What on earth has made you fix on such an abominable hole, where prisoners are sent to rot and die ? *I* will find you a place in the country fit for a Queen."

"Oh, I don't want a place fit for a Queen. I want a place where nobody else will come, fit for a girl who wants to forget, and a. woman who is tired, and wants to go to sleep and dream——"

"To commit suicide you mean!"

"Dr. Rackstraw, I am a Queen, and not used to be disobeyed. If Crossmarsh is so bad as you say, all the more reason why I should buy it, to keep other people from dying of fever or murder. I must see such a place, just for the sake of knowing the exact opposite of Apahu. What is the use of having crossed the ocean of death unless one gets a glimpse of Hell ? I thought I had seen it, here in London: but—go and buy Crossmarsh : it is my will."

"Yes," muttered Dr. Rackstraw, "a woman always calls her whim her will. But I say won't: and where there's a won't there's a way. . . . Well," said he, sullenly for him, "I will see about it. Seeing about it will do no harm."

"Give any price they want," said Rosamond ; "I don't want bargaining—and I want to go to-morrow, if I can."

Eagerness was imprudent: But then nobody thinks of analysing the whims and caprices of a Queen.

Only that morning, and by the merest chance, for she was no newspaper reader, Rosamond had learned that her old home was for sale. That at least remained, whoever the owner who wished to sell it might be. That she would soon learn ; though that Sophy would part with Crossmarsh while one brick remained upon another and while one wave struck against its cliffs was among the things too impossible to suggest themselves. Crossmarsh might in some way act as a link to bring her to Sophy—if not, Rosamond would have conscious and tangible possession of all that was left to her of her childhood—of that home-life that had been hers before she became an exile and a Queen. She could have almost struck Rackstraw, for his abuse of a place, that

obviously he had never seen, for its actual merits and for its
imaginary vices. Whether she would actually visit that old home
she had become doubtful. That moment was over when the name
of Crossmarsh, standing out from a lawyer's or estate agent's
phrases, made her quiver with the wash of waves, more musical
than all the rest of ocean, and with the scent of flowers more
fragrant to the heart than all the southern profusion of Apahu:
Perhaps she would let it all remain a memory and a dream—all
the rest of her home-coming was a failure: why should this also
be spoiled ?

As he went in the direction of Lincoln's Inn Fields to make, or
at any rate to pretend to make, the enquiries with which he was en-
trusted, the Agent-General of the Goblin Islands recovered his
wits and laid his plans. There was one obvious course open to
him—he could report that the purchase was impossible, for want
of title, or for a hundred other reasons that would satisfy any
ordinary woman with confidence in her business adviser. But to-
day he had seen her in an altogether new light capable of indulging in any caprice however unreasonable, and rendered the more
resolute in it by opposition. She was quite likely, he felt, if he
should disappoint her, to rush down herself to the lawyers who
had the sale in hand and of concluding the affair at any cost and
any risk—the greater these, the more likely she.

But then another idea came into his mind. The great thing
. was to prevent her learning that Sophy was selling Crossmarsh :
because that would inevitably lead to a general communication
between Oswald Hargrave, the Senhora, and the supposed Miss
.: Gray, to the loss of his own influence—for it was entirely a
question of the greater influence, he felt, upon which his success
depended in a love affair which by its very difficulty was now
absorbing all his desires. But if he himself became purchaser in
the first instance, he could afterwards lengthen out proceedings as
long as he pleased, and could even keep Crossmarsh out of the
market altogether, besides making what would be probably a good
investment, and having a magnificent hold over Sophy, as the lord
and master over her old home.

As it happened, however, he did not reach the lawyers until
office hours : and the next day he was intentionally too busy hoping that some new purchaser might intervene. But it would not
do to keep so impulsive a savage as the Queen of Apahu waiting
too long: so on the next day he called in good time to see

how the land lay. He could not make any sort of report to his principal unless he knew what all the circumstances really were.

In the outer office two gentlemen were talking; one with his back to Dr. Rackstraw, the other, evidently a member of the firm, or perhaps their managing clerk, facing him.

"I am very sorry, sir," the latter was saying, "since you were so anxious for the property. But the lady was a human steam-engine hung on electric wires—she put everything into our hands, and positively got the business put through in four-and-twenty hours—deeds handed over, purchase money actually paid, and all. I shouldn't have thought it possible; but of course when a lady produces the cash in Bank of England notes, and insists on signing everything at once and taking our word for the title—all I can say is, *Caveat Emptor.* Not but what it's all right enough—though I scarcely now know whether we're on our heads or our heels."

"And who the devil," broke out the other in a voice so loud and rough that Dr. Rackstraw barely recognised it as that of an acquaintance of his own, "who the devil is this mad woman? Where is she to be found?"

"There's the oddest part of all, Mr. Harding," said the lawyer. "She calls herself Senhora Miranda Ngahoung—there's a name for the nutcrackers!—And it's a fact, sir, but she's a Real Queen! —and as rich, sir, as—as—"

Mr. Harding, otherwise the Man from Nevada, otherwise Lawrence Derwent, turned on his heel and strode off without another word.

A woman's caprice had cost him the house that held his rights, his liberty, his good name: and that woman she who had goaded his passion into open war.

But sudden rage revealed the man who, in cold blood, had defied detection with ease.

"I came about Crossmarsh too." said Dr. Rackstraw to the lawyer, "but I see I'm too late now. Good day." So he departed, meditating many things on the return of Lawrence Derwent rich and disguised: on girls who are coy and hard to win: and on the difficulty of dealing with a woman so deplorably uncivilised as to pay hard cash before examining her title deeds.

CHAPTER XXVI.

They dead ?   Not they !   For vain the boast
Of flesh or blood to slay a ghost :
Dead ?   Nay—when phantoms feign to die
They but increase and multiply,
And ghosts of faith, when hunted out,
Make double room for ghosts of Doubt,
Who, like Sir Hercules of yore,
For ten crushed heads finds twenty more.
An honest Goblin's twice as true
As half the lights that dazzle you.

IT may be remembered, or forgotten, that in the days when
Silver Moldwarp was in business as a practical archæologist
at Crossmarsh, he used, by way of recreation in the evening, to frequent an unpretending tavern called the "Feathers."
The "Feathers" still flourished, in spite of time and change,
though the thirst of not a few of its customers was quenched
for ever.   To say that one evening a number of the parishioners of
Crossmarsh were vainly endeavouring to quench theirs would be
an entirely safe proposition, because there never was an evening
in the year when some of them were not, while it would be
altogether too vague for the purposes of History, who insists
upon accuracy in dates, in order, no doubt, to be as loose as she
likes in all really important things.

When, however, the choice lies among some thousands of
evenings as the date of a proceeding which remained the same in
its incidents, however often it was repeated, accuracy becomes
obviously impossible.   So after all it must suffice to say that
the sun set, and, in that same sense, that once a number of
parishioners of Crossmarsh were at the "Feathers," drinking
ale.

"Yes : 'tis true as gold," said Giles Fletcher.   "I was at
Laxham market my own self, and nobody else's : and I heard it
as plain as that mug there.   And so you'll see."

"Ah, but, Mr. Fletcher," said the new rector's groom, " if
everything was to be true one hears, this would be a muddlesome
sort of a world.   It doesn't depend on ears if a thing's true, but
on the tongue."

"And not too much on that," said the parish clerk.   "Seeing's
believing—I goes by the eye."

"Then, Mr. Crow," objected a mild shepherd in a corner, " if
you was a blind man, you'd believe nought, nohow ?"

"That's gammon," said the clerk.   "That's what that is, gammon. When I say the eye, I mean what I see by. And a blind man with a bit of sense can see cheese from chalk just as well as if he'd got an eye for every finger——"

" Aye, but, Mr. Crow—suppose he'd lost his fingers too ? I seed a chap once at Laxham fair that got no arms nor legs, but stood on his head, and swallowed his drink topside down. A wonderful sight for to see ! "

" And so you'll see!" resumed Giles Fletcher, whom these metaphysicians had for the moment thrown out of the running. " When I hear with my own ears a man tell me something with his own tongue, and when that man's own father to the lad that runs of a lawyer's errands, I ain't far out, I reckon, though I never lost so much as a toe. Topside down, indeed! What's that to Fane's cottage being sold ? "

" Come, Mr. Fletcher," said the groom, " nobody meant no offence, I'm sure. I'm uncommon pleased to hear it, for one. Crossmarsh is a nice place, but there's no saying but what, for anybody that's lived t'other side of Lowmoor, 'tis dull. The 'Feathers' is a good house, and so's the home-brewed, however 'tis took: but there's a terrible want of company. There's my master: but of course, I don't reckon him : and there's the doctor but he don't count neither ; and there's Mr. Hargrave, but he's never at home; and that's all. What we want is a real, good, comfortable family, that'll keep company all the year round, with London gentlemen and ladies in the servants' hall, and keep the place alive. We'll get along then."

" No, no, we was never like that at Crossmarsh," said Mr. Crow. " That's not our style. Ah, we'll never see the like of the old times, when Squire Fane were grubbing up the Knoll, and Squire Hargraves were riding his mare over nigh every day, and a chap from foreign parts—Moldwarp by name—was fiddling your head off, and conjuring your nose into somebody else's shoe, and Parson Pitcairn was preaching, and I were first helping him : those were the days; nothing like 'em now. Life —ah, that was the life for me."

" *I* mind old Moldwarp," said Giles Fletcher. " But there was one thing he couldn't do : he could whistle, but he couldn't sing. You'll mind, Mr. Crow, how he and I sang ' Brakes o' Barley,' verse and verse, for a quart, and how he stuck at the nineteenth, and I went on to the end ? "

" Aye, Giles ; and how when you'd finished you found yourself tied fast in your chair, and couldn't get out—Ha, ha! Ah, what times were they—nothing like 'em now. Talk o' life! 'Twas because we lived too fast, I'm afeard, in the times of Squire Fane and Parson Pitcairn. I reckon we burnt our candle both ends and the middle as well. I wonder who the new folks 'll be."

"The lawyer's lad's father thought 'twas some sort of a lady," said Giles. "He said, to the Queen. But I told him I didn't come to market to buy gammon—so that were one for he and two for I."

"Aye: they think they're uncommon sharp, at Laxham. The Queen, indeed! Well 'twon't make much difference, whoever it may be. We've done without anybody at the cottage now this twelve year, and got used : and 'tisn't like as if Miss Rosamond or Miss Sophia was coming home."

"And who might they be?" asked the groom.

"Eh?" asked Mr. Crow, with some surprise. "Well, my lad, never you mind if you don't know. How was sheep going at Laxham, Mr. Fletcher, pretty fair?"

The groom, as indeed he seldom lost an opportunity of letting Crossmarsh know, had come from a greater and wider world, felt that the change of topic had been made with an intention—either with the favourite object of excluding a stranger from too intimate an acquaintance with the hereditary mysteries of Crossmarsh, or else of piquing his curiosity into asking a question. Curiosity was just getting the better of the dignified indifference of a man of the world, when—"

"Good evening, gentlemen," said a strong, but not very genial voice: and the parliament of Crossmarsh perceived that to-night's was to be no ordinary session. A stranger was among them; and not only a stranger, but one who, in calling the company gentlemen, spoke with knowledge of the article. "I suppose there's no objection to my smoking my pipe in here? The land-lord wanted to put me into solitary confinement—but a man's own self isn't very likely company, so——"

"And you're welcome, sir, I'm sure," said the clerk: for it must not be supposed that the people of Crossmarsh were boors. They were not of the north, where every man is better than his neighbour, nor yet of the east, but of the west, where churls are few, and men do not hold it impossible that they can have betters.

The visitor, a large man with a big beard, took the first seat that came to hand, filled a meerschaum pipe, and ordered cider.

"It's a fine coast you've got here," said he, to break the spell of observant and curious silence caused by his coming. "You're a bit behind the times down here, it seems to me. You ought to have a branch line to Laxham, and build an hotel—you'd have visitors by the shoal."

"Yes, sir," said the rector's groom, instinctively lifting his thumb to his forehead. "That's what I say myself—having lived in places where they makes the most of theirselves."

The gentleman might be a painter, or he might be an angler: for both painters and anglers, those pioneers of the bricklayer, had discovered the cliffs and the streams of Crossmarsh full half a dozen years ago. However, time would show. Even curiosity was patient and leisurely there as yet, and took its time.

"I walked over from Laxham," said he. "Not much to see by the road. By the way, though, what was that big building I passed to the right, about six or eight miles from here, beyond the downs? Do you know?"

"Aye, sir; I know," said Giles Fletcher. "That be one of Queen Victoria's palaces—that be: where she asks you to come and stop, and plenty to eat and nothing to pay."

At this venerable joke, cracked so often at Crossmarsh that it had become to be looked upon as an unsurpassable gem and inexhaustible fountain of humour, Giles Fletcher chuckled as if he had invented it on the spot, and a grin spread over the parlour.

"Queen Victoria's palace?" asked the stranger, gravely. "I smell a joke——"

"'Tis Lowmoor gaol."

"Oh—Lowmoor gaol! Of course I've heard of Lowmoor gaol. I must get an order to go into it some day——"

"Aye, sir," said Giles Fletcher; "that's fine and easy, to get in. The thing they mostly want is to get out again."

"They may want, then," said Mr. Crow, recovering his social monarchy, which the stranger had disturbed. "Lowmoor gaol is the strongest, I'm told by them that's been in 'em all, the strongest, sir, in the whole world. There's none that comes near. There's been but two escapes out o' Lowmoor ever since 'twas first a gaol."

"Indeed?" asked the stranger, carelessly.

16

"And one of 'em wasn't much of an escape after all—'twas a man that was picked up next morning under Furnace Point, where you'll see the very spot, if you goes there, to this day. I were a little chap then; but my father saw the man, and there wasn't a whole piece of him left more than would fill a thimble."

"That was out of the frying-pan into the fire, eh? And the other man," asked the stranger. "What became of *him?*"

"Ah, sir, but if anybody could answer that, he'd have a hundred pound this very day. Some say he went over Furnace Point too, but if he had, he'd have been found—leastwise some of him. I had a look after him my own self, along with young Squire Hargrave of Windgates, that was after him like a red hot needle. He was out quarrying with the other gaol-birds, that man was, and all of a sudden he was gone. They fired the gun, and all the country was up and after him—Silver Moldwarp and all, that could always find whatever he pleased; p'r'aps he didn't please—leastwise, he didn't find."

"What was the gentleman's name," asked the stranger, refilling and lighting his pipe, "who was so hot on catching a poor devil who did what any man would do?"

"Young Squire Hargrave, of Windgates. But what any man would do? No, sir; not any man. An honest man what's sent to gaol—there he'd stay. Speaking as clerk of this parish, a man's got to do his duty in that state of life whereto he's called. We might every one have been murdered, for ought we could tell; and no man's got a right to fight a whole parish because he don't like what comes of his own misdeeds. Ah, that was a terrible time—we don't have no more times like that now. We'll never see the likes of 'em again."

"Ah, Mr. Crow," said Giles Fletcher, rubbing his hands gently and slowly, as if he were caressing exciting memories, "times, as you say. 'Twas the very next dry Squire Fane's niece suicised herself——"

"Your memory aren't quite right there, Giles," interrupted Mr. Crow. "Nobody knows the ins and outs o' that but me. 'Twasn't the very next day—'twas two days. And 'twas no more suicide than you be. But 'tisn't best to talk too much o' that, with the house just sold. Best let bygones be bygones," say I.

The rector's groom pricked up his ears, for an opportunity seemed to present itself for satisfying curiosity without losing dignity.

"We're all friends here, Mr. Crow," said he, "and if so be this gentleman likes to know what *we* know——"

"I should very much like to know," said the stranger. "Your conversation, and your opinions, interest me, Mr. Crow, more than anything for a long time."

"I quite believe *that*," said Mr. Crow, ignoring the groom. "When a man's been parish clerk of Crossmarsh from before Parson Pitcairn's time, 'tis his own fault if he don't know something o' most things. If a man don't know Crossmarsh, he don't know all England : but if a man do know Crossmarsh, he do know Crossmarsh ; and so he knows what t'other chaps don't know."

The stranger waited. Mr. Crow, having seen that everybody's attention, coughed, drank, and began ; and there were but two in the company, the stranger and the groom, who had heard it less often than five hundred times.

"We used to think there was some'at uncommon about Squire Fane's maggot for picking up pebbles and such like things. He groped about for what you'd call rubbish—lumps o' chalk, and snail shells, and lobster claws. And he wasn't content with what lay a'top o' the ground. If you come, sir, from Lowmoor straight over the downs, you passed by a bit of hillock, called Pix-Knoll. Squire Fane cut through it crossways, end to end and twice athwart ; and he'd go poking in and out as if he was a coney in a gold mine. Now I leave you to guess, sir, what a gentleman should want with a lot of lumps of chalk out o' Pix-Knoll. We didn't think so much of it at first—at least the others' didn't, though I always had my own thinkings. One day I spoke to Parson Pitcairn. 'Oh, the Squire's a great scholar,' says he, 'and he's after the treasures of the Ancient Britons'—those were his very words. But he didn't seem to find 'em. So all of a sudden there comes into his service, from the Lord knows where——"

"Aye, Silver Moldwarp !" interrupted Mr. Fletcher.

"I say, from the Lord knows where—a man without his like, neither here, nor there, no nowhere all the country round. They were good times, but I don't care to talk too much of 'em late at night : and of how we used to make merry with a man that mightn't ha' been a man at all. After all, sir,"—he looked severely at the groom—"fun and good company's all very fine but the soul comes first : and you may talk of your hotels and your railroads, but when I say the good days be gone for Cross-

ma sh, I mean more as goes to the ear. Silver Moldwarp—that
was the chap's name. There wasn't a mortal thing he couldn't do.
H, could fiddle, and he could whistle, and he could sing. Aye,
G les, *sing*. But he could do things nobody could believe, if I was
put on oath, except Giles Fletcher, because he knows of his own
eyes. I've seen him turn a boiled egg into a live mouse, and pull
erty fathom of blue ribbon through his mouth out of his own
inside. I've heard him talk queer talk with a spirit that was up
the chimney, and make one quart pot dance while another quart
pot sang a song. I've seen him make a table dance, too ; and
conjure the money out o' my pocket into his own. . . . and things
I wouldn't dare tell to none but Giles Fletcher, that knows. We
used to laugh, for he was a jolly chap at ' Feathers : ' but he lived
all alone, and all his work was to help Squire Fane grubbing in
Pix-Knoll. And when you gets together a great treasure-seeking
scholar and a devil like Silver Moldwarp, come express to help him
from Lord knows where—well, sir, it seems to me as how there
you are."

"A wizard and his familiar," said the stranger. "I see."

"Anyhow, they was always too familiar to please me, though I
was young and giddy then, and used to go to the ' Feathers ' more
than, maybe, I ought to ha' done. Well, sir, this Squire Fane
had two young nieces, as nice children as you'd wish to see. And
they was Miss Rosamond and Miss Sophia, young man," he added,
severely to the groom.

" Well—to be sure ! "

" Young Fletcher, up at Fane's cottage, used to tell me there
was a sort of a empty lumber room where nobody never dared to
go——"

" The magic chamber ? " asked the stranger.

" Eh, sir ? You seem uncommon knowing about them sort of
thing. Where nobody never dared to go—But one night Miss
Rosamond, being a female, and therefore curious by nature : 'twas
midnight, maybe—she, I say, went into that there very room.
Think o' that, now—into that very room after dark : and she but
a female girl ! "

He paused for drink, and for the enjoyment of the indrawn sigh
of anticipation that thrilled the room.

" Ah ! And she saw—— ? " said the stranger.

" God alone He knows—if He knows ! " answered Mr. Crow.
" for never was that young creature seen, herself, again ! "

" Carried off by the devil ? "

" Don't ask *me*, sir. I only tell you this—*Silver Moldwarp vanished too.*"

      *   *   *   *   *   *

" I'm glad I came to Crossmarsh," said the stranger. " That's the best original story of the black art I ever heard—it leaves such a lot to the fancy. Yes—the old wizard, the magic chamber, the innocent girl, the fatal curiosity, and the devil, half comic, half tragic, like all the best specimens, to fly away with her through the midnight air. But what became of the wizard uncle ? And weren't there two girls ?"

" After that, sir, Squire Fane threw all his gettings out o' Pix-Knoll into the sea, 'twas may be chalk, or may be gold; and then he with Miss Sophia went to foreign parts away, and died in London town. And now the cottage is sold; and she's a bold woman, say I, that's bought a house to live in where there's been such-like goings on."

" Then has nobody lived in that house all this time ? Is it empty at this moment—Now ? " asked the stranger, with an air of such absolute indifference that a quicker brain than was used at Crossmarsh must have seen that it was too complete to be sincere.

"Not a soul, sir. Leastways not a body I should say. Bless you, sir, the folk hereabout are that coward they won't go by the place after sundown. Of course I would, if I had occasion—only it don't happen to lay my road home."

" Ghosties and bogles ! " broke in the sceptic in the corner. " Not a bit of 'em. There's no such things."

" And who said there was ? " asked Mr. Crow. " But p'r'aps you don't believe Miss Rosamond was spirited away——"

" She jumped over the cliff," answered the sceptic.

" P'r'aps you saw her jump ? " asked Mr. Crow. " And p'r'aps she told you why ? And p'r'aps as you're so bold, shepherd—— look here, if you'll go and sleep to-night in that cottage, I'll stand you a gallon ; and then we'll know if there's ghosts or nay."

" No, no ! " said the sceptic. " 'Tis *you* ought to try that ; " and he looked round with a grin, for a laugh, but none came. It was getting late, and the subject growing somewhat serious for the hour. At Crossmarsh the people prefer talking of ghosts by honest day.

" And so I would," said Mr. Crow, stoutly, " and for no better than a quart, only I'm a married man, and my home lies t'other road. And what's more, a new shepherd's easy got; but as a public officer, I've got to think of the parish. No, shepherd, 'tis you said going into that room meant no more than suicide; so 'tis you ought to see."

"There is such things as a haunted house," said the groom. "There was one near my last place, where an old man without a head and fiery eyes used to slide down the bannisters every first Tuesday in the month at twelve; and I've heard tell of another, where a big black dog used to howl in the scullery when anything was to happen, and when they used to look for him there was nothing to be seen. And there was yet another where a skeleton used to jump out on the maids from behind the haystacks, till they didn't dare to go by. P'r'aps the new lady that's took the cottage will keep her servants, but they'll have to be plucked ones, and their wages 'll have to be high. What'd you take to sleep in that there room, Mr. Fletcher, where the poor young lady went into and never came out again?"

"Take!" said Mr. Fletcher. "There's none of your common ghosts in Crossmarsh, mind that, young man; but I'd like to see the man that would take five hundred pounds to sleep a night all alone by himself in Squire Fane's back room."

"Nevertheless," said the stranger, who had not spoken for so long that his presence had become almost forgotten, "nevertheless, gentlemen, that man will have to be found. I have never seen a ghost, and I should like to have a talk with one of all things. I want to get at the bottom of all this. I want to know what the wizard conjured out of lumps of chalk and lobster claws. I want to know whether he really sold his soul to what's his name—Silver Moldwarp, and how it was done. You see, I weigh near twelve stone; I'm not so easy to fly off through the floor, or the celling, as if I were a slip of a girl. Moreover, I am a bachelor, and I am not a parish clerk, so that my loss would not amount to a parochial or even to a domestic misfortune. In short, I will spend to-night in the ghost-chamber, and I'll meet you all here to-morrow and tell you what I've seen. Of course, if I don't come—well, gentlemen, you'll understand that I shall be elsewhere."

It was certainly a chance in a thousand for a man who wished to have the run of a house while it was empty, and which he had no reasonable excuse for entering and searching. For had he advanced the true one, that he was searching for an alleged will, it would not be long before he would be considerably

nearer to Lowmoor again than Crossmarsh was, while a man
like Rackstraw, as the pretended Queen's fellow conspirator
and employer, would at once be put on the scent of such a
search, and, being once put thereon, would take every efficient
care that no will should ever be found. Everything, indeed,
depended on working with the most absolute secrecy, and with
so much suddenness that no sort of risk could possibly be run.
He could not go to the house and say, " I am a stranger from
America, but I have reason to believe that an important document belonging to myself is hidden in this house with which
I have never had anything to do, and why I think so I cannot
tell." Such an application as that would assuredly have to be
decided upon by Rackstraw—and it was not likely that the same
man would escape twice from Lowmoor gaol. Nor, if he could,
would the all-important document remain open for finding. He
had come to Crossmarsh in search of a plan of undisturbed
entry, and had lighted upon an absolutely ideal plan. A house
empty and haunted, at a ghost-hunter's sole disposal for a whole
night—why it was almost as good as having bought the place,
and in some ways even better still.

He certainly had ample time for thinking things out during
the startled silence that followed his offer to beard the very
devil in his den.

It may be that the fathers of the parish senate were distracted
with conflicting emotions, and that there was some charitable
unwillingness, perhaps sense of shame, at letting a stranger
expose himself to the mysterious perils of the invisible world.
But his calmness was even more impressive than his courage;
he was certainly sober and apparently sane. And, after all,
Crossmarsh was not so very different from Laxham, Windgates, and the rest of the world so far as human nature was
concerned. When a man deliberately throws himself into a whirl-
pool, horrified crowds gather from far and near, not to forcibly
restrain him from his purpose, but to look on. If he succeeds
he is a hero; if not—well, he gives people something far more
delightful than heroism to talk about to their grandchildren.
If this venturesome stranger emerged from his adventure safe
and sound, the old story of the place would still be just as good
as new. If something happened, the old story would be a hundred
times better than new. But if the stranger vanished from mortal
sight, even as poor Miss Fane—why then an ineffable horror

would give Crossmarsh a glory of wonder and awe, and enable every man there present to boast to his dying day, "I seed the chap just afore he went in."

"Well, sir," said Mr. Fletcher, licking his lips as if they had a pleasant flavour, "you be a good plucked 'un—that you be!"

"Oh, it's nothing," said Lawrence, "I'm only afraid, with our friend in the corner, that there'll be nothing to see. Ghosts are shy birds, except when they're not wanted. Somebody, I daresay, will lend me a lantern; and I've got a pipe and a flask, and I'm used to sleeping rough out West, so I shall do very well. The only question is, how am I to get in and find the room?"

"You'd better not go, sir," said Mr. Crow. "But, of course, if you will—why there's nought more to say. About getting in, you can do that, for I keep the housekey, leastwise 'tis at my house nigh the church, not a quarter of a mile off here. About the room, you go straight through the hall, and up the stairs straight in front of you, and then along the landing, that looks over into the hall, to your left till you comes to the end, and then down three steps, and along a long passage to your right—a main long passage; then you gets into the back part o' the house, but you never turn; and when you have got through a old loft with a lean-to, there's the door afore your very nose. A child couldn't miss the way."

"No; that's plain enough. First landing, left as far as you can, right as far as you can: room. Now, gentlemen, drink me good luck and a lively ghost, and I'll go, for it strikes me the witching hour isn't far away."

"A minute, sir, if you please!" said Mr. Crow, for the rest were falling into somewhat ghoulish silence, save the groom, who whistled to show that he, as a man of the world, was not to be impressed with a mere Crossmarsh mystery. "If anything *should* happen, sir—not that 'tis likely, nor I hope it won't—wouldn't it be best to leave your name and where you belong to, so as your friends might know?"

"I'd rather not," said Lawrence, lightly. "If your Silver Moldwarp carries me off it shall be name and all. Think what it will be to say, 'There wasn't so much as his name left of him.' As for friends—perhaps if I had friends I shouldn't go. It's having wives and children, and comrades, that keeps back brave fellows like you."

"That's it, sir," said Mr. Fletcher. "'Tisn't that a man's afraid.'

" No, no. Of course not. Good-night, gentlemen—good-bye, in case I shouldn't see you again. Now, Mr. Crow."

" I wouldn't be in that there chap's boots," said Mr. Fletcher, " not for all the money in London town, and Laxham besides."

And none said him nay.

CHAPTER XXVII.

It's hame again, and hame again,
And hame ; sae lilted she :
But a' was lane and a' was gane
Whaur the kindly licht suld be.

And a' was leer and a' was bare
Of a' she fared to see :
Sae it's hame nae mair, and name nae mair,
And never mair for me.

"SOPHY," said Rosamond, " I am going away from London —really, this time. So please find out all about the trains."

" Oh, Madam ! You are going home ? "

" Yes—Home."

" Then—you will not want me any more ? "

" Not want you, child ? Why, I thought it was settled you had transferred your allegiance from Queen Victoria to Queen Ngahoung. Are you not coming with me even to the other side of the world ? And not want you when I am only going a few miles for a day !"

" Yes : you are my Queen ! " said Sophy, " I only want to serve you till I die. But you might not want me in your own country, where everything is so beautiful and so happy—and you said you are going home."

" Well—isn't one's house one's home ? I've been buying an English house, you know, where I can escape from the smoke to the sea till I go really home. And, dear—but don't tell—I think I want to get a little away from Dr. Rackstraw too. Of course he is a wonderfully clever man, and explains to me all about the parliament, and the Church, and the peerage, and politics, and commerce—particularly commerce—in the clearest way, so that I really think sometimes I'm beginning to understand them. The only thing I can't make out is how it is we get on so well without them in Apahu, and how you seem to get on so badly with them here. I suppose it's a shocking thing to say, dear, but I don't like civilisation and enlightenment—but then

I'm only a savage—and, Sophy, don't breathe it to Dr. Rack-straw : I shall never be anything more, I shall just take one thing back to Apahu, and that's *you.* Now find out all about the trains to a place called Laxham, like a clever girl as you are."

" Laxham ! " Sophy exclaimed.   But Rosamond's mind was busied with lands beyond Laxham, and had no reason for noticing any peculiarity in Sophy's tone.   However, the word had put an additional seal on the latter's lips.   If she were going back for a little while into her own country, it should be simply as Senhora Miranda's companion not as that poor Miss Fane who had to sell Crossmarsh because her uncle had robbed her of her last penny for the sake of his own whims.   She was grateful to Dr. Rack-straw for having turned her into Miss Gray, and to fortune for not having let her visit her own country since she was a little child, so that nobody could recognise her as the Miss Fane whose lands were being sold.   She had not a tie left to link her with her past, and intended to have none for evermore.

A good deal to her surprise, and a little to her disappointment, nothing was seen of her friend and patron before they started for Laxham.   Indeed, though Sophy had always found the grace and dignity of her mistress a good deal mixed with sudden and a sometimes unintelligible impulse, as was natural enough in a lady from the South Seas, the Senhora had never appeared downright capricious until now.   The purchase of this house must have been a strangely sudden caprice : her departure for it seemed like the rush of a child upon a new toy ; and she would not take a single servant with her, not even her Swiss courier. The inexperienced traveller, utterly unversed in railway com-plexities, threw off her leading strings and corks, and cast her-self upon the world with none but Sophy to counsel and protect her.   However, Sophy had been a wanderer in the labyrinth of civilised travel all her life, and to avoid arriving at Laxham was not an easy thing.

Here they dined : and here Sophy expected they would stay for the night.   But a demon of unrest appeared to have seized upon her Majesty the Queen.   A carriage with a pair of horses was ordered, and the travellers, with their very moderate amount of luggage, were once more upon the road.   It was already the latest shade of twilight, and Sophy knew not whither they were bound.

"Is your new house far from here?" she asked.

"Yes—no—" said her mistress, who had fallen into a silent reverie, and appeared to be gazing farther than eyes can see. "No doubt," thought Sophy, "she is wearied out with being an English lady—and no wonder. I wish all this time were over, and that we were gone. I wish we were in that wonderful island, where people dream that they are happy and never wake from their dreams.

Presently the road lay over the chalk downs. All at once Sophy felt one of her hands clutched by both the Queen's—and these were fevered and trembling. "Oh, Sophy," she exclaimed, throwing herself back, and drawing a full breath—"the sea—the sea!"

Sophy was not an imaginative person, and could not see what was not to be seen. Moreover, her thoughts were exceedingly far away. But her mistress's fevered clutch and excited manner called her back from her own thoughts half alarmed. She could almost hear the Queen's heart beat: she could see her bosom heave; she felt her trembling.

"What is the matter, madam?" she asked, growing really frightened. "Are you ill?"

"No, no. Don't speak to me—don't think of me : that's all." She spoke almost sharply—she, who had been so unfailingly and generously kind. But she grew somewhat calmer : and Sophy wondered if she knew that she had heard or answered a word.

At last they stopped at a cottage by the roadside, with a light burning in the window. The driver tapped with the butt of his whip at the door, and brought out an exceedingly respectable old lady, who curtseyed at the carriage window.

"Are you Mrs. Crow?" asked Rosamond, still speaking as if she were but half awake from a dream. "I am Madam Miranda, who have bought the house that used to belong to Mr. Fane, and the lawyer at Laxham told me I should be able to get the key from you. Here is his card."

"*Our* house—Crossmarsh!" cried Sophy to herself, and crouching back into her corner of the carriage as if there were need to hide on a dark night from an old woman who had not seen her since she was a little child. She was utterly scared by the coincidence; and yet what could there be more in it than that a house wanted a purchaser, and a purchaser a house, at one and the same time? Every purchase is a coincidence in that way. But at the moment

Sophy did not know what to think, still less what to say
or do.

" *You're* the lady that bought the cottage ! " exclaimed Mrs.
Crow. " Why you don't ever mean to say you're going in now ?
News come from Laxham market that 'tis sold : but to think of
your coming down all at once, so soon ! Why, ma'am, the house
hasn't been slep in since Squire Fane he went away. To be sure
I've got the key——"

" I suppose it is sudden, but never mind," said Rosamond, in a
less dreamy tone. "But my friend and I have brought down
all we shall want for a night, and we must see about making
things comfortable to-morrow. We were in a hurry to get home
and we like roughing it, and we hate inns."

In country places it is not good form to express surprise : but
Mrs. Crow looked decidedly grave.

" I think you'd best not go to the cottage to-night, ladies," said
she. " 'Tis sure to be terrible uncomfortable, and empty and
cold ; and, begging your ladyship's pardon, of course it's all nonsense, but there's tales."

"Tales ? " asked Rosamond.

" You haven't heard, ma'am ? Ah, then, tis no business of
mine: and 'tis all nonsense—there aren't no ghosties nowadays."

"And if there were," smiled the purchaser of that worst of all
bad bargains, a haunted house, " we shall get on very comfortably
with them, I dare say—though of course now they'll have to go :
but all the same it seems a little hard to disturb old tenants, Mrs.
Crow. I'll take the key now, and you shall hear from me pretty
early to-morrow——"

" Yes, Madam : 'tis for you to do as you please, to be sure—but
all the same—Why, bless my heart alive ! wherever *is* the
key ? "

Rosamond leaned back patiently while the search was being
made. Sophy was still trying to reconcile herself to the complication of being thus brought back, under a changed name and
as a stranger, by a stranger to her own old home. Sentiment
had little or nothing to do with her state of mind, for in truth
her only desire had been to cut herself away from her past altogether, and never have to do with the world that held Horace
Derwent again. Her childhood at Crossmarsh had ended in pain
and trouble, her after-life in ruin, and the death of her one
dream had crowned it all, making her believe the whole world,

save Senhora Miranda and Dr. Rackstraw, an abyss of fickleness, falsehood, and greed.

The key could not be found. "I *know* I put it somewhere," said Mrs. Crow, "and have kep it somewhere: and I could have laid my life 'twas on that nail. But it can't be gone, and to-morrow I'll hunt high and low. 'Tis a sort of a providence, ma'am. They can make shift at the 'Feathers,' I dare say—'twill be better than you'd have found at the cottage."

"There used—" began Rosamond, "there ought, I mean, to be a key of the servant's door, at the side."

For a moment Mrs. Crow did look surprised, and vexed besides. "Oh yes, ma'am, I've got *that* key. But 'tis hardly fitting a lady should go into her house after dark, by a back door, and no beds aired——"

"I prefer it," said Rosamond, in her royal manner. "I'll take that key now. Good-night, and thank you, Mrs. Crow."

When Mr. Crow came home, rather late, from the "Feathers," there was news for him indeed. His wife had been good enough to wait up for him, so that he might have the very earliest word —"Peter they're come!"

"Come?"

"Aye, Peter: Squire Fane's is sold to two young women, with their bonnets choke full of bees——"

"I know; Giles Fletcher heard all that at Laxham market. Ah, *they* won't stop here long."

"But you don't know they're in *now*, by the back door! They come here for the main key—and I couldn't find it, high nor low —from Laxham, in a fly and pair, baggage and all."

Mr. Crow glared aghast. For his nerves had been considerably fluttered by his own ghost story, and the result of his return to the "Feathers" had by no means cleared his brain. The con-sequences of having betrayed his trust as key-keeper might be disagreeable unless he took precautions to hide his past transaction; and he had not the least intention of going to a houseful of bogeys, bogey-hunters, and other strange creatures to see if anything was wrong. And so, with plenty of beer in his brains, he did what every blockhead is almost sure to think wise—he said nothing to his wife about what had become of the missing key. For he was well up in proverbs like, "You may tell who's new married by his telling his wife news:" and "Silence is the hedge of wisdom," as some exceptionally long-eared saw-coiner used to say.

But Rosamond knew what she was about exceedingly well. It is true she had no practical purpose in view : all she felt was that there was nothing left her at the end of a vain search but to go back to Apahu, and there to live and die alone—only first she must see the old sights, and hear the old sounds, and bid good-bye to the ghosts of old times. Moreover she must keep the tomb of her life in her own hands : she loved it too well to let it pass to strangers, and there was always the chance of its proving something more than a tomb so long as it remained hers. Sophy, if living, would surely come back a pilgrim to the old home some day, even as she was coming back now, and before she left England for the land which had married her, she could take steps to ensure that such a pilgrimage should not be made in vain. The hurry of her flight from London had been deliberate : she desired to throw off her queendom, and not to have the sacred places of her heart intruded upon and dissected by her philosopher and friend. Dr. Rackstraw would, of course, in due time recover his pupil, and she would in due time need again his help and his counsel : but not now. And she entered her own house, her Mecca, like a thief in the night not out of impatient caprice but because it was her heart's desire to come unseen and to find as little unchanged as could be found. A hint of the new mistress coming, she thought, and it would be somebody's business to sweep, and garnish, and drive out the very ghosts whom she was coming to see : and she would have to face all the stares in the parish instead of creeping in silent and unknown.

Dumb must be the pen and deaf the ear that have failed to tell and to gather what this home-coming meant to Rosamond, Queen of Apahu. Many times, and in many ways, has her strange story been told—the story of a home-bred English girl carried off in the simplest way and yet as if in an Arab's dream, and at once transformed into the Queen of an unknown land. And now, after many years, with her mind full grown, her soul enlarged, but with her heart of hearts unchanged, she was coming back to her cradle wherefrom all but her heart had died. She had thought to find all as she had left it—Uncle Æneas groping for his fossils; Sophy running about like a wild bird—just because the same Rosamond was coming back again : and she, the dead was coming back to life, and only the living had died.

It was a ghastly business, after all, when the side-door had been opened, the luggage carried in by the driver, and the fly discharged.

As to reasonable comforts, there was no lack of them, for she had made Sophy pack almost as if for a campaign. But these things were of no moment, seeing that she had only thought of them for her companion's sake. She passed into the square hall, holding her lighted lamp, Sophy following. Not a chair had been disturbed. Sophy regarded her with a sort of awe, she was so silent and her eyes were so full of the light of April. The younger girl was on the very edge of taking the Queen into her confidence, but did not dare.

Imagine the feelings of a ghost permitted to return, after many years, from the grave, with the wisdom of death in its soul, to find all changed. Or rather, a woman made a child again without losing her womanhood, to find that even childhood also is dust and vanity. Now she seemed to hear her uncle calling: now Oswald's mare upon the drive: now Sophy bounding down the stairs. Now again she was only conscious of all the emptiness and the end, and her home-sickness turned into a longing for the blue skies and human sunshine of Apahu.

"Come in here," said she, opening the library door. That room was empty indeed. "We will make this our parlour for to-night," said she. "And now we must look for night quarters. Let us go upstairs. We will make some tea with the spirit lamp, and——"

Her eyes caught sight of something on the floor. It was a sharpened flint, labelled, "Found by Moldwarp," with the date "in Pix-Knoll."

She gazed at it in so long a trance that Sophy knew not what to do. "Leave me," she began to sob. "Don't you hear me? For God's sake leave me alone."

A Queen must be obeyed. Sophy, frightened and miserable in that ghastly house, alone with this woman, who seemed falling back into the savage more and more every hour, crept back into the hall, but left the door ajar. The heathen queen seemed to have found a fetish in the pointed stone: for she was on her knees with it in her hands.

"Oh, if something would speak to me,—if I could only hear a voice!" Sophy heard her cry.

"I am not myself to-night," she said, after they had looked into one or two of the upstair rooms. "I suppose civilisation is telling on my nerves. You mustn't mind me to-night, dear. To-morrow I will   down to the sea, and swim my nerves and my follies away. We will sleep here. Come, let us make up our beds. These couches and our blankets will do for to-night. We don't have feather beds in my country, and you must learn our ways."

The room she had chosen was that which had been her own; and it was even curiously little changed. Mrs. Crow who had the care-taking, evidently was of strongly Conservative views, and had taken no liberty with the place as it had been left by the Fanes. It may be remembered that the room was double, so she bade Sophy take the second and inner room. Sophy would rather not have left her mistress even to the extent of having an open door between them : but the Queen always made a point of sleeping alone.

"If you wake and chance to hear me moving about, or miss me," said the Queen, "never mind. I don't feel much like sleeping : and I may be inclined to explore."

"Oh," cried Sophy, "pray don't go wandering about this—this strange house all alone! Do wake me, if I'm asleep, and take me with you, if you do."

"Go to sleep, my child," said Rosamond, "you must be dead tired. Now kiss me—and if you wake before morning, you will have disobeyed your Queen."

It need not be said that Sophy was tired—very tired : with travelling, with thinking, with grieving, with fearing, with wondering. Her bed was anything but luxury, and her whole situation was trying and exciting to the nerves; but, after all, Sophy's nerves and troubles were mostly apt to let themselves out in one good cry. Her disillusion about Horace Derwent was the only trouble over which she had never cried. That had gone deep : but mere sentiment was as healthily unknown to the grown girl as it had been to the child. Her tears floated her into slumber very soon.

Rosamond was fully as restless as she expected to be. She closed the door between Miss Gray's room and her own, placed the lighted lamp in a dark corner, threw up her window, and looked out to sea. The water had been like glass when she last saw it; now, even through the dark, she could see the white horses tossing their manes. What was she getting out of this visit, after all? Well, she would have been miserable if she had not come—it had at any rate the advantages of exorcism. She would never wish to set eyes on it again. She had come there, and freed herself of the hunger: and now, since all was lost and dead in her old home, she would be able, with a freer mind and an emptier heart, to devote herself to her new.

But, meanwhile, she must go through it all. Without the least trembling of the nerves, for she was in far too exalted a mood, she carried her lamp along the gallery over the hall, and along the white-washed passage, until she reached the door of her bower and citadel of old time. Surely she had been there but yesterday —not full ten years ago. For her, at least, was absolutely no change: this back part of the old farm-house had always been empty, deserted, and her own.

She almost expected to see her bundle of romance lying upon the table: but that had gone. So also had the heap of straw from which her real romance had appeared in living form. She went to where it had been—the only spot on the floor which she had never seen.

If she had only seen that spot, how the charm of her bower would have been multiplied; for, as is not unusual in old loft and lumber rooms of farm-houses on the west coast (the farmers who made them, and sometimes the preventive service, knew why, there was a trap-door that was not hard to pull open: and not only a trap, but a half-ladder, half stair-case, below.

In a word, the nature of the apparition that terrified the child out of her wits stood revealed: and all her history had hung upon a straw. . . . But that was an old story now, and courage had grown—perhaps for the moment morbidly high. She turned the trap well back upon its rusty hinges, and carried her lamp a few steps down. Who of the sex of Eve and of Bluebeard's wife would not have done the same—or of Adam's either. So it was thus that the man had hidden himself who had brought her fate, and whose voice had found her again and summoned her after ten years. The mystery had been exposed thus far: but she shuddered at the remembrance of its misery—perhaps of its recurrence, unless she hastened back to what seemed the only spot on earth where these mysteries and miseries were alike unknown.

It seemed strange that there should have been a nook or corner of the cottage that she, and still stranger that Sophy, had never found out in their exhaustive explorations. The steps led down, through an atmosphere of close air and choking dust, into a bare room exceedingly like the one she had left above ground, though not quite so large. What a find, what a castle, what a secret bower

17

it would have made for her once upon a time! She would explore
no further now, although the discovery of so much promised so
much more. Besides, she was half choked and stifled, and new
things were not what she had come to see.

The room must have been used for some purpose or other by
former generations of Fanes, or whoever were there before them,
for there was an old three-legged stool there, and some hoop-staves,
and similar odds and ends. At present, however, it was given
over to the spiders, for whom it must have been a veritable Apahu.
There were plenty of mouseholes; and a corner cupboard with
broken doors. Before leaving the place she looked into this, and
stood on the three-legged stool to look higher: and on the top
shelf she found a folded paper, covered with dust, but showing no
special signs of age. She opened, it seemed to be, some sort of
law paper, and the first words were, "This is the last will." It
was not likely to concern herself; but it must needs, she supposed,
concern somebody: and when she was a child she had read
plenty of stories about the curious places where wills are found—
after all, remembering these stories, a cupboard in a hiding hole
in an old farm-house was just the very place to find somebody's will.

"Derwent!" thought she, looking at the names. "I don't remember any Derwents about here—or any Derwents except those
people that Dr. Rackstraw knows. I had better send it to him;
and he'll know what it is, and what to do."

She placed the paper in her dress and returned up the stairladder.
It was a relief to close the trap again, and to breathe less stagnant
air.

Hitherto her nerves had been strangely calm, as calm as if she
were re-visiting a grave after many years. But, whether the calm
was false, or whether the last impressions she had of her bower
crowded back upon her in the rush of a moment, she was seized
with a panic the like of which she had never known. . It seemed
to her as if a human form were in the darkness of the door—as if
with her the shadow of her life had returned to the same spot
where it had first been thrown between her and the sunshine of
her days. Yes, the shadow was now all that was left to come.
She did not stop to reason. She, Queen as she was, flung her lamp
into a corner, and in the crush and darkness, flew through the door,
slammed it behind her, turned the key twice in the lock, and then
sped at double pace till she was at her bed-room window, again
drinking the wind from the sea.

"It is the last time!" she panted. "Never while I live will I open that horrible door again!"

CHAPTER XXVIII.

COBBLER.—Of your good learning, unriddle me this master:—
Sworn to Sue, and plight to Prue,
Robin's false, and Robin's true.
DOCTOR.—Nay,'fellow: never was he true wight that is forsworn.
COBBLER.—Then must I e'en resolve mine own maximum: e'en thus:—
If Sue were Sue, and now is Prue,
Unforsworn he were not true;
Since Prue is Prue and was not she,
Being true swain, most false is he.

OSWALD HARGRAVE was necessarily aware of the conveyance of Crossmarsh to Senhora Miranda. He was vexed; though, of course, he had no business reason for being so. On the contrary, everything had gone miraculously well and smoothly. Of course, Sophy would not be a penny the richer for the sale, which would be swallowed up by the payment of debts and mortgages: but she would be saved having to pay heavy annual interest, and be free from a legion of responsibilities. Indeed, to say that she would not be a penny the richer is to speak too conventionally: for the Senhora had been in much too great a hurry to bargain, and had paid what the amazed lawyers had chosen to ask her in the expectation of having their terms beaten down. Moreover she had paid in hard cash, and had asked no questions: so that nobody but herself had a right to come. I have abstained, and claim credit for it, for not having detailed the proceedings which resulted in the leave of the Court of Chancery to sell an estate in coparcenary on security being given to satisfy the claims of the co-heiress should she ever come to life again. I claim credit, because, in the position of Miss Fane's counsel, the case has given me an infinity of thought and trouble—all to result in these half dozen lines. Oswald found the security by a mortgage on his own farm: nor was he advised to the contrary, seeing that unless the court had been reasonably satisfied of Miss Rosamond's death without issue, leave would have been withheld. As things were, even he, loyal to the possibility of her life as he had been all these years, was bound at last to surrender his dream, so far as she was concerned.

All these things belonged to his talk with the lawyers at Laxham: the whole business was settled, and he had once more to face the fact that he must either quit his search or forthwith force it to an end. Moldwarp and Rackstraw were still his only clues: and he had absolutely no means of forcing their hand. For still through Lawrence Derwent lay his only road to Rosamond. The weak and easily turned—that is to say, all the worshippers of resolution and strength of will—will feel that he ought to have cut through the knot somehow, though they know not how. But such must learn to realise first what it means to love a ghost for ten years. Rosamond had never been his, even in name, he would not know her if she came before his eyes, as he very well knew. He himself was ten years older than he was ten years ago: and the probability of her death grew stronger and stronger, while his hope, which meant his faith, grew weaker day by day. In such a cold fit he could only perceive that Rackstraw meant to be inscrutable, and that Mold-warp was as slippery as a serpent, and would know his purpose besides.

Well—it came to this, that at any rate there was no middle way between beginning life again, or driving on to the end. And whichever way he decided, he would leave his own country, where he could neither follow his search nor begin life again For Sophy he had now done all he could: there was nothing left to bind him to the lives of others. He would see the last of her, and then make his own decision, once for all, and stand by it without further wavering, whatever it might be. It is just the most stubbornly faithful hearts that have the faintest hours, if all the truth could be known.

So, though her business had been carried out for the best, that she should have been brought back to Crossmarsh was odious to him in the extreme. He shared to the full all Mr. Harding's disbelief in the Senhora, and none the less because he had but once seen her, and had never spoken to her; and her connection with Rackstraw only confirmed him in his idea of her as an adventuress—though it can be no ordinary adventuress who buys real estate with hard cash, and whose wealth on that occasion was beyond disputing. If Harding was a king of the silver mines, she was an empress of emeralds and rubies. He was afraid of her for Sophy—and yet even in this there was nothing to be done. He could not forget how the girl had fired up at the least suspicion of her friend.

Thus it happened that Rosamond, standing at the library

windows and looking out upon the drive, and thinking, not merely dreaming, of her own, her real own people of Apahu, for whom she was answerable to the King of Kings and Queens was brought back, all in a moment, to the Crossmarsh of old. For, as if it were but yesterday, there was Oswald Hargrave, he and no other, leading his horse past the greenhouse where he had told her to wait for him, the last words of his that she had ever heard : words that she had forgotten the moment they were spoken, but which now came back as if they had been seeds that had taken ten years to grow.

And she had thought he, too, had vanished out of the world like all else that had belonged to her when she was young. . . And would *he* know, perhaps, what had become of Sophy ? . . She felt herself turn faint and pale. If he could tell her nothing ; if he could only tell her that the child was dead—but then, if he could say, " The child is alive "—Rosamond felt like a prisoner before her judge, before doom is spoken. She left the window and paced the room. " Has he found me out ? " she asked herself. " *Can* he have learned I am here ? " She did not know whether she hoped or feared. " If he knows me, he knows me—but if he does not ; and if Sophy is gone—There must be no chance then ; Rosamond Fane must be dead, and I must be for ever what I am. Have I come for life and death ? It is no use praying. What is done is done."

The house, with the help of Mrs. Crow and of the village carpenter had very soon been put into sufficient living order for two ladies who required for the present only three rooms; for none of the needful furniture had been removed. Sophy had not yet found either the courage or the will to tell her mistress of her own former connection with the house to which she had come as a stranger ; and, for that matter there was every reason why she should put off that perfectly useless confession for good and all. She, also, was beginning a new life, and meant to be Miss Fane no more; and besides, it would be a breach of faith to Dr. Rackstraw, and oblige him to make explanations which she knew he wished to avoid. So when Oswald was shown by Mrs. Crow into the drawing-room where she had been meditating, as became a lady in waiting, on less lofty matters than became the mind of Majesty, she said at once—

" I know what *you* think, Oswald—but I am still to be Miss Gray.'

" And for once," said he, " I *don't* think you are wrong. It isn't
that that troubles me. It is your being with this woman, here at
Crossmarsh, at all. Being here—since nobody will remember you
—it is as well you should avoid the false position you would be
in as Miss Fane."

" Ah—I am so glad you think me right!" said she. "And——"

" We must fall out, Sophy, about no small things. I may not
see you for a long, a very long time."

" Yes, Oswald—and I—I am going to Apahu."

" Apahu ? "

" Don't you know ? It is the country of my mistress, the
Queen."

"Good God, Sophy! But I can't match reason against a witch,
and a—Rackstraw : if there be an Apahu, or whatever the name
is, anywhere out of the world of dreams: or of frauds. That
woman——"

" Hush, Oswald! Here she comes—the Queen."

Sophy rose, and stood in all respect : for she believed with all
her heart in her mistress, and in her own office, and publicly indulged in no favourite's liberties.

Oswald was already standing ; and he bowed, but under protest ; and certainly not to the Queen. Rosamond merely inclined
her head, and did not hold out her hand; it was not the custom
in her own country. But, for all her cold stateliness, her heart
was throbbing, and she was searching him with her eyes.

" He does not know me," her own eyes answered her. " And
yet he is not changed."

Strange enough, in all conscience, would it have been if the
man who had been moving round in the circle of one idea for ten
years had known again her who in that time had grown up
from a child into a queen, and from a queen into a woman.

Yet she was saddened by his want of knowledge : the woman
had not yet grown up to the height of pure reasonableness—nor
would, may be, until her time came to grow into something higher
still.

As for him, with all his doubts of her, he was far more impressed
by her presence than when he merely saw her in the midst of a
crowd on the night when Æneas Fane died. He had to harden
himself against a certain magic: for he could not feel that she was
what he believed her to be.

" I am a neighbour of yours, Madam," he said. " My name is

Hargrave; I live at a place called Windgates, not many miles away."

"And you have come to call upon your new neighbours?" asked Rosamond. "That is friendly. This is my friend, Miss Gray. . . . Of course, you knew the people who lived here before——"

"The Fanes? Well."

"Of course—being in their house—they interest me," said she. She was so eager to reach her question, and yet so dreading it that she fancied she needed excuses for the most natural curiosity about the traditions of the new home.

"There are so many relics of them about that I almost feel as if—as if I belonged to them. Are you sorry they are gone?"

"They were very dear friends of mine," said he.

"Let me see—I have heard something of them already; they were an old man and two girls. He is dead; and they—what has become of *them?*"

Sophy glanced at him quickly.

There was certainly no reason why he should betray what she chose to make her secret to satisfy the idle curiosity of a stranger.

"I cannot tell you," said he. "The elder is thought dead——"

"Yes—and the younger?"

"I cannot tell."

Sophy's eyes thanked him. And so Rosamond had her answer. So this was friendship: she came back to find that Oswald Hargrave could not tell. "Then neither can I tell," she thought, all cold with a dull pain.

"Perhaps," she asked, "she is thought dead too?"

"She went abroad," said Oswald "and what has become of her —I have said—none know." That was quite enough truth for one whom Sophy's fate could not concern.

"Or care to know, I suppose," said Rosamond. "That seems to be the way of the world." A queen from the South Seas might speak a little strangely without seeming strange. "So *she* is dead too—for that is all it can mean. How long have these people— the Fanes—been gone?"

"Ever since the elder girl——"

"Died?—Ah, I see now."

It was as if she had seen her sister die. For if Sophy had vanished out of life on that terrible night ten years ago, even so would Rosamond have broken her heart and have died of love and sorrow.

Nothing on earth could have made her say to Oswald now. " I am Rosamond Fane, come back from the grave." All was lost that she cared for : he knew her not : he was so indifferent that he had even forgotten how and when her sister had died. What would she signify to him, or he to her? It would merely confuse her plans, and roughen her return to Apahu. . . . Let all the past go now : for all had gone.

"It is a strange old house, this that they call a cottage," said she, with a sudden change of manner, bright, but hard, like one of her own gems : and a little bewildering to a man who knew little of women's whims. " I have been groping about all over it, and look what I found. Is it of any use do you suppose ? "

He looked at the paper which she gave him. " Why," said he, "it is a will. And Derwent—there have never been any Derwents here. I know some Derwents——" Sophy's heart came into her ears.

"So do I," said Rosamond. "Can it have to do with them ? "

" Impossible, I should say," said Oswald. " And of course, if it could, there's no saying whether it's any use to them or no. . . . . . But wait——." He turned deeply grave. " This *is* of use, I should say. Where was this found? " he asked, with his eyes fixed on the paper in his hand.

"In an old cupboard. Of course it means nothing to me. I thought of sending it to Dr. Rackstraw——"

" Would you trust it to me ? " he asked, eagerly. " I know the Derwents, and they *are* the people it concerns."

" Certainly," said Rosamond. " I don't mind who takes charge of it, as long as it is in the right hands. It is very strange, though it should be here. But no. There is nothing in the world that is strange."

That, however, was not Oswald's opinion as, after some further talk that wandered farther and farther away from what was in the hearts from those who made it, he rode back to Laxham. To find further evidence of a connection between Moldwarp and the Derwents, in the former's witness to a very obvious experiment in forging something more ambitious than flint arrow-heads was certainly not strange. That was merely useful; and he would employ it without further delay. What he found strange, and what, all the way to Laxham, and all the way that same night to London ran in his mind, was the woman to whom he had spoken for the first time that day. He, the lover of a dream, felt as if a living woman had thrown him under a spell.

He had come scarcely meaning to see her; or, if seeing her merely to gain such knowledge of her as might enable him the better to warn and protect Sophy. He found a presence, now soft and eager, now keen and brilliant, that, in its sudden moods, startled him into something beyond observant interest, and a voice that seemed to make music in him at once old and new. He had felt this in some measure even at the outset, when she was merely asking questions about the Fanes and showing him the paper she had found. But it was afterwards, when the talk ran upon her own country and her thoughts of England, that he began to comprehend the devotion of Sophy. The truth was that the Queen of Apahu was energetically throwing away the last remnants of Rosamond Fane.

So he who was searching the world for Rosamond found a charm in another woman that he had surely never known in that poor child. His excuse must be that he came to her doubtful of himself and disheartened, and that his heart had lived empty all its life, of all but hopes and memories, and these are sorry food.

CHAPTER XXIX.

If thou could'st change each moment of thy past
    Into the sands that marked it as they rolled,
And every sand, so scattered, could'st recast
    In time his crucible, to make it gold:

If from such gold a ring could forged be,
    And for a gem therein thine honour set
To wear upon his finger—yet were he,
    All unrepaid for even a moment's debt.

MRS. DERWENT'S son Horace had not shown himself an interprising lover; but he was at any rate a true one And indeed, though his enterprise had stopped short of the point of success, still it had been enough to achieve success under all ordinary conditions. When a young man has persistently called upon the mistress of his heart some half-dozen times only to find out at last that her invariable "not at home" is untrue, it would be natural enough that he, having obtained no claim upon her, should conclude that his visits are disagreeable things, and cease to make them. He could not write to her in the tone or manner of a discarded lover: but he could make her uncle's death an excuse for writing a letter—which remained unanswered. Such was the manner in which Oswald Hargrave had, all unconsciously, played into the hands of Hermon Rackstraw. And of course when Sophy once changed her name and went out to service, Dr. Rackstraw himself was able to take the whole play into his own hands. In the face of such complete indifference even to his friendship, and such proof that she classed him merely with common morning callers and troublesome correspondents, it would have been strange if the young man's enterprise had not frozen. The only wonder is that he continued to care in any fashion for a girl who had dealt such a mortal wound to what we call vanity in others and pride in ourselves.

Perhaps he would have been somewhat less constant if he had, less than eight thousand a year; at any rate if he had very much less, because then he would have had to put the extinguisher of work upon the spark that had, indeed, never been fanned into an open flame. As things were, he had leisure to be broken-hearted, and even as Sophy had turned misanthrope for his sake, so he turned misogynist for her's. One morning at breakfast he announced his intention of leaving town.

"For Scotland already?" asked his sister Anne.

"Scotland! No, indeed. What on earth should anybody go to Scotland for?"

"Oh, I don't know," said Ann. "To shoot things, or catch things, I suppose. Isn't that why *you* go?"

"I suppose it's why one's supposed to go. But it's got to be a cockney sort of business at best. I'm thinking of trying Kamschatka or Patagonia for a change. Which shall it be?"

"Horace!" exclaimed his mother. "But you're joking——"

"Indeed I'm not though. I've felt for a long time that I've been wasting my life on such trumpery as grouse and venison when there are tigers and bears——"

"Tigers in Kamschatka! oh!" cried Anne.

"Well, elephants then, or—or—whales. Something big, either way. You must see I'm wasting my life here, mother. Look at other men. Look at Hargrave. Look at Harding. Look at Rackstraw. They've been everywhere and seen everything——"

"Why, I believe you *are* serious!" said Anne. "It's just like what they do in books, when they have been rejected, or when the girl dies. Only they mostly go to Africa after lions——"

"Great Heavens!" cried Horace, flushing, "can't a woman get anything into her head without twisting it into love, and marriage, and all that rubbish ? I believe it's the only idea that girls and women have got among them. A fine world it would be, if men were the same."

"Well, Horace," said Anne, gently, "I'm not sure it isn't a better idea than killing things. Of the two ideas in the world, we've got the best of them. But oh, Horace—to think you wen't find things just the same in Kamschatka as here! And what on earth will you do for a thirty-sixth flame ? Or, let me see, thirty-seven, reckoning that Miss Fane whom we invited, and who never came : unless indeed the Kamschatkans are better looking than their pictures are——"

"Hang Miss Fane !" exclaimed her once good-tempered lover, who had let his sisters chaff him about his innumerable first passions hundreds of times, and had never failed to laugh with them. "Mount Athos—that's were I'll go."

"Mount Athos ? Why ? "

"Because no woman is allowed to set foot there."

"Not allowed, Horace? If she isn't allowed—then depend upon it a woman will be the first thing you'll see. Fancy expecting not to find a woman where she isn't allowed ! A double knock, this time ? Who can that be ? "

It was a gentleman to see Mr. Derwent : and, glad of the excuse —for he was ashamed of having lost temper—he left the room.

"Mamma," said Anne, gravely, "something has happened to Horace, I know."

"And this going abroad ! My dear—if it wasn't impossible, I should be convinced he had been proposing to that Miss Fane."

"It's not impossible, mamma. He wouldn't have said 'Hang Miss Fane' if he didn't care. I brought her in on purpose to see. If anybody said, 'Hang Anne Derwent,' I should know he was thinking about me a good deal."

"It's impossible, Anne," said her mother, "because he wouldn't have been talking about tigers and whales if she hadn't said No."

"But that's it—she *has* said No."

"What—a penniless orphan say No to Horace, with Longwood and eight thousand a year ? "

"But about his going abroad ? "

"I must consult Dr. Rackstraw," said Mrs. Derwent, with a rather anxious sigh. "It might be for the best—I don't know. And if Horace could go abroad under his eye—Anne, I thought at one time there might be a chance of Horace and that Queen :

Senhora Miranda, you know. She is quite a lady: and Dr. Rackstraw says that the jewels she has brought over alone make her a
millionaire."

" A heathen!—Oh, mamma ! "

" Of course we should convert her. Dr. Rackstraw says conversion's the easiest thing in the world—he has known natives
who will let themselves be converted over and over again."

" Why doesn't Dr. Rackstraw marry her himself, mamma ? "

But to this Mrs. Derwent said nothing : and Anne was quite
sharp enough to guess why.

Meanwhile Horace had gone into his library (so he christened
his sanctum when he amazed the family circle by taking up with
book-collecting), and there found Oswald Hargrave.

" It *is* rather early for a visit," said Oswald. " But I'm always
in a hurry, you know—and a curious document has come into my
hands in a curious way. You won't think me impertinent if I tell
you that I know you have a brother——"

" A half brother, if you please," said Horace, flushing; for such
a beginning as this was not the way to get his temper back again.
" He was my father's son. I suppose you have some reason for
mentioning *him*. Well ? "

" Of course I have," said Oswald. " I would give the rest of my
life to find him—if he is alive : and he *is* alive."

" You know Lawrence Derwent ? "

" Never. I never saw him even. But he alone knows what I
would give my life to know—it is not that, however, that concerns
you : except that you can help me, and I am sure you will, when
I tell you why. . . . I have every reason to know that—but,
by the way, what is your opinion of Dr. Rackstraw ? "

" Only that he is a conceited cad," said Horace, frowning. " But
he has somehow become one of us—my father had great confidence
in him : and I have no doubt it was deserved."

" It comes to this, then," said Oswald, " I connect this document,
which I have here, with a particular house, in which it has been
just by chance discovered. I connect that house with Moldwarp,
of whom you bought the *Flora*—the most ingenious of professional forgers. I connect Moldwarp with Lawrence Derwent ·
and lastly, I connect Lawrence Derwent with this will. Look at
it and see whether it concerns you or no."

Horace Derwent took the will, and glanced at it. But his
glance became a look of the most profound attention as he ex-

amiued every letter and every word. At last he folded it up slowly and laid it down.

"It does concern me—a little," he said, at last, slowly and gravely. He lighted a cigar very carefully and deliberately, and then spoke again. "I suppose you've read this?" he asked.

"Of course. It seems to be an old will in favour of Lawrence Derwent. As to what it really is——"

"I know you think it's forged. Why?"

"Because I know Silver Moldwarp: and because I suspect Hermon Rackstraw. As you see, this is a will that would establish Lawrence Derwent's innocence. I have the best reason to believe that he is even now hidden in London, and in communication with both Moldwarp and Rackstraw. Moreover I have even better reason to believe that he was in communication with Moldwarp at the time of his escape from Lowmoor. And look the witnesses' names Silver Moldwarp—Hermon Rackstraw. If were it not forged, would it not have been brought forward long before now? Moldwarp has forged much more difficult things than wills."

"I see. And who found it? And where?"

"Strangely enough, Madam Miranda. At Crossmarsh, near Laxham: and near Lowmoor: and where Moldwarp was once in service with the Fanes."

"Then your theory is this, Hargrave," said Horace, quietly—for all the world as if he were discussing another man's affairs: "you think that Lawrence Derwent and Rackstraw have invented a plot: that they have employed Moldwarp to forge and hide, and Madam Miranda to go down and find?"

Oswald started. That she also might be in the plot, whatever it was, had never occurred to his mind; though it was certainly remarkable that she should not only have bought Crossmarsh in such frantic haste, but have discovered a document bearing Rackstraw's signature the very next day. Nor was his opinion of the lady altered by his change of feeling—fascination would naturally be her stock in trade.

But "No," he answered quickly, "she would hardly have parted with it to me—"

"True. 'Crossmarsh, near Laxham,'" he said, noting the address down. "Will you do me a favour, Hargrave—or rather several favours? Don't say to any living soul a word of what you have said to me. And take charge of this will yourself: don't let it come into my hands till I ask you for it in writing. If you'll do this for me, I pledge myself that you *shall* meet Lawrence Derwent, if he is in London, and alive. . . . . . Where are you staying? Where are you to be found?"

"I must get down to Laxham to-night. Here is my addrsss there. But about these conspirators—what is your plan? You know my interest in all this; to meet with Lawrence Derwent——"

"I have said you shall—if he is alive. You won't think I mistrust you, Hargrave, if I go to work alone?"

"I am afraid you must act alone," said Oswald. "I have tried, and failed ; and it is only you who can know how to deal with Rackstraw. Of course I will say no word to a mortal soul; and of course, I will keep this forgery as long as you please."

There was an altogether new decision of tone and manner about Horace that rather surprised Oswald, and at the same time gave him greater confidence in his acquaintance's capacity for action than he had hitherto been disposed to place in him. But then it is true, that to have one's whole fortune attacked by a gang of robbers is enough to find a man in energy and decision, however little may have been given him by nature. And such a series of accidents had renewed Oswald's faith that at last the work of his life was about to prove not in vain.

But infinitely more surprised would he have been, could he have seen Horace Derwent after the consultation was over and he had gone his way. The young man tossed away his cigar, and covered his face with his hands.

"My mother—the girls—what is to become of *them?*" he groaned aloud.

For he knew it was no forgery that he had seen. He knew as a matter of family history, what the nature of his brother's defence had been—that he had, at his father's own request, destroyed the will disinheriting him, so as to make him safe in his right as heir-at-law in case there should be no time for another will to be made. He knew all the history of that death-bed as no stranger, like Oswald, could guess them. And there were solid reasons, besides his father's signature, and the kind of paper the colonel had always used, and the allusions and turns of phrase that nobody could possibly have reproduced, unless indeed it might be Rackstraw. Nobody could have done it but he; and he would surely have not inspired the forgery of a will that abused him in good round terms as a knave and a scoundrel who had done all he could to make mischief between a father and his son. Nor would he have inspired a forgery that revoked a handsome legacy, and left him nothing at all. But, on the other hand, that last reason made it his interest to suppress a will which as his signature in witness showed, he knew had been made.

But why had he not destroyed it? If he had only done his work thoroughly, the younger son, whom he had served, would not have had to wake up from his idle dream of life to find himself a beggar in the land. Was it partly to keep himself from a terrible temptation that he had bidden Oswald keep the will? Very honest men do not know what they are capable of until they are tried.

"The infernal scoundrel! And for the sake of a few thousands he has robbed an heir of his inheritance, and sworn an innocent man into gaol. And I have been amusing myself with stolen goods all these years—and my brother—it is horrible! What has become of *him?* What it must be—to lose liberty, honour, everything worth having on earth, and to think that thieves and fools and idlers are pampering themselves on one's soul. . . And my mother will have to know; and though he is my brother he is not her son——"

So he thought and felt; and yet not for one moment did it enter even his very deepest heart to upbraid Rackstraw for not having destroyed the will. Nor did he even hate Oswald Hargrave for having meddled in another man's concerns.

There are cases in which one must be either a scoundrel or a hero—in which it is impossible to be merely an honest man. Had Horace Derwent been tempted to frame such a wish, even in thought, he would have been a worse man than Dr. Rackstraw, who, after all, probably did not consider that he had done unto others worse than they would have been justified in doing unto him—if they were able. Nevertheless, it is not common honesty that does not think twice about the right and the wrong of giving up a fine estate, a large fortune, and all the pleasures and luxuries which have become the necessaries of life, and to ruin one's nearest and dearest into the bargain, and all for the sake of one whom one has been brought up to fear, to hate, and to scorn. Common honesty would have done right; but it would have thought twice about where the right lay, perhaps three times.

He did not see his mother before he left the house ; and for the simple reason that he was afraid. All men think that all women are more apt to judge by prejudice or interest than they ; and, though he did not frame the thought, he felt that a mother so wholly under the influence of Dr. Rackstraw, would not be entirely competent to advise her own son to ruin both himself and her. And why should he call upon her to face trouble before he could tell her its extent, or suggest how it was to be remedied ? So, without a moment's delay, he went out and drove straight to the Agency-General of the Goblin Islands. He thought, in the conceit of good intentions, that he would be able to compel a confession from one who, being a knave, ought, according to a common superstition, to be a coward besides, and no match for resolute honesty.

It was more fortunate for the knave than for honesty, however, that Dr. Rackstraw was not within.

" I will wait," said Horace, to the sharp lad, "till he comes in."

" I'm afraid you'll have to wait a goodish while, Mr. Derwent," said the sharp lad. " The Doctor's gone to the Goblins."

There was nothing unusual in that, for Dr. Rackstraw thought nothing of a sudden trip to the Antipodes and back again, and, more often than not, said nothing before hand about such expeditions, any more than if Port Rackstraw, or Atlantis, or Xanadu, or wherever he might have business in cotton, hardware or rum, were but just across the Thames. Had Horace been aware of the Doctor's close relations with Senhora Miranda, and of his feelings towards Sophy Fane, he would no doubt have been very much surprised by such sudden and unreasonable absence : as it was, he was only disappointed. For it was the last pitch of cruelty to leave justice undone and injustice triumphant even for a single hour.

The next best thing he could do was to set to work upon Mold-warp whom Hardgrave had no doubt rightly judged to be implicated—though in the concealment, and not in any forgery, the last being utterly out of the question. He remembered the shop where he had bought that new historical *Flora* for Æneas Fane ; and was this time fortunate enough to find the person he wanted at home.

" It's a time since you've been our way, sir," said the bookseller, politely, " I suppose you're like the rest of 'em ; everybody's found out now where books is to be picked up like flint stones, for the price of an old song. I've got some real uniques, that'll be worth their weight in gold in a year or two, but I can t afford to keep 'em these bad times, and you may make your fortune out of 'em. Here's——"

"I have seen a will executed by my father, Colonel Derwent," said Horace, at once, "and witnessed by you and Dr. Rackstraw. I want the address of my brother, Mr. Lawrence Derwent, if you please."

"The Devil!" exclaimed the bookseller: a heavy folio falling from his hands and raising a dust from the floor.

"You had better lose no time," said Horace. "I am in a hurry —and there is none to lose. It will save fencing if I tell you at once that a will has been found at a place called Crossmarsh, and that it has come into my hands. I am told also that my brother is in London, and that you know where."

Moldwarp raised the folio, dusted it, and found a place for it on the shelves. Then he took his gold spectacles, carefully rubbed the glasses, and returned them to his nose.

"Mr. Derwent, sir," said he, "then all I can say is, now you've got hold of the thing, nothing could please me more: no, nor half so well. Of course you'll say I ought to have destroyed that there will. And you'd be right, sir. For once, instinc' has led me wrong. No—'twasn't instinc', neither; 'twas because for once tried to be too wise for instinc'; that's what it were. And I'll never do it again. I ask your pardon for not having destroyed that there will, Mr. Derwent—on my bended knees, I do."

It no more entered the heart of Silver Moldwarp that Rackstraw and Horace Derwent together, or Horace Derwent alone, had not destroyed the will which unlucky chance had brought into their hands, than he could imagine any other possible combination of circumstances under which a man would risk the loss of eight thousand a year. But it took Horace at least a whole second to realise that Moldwarp assumed him to be, as a matter of course, an accomplice in the original fraud—at any rate after the fact: and this moment gave the other time to shift his ground further still.

For the game was up, anyhow, so far as making his fortune out of the rightful heir was concerned. He could only curse the evident stupidity of that rightful heir, who must have bungled matters in a most marvellous manner before the will could have

18

come in those hands to whom its existence meant ruin. " 'Tis just my regular luck all over again," he mentally groaned, "First and foremost I lose my place with old Squire Fane: and all by chance like, and no fault of mine. Then I fall out with old Rack-straw, for him being ungrateful—no fault of mine again. Then I go and trust a fool. 'Tis hard. Instinc's own self's no match for a fool. I do believe if instinc' led me straight down to the bottom of the diamond mines, some fool would go and cut away the rope I came down by. 'Tis enough to make an honest man give up in-stinc' and turn Rogue."

He saw, as plainly as he could see other men's blunders, that Lawrence Derwent must have bungled matters in such wise as to let the will slip back again into the hands of Rackstraw; and his knees felt ready to bend themselves with shame and reverence be-fore that great and unconquerable man. Remorse and repentance overwhelmed him for having dared to pit his wits against those of his master, who was no doubt aware of the whole extent of his treachery in the interests of justice and law. There was only one thing to be done—to return abjectly to his allegiance, and to make the best bargain left him.

" You see, sir," said he, " now that document's back again in the right hands—which in course is yours and the Doctor's—there's no harm done. And you're quite right: you nor yours will get no peace till that there Lawrence is safe again in gaol. I tell you, Mister, he's a regular dangerous man: and he'll now be that des-perate, now he's lost his rights—I should say his chances—that your life won't be worth a minute's purchase ; nor Rackstraw's nor mine. I'll do, to rectify my bit of a mistake through not trusting instinc', the best I can. You're a gentleman, Mister: and I'm but an unlucky customer that's come to grief by no fault of his own——'

" I understand," said Horace, with a passion of indignant scorn too deep to express itself in word or tone. " You were employed by Dr. Rackstraw to destroy the will, in order to cheat Lawrence Derwent. Instead of destroying it, you concealed it, in order to cheat Dr. Rackstraw. Because you could not get as much black mail as you wanted, I suppose, you try to sell the will back to Lawrence Derwent. Finding the will in my hands, you are will-ing to sell Lawrence Derwent to Dr. Rackstraw, Lowmoor, and me. Very well. I will buy him—such perseverance ought not to go without reward. What was Lawrence Derwent to give you for his estate and his good name ? "

"No, sir—no, Mr. Derwent! If I'd destroyed that there will I should have committed a crime. And if Dr. Rackstraw chose to be ungrateful, that was no fault of mine. And if I tried to get back the will for its lawful owner, *that* was no fault of mine. And if I consent to give up a convict—'tis hard times, Mister: for though duty's duty, like instinc's instinc', that there convict he promised me ten thousand pounds: which is a goodish bit to lose."

"And for how much—if you had one—would you sell your soul?"

"Well, sir—it seems to me Rackstraw's selling his pretty cheap, and your selling yours pretty dear. As there's souls going, I don't see why I shouldn't go to market with mine."

"It is certainly hard you should sell it for nothing. Of course you are putting yourself in a position to renew the black mail trade—so we can talk afterwards of terms. Where is Lawrence Derwent now?"

"Begging your pardon, Mister, you seem to take uncommon kindly to the trade. When old Rackstraw goes off, he won't want for a better to come after. Well—'tis all the same to me, since you put it like a gentleman. There's only one bit of advice to give you, sir. You shouldn't have let me know you'd seen that will. You see, sir, that puts you in a man's power. But for the rest, Mr. Derwent, you've done it beautiful: well-nigh as well as Rackstraw."

"Then—where is Lawrence Derwent to be found?"

"Where that will come from, to be sure. Crossmarsh: Lowmoor all handy by."

CHAPTER XXX.

Though way-worn steps for refuge seek
Where hands that builded well,
Of Duty raised on granite peak
The maiden citadel :—

WHEN Oswald had taken his departure, Sophy, her attendance on her sovereign not being immediately required, set out upon a tour of exploration over the old house, from which she had been absent very nearly as long as Rosamond. Not being of a sentimental nature, nor a slave to association, its nooks and corners had but little significance for her

18 ▲

save as signs of a childhood that she had almost forgotten and did not wish to recall. Still she could not help having a natural curiosity about seeing how the old place looked, and how far it had changed. It was wonderful, now that she saw it by day-light and in sunshine, how little change she was able to find.

Naturally, in the course of her rambles upstairs and downstairs she arrived at length at the passage leading to Rosamond's castle. But, from the far end of the passage, she heard the sound of voices: and, when she reached the castle door, found a couple of workmen busily engaged.

"What *is* being done here?" asked she.

"Only doing Madam's orders, miss," said one of the men, "to fasten up this here door—we've finished the trap inside. And a good job too."

"How strange! Why does Madame Miranda want to close this room?"

"Yes, miss: and we've to brick up the passage. And a good job too, as I said afore."

"It's a very strange order, pondered Sophy. And why do you call it a good job, please?" she had become to some extent used to the caprices of her mistress; but this sudden order, to brick off a passage and a couple of rooms for no imaginable cause, seemed to go beyond the bounds of even uncivilised eccentricity.

The two men looked at one another, as if to consult before answering the question. The village mind is prodigal with hints; but it is a dangerous thing to be the first to give a haunted house a bad name. It may drive away money from a place, as well as residents and their company: and so, all who take haunted houses learn to their cost, they have at last to find out from their servants the sort of purchase with which they have saddled themselves.

"Well, miss," said one, "Madam didn't say why—but maybe 'tis foreign fashions——"

"But you said it was a good job yourself," said Sophy, persistently. One need not be sentimental in order to feel aggrieved at a new owner's taking liberties with a house that was one's own but a few days ago. Nay, the feeling is sure to rise up even when the days are years. For our house is but our outward body; and our life is its soul.

"Yes, miss—most jobs are good, these times——"

"No," said Sophy, getting provoked, and using her quick eyes,

" You didn't mean that. Is there anything—said—said about this room ? "

" Well, miss—if you put it that way——"

" Yes : 1 put it that way."

" Then 'tisn't me nor my mate here that says it, miss; but 'twas in that room Old Harry carried off Miss Fane."

" Oh ! "

" Yes, miss; it do sound queer. But that's the tale. And when a room gets thought on like that——"

" I see ; it is best closed."

So she wandered back again to the staircase, supposing that some idle nonsense had already found its way to the Queen's ears, and wondering that a woman of such shrewdness should be such a slave to her native heathen superstitions as to imagine that a disembodied phantom could be imprisoned by bricks and nails.

And no doubt, it was superstition; though not quite of the gross kind that Sophy supposed. Rosamond's panic of last night, when she dashed her lamp away into the darkness had been extreme. It was a sudden and violent renewal of the old influence that had well-nigh driven her into brain fever years ago: and it was a great deal more. It was as if one were suddenly, when full grown, to meet in sober earnest with some imaginary horror that had been the dread of one's childhood—that horror which, if one lives to be a hundred, one never forgets, come what may. Her very first thought, when the sunlight came, was to close this book of her whole life for ever, before returning to her Arcadian people and their golden age. And the wood and brickwork she had ordered was but the natural, outward and visible sign of that final closure. There was something terrible about that old room of hers, but there was something sacred also. Its further use would be fully as much profanation as peril. For that room was the tomb of all her hopes and all her dreams : it was haunted indeed. And all nations close their graves.

In this manner she settled all accounts with her past : it was as if she had travelled all the way from the other side of the world solely to fasten the door of an empty room. She had only to make one last pilgrimage to certain old haunts and scenes before blotting them all out altogether. Nor, since Oswald's faithlessness and indifference to his kindred in friendship, was her last pilgrimage touched by any sort of regret or sorrow. She had convinced her-

self that it was her pleasure as well as her duty and her destiny
to leave all behind, and she had not, even in London, lost the
health which enabled her to face the future, though a Queen
and alone.   She did not even regret having come to England.
It was only right to know the worst, and not to live in a fool's
paradise of illusions.

So she purposely rid herself of her secretary's company before
strolling off to the cliff path whence she was supposed to have
thrown herself into the sea, and to the boathouse on the beach,
and to Crossmarsh Church, and to Pix-Knoll.   That mine of im-
posture still showed the excavations, longwise and crosswise, from
which her uncle had sought to recover the history of the prehis-
toric world: but the grass had invaded these works from the
Downs, and was covering away the old Squire's folly.

As she rambled, she more and more consciously and resolutely
forced her thoughts away from herself, and bent them upon what she
should do for her people, for whom she must henceforth live wholly,
and whom she must strive to love, for her own sake as well as for
theirs to the utmost of her power.   And she could reach but one
conclusion—she could not perceive that England, with all its great-
ness, had given her anything to carry back to Apahn.   Even the
religious part of the question was ceasing to trouble her, and for
what seemed to her the best of all reasons: that by their fruits·
are nations to be known—and that to seek to carry grapes and
figs from a country where men only preach to one where they
however ignorantly practised would be a fool's labour.   She had
no sort of doubt herself as to what she had learned in the very
church where she had been christened and under which she was
standing; but she could not comprehend how the Christianity of
a country whose people regard money as of value could be worth
exporting to one which thought doing right the only thing about
which any sane creature could care.   And then there was Lowmoor, within but a few miles of her.   To bring England to Apahu
would be to bring its gaols: for what is civilisation without a
gaol, and all that leads there?   Surely, she thought, what we
are, and not what we call ourselves, is the great thing.   They
were right—Apahu ought not to be so much as named across the
sea.   Well; it shall never be named or heard of again.

It had been a solemn day for her, but, though melancholy as
well as solemn, not wholly unhappy, and she returned late in the
afternoon to the house in a quieter mood of mind, and with better

courage for the future, than since she had left her kingdom. She had persuaded herself that Rosamond Fane was buried in her empty bower, and that nothing remained alive but the duties of Queen Ngahoung.

Sophy also had left the house, so she learned from Mrs. Crow, who was acting for the present as cook and housekeeper, and had not yet returned. Rosamond was a little vexed, for, having thought so much, she wanted to talk a little, and she learned to need the companion who seemed to worship her, and was vowed to follow her to the other end of the world. However it was natural enough that Miss Gray should be making the most of a first day of country freedom by the sea. But Rosamond was not fated to be left without company, for she had not settled herself in the drawing-room window over a book for half an hour, when Mrs. Crow disturbed her with the announcement of a gentleman to see her.

"Mr. Hargrave, again?" asked she, with a frown.

"Oh no, my lady," answered Mrs. Crow—for some vague idea of the new comer's rank had followed her down even to Cross-marsh, in the unaccountable manner of such things. "He's Mr. Derwent, says he."

Rosamond sighed: for she had made up her mind to cut herself adrift at once from every English connection—and especially from those which had to do with Rackstraw. Her acquaintance with the Derwents was slight enough, but still it had to do altogether with Rackstraw: and what should so slight an acquaintance mean by coming down upon her here? Had her professor of civilisation discovered her flight, and did he intend to return? If so, then he should see that she intended to rebel: for the Doctor's guidance had become exceedingly like tyranny now that she knew how to walk alone.

However, there was nothing for it but to receive him graciously, and to hear what he had to say.

She hardly knew him by sight: and indeed his mood, on the occasion of her introduction to English society at his mother's house, was not such as to enable him to remember her very clearly —he had been the only man there who had been impression proof during the short season of her being the rage.

"I am on too important business to apologise for intruding on you, Madam," said he. "I understand it was you who discovered my father's, Colonel Derwent's will."

"Oh—that paper!" said she, relieved: for she had forgotten that insignificant accident of her adventure. "Yes: I found a paper which I gave to Mr. Hargrave. Is there anything you want to ask me? Though I hardly guess what it can be."

"Surely, Madam, you know——"

"Indeed I do not, Mr. Derwent," said she, a little proudly—Queens are not used to contradiction, even in Apahu; and henceforth she was to be more than ever a Queen.

"Of course you know that your forwarding me that document through Mr. Hargrave gave me only one thing to do; and I thank you with all my heart for letting there be no delay. Can I see my brother at once—now?"

"Your brother, Mr. Derwent?" asked Rosamond, beginning to wonder if the young man was quite right in his mind.

"My brother—Lawrence Derwent, who is staying with you."

"You are under some strange mistake, sir. I have nobody with me but my friend, Miss Gray. As to Lawrence Derwent, I never heard the name."

"Did he not come down here to find this very will? Did you not find it just where he knew it was to be found? Did you not know from him that it gave him back what I have been robbing him of nearly all my life——"

For how can men judge but by their own natures? Even as Silver Moldwarp assumed that the will could not come into the hands of Horace without instant destruction, so Horace took for granted that it had been forwarded to him in the confidence that he would do justice. And, instructed by Moldwarp, he could only suppose that this lady was aiding the rightful heir in this affair. It was natural that Lawrence should keep in the background until his innocence as well as his rights should be made amply clear.

"Pray explain yourself," said Rosamond, with a touch of impatience. "I never heard of your brother, or knew you had one. I found this will by the merest chance—in a cupboard, in a lumber room, under a trap door——"

"Yes: exactly where he was told. Madam," he went on, eagerly, in a low quick voice, "I thank you with all my heart for your protection of my infamously wronged brother: but there is no need for your loyal, generous secrecy any more. Let me see him face to face, and take his hand—if he will give it me: I come to give him back his rights and his good name."

Rosamond could only wait for light. He could only take her silence for hesitation.

"You and he trusted me with the will," said he. "Can you doubt my good faith *now*? You see I have not lost a single moment in coming down. Imagine if you can, what it is to me to have had all my brother's wealth, and to have been in his place, while he has been a martyr to villainy—a convict: an out-law:——"

"I think I understand," said Rosamond, thoughtfully, "that you are come here to do some just or generous thing. And so I am glad of the chance that made me find the will. Will it cost you much money to do what you wish to do?"

"For Heaven's sake, Madam," cried Horace, "don't keep me on the rack any more. Don't you know that every penny I possess on earth, and every inch of ground, is shown by that will to be my brother's, and that I have come to give back to him all—to him, who has been made a felon in trying to rob me, while I, though not knowing it—thank God for that—have been robbing him of wealth, honour and all?"

Very different indeed was the young man whom Rosamond saw and heard from him who examined Moldwarp so quietly. The Queen gave him her hand, with a royal smile.

"Why, here is one at last who only thinks of doing right!" said she: thinking of what her thoughts had been in the church-yard that very day.

"I should be a greater cad than Rackstraw else," said he: not caring to remember that the Doctor was this lady's friend. "But as to my brother——"

"You want to see him, of course: instantly. I understand now. If I knew where he was! But I told you simple truth when I said I never heard of him, or his name. What made you think he was here?"

"Because he knew where this will was to be found. Thank Heaven, any way, that it came into my hands first and thank you too for that, Madam. It is something that I may give him back his own freely, and with my own hands."

"I should think it would not be very difficult to find him," said Rosamond, "considering what he is wanted for—if he was coming here to search, as you say, perhaps he will come, still."

"But you don't know all," said Horace, bitterly. "He is in the position of a convicted felon, who escaped from gaol from Low-moor. He would not dare to risk an open search——'

"Escaped from Lowmoor!" exclaimed Rosamond, who could almost fancy that she again heard that signal gun which had broken her life in two. "There have been but two escapes from Lowmoor: one man was dashed to pieces over Furnace Point: the other—Ah! then when he called himself guiltless, it was true: and he must have been hidden in the same room with this very will— why did he not find it then? Oh, God, what I should have been spared!"

She had forgotten herself and her part: and no wonder, for to her all was as clear as day. Indeed she had become blind to her companion's presence in the hideous knowledge that her life had been cursed and her heart well-nigh broken by reason that Lawrence Derwent had not discovered a scrap of paper that had been literally under his very fingers for days.

"Madam! What made you start when I named Lowmoor? Then you *do* know ——"

"Forgive me: I'm afraid I *was* startled—I only mean that what you have said—yes: you may be at ease: I do know your brother after all: I do know where he is to be found. But I know him under another name—and there are reasons why he must never know nor hear of me. And so long as you meet him, it is enough for you and for him; you will not ask my reasons, and he will not know from whom your knowledge comes—and indeed before you can meet, I mean to be far away. Have a little patience; for all this means as much to me as to you—ah, and more. Have a little patience; he nor you can lose by it, and I shall gain—all I have left to gain. Forget all I said just now. You shall meet your brother; but it must be in my own way." For she had not closed the tomb in order that her life might be haunted still, or buried her past self in order that he whom she had recognised with terror in the man from Nevada should recognise Rosamond Fane in the Queen of Apahu. It would be easy to make her escape unbetrayed so long as she kept matters in her own hands. "I promise you," she said, holding out her hand, "on the word of a Queen . . . Ah, Sophy—you are a good child to have found so much to say to the sun and the wind, as we say at—home. Mr. Derwent, this is my dear friend and daughter, Miss Gray."

"Good God—Sophy!" cried he; "Miss Fane!"

Sophy bent herself towards him coldly and proudly. But, hearing her name spoken, and all miserable at meeting this false friend, she stood trembling like a detected impostor before the Queen.

CHAPTER XXXI.

Yet soon as from the vale below
A breath hath reached their air,
The granite crumbles as the snow,
And Duty bideth—Where?

TWILIGHT was too far advanced for anything but a lover's recognition of his lost mistress; so that Sophy's downcast and tearful eyes did not perceive how the Queen's looks received evidence of an untruth which, however slight, should unfit any creature for the society of Apahu.

"Mr. Derwent," said Rosamond, in a voice that seemed to tremble faintly, as with vibrations that follow the stroke of a bell, "you have my promise—I will see you to-morrow, at whatever hour you come. I can say nothing more till then."

"I *will* come," said he, and it was to Sophy he spoke though he addressed the Queen. "I trust your promise, Madam. And you may trust mine, that not one of these mysteries in which you live shall remain by the time to-morrow is gone."

So he went back to where he had met Moldwarp at the "Feathers," hardly knowing, at the last, whether this woman were friend or foe; yet failing to imagine how or why she could be otherwise than friend. Had it not been for that sudden sight of Sophy, and in her company, he might not have let himself be dismissed in such royal fashion. And could it be Senhora Miranda who was at any rate his enemy there?

"Madam—" began Sophy.

Rosamond was silent.

"It is quite true. I am Miss Fane from whom you bought Crossmarsh. I had a reason for not wishing—for not wanting to keep my name; of course it had nothing to do with you; and it seemed wise at the time: and Dr. Rackstraw advised——"

"I have never told you *my* story," said Rosamond. "I will tell you it now."

"You are not angry, then, Madam?"

"You shall see. Had you ever a sister?"

"Yes, indeed——"

"What became of her?"

"It is a sad story, Madam. Something happened to her brain·

and she—she fell one night over the cliffs : close by here. We—
we never lived here after that time."

"I once knew a woman who had a wonderful story.   She had
a sister like you. She, too, lived close by the sea. She was an
odd sort of girl, living all alone with her own foolish plans and
fancies, until she was fifteen years old."

"Our poor Rosamond's age!" said Sophy : wondering what
all this preface could mean, relieved at having escaped instant dismissal, but giving all her real thoughts to that unlooked-for meeting with him on whose account she was going
into exile.

"Indeed ? Well," said Rosamond, "I suppose we have both
known what fifteen means. A poor fellow, wrongfully imprisoned,
had escaped from gaol——"

"I thought there were no prisons in Apahu ?"

"Nor ever shall be. This was not in Apahu. . . . . He
threw himself upon the protection of this girl. She concealed
him, and helped him to escape from his enemies. But he did not
trust her. He left the land in a boat : and that there might
be no witness of escape, he forced her away with him—away
from sister, friends, home, without a word to say how or where or
why she had gone, or if she would ever return. Think, if you can,
what that voyage must have been : for they were carried by a
passing ship to the other side of the world: and not a word or
sign could she send home.   At last there came a storm, and the
ship went down. The girl was saved, and thrown by the sea upon
a shore that none but they who dwell on it have ever seen. It is
laid down on no map ; no ship ever passes by : it is another world
than ours, in all its thoughts and ways. The people thought this
girl borne there by miracle from the sea, which divides the world
of men from the world of spirits ; and they made her Queen.
They were good ; but she became more and more unhappy, year
by year, and day by day. . . . You have had a home ; a
sister; you will know why. . . . At last what *she* thought
was miracle allowed her to escape—are you listening ?"

"Indeed, Madam, I am !"

"She took certain vows to the gods of her people, and hastened
home—Oh, what hopes and fears ! But her Uncle Æneas was
dead, and her sister Sophy——"

Sophy gave a cry, and started to her feet. "What are you
telling me ? What does all this story mean ?"

Rosamond opened her arms, and her heart—.

"Oh, Sophy, Sophy—Don't you see ? I am Rosamond—come back from the grave ! "

It was the supreme moment for which her whole soul had been hungering, and of which it had at last learned to despair. But there was no more despair now—all was forgotten and swept away, save that she and Sophy were together at Crossmarsh again once more. Home became home in an instant's flash ! Apahu became the dream. She sobbed with joy—joy that had been suppressed and distorted into one great heart-ache for twelve long years.

But alas ! It was not thus with Sophy. She had not been living and breathing in one thought all this while. She had mourned and wept for her dead sister like the quick-hearted child of April that she had been from the beginning; and then, in her life of travel abroad, in her studying, her pleasures, and her excitements, she had lived in a new small life nearly every day. Rosamond had been talked about until the subject was worn out: and then not talked about until she had become, if not a myth, yet a family legend. And then came the other household troubles : and then had entered into Sophy's life that element which well-nigh slays all others. The memory of a dead sister can scarcely count for much against the fact of a living lover, be he false or true.

This woman Rosamond ? Why, she had well-nigh forgotten Rosamond's very features, save in the very vaguest way. And then it was as yet all too real to understand—bewildered as Sophy was, such an undreamed of resurrection filled her less with joy than with dismay.

There is surely no such mistake in the universe as to return from one's grave. Let every corpse rest at peace ; let it assure itself that its survivors are very far from being heart-broken. It will only come back to lose its way among a labyrinth of new growths, and find its place filled. Rosamond had been put away and forgotten ; and Sophy, instead of being overjoyed, was only amazed.

But Rosamond felt for Sophy as well as for herself, and gave herself welcome.

" Oh, Sophy," she cried, pressing her sister to her heart, " I am glad of everything now; I am glad that I learned to like you and love you for yourself before I found out who you are. And to think that we two have been living together all this time without

guessing—and I, trying to find you and hear of you while you
were with me all this time—I thought at last you were dead,
just as you thought me. Don't let us tell all our stories yet—let
us feel that we are together again, just as we used to be."

"You *are* Rosamond?" asked Sophy, with a sort of awe.

"And you are Sophy—and I don't know what to do and what
to say. I have been dead—a Queen of shadows—for years. My
dear, my dear—don't speak to me ; let me wait till I feel awake
and alive."

And indeed Sophy was glad enough to wait; for she also knew
not what to do or what to say. She could not at two-and-
twenty, take up life again, all at once from the point where it was
broken off at twelve years old. Nor was this Rosamond the Rosamond who had been lost, after all. This foreign Queen, with her
barbarous jewels, her high thoughts, and her strange ways, was not
the dimly remembered sister who used to hide in the lumber room.

However, Rosamond herself as yet missed nothing, because she
knew, or thought she knew, how she would have felt had she
been Sophy, and Sophy she. They sat together, hand in hand,
while she poured out a thousand questions and told a thousand
things ; too many thousands to tell coherently what they were.
She had to ask of her uncle's last hours, of Sophy's foreign life ;
of how Crossmarsh came to be sold ; of Silver Moldwarp; of all
things and creatures save Oswald Hargrave alone. And she had
to tell of her strange life in a strange land, and how her spirit
sickened till it almost died, and how her heart had gone out to
Sophy the first time they met—

"And no wonder !" said she. "But why did you come to me
in another name ? "

"Dr. Rackstraw said——" faltered Sophy.

"And what do you know of Dr. Rackstraw ? What had you
to do with him ? And you know Mr. Derwent ? And—Sophy—
I have learned how all this happened—but never mind all that.
We will forget everything except that we are together, and you
and I—don't cry, dear, it is all over now."

But it was Rosamond herself who was crying, and did not
know.

"Are you still going back ? " asked Sophy, " to Apahu——"

"You haven't once called me Rosamond ! "

"—Rosamond ? " Sophy finished her question. "But it *is*
all so strange—Rosamond ! I feel in a dream——"

Rosamond shuddered : and all her royal duties shrivelled up and were no more. "No, dearest : they will do without me now. They have done without me for ages, and will for ages more. But I can't do without you and home. We will go on living here, just as we planned when we were children : I am going to blot out all that has happened as if it were a nightmare, and I am going to be fifteen years old. Yesterday was my fifteenth birthday, you know : and you will be thirteen next June. If only poor Uncle Æneas were alive ! But for the rest we will be as we used to be, all but the castle, which shall be blotted out like the nightmare ; and I am rich enough for both—terribly rich : richer than anybody knows. I soon found out in England what diamonds and rubies mean, and Dr. Rackstraw has—taught me a great deal, Yes, we will go on living here all by ourselves, and never change. . . . I suppose I shall have to be a nine days' wonder : but never mind. It won't matter here. Whatever happens I must be Rosamond Fane once more."

"And your people ? " asked Sophy, who by no means felt fascinated, after her vision of a golden age in the tropics, by the prospect of an old maid's life in a village she had learned to abhor.

"I have no people," said Rosamond. "They are all a dream. . . . . Yes, I have : you are my people, Sophy."

Alas ! Sophy began to feel that, despite her abdication, her long lost, unknown, scarcely welcome sister did not mean to cease to be a Queen.

CHAPTER XXXII.

When nations rise to pull their tyrants down,
Each blood-stained hand is given a hero's crown :
Dies Freedom's right because, when wrong is done,
A nation's sword is many—mine but one ?

THAT same evening Oswald Hargrave, having transacted his business at Laxham—indeed having there wound up all that remained, so far as he was concerned, of the conveyance of Crossmarsh and the mortgage of Windgates in order to provide the security on which the conveyance had been made conditional—rode over to the " Feathers" where he had often put up on occasion. The present occasion (so he told himself) was the duty of calling on Sophy next morning in order to give her a clear understanding of all that had been done in her interest : but more especially to make yet one more attempt to compel her to see the madness of sailing for a non-existent island in company with an adventuress whom he vehemently suspected of being the confederate of a knave.

But this was no more his real purpose than are the purposes which we believe to be ours, really ours, nine times out of ten. Adventuress as Senhora Miranda might be, her influence was upon the man whose nearest approach to love had been the resolution to some day marry a child who had perished long ago. Whether there was any occult recognition, others must decide: and we all have read or heard of how Carolan the minstrel, when old and blind, recognised by the mere touch of her finger the lady whom he had known and loved when both were young. It may be so: though it is hard to believe that either touch, or glance, or voice, or anything more subtle still, could connect Queen Ngahoung of Apahu with Rosamond Fane. If this is to account for her influence one must be driven to compass the secret of it with the magical perfume of a flower, which will bring back with it phantom memories so far off as to belong to times utterly forgotten—perhaps of the world in which our souls were born: which may, or may not be, beyond the moon. One need not wander away so far as that to discover why a man who has lived the life of a knight errant under the vows of a monk should feel the fascination of a strange and beautiful woman, with all the prestige of mystery and a certain witchcraft of her own about her, adventuress though she be.

In short, he feared for his own constancy: being deceived as the needle of a compass might be, which, having been held for years to the east by a certain magnet, should be compelled by that same magnet to point westward. It would believe itself false because it was true. He would never see this woman again. But such a vow implies the privilege of a Once More.

No sooner had he reached the " Feathers " than he was accosted by Mr. Crow, who of course knew Mr. Hargrave of Windgates well.

" I be main glad to see you, Mr. Hargrave," said he : " for there's some of us be in mortal trouble, to be sure. "

" What is it, Crow ? "

" Well, sir : it be this ways—'tis about that there place that used to be Squire Fane's—"

" What has happened there ! " asked Oswald, vaguely alarmed.

" Ah—*what*, sir ! What'd be likely to happen when a gentleman, as might be your own self, goes in there last night to lolnob with the—never mind who, and never comes out no more ? "

"I should say it's likely to happen that he's there still. But what the devil do you mean, Crow? You look as if you'd just seen a ghost in a dark lane———"

"Don't name him, sir, if you please. There's them as think 'twas He flew off with Miss Rosamond, as may be you remember —her that was niece to Squire Fane: and till last night there wasn't so much as a child would put foot into the room where 'twas done. . . . But last night a artist gentleman dropped in at the 'Feathers,' and we got talking about the new ladies, and the house, sir—and naught would do for him but to go and sleep in that there room. And he went, sir: for he was a dare-dev—a dare-never-mind-who. And dead nor alive, he's never been seen no more. 'Twas just like what happened to Miss Rosamond, sir— just the same."

"But how do you know he never came out?" asked Oswald: not in the best humour at having been alarmed without cause.

"Because he hasn't, Mr. Hargrave. Nothing's been seen of him from that minute till now."

"Then what in the world makes you think he ever went in?"

"Because naught's been seen of him from that minute till now. There's none but four of us know of it, sir—me, and Giles Fletcher, and the new groom at the rectory, and the shepherd at Johnson's. I haven't even told my old woman, because I gave him the key to let him in: and she'd go telling the ladies, and setting all the parish afire. 'Tis awsome to think of, Mr. Hargrave. We can't eat, nor shut an eye, not we four: and the beer's got to taste like Brimstone, sir: it do indeed."

Oswald knew that country side too well to give himself the airs o' a rationalist or sceptic. "Are any of you four at the 'Feathers' now?" asked he.

"To be sure there's Johnson's shepherd—he dursn't go out of company now."

Oswald went into the parlour, followed by Mr. Crow: and though its atmosphere was always dull enough to a man not Crossmarsh born, this evening it was something more than dull. For the news had not yet spread abroad, and those who knew it felt like members of a conspiracy: burning, yet afraid, to be the first to tell the world. There were the sceptical shepherd: and old Fletcher: and a stout person in black absorbed in a newspaper in a corner: and there was beer, and there were pipes: but no man was saying a word.

"So I hear the Devil's abroad in Crossmarsh," said Oswald.

19

"What does it all mean, Master Fletcher? We must get to the rights of this—we mustn't have the ladies frightened out of their lives."

Then, at last, the door was opened to speech: and Mr. Crow's story was even improved upon, if such a thing could be. Despite all that could be said to dissuade him—Oswald learned—the stranger had determined to spend the night in the chamber of evil fame, and had never been seen again—

"And 'tis my belief," said Giles, "that whatever came to Miss Rosamond Fane, that's come to he."

No man on earth was less superstitious than Oswald. But none else remembered Rosamond's story in her supposed delirium, and on the faith of which he had connected her disappearance with the escape of Lawrence Derwent from Lowmoor. There could be no imaginable connection in the shape of reason between that story and this: but then the whole thing, from first to last, was outside reason.

One of the company gave a long solemn whistle. "And 'twas this very afternoon I was saying to the young lady 'twas a good job too—and Bill here can swear 'twas my very words!"

"A good job!" exclaimed Mr. Crow, aghast—

"Surely—fastening up that there room. 'Twill take a toughish ghost to get through our work when 'tis finished; mine and Bill's."

But there were so many anecdotes to prove the contempt of ghosts for carpenters' work, nay, even for coffin makers', that Oswald, for the present, was compelled to listen. Nor had he listened long, when the person in the corner laid down his newspaper, crept round the room, and at last whispered in Oswald's ear.

"Don't seem to know me, Mr. Hargrave, if you please. If you want to know something, we'll step outside."

"Moldw——"

"Hush, sir. You come along of me. . . . When I told old Squire Fane I'd find Lawrence Derwent by instinc', you as good as said I lied. Well, sir, it's took instinc' a matter o' ten years to do it; but she's done it, and she'd have done it if it had took her, for ever and ever Amen. I've heard them fools talking, and I know 'em of old—Lawrence Derwent has been and got nailed up in that there old lumber room as sure as you're alive."

Oswald seized Moldwarp by the shoulder, as they stood before the tavern door. Moldwarp felt Oswald's arm tremble with the strength of the grasp.

"Good God! he exclaimed. "Speak out at last—and if you lie now——"

"I won't, Mister. I've come down after that convict in the interest of justice——"

"Of the reward?"

"'Tis all the same. And he'll be in that house: *and I know where.*"

"Man—all the world knows I would give half my life for one minute with Lawrence Derwent before the law can touch him.

"I know, Mister. But half your life'll be no manner of use to me. 'Twas something more substantial you offered ten year ago, you and old Fane."

"Then if you're not lying you may earn it twice over. But is it *there* he is concealed?"

Even in his sudden excitement, and with the hope of finding this man, startled from its ashes into flame, his heart sank—for was it not in Senhora Miranda's house that Lawrence Derwent was being concealed?

As for Moldwarp, his course at last lay clear before him. If he could save Horace Derwent from the scandal of delivering his own father's son up to justice by transferring that work to Oswald Hargrave, he would have a double claim upon the gratitude of both, besides earning a double reward. He even had visions of renewing his hold upon the great Rackstraw himself—in short of having the whole of this story under his hand.

"There, Mister, sure enough. And now we're two of us after him, he's safe enough for Lowmoor this time. Do you know a party calling himself Harding, from the American silver mines?"

"I have seen him—well?"

"That's the man. That's Lawrence Derwent, Mister."

"Ah! And *her* friend! .... Moldwarp: I'm going to trust you. I am going to unearth this man now. And if you are tricking me—Heaven knows why you should, but if you are——"

"You needn't finish, Mister. I'm not game to give half the rest o' *my* life, whatever you be."

"Will you come with me, now?"

"Surely, Mister. I came down with a friend, but he's gone out, and won't miss me for an hour or two."

"A detective? Well, I want no constable to forestall me. I must see him, man to man. Let me see—if one goes by the cliff path, one can get up by the wall to the tiles of the dairy, and so to the window of the loft: I've done it dozens of times, when I was a boy. It will be easy enough to see if what you say is true —if he is there. . . . . Yes," he told himself, "to set a ghost story going: then to hide the man in the haunted room and to fasten up the door till a chance of escape comes: she who can invent such a plan as that will be quite clever enough to feed him too, in spite of the nails. But—She! And Sophy in Her power!"

That it is quite feasible by means of the cliff path, the wall, and the tiles, and a trifle of further climbing, to obtain a complete view of Rosamond's castle had been proved not only by Oswald, but by Lawrence Derwent himself, who could only have made his original entry into the cottage, by this or similar means. What would be the next step must be dependent upon circumstances: in the first place it was needful to see if the convict was really thus hidden, according not only to Moldwarp's story but to all the unhappy likelihoods dependent upon the Senhora's acquaintance with Madam Miranda. And even if nothing more could be done to-night, the convict's escape from the house before morning could be prevented by standing guard.

So—it was moonlight now—Oswald, in company with the rascal whom of all the world he least expected to prove his ally, doubting, hoping, anxious, and yet believing, and all the while with the heaviest weight at his heart he had ever known, proceeded to that path overhanging the sea where the last vestige of Rosamond had been seen. There were no lights at the back of the house, and no passing constable was likely to mistake Mr. Hargrave of Crossmarsh for a housebreaker, despite his suspicious company: nor for that matter was the ragged Silver Moldwarp likely to be recognised in the stout and gold-spectacled London tradesman.

"Stay here," said Oswald, "while I climb the garden wall."

The full light of the moon was on the back windows, so that he had no need of a lantern. He had one knee on the low wall, when, looking up, he was arrested by a sight that made his heart beat with exultation, and yet sink again at the realisation of his worst suspicions of the Senhora.

At the window of the loft itself—easy of access from without, though, from its being near the ceiling, not from within—appeared a bulky shadow, which presently emerged into the moonlight in human form. Well was it for their sanity that neither Mr. Crow nor Mr. Fletcher nor Dr. Johnson's shepherd was there. Oswald dropped back into the path, so that the coming encounter might take place on level ground. "Stand back," he whispered to Moldwarp. "We are two to one, so he can't escape—but I must meet him alone."

The human figure let himself down from the sill to the full length of his arms and then dropped heavily, and with something of a clatter upon the tiles. Moldwarp, black traitor as he was, must have felt something of the honest excitement of the hunter, and his heart, or whatever he had in place of it, laughed at the prospect of the triumph of Instinct over Fortune after all—Oswald his debtor: Rackstraw his subject: Horace Derwent his slave: all the revenues of Longwood his pasture. . . . The man crept slowly along the tiles: the man from Nevada was not quite so lithe and active as ten years ago. But he knew his road. At last he stood upon the wall and looked round to see that all was clear.

He dropped on the path : and then Oswald sprang forward. It was the man from Nevada indeed.

"Lawrence Derwent—" he began—

But well-nigh before the words had left his lips, the desperate, hunted man, who had lost all that he had come to find, and was now at bay put his hand to his breast: a quick shot broke into the roar of the rocks and waves: and the last words that Oswald's ears heard were :

"Traitor—bloodhound !"

As the body of Silver Moldwarp went flying over the cliffs to the rocks below—

Rosamond turned in her sleep : and thought she had heard the signal gun of Lowmoor in a dream

CHAPTER XXXIII.

GITANA. Why dost thou weep, fair lady ?

ISABEL.   For my lord,
My dear, dead love, whose death made dark the sun !
See, I would give my wealth, my soul, my all,
My more than all, to see him live, and say,
'Twas but a dream I died in : here am I.

GITANA. No more than this—to make a dead man rise ?
The Witch of Endor did as much : and thrice
The secrets of her craft are known to me.
I'll use my spell for pity, not for gain.
Come forth, Count Arcos !

ISABEL.   Hold : in mercy hold !
Tears shed for love must not be shed for naught—
And should he come—
GITANA.   Enough, I understand.
Tears wept for one, another's lips must dry.

A FTER so dark a night, in so many senses, it was natural
that the sun, who has no sort of sympathy for what goes
on beneath him, should rise with unusual brilliancy.
Rosamond sprang from her bed early, with a delicious sense that
the weight of her unsought crown had at last fallen from her, that
she was released from the spell under which she had been living,
and was free to resume the life she had always longed for—even to
begin again from her fifteenth birthday, so far as that might be.
It was not that she had become false to the good resolutions she had
been making for her people's sake—it was that Apahu had
ceased to be real to her, in the fresh birth of an English
morning.

Her first action was to kneel down beside the bed of Sophy,
who still slept— who, indeed, had never been robbed of a night's
rest either by joy or sorrow — and to sing a song of thanks
without words. She knew how she would have felt had Sophy,
been lost out of life and then, after many years, had risen from
the grave : and what she herself would have felt, she believed
that Sophy dreamed. And then, throwing open the window, she
let her plans of life make themselves all over again.

She would never marry. She remembered what Oswald Hargrave had said to her when she was a child, and even in Apahu
she had come to comprehend his meaning. Indeed, where in the
world are such meanings not to be learned? And if he had been
ever so much loyal as to have known or cared whether her sister
was alive or dead, she might easily have been tempted to be as
false to her childish vow of singleness, as to her vow of self

devotion to her people made in the belief that her people had become her all. But even Oswald, the only man she had ever met, whom insight bade her trust wholly, had, by showing how quickly forgetful the staunchest of all men was, shown her what all other men must be. It was not that he had not recognised Rosamond herself in the Queen of Apahu; that was nothing; even Sophy had not guessed at what lay beneath her disguise. But not even to know, not to speak of caring, what had become of Sophy—that was treason; that left no name for the nature of a Rackstraw, or a Horace Derwent, or for any other example of civilised man. Had not her heart been overflowing with joy at finding Sophy herself alive, and well, and with her once again, and all her own, and maybe if the sun had shone less brightly, she would have let her heart turn bitter. As things were, she contented herself with a royal and lofty scorn for Oswald's sex, and was far too much assured of her contempt for it to make vows against a temptation by which she could never, by the remotest possibility, be assailed. In her narrow world there had never been any man, who could be called such, save Oswald; and there was no place in it for a worse, the best having been expelled.

Why, he had not recognised Sophy any more than he had recognised Rosamond; Sophy had found concealment as easy a game to play as she. Of course, he, as their neighbour at Windgates, would now have to know who the ladies at Crossmarsh were. And yet—it suddenly struck her—why should he, why should any living creature know? It would be hideous to have to play the part of a nine days' wonder, as the heroine of some newspaper romance about the conversion of a missing heiress into a barbarian queen, who had returned home after years of adventure such as none of imagination inferior to a professed journalist's would dare to conceive. She shrank, as any woman would, from feeling herself a heroine of such sort even for a single hour. And then Sophy would have to be dragged into the exposure, with her own concealment to account for —a concealment which no human being would ever be able to comprehend. All this would be saved if they remained as they were — Sophy and Rosamond to one another, but to all the parish Madame Miranda and Miss Gray. Crossmarsh would become used to them in time, and the wider world would soon forget even the tradition that there had ever been a foreign woman calling herself Queen of a country that would never be heard of again.

For occupation, home and rest looked ample to satisfy one who had known neither for many years : and who does not fancy that what she feels now she will feel for ever—nay, that all the world will feel for ever what she feels now ? So, single and at rest, she and Sophy would go on living at Crossmarsh, which was at any rate full and large enough to give two pair of hands as much work as they could do. It was not idleness that Rosamond wanted, but to work out her life in peace, and she had at any rate studied the art of government enough to have learned that there is work enough to be done anywhere and everywhere.

She knew when Sophy woke even sooner than Sophy herself : and the first sight upon which the opening eyes fell was Rosamond.

" Wake up, Sophy ? " cried she ; "and wish me many happy returns of the day ! At last I am fifteen ! "

" Fifteen ! " exclaimed Sophy, starting up in bed, and feeling herself compelled to face a new day in company with one whom her inmost heart could not receive as the sister who had died while she was a child ; " why—you were fifteen when——"

" Never, Sophy. Nothing has ever happened since I—since I was ill. That was yesterday. I am well, and fifteen to-day."

Meanwhile Horace Derwent, utterly baffled by his reception of yesterday, had spent his evening in a long ramble along the coast, in order to think matters out by the help of hard exercise: for he was little used to sit thinking, and had to balance the action of his brain with that of his limbs. And the more he thought the less could he believe in Senhora Miranda's good faith, even though he could not invent any shadow of reason for her continued concealment of his unfortunate brother from one who so clearly meant him well. But there is no need to narrate in detail the inevitable mazes in which the mind of one was compelled to wander who had no better light than Silver Moldwarp's for a guide. And then he was angry with himself for having been startled out of needful persistence by recognising Sophy in the Senhora's companion; and still more angry in that one who had so plainly shown her contempt or aversion for him, or both, should still have had the power so completely to overthrow his presence of mind.

Only one thing remained certain and clear —that Senhora Miranda must be compelled to give up her knowledge that his half-brother must forthwith be restored to his inheritance, that

Sophy must be blotted out of his life, and that he must henceforth devote himself to the work of holding up his mother and his sisters above the ruin that justice would cause by the strength of his own arm. Of one thing he did not as yet dare to think; for the bravest and honestest of men was bound to be a very coward of cowards before the prospect of having to announce to his mother the catastrophe that was about to befall. No man believes in the power of a woman to sacrifice those who are dear to her for the sake of justice to an enemy; and doubtless in Mrs. Derwent's case, her son's disbelief in the capacities of her sex were not unjustified. Even he had had to thrust himself out of temptation, though a man. At length his thoughts succeeded in tiring limbs that were untirable while left to themselves, and brought him to the condition in which To-morrow appears in a hopeful light, simply because it is not To-day. So he returned to his bed at the "Feathers" at an hour that would be considered late in Crossmarsh, and in a humour of too little desire for the company of Moldwarp to make enquiry whether the latter was in the parlour or in bed, or where.

When next morning came, with its fresher if not better counsel, it seemed of but small moment to him that Silver Moldwarp was still missing: and to others, who knew not that this elderly gentleman in black clothes had been in the neighbourhood of the haunted chamber, of no moment at all. Now that Horace was in direct treaty with the lady who, a mystery herself, appeared to hold the key of all lesser mysteries, his original guide could be dispensed with, and would doubtless take good care to turn up in time for his reward. Had he cared to make enquiries, he might perhaps have heard news; as things were, he saw nobody but the country maid who brought him his dish of eggs and bacon, and then set off at an hour, fixed rather by impatience than by etiquette, for a second and final interview with Senhora Miranda.

"She knows where Lawrence Derwent is: and both of them trust me, or they would not have trusted me with the will. I forgot I was dealing with a woman, who doesn't know how to be straightforward, and must needs make a secret of everything, so that she may be important, and let it out piecemeal," thought the young man, whom everything was combining to confirm in his misogyny. "If she had anything to hide, she would have let it out long ago—one may be sure."

With such venerable traditions he sought to transform himself into a philosopher, and labeled and disposed of one woman so that he might not be troubled in his social ruin by vain thoughts of another—rather than call Sophy a coquette, he laid other offences upon the shoulders of any of her sisters in Eve who might happen to be nearest to hand. Nay, he believed that he had steeled himself, by dint of common sense, strength of resolution, and half eagerness for the hard battle of life in which he must presently engage, that he honestly felt capable of meeting Sophy herself face to face without again losing one iota of the most dignified self-possession. In returning to the house that held her, he was no mere moth stupidly fluttering about a fatal flame, but one inspired by the conviction that one may learn from experience how to avoid being burned again. A burnt child, as they say, fears the fire : a philosopher is not, or ought not to be, a slave to childish fears.

Indeed, he was so confident of himself that he even looked forward to meeting her for the last time, solely, of course, in order that she might plainly see how mistaken she was if she fancied that any conduct of hers had so much as singed a single feather of his wings. He would confine himself solely to his all-important business with Senhora Miranda, and so, it may be, have the triumph of wounding a coquette's vanity for love delights to give pain, and to share all things it feels; and somehow the very brightness of the sunshine, as it were, hardened him : for it shone so apart from all things that went on upon earth, and upbraided his life with all that other sunshine that might so well have been but for a villain and a flirt—and but for the flirt the most of all.

For exactly one thing he was not prepared : and that was in the midst of his thoughts of her to come face to face with her of whom his thoughts were. He had not expected to see Sophy till he had entered the house : and he met her, all on a sudden, in the middle of the drive.

Had he been prepared for this most simple of chances, he would have raised his hat and passed on, so as not to press his company upon a girl who had so plainly shown that she wished to have nothing to do with one whom she had no doubt learned from her new friends to be a ruined pretender to a fortune that was none of his own. Indeed, he had already felt—for he had thought of all things save this meeting with her alone—that had she ever promised to be his wife, he would have had to have given her her release, and that he could never have kept her even if he had had the evil fortune to win her. But, unprepared, he wavered: and it was for Sophy to vindicate her own dignity by not showing a sign of having so much as noticed his neglect of her in her time of trouble.

"Good morning, Mr. Derwent," she said, with an effort after easy indifference that made her seem almost cordial. She even forced herself to hold out her hand, even at the risk of his finding it too warm or else too cold. "If you wish to see Madam, you will find her at home."

"Thanks, Miss Fane. Yes: I have business with Madam." He did not notice anything about her hand, as he held it lightly for a moment: and indeed if it had actually trembled, he would have thought his own to blame. "It—it is a long time since we met, Miss Fane."

Of all things this was the last he meant to say: and so he said it according to the law of such things. They were standing hard by that very greenhouse where, in old times, Oswald Hargrave had asked Rosamond to wait for him, and had tried, as it seemed in vain, to give her first lesson in love to one who in some ten years had never received another. Thus, seeing that this greenhouse (as may be remembered) had been Sophy's main watchtower, they were in the worst possible position for confidential talk; for if stone walls have ears, glass ones have ears also, and eyes as well. But nothing was more remote from their intention to talk in confidence: and Sophy's recollections of her childhood were as faint and dim as her sister's were strong even to passion.

"Is it?" asked Sophy.

"Well, perhaps not," said Horace. "A good many months isn't much for people not to meet in London, I know—especially as it will have to be a good many years now."

"Yes," she answered. "I dare say it will."

"Yes—I am not likely to trouble my friends any further, after to-day."

"I am sure of that," said Sophy, trying to be sarcastic and cool. "I should say there is nobody in the world who is less likely to be troublesome to his friends."

"To trouble my acquaintances then. But I should have thought you the last to give me so good a character, Miss Fane. I have it on my conscience that I ought to ask your forgiveness for having been something more than troublesome."

He knew he was not speaking as he had planned: but her cool·

ness stung him : and for that matter it now seemed better to part from her in a quarrel than simply to lift his hat and pass on.

Perhaps he felt, though he certainly could not see, that she also was growing a little angry : for she had meant to make some sort of point against him, as she would hardly have done had she been honestly careless, or as clear in her conscience as he felt himself to be in his own. "I really," said she, a little sharply, "cannot guess what you mean."

"Then all I can say is," he broke out plainly, "you must be forgiveness itself—as for me, I declare that I can't look back upon the way I tried to force myself upon you in the midst of all your trouble without shame. Only I thought I might be able to help you—and I could not know then, as I know now, that I had neither the right nor the means to help the weakest of all creatures in the world. I never meant to say a single word—but it is said now. I think, if you knew of my position from your friend, the Senhora you might have let me know it at once, and saved me a great deal of pain. One does not generally go out of one's way to wound those for whom one cares nothing—at least a man would not, whatever a woman might do. There—it has said itself, and it certainly will not be said again. I ought to be thinking of my poor brother, and of him alone. Perhaps *you* can tell me where I may find him—or must you wait in everything upon the will and pleasure of your Queen ? "

"But it must be said—everything must be said ! " exclaimed Sophy, with a sudden change of tone, and an eagerness that she might have caught from Rosamond. "What do you mean by forcing yourself upon me ? You must tell me—you must indeed."

"Why 'must' ? What is the use of another word, when I never meant to say a single one. However, if you *must* know— well then, a man who finds himself denied and unanswered may go on persevering up to a certain point: so long as he cannot guess why. But when he finds that, unknown to himself though not unknown to others, he had lost a fortune, he can only put the two things together and—beg pardon for his troublesome folly, as I do now."

"And what, then, are his friends to think, when he seizes every chance of flattering their weaknesses while he thinks them rich, and quietly throws them over as soon as he finds *them* ruined and poor ; yes, who is so afraid of their wanting his help, I suppose, that he flies even from their deathbeds, as if it were the plague ?

. . . . There, Mr. Derwent; we have both said our say now—"

" Good God! *I* fly from *you*—and because I was afraid of your being poor ? Have you forgotten how I tried to see you day after day, and was always denied—how I wrote to you (and it shames me now to think of how and what I wrote) and was never answered: how——"

" You *did* write ? You *did* call ? "

" How can you ask me—when you know it as well as I ? "

"But I do not know it—I never knew it—it must have been kept from me; though Heaven knows how, or why, or by whom. Oh, what have I thought—what have I done ? "

" You never denied yourself to me ? You thought me some miserable fortune hunter, who found himself disappointed, and was not even civil enough to let himself slide away by decent degrees ? Sophy, *you* thought this of *me !* "

Surely she was sharp enough to have retorted, " And what better did *you* think of *me ?* " But she had no heart left for retorts; that part of her was wholly engaged in the new birth of an old dream of hope from its grave under the warmth of looks and tones that it welcomed almost too much to understand. So she only answered,

" Is it possible for friends to forgive friends ? "

And while her heart was thus engaged, all her wits were at work upon what that letter had said, and whither it had gone. Little indeed had she guessed, when she went out that morning, what its sunshine was to bring ! After all, the sun is not always cold-blooded, and can laugh with his subjects now and then.

" They can try," said Horace, magnanimous with love, and forgetting that if mistrust was treason, he was himself no less to blame. "Sophy—my darling—you know what I would have said if this strange cloud had not come between us, ages ago. I was going to tell you all I felt that very night when you were to have come to our house, and never came. Sophy—whatever you would have said then, or after, say it now ! "

Then Sophy also learned what it means to wake up suddenly and to feel as though all past sorrows are a dream. There was no need to stand out for the formalities of wooing : for she felt herself alone in the world, despite those new found ties which meant so little to one who had lived without them until she had forgotten them, and indeed the most gracious and generous honesty

was only the due of one who had waited under so dark a
cloud so long. . . . . And so the word she would have said
before she disbelieved was whispered and sealed, despite the
blundering of Oswald, the plotting of Rackstraw: in short, despite all the world of men and women they knew.

Indeed it had needed but a look and a word to clear the air
between them, and it was a little wonderful that the process had
taken at any rate so many words. Had they not been true lovers,
after their manner, they might doubtless still have found many a
matter left that needed removing before the air could be considered wholly clear. How, for example, could Sophy's presence
at home and in London be without her knowledge so often and so
systematically denied? How could he have written a letter that
had failed to reach her hands? But though reason be helpless all
at once to exorcise such doubts, reason, happily, was wholly
absent, as she should always be when two lovers have found one
another again, and stand hand-locked in a garden of sunshine.
Let ruin come now, and welcome—

But no; less welcome now than ever. Ruin had been only
welcome when it meant escape from self—not now, Horace,
though it was he who loved the better, as one needs must out of
every two, was the first to recover consciousness that the cloud
had been no dream, and hung over them still.

"My darling," he said, "don't forget that you are giving yourself to a poor man; who can call nothing but you his own——"

"Did I ever think of you as a rich one?" asked she.

They were as close together as could be; for they were out of
sight of both house and road, and there was nobody to watch from
the greenhouse now.

"But you know that everything I have seemed to have, I have
been robbing from another man—or rather has been robbed for
me by others: and must all be given back again. And I have
others to work for—not only you. For I cannot suppose that my
brother, since he has been so treated, will show much mercy to me
and mine: and, for myself, I would ask for none. There is only
one thing for me dearest—I must go abroad. The colonies were
made for men like me,—so that scoundrel Rackstraw has told me
and proved to me over and over again. I must work my way up
—can you wait for me, Sophy? With you to work for, waiting
can't be long."

More than half his speech had been wasted. That his brother

had been ill-used, and that Rackstraw could be called a scoundrel, were things too dead against all her beliefs to be understood all at once, though since he said them, they must needs be true—she could not believe and trust him enough to make up for having mistrusted him so long. But what was not wasted was as clear as day.

"No—I will not wait," said she. "I am beginning to understand things—not much, but enough for me. You must not have all the work, and all the trouble, while I have none. Oh, Horace, you must not ask me to stay waiting for you here—waiting, and wondering, and perhaps not hearing from you, like—like I did before——"

"What!" he cried, looking down into her eyes with joyful wonder ; "You will come with me?"

"Why not? I could help you—I should not keep you down——"

"Darling! But to the other end of the world——"

"What is to keep me here? Yes, and farther still."

So spake she who but a few hours ago had been full of longing to place herself indeed at the other end of the world, but in other company. Heart was speaking to heart now, so that their words were not loud. But their whisper was loud enough at least to reach the ears of Rosamond, as she stood and listened behind the glass and under the vine.

It was not a case in which one calamity waits to decide whether listening is right or wrong. At first the words she heard were such as were open for all the world to hear. The line when they ceased to be such was far from being clearly drawn; and, when that line was passed, she could not lose the rest without stopping her ears or letting Sophy and Horace know that they were being overheard. Indeed she was not conscious of being a listener, but of a sudden blow.

She was dead then: after all.

Why had she ever come back from her grave? The folly of ghosts who come back to trouble the living was at last being borne sharply into her mind. Only yesterday Sophy had regained her lost and buried sister; only to-day Sophy was eager to leave her, "for the other end of the world, and further still." Rosamond had come back, with her heart on fire, only to find all things void and barren, and herself forgotten, not wanted, and in the way.

And so it was for a common love-pique, and out of no instinctiv affection for the sister who had become a friend, that Sophy h: d been so anxious to escape to Apahu. And so this was the end of the poor Queen's fantastic plans of throwing her crown away, and of living with Sophy, in such manner as wise maidens will who have discovered in time the vanity of love, marriage, foreign friendships, and of all things but nature, duty, and home.

She had been wasting all her joy upon a heart that never knew her, and turned from her without a thought as soon as some young man came by. I know that love is the only passion which poetry and prose too, permits to set hearts breaking; and that for a sister to break her heart over a sister is out of all rule. Yet I doubt if many a man has gone nearer to breaking his heart over a mistress than Rosamond went to breaking hers over Sophy, just then. Think how it would be if you, having been dead, were suddenly to come back, full of passionate life, to find yourself conventionally mourned indeed, ut—in the way! If you were wise you would straightway crawl back to your grave. And who among us could count upon welcome to the midst of all the new growths and the new interests that had sprung up since he was dead, and that he would only come back to disturb?

That is a thought solemn enough to comfort the dead (if they could feel) in their graves. But it brought anything but comfort to Rosamond, as she watched her sister and her sister's lover move slowly toward the house, and with none but themselves in their minds. Her uncle was dead—well, that was a disappointment rather than sorrow, and he had always been one of those men to whose loss a younger generation soon grows reconciled. The friend of their household had forgotten them; but to accept this she had been aided by pride. She had found her home lost and broken, and herself forgotten; and this had been hard at first to bear, but it could be borne. But Sophy was not only Sophy, but had come to unite in herself all that was left of friends, family, and home, all in one. And while Sophy was thus all in all to her, she was no more to Sophy than if she had never been born.

It was a tragedy; and none the less for its being wanting in all the elements whereof tragedies are made. She was young, healthy, rich, a crowned Queen, who had lost no lover, and was free to do with her life well-nigh what she pleased; neither had she sinned against any, nor any against her. Why should she wish to stand between two true lovers? She did not wish it; she wished nothing. She could only feel dead in the midst of others' lives, and infinitely, hopelessly alone. If only a dog could have let her see that he remembered her, she could have cried. It would have been more bearable had she felt less full of life and strength, or compelled, like her sister, to fight the world. And if other real kings and queens ever feel in this like this one, then it is the beggars who have the best of the world.

She had not the heart to follow the lovers towards the house which had once again ceased to be home—or indeed, for anything. So she crossed the lawn, and passed through the side door in the garden wall to the path along the cliff's edge whence she was supposed to have thrown herself; it had been an old haunt of hers when she was alive.

CHAPTER XXXIV.

E'en till the gate shall close,
Thus shall it be—
Waking, to seek and lose,
Sleeping, to see.

THE last sight and the last sound which made Oswald Hargrave conscious of life, as he fell forward upon that same cliff path into which Rosamond had turned for solitude (as if loneliness can be made more lonely) was the sight of Silver Moldwarp whirling through the air out of this world, and the evil echo of his fall into another. The next experiences of life were such as are not to be told, for they were painted by fever. So wildly impossible were they that at last he could have sworn, had he the strength, that he was lying on a bed of spikes in the midst of a flock of wolves, while Rosamond herself, looking and speaking as he had last seen and heard her ages ago, was by his bedside guarding him. Whatever he might now and then doubt as to the truth of the rest, she remained always real. He could hear her very voice; nay, though less often and less clearly, he could feel her very eyes. Nor did she ever change into any other creature, as did the wolves. So far from this, he once or twice found strength to doubt whether he had not really found her at last, and feebly tried to decide whether he, living, had found her dead, or whether, being dead, he had found her alive.

At last, however, there came the time when other powers than his own had to decide whether he should actually live or die; and they decided for his living. A long, deep darkness seemed

20

to roll away from him, and left him with a body miserably weak, but with a mind strangely calm and clear. When this happened, he found himself stretched out in bed, in a room at once familiar and strange, and with a general consciousness of having been terribly ill. He tried to rise, but had not strength enough to bring himself to his elbow. The effort only brought back the memory of how it was he had been brought to this pass, and the knowledge of where he must be lying; and, alas! the knowledge also of how he had brought himself face to face with Lawrence Derwent at last only to let the ruffian slip through his hands. The memory of what he had last seen and heard of Moldwarp made him shudder; but at that of his own blundering failure he groaned aloud.

The slight rustle of a dress seemed to answer him. Then clear though his brain had grown, a desperate hope, born of past fever, came to him.

" Is it Rosamond ? " he asked in the ghost of a voice, so much a ghost that he scarcely knew whether he spoke or no.

" Do you know me ? " came an eager and anxious answer, close to his ear.

The desperate hope vanished, " You are Sophy Fane," he sighed, " unless I am dreaming still." He was so weak that he could hardly keep from weeping over his vanished vision, as if he were a child who had dreamed of having grasped the moon, and wakes with clenched but empty hands.

" Thank God ! " exclaimed Sophy. " The doctor was right—the danger is gone ! But how *did* it happen ? How came *you* to be found lying on the cliff—But I mustn't ask questions now——"

" And——"

"Hush ! Nor must you."

Indeed, what between sleep and weakness, and the first passive indifference of one who had just returned from a journey to death's door, Oswald took four-and-twenty hours to learn that it was over four weeks since he had been discovered lying stretched upon his face, all unconscious, bleeding to death, and so near the cliff's edge that it was wonderful he had not rolled over and been swept away by the tide. Who had found him there ? But at this question Sophy only shook her head, and answered that it was nobody in particular—indeed, that she had forgotten, and would have to enquire. Who had shot him ? asked she in turn. But not having yet settled in his own mind how, when, how far, or to whom he should report this portion of his search for Lawrence

Derwent, he answered, somewhat in her fashion, by turning round, and affecting a sudden sleep that very soon became a reality. Clearly the murderer of Silver Moldwarp, and his own half murderer, was not arrested, or Sophy's question would have been put in a different form.

By the time another long bout of sleep and food was over, he had seen both his doctors, one of Crossmarsh, and the other from Laxham, as well as Sophy once more, and was in better possession of matters, so far as they were known, and as he could be told them. He was truly at the house that was now Senhora Miranda's, whither he had at once been carried, and where he had been nursed back into life again. It had been a formidable wound, a bullet having entered the chest, and having spared life as if by a miracle; as things were, there was still fear of permanent lung mischief, and of his being never wholly the same man again. No mention was made of Moldwarp, whom there was nobody to miss; and no reason for missing; and Oswald preferring to keep his own counsel, at any rate till he should have seen Horace Derwent, readily fell in with the general impression that his assailant must have been a burglar whose work had been disturbed. What was more likely than burglary upon a house just occupied by two unprotected ladies from London, where thousands of people knew that one of them was a very queen of ruby mines? Nobody had been taken; indeed the police were altogether without a clue.

There was little more to be spoken of, so far as concerned Oswald. His only interest in the disposition of the Derwent property depended upon its enabling him to meet the rightful heir, and this seemed now to have become more impossible than ever. The assassin had no doubt fled the country by this time and Oswald, dogged, as he had proved himself, shrank from the prospect of beginning to search the habitable world all over again from the beginning. However, his strength increased as the days went on, though slowly, and, as he gathered, much more slowly than his doctors expected. Had he not been healthy in himself, he must have died: but in truth, he was in no great haste to live, as having nothing left to live for—unless he might discover something new. Loyalty, at least, had proved but a poor career.

Thus fortune had at last given him plenty of time for reflection on the use he had made of the ten best years of his manhood, and for finding out, if he were able, that his loyalty had stagnated into something sadly hollow and empty — bitterly like dogged

20 ▲

revenge, and the vanity which will be false to the trust that life is rather than confess to defeat or folly. Suppose it had been Rosamond herself instead of Sophy who sat by him through his fever—would he have known her on waking? Would he not sooner have seen his enemy, so that he might find a better chance on a fairer field? "No," thought he, wearily, "I love Rosamond no more." And he knew not whether he were the more ashamed for his unfaith, or for his life thrown away upon a barren craze. Rosamond had been right—even from a lover ten years is too long to stay away.

He knew he was in Senhora Miranda's house, and yet the mistress had never yet paid him a visit—nay, though she doubtless made all courteous enquiries after the recovery of her guest, no such message was ever brought to him. Even without such seeming neglect, she would have been much in his thoughts; by reason of it, she was in them all the more. But, for that matter, he had been struck down even while his thoughts had become filled with her, and the bullet of his enemy had thus served to emphasise the influence over him, of a woman who was more of a mystery than even her sex had made her. Between the dead child and the beautiful living woman, all the more fascinating for the possible danger to which her spells might lead, the battle was wholly unfair. No thought of love for one of whom he knew nothing but that she was strange, and beautiful, and likely enough to be unfit for any true man's love, entered his mind. But then love, alone among passions, has ten thousand names. It is harder to say when love begins than when it ends; and even that is hard enough to say.

Sophy, however, came and sat with him two or three times a day : the Crossmarsh surgeon made a daily visit : the Rectory was attentive : and neighbourly visits from Windgates and Laxham were not rare, not to speak of calls of enquiry from Mr. Crow, and other fathers and mothers of the two villages. So, as he advanced in convalescence, he did not want for company, and this made it all the stranger, at least to him, that there was no gossip worth mentioning about Senhora Miranda. Instead of being a wonder of the country side, she seemed ignored. Of course the reason was plain enough—that she held a place in his mind which forbade speech of her. He was too proud, or too shamefaced, to seem curious about one of whom he could scarce reconcile his honour to be thinking at all ; and more—though he dared not own it, he was afraid to hear. None knew better than he how a foreign woman, who was either heathen, papist, or worse, and far more beautiful than she had any business to be, would fare in village talk; and it was only too likely that such talk might in her case be only too true. At last it seemed that his visitors' very silence came from fear of giving offence to a neighbour who might be the lady's friend as well as guest; and so it came to pass that his silence created theirs.

Besides there was everything else to talk about—not forgetting, when Mr. Crow happened to call during Miss Gray's absence, the fatal mysteries of the haunted room. Despite the conspiracy of silence, the great village story had spread and grown beyond the recognition, though not beyond the belief, of its first inventors who had almost daily to lay on fresh colours in order not to lose the prestige of original authority. Even had Oswald cared to set things straight, it would have been out of the question now— Crossmarsh would have gone to the stake as one man rather than give up the faith that it was the devil's own playground.

At last it came out that a Windgates man had seen, with his own eyes, a dark shape with horns like an ox fly thrice, on that fatal night, round Windgates steeple with a struggling body in its claws.

This was too much for patriotism. "'Twould take a Windgates man," said Mr. Crow, with scorn, "to think an owl and a mouse for a man and—*him*. For 'twas round Crossmarsh steeple; and 'twas four times—not three. And harns like an ox's! Why, they was harns like a bull's!"

"And what are your own plans?" he at last asked Sophy. "Are you still bent upon that voyage——"

"What voyage?" asked she, with an air of wonderful innocence though she knew what he meant, perfectly well.

"You mustn't expect me to remember the name of a country of which nobody ever heard. But I can't forget what you told me, before——"

"You mean Apahu? Oh, that idea is given up long ago. Of course it must be, now."

"Then I am glad of it with all my soul. You have taken a weight off my mind! But why *of course?* I thought your friend's will was law."

"Ah, but it was never her will, Oswald," said Sophy. "It was mine. But—has nobody told you? Haven't you heard?"

" Heard what ? " he asked anxiously : for he was not likely to
be in ignorance of any news that would be good to hear.

" You have always been so like a brother to me, Oswald," said
she, busying herself in rearranging the table. " I almost feel as
if I ought to have asked you to approve. I am engaged."

" Engaged ! what—since you have been down here ? Why,
who on earth have you seen ? Not—not to Rackstraw ? "

" Rackstraw—that scoundrel ? " she exclaimed, hotly ; for her
views as to her friend and patron had undergone an exceedingly
violent change, and, in describing him, she could only use her
lover's word. " Why, I took a hatred to him the very first moment
I ever set eyes on him—as you must remember : and first impressions are never wrong. Dr. Rackstraw ! No ! "

" I thought you told me he was the best and kindest of all your
friends——"

" I couldn't have said it ; for it wouldn't have been true." For
where is the woman who can even remotely suspect herself of
ever having been in the wrong ? " He has been Horace's worst
enemy : so how could he ever have been my friend ? "

" Horace's ? "

" Horace Derwent's. I am engaged to *him.*"

" Well, that *is* news," said Oswald. " And I do approve : for
he must be a good fellow and really in love to take you without a
penny, and—but wait : what am I thinking of ?——"

" What indeed ? Why, he was as poor as I was until——"

But Oswald was but half-listening : for he was recalling his
own former fears lest this very thing might be, and how he had
done his best to delay a crisis that promised to end in the engagement to the brother of the man whom he still held answerable for
her sister's death—for that Rosamond must in truth be dead, had
at last been borne in upon his mind. Then other matters had
made him forget the danger : and what could he do now ? It was
true that Horace Derwent could not be held answerable for his
brother's crimes ; but such had become his own relations to the
name of Derwent that he could only feel as a Corsican who hears
that his own sister is about to wed into the family of their hereditary foes.

Sophy herself, ignorant as she was of any possible reason for its
cause, could not fail to read the trouble in his face ; and then she,
for her part, remembered how hard this man had always seemed
towards her and hers—as hard as he had been kind, and kind only

so long as it was in his own way. He had sought to oppose her in everything, since her uncle died; and some secret certainty that he would oppose her in this also had much to do with her timid postponement of her great news.

" And there is so much to tell you," said she, " and I should have told it long ago, if—if the doctors had not forbidden your being told anything real——"

" I have certainly been allowed to hear a great deal of unreal, Sophy," he said. " And as old Crow's stories haven't done me much good, perhaps yours will. I can't lie here for ever, you know; and before I go out into the world, I should like to know how it stands."

" Of course when I became engaged to Horace, there could be no more thought of my going to Apahu. Indeed I never really wanted to go, only—there was nothing else to do. Don't you like Horace, Oswald? You looked so strangely when I mentioned him. Is there anybody else in the whole world who would have given up everything, even to his last farthing, when he might have kept them just by holding his tongue? You remember that story Dr. Rackstraw used to tell of how Horace came to be his father's heir while his elder brother was alive. That story was false, Oswald. The elder brother was the real heir; and Horace found it out, and—he is a hero, Oswald! He is seeking his brother to give back everything to him—seeking him high and low."

" What he is seeking Lawrence Derwent too? And with a great fortune for a bait? Well, Sophy—I do know enough of that story to see that you have engaged yourself to an honest man; though——"

" There's no 'though' at all, Oswald. Honest! of course he's honest. I said he is a hero. And I'll have no meaner word."

" And how are you to live?"

" When he asked me to be his wife, he thought I was as poor as he. It is a strange story I have to tell you, Oswald, so strange that I have not dared speak of it till you were strong; and because I am rich, Oswald; and thank God for it, since he is poor. You are in *my* house, Crossmarsh is mine again."

" Why how in the name——"

" Madame Miranda——"

" Well?"

" She approved of everything; she thought as much of Horace

as I do ; she knows Lawrence Derwent ; and has put Horace in the way of finding him ; and she is so rich that it was nothing to her to give me Crossmarsh, and——"

"And an income besides ? Is she a princess of an Arabian tale that she buys estates as if they were yards of ribbon, only to give them away ? And she *does* know Lawrence Derwent ? And you take such gifts as though she were your own sister, instead of a stranger to us all ? "

Then he set his teeth, while his heart seemed to turn to one vast ache ; for she did know this Lawrence Derwent, and it was from her house that he was escaping at midnight, and armed.

"Is she here—in this house—now ? " he said, in a voice so strained and hard that Sophy started, thinking him in actual pain —as he was, in very deed.

"No, Oswald. I ought to have told you nothing—you are not strong enough for real talk, after all. Are you in very much pain ? What can I do ? Can you sleep, if I go ? "

"I am in no pain. I am strong enough to hear everything— but not strong enough to sleep upon half words. I can't guess what you can have to tell, but there is something I know from the very sound of your words. Where is this woman, then, if she is not here ? "

"She would not stay here, Oswald. She had made a life for herself, out there. You see, she found everything so changed that she only got restless, and homesick for her new country. And indeed you would not know her, any more than I. . . . So she waited till you were out of danger . . . . and had settled her affairs . . . . and she is gone back to Apahu. That is all, Oswald You may go to sleep now."

"Sophy," said Oswald, very quietly, "you are telling me, more plainly than words can tell, that I was not mad when I saw Rosamond by my bedside."

"Oswald ! I *never* told you—for I had promised not to tell ! She had her reasons—oh, what *have* I done now ! "

"Nothing, Sophy. And since it is a secret, leave it alone. Let us talk of other things."

He took the news with such strange, nay, incredible quiet that his nurse and hostess forgot her own lapse of speech in alarm for his mind.

Never again did he mention her name. And yet his doctor,

hitherto surprised at the slowness of his recovery, was thenceforth amazed and bewildered at the rapidity with which his strength came back again. Yesterday he seemed destined to be a hopeless invalid; to-morrow found him rebelliously well.

CHAPTER XXXV.

FORTUNIO.—Not even such dross is mine as mocking sprites
Twist into crowns of straw for phantom kings.

WHAT Sophy had told, as practical people can, in twenty words, was the true and faithful story of what had happened while Oswald lay ill—so far at least as practical people know truth when they see it : which is neither clearly nor far. And the reason why all who tell stories should be practical minded, and confine themselves to bare events without trying to explain them or account for them, is perfectly clear. It is not because the latter method is difficult, because it is not difficult at all. A flight to the sun is not difficult. It is impossible.

And even so Rosamond Fane had found it, not difficult, but impossible, to make the world move backwards, and to resume life at the point where she had laid it down. From the moment of bitterness when she found that she existed in the heart of Sophy only as a passing friend, to be forgotten in a moment at the first word of a lover—as one to be discarded without a thought so soon as she ceased to be a convenience, she shrank within herself, and did her best to make Sophy feel that her sister's ghost did not mean to embarrass or encumber her. It was easy enough, by means of easy speech and suppression of every sort of emotion that could lead to a scene, to re-establish the authority of a mistress, at least in form. The sisters continued good friends, though they neither shared a thought, nor had a single feeling in common. There was even a hollowness in their friendship, seeing that Sophy, who had got on very well without a sister for ten years, was now in no want of one whatever, while Rosamond was in want of a sister who had never been so much as born.

But all this was of the past now. Lover and friend had been put far from her : but there still remained the island which had given her all that her life had to give, and where lay all of home that was left her in the world. Why had she dared forget her own home, that contained nothing harsh, nothing evil, for a single hour ? Why had she been such an ungrateful fool as to fancy that her empty chair was still kept sacred in the home she had left behind?

So—" I will go back to my own people," thought she. " And I will never leave them again, for the sake of a dream."

Her plans were easily formed, and rapidly put into execution. The lawyer at Laxham must have shared in the bewilderment into which his new client from Crossmarsh had thrown his brethren in London: but he knew how to keep a secret, and the re-conveyance of the estate to Sophy presented no difficulties whatever. Alas, that the parting of the sisters should have presented fewer still. Sophy had her lover: and her lover, fortunate as he was, could not regret the loss of a sister-in-law whose life had been and still was an outrage upon all social laws. Sophy was irreproachable: but who would wish to be talked about as the young man who married the sister of that woman who began life with an intelligible elopement, lived abroad for years, heaven knew how, and came back calling herself Queen of Cannibals—for so the story would be safe to run? Indeed he thought her dangerous, and with impulses not to be trusted from hour to hour—in short, altogether away, and with his wife safe from an influence under which she had very nearly been lost to him. It was almost with a sense of relief that Rosamond turned her back at last upon Crossmarsh, without bidding any spot a special farewell—her last kiss to Sophy (who wept a little, while Rosamond's eyes remained dry) was a good-bye to all. Her own last tears were shed alone. And when she was fairly on her way to the Goblin Islands, and England had become but a faint grey cloud, her heart began to flutter its wings, and to fly before her towards Apahu. With different feelings indeed, brimful of passionate hope, had she sailed towards that faint grey cloud. Every one of them had been shrivelled and chilled. She set her face to the wholesome wind, so that the dead leaves might be blown away.

It was Rosamond's third voyage—the first made in despair, the second in hope, the third in the spirit of one to whom both hope and despair alike have come to be but empty names. This voyage save for the commonest incidents, was as uneventful as to suit her humour, and as the most wearied of adventure could desire. There is therefore no need to speak for the third time of a route so familiar to all who have visited the Goblin Islands and of so little interest to the many who have never made that long and tedious voyage. Port Rackstraw is still but a young colony, and with but little prospect of ever becoming a great one, and has always had a way of disappointing those who, like Horace Derwent, imagined that everything needful for success abroad is to have been ruined at home. But so long as Hermon Rackstraw represented the Goblins in Europe, they were never likely to want for sanguine spirits who were willing to invest in uncleared lands for a song, only to find their bargain dear at a single stanza. Moreover there was more or less constant exportation of British goods which, being unsaleable in any ordinary market, sold at Port Rackstraw for double what the best of their kind went for elsewhere. So under these conditions the presence on board of so exceptional a passenger as Senhora Miranda was an event for her fellow-passengers, from whom she held herself, so far as might be, in the seclusion of royalty *incognita*. And when at last she reached Port Rackstraw, she made no official visits, but—disappeared.

Yes—the truth must out. It is not for nothing that one lives among ¦barbarians from childhood to womanhood, gentle and virtuous as they may be. Rosamond herself knew not how she herself had grown out of sympathy with the old world, or how much even she herself might be answerable for the forgetfulness of her and the estrangement she found. In London she knew how to hold to perfection her part as a lady, so that people wondered at the resemblance of a heathen savage to any princess in the almanac of Gotha. But in Crossmarsh, had she stayed there, second nature must have proved too strong for her at last: and now came a glorious plunge into a very bath of liberty that, while the first excitement of it lasted, made her cease to regret the lost affection that had been put to her lips only to be dashed away. She was Queen Ngahoung of Apahu once more—Queen of an almost amphibious race who were the finest sailors and swimmers in the unknown world. Nor had a season's confinement of her limbs and her brains robbed her of those results of health and delight in action which had gone far to establish her on the throne.

Less regret than ever would have been felt for her second and voluntary death had her sister and her future brother-in-law, and the ladies of Longwood, seen the lioness of a season, as she sat alone in the stern of a long canoe, while a sail of strange fashion carried her before the wind. She knew where lay the country whence she had set sail in such solemn state, and the wind that would bear her there, and the season, when, in that most regular of climates, she might count upon its blowing. A canoe to fairly suit her was easily procured and provisioned : and she had set sail at nightfall from the creek where her native crew had bidden her farewell many months ago.

When the sun rose next morning, in one sudden moment, out of the sea, without any of the changing lights and flushes that give our northern skies the look of a maiden tenderly wooed and slowly won, she who had once been Rosamond Fane (how long ago?) would have been seen—were there a magic mirror and any eyes that cared to glance therein—speeding before the steadiest and most fragrant of good winds out of sight of land.   Nay: out of sight of this mortal world : for was not the ocean held to be the border between life and death in Apahu ?   As she sailed thus, I would make her picture, if I had the power: only that her dress had more of Europe in it than became her new freedom. Of course she was in peril : for even as there are no seas that know how to be so calm and radiant, there are none that know such fury: and their fury is as sudden as their sunrise.   But something had to be dared now for the safe-keeping of her people's secret, which had already been only too heedlessly whispered abroad. And even the peril was welcome : it was all the more relief from the mere death in life she had left behind. Meanwhile, all was well and there was reasonable hope that no change would come. If it came—well, there must be an end some day of all this : and not a soul on earth would mourn her : she had outlived all that delusion now.

Meanwhile it must have been another than Queen Ngahoung who would dream of danger when floating as smoothly as a swan between the blue sky and the blue sea, and through a golden air that went to the senses like wine. The fragrance was not so keen as if the breeze were from Apahu, the first known perfume of which was in her nostrils still, but the breath of the wind on her cheek, at once sharp and soft, was the same that had for the first time welcomed her. It was an ideal voyage, such as makes those who have sailed in the far south believe that every poet must have once sailed them also, if only in a dream. And then to think of what awaited her beyond ! Loneliness, perhaps, for her heart was still English born ; and hunger, it might be, for the rest of an English churchyard when the time came for her to pass the borderland of life and death, in truth and in deed. But meanwhile it would be loneliness that a healthy mind, with a sense of duty, might well manage to bear. No more sights of men and women suffering and poverty stricken beyond the wealth of all the rich combined to aid them : no more struggling for gold, to the loss of what no gold can buy ; no more crime; no more sin. There at last she would be free from the enemy who had forced himself into her life for no cause, and from whose presence she could not escape, except by flight into an unknown world. And there, too, she would be as free from friends who could forget as from enemies who could remember.

The wind favoured her, no less than on her last voyage : indeed it carried her far more quickly than she hoped, when she trusted herself to it alone, and she had nothing to do but to let it steer her straight for the shore, which she could not lose unless the weather changed. Already she pictured to herself the joy and the wonder that would greet her return: how old and young, noble and peasant, man, woman, and child, would troop down to the shore where she had been first given to them by the waves. to hear of the wonders of the world of evil that she would scarce dare tell them for fear of their scorn.

At last, in almost a day less than her last crossing of the same sea, a faint familiar outline told her that the wind had been loyal to her trust, and had steered her well and true. And, as the far-off vision began to melt into lights and shadows, even so the world she had left melted from her mind. Then, by exquisite degrees, the lights and shadows grew into colour : and, in a word, the Queen was coming home, after the most royal passage that ever queen has made.

Some three hours later, she struck sail, and let the rising tide carry her canoe high on a beach of sand, and then waded ashore. She was glad that her landing was unperceived : she would be gladder still if she could remain invisible till she had seen the old priest who had blessed her when she had departed, and prayed for her return. Long as her many months of absence had been, she feared to find no change for she had not left love enough here to fear lest her treasure had been stolen. But before setting forth, she knelt down and kissed the shore. This was her grave : and here her troubles were to end.

Boom !

She sprang to her feet, almost with a cry. Never, to her dying

day, would she forget the sound of the signal gun of Lowmoor.
And it sounded here—here, in Apahu!

What could it mean? There was no mistaking it: and a
people before it invents artillery must invent war. And it could
not to be fancy: for she had scarce recovered from her start when
the sound came again. The Queen looked round in dismay,
doubting whether to believe her ears or her eyes. But her eyes did
not deceive her: she knew by heart every mark in the cliffs, and,
every curve in the bay. She was most surely in Apahu. And so
how could she believe her ears?

She hurried across the beach, and entered the narrow strip
of bush that lay between her own palace and the sea: and, as
she entered, again came that incomprehensible sound. As quickly
as she could walk through the tangle of stems and brushwood,
she reached the confines of the glade that formed the royal
domain. And there she came face to face with a long, low, log
hut, over the door of which was painted up, in the English
tongue,

Whisky sold here: by Jacob Green.

As for her palace—it had vanished, like a castle in the air. And
instead of the glade, which had been another Eden, it had been
grubbed and cleared, and the timber of its margin used to build
some two dozen other huts, in regular rows, only differing from
the first in being lower and less long. In one direction, a complete clearing had been made, so as to give a view of the mouth
of the river that rose among the hills whence the rubies came.

The settlement showed no signs of life, however: and Rosamond
drew back among the trees, bewildered and alarmed. She knew
all the tracks, as well as she knew the path from Crossmarsh to
Pix-Knoll: and so she was able to give the transformed glade a
wide berth, and to make straight for the college of priests which
stood on a plateau overlooking the entrance of the river into the sea.
It was not far, and the way was easy: and vague anxiety gave
her wings.

At last she reached the plateau, where a still smoking wreck
showed where the college of the venerable fathers of a blameless
people had been standing some months ago. But this was not the
first sight on which the Queen's eyes fell, as she stood on the edge
of the open space, not venturing to draw nearer to the ruin. Nor
was it the glorious view of the river, sand, cliff and sea that
formed a vast, sunlit circle as far as the eye could travel. For she

was no longer alone. Some scores of rough and bearded men, such as she had never seen either in Europe or in Apahu, and all variously armed with rifles, revolvers, or knives, were mingled with perhaps a dozen women well-nigh as rough-looking, and with two or three persons better dressed if not of better appearance, were crowded round a pole planted in the very midst of the plateau. Pointing seaward was a ship's gun, attended by a smaller group— no doubt the cause of the sound of evil omen she had already heard. Not a native of the island was to be seen. Then emerged from the greater crowd, and climbed upon a stone of the smouldering ruin, a long, lean, grave figure in a black frock coat, and a broad-brimmed straw hat, and waved his hand. " Silence ! " he cried, in a voice that she knew as well as she knew that figure, so vulgar in its every detail, and yet so expressive of persona power.

A flag ran up to the head of the pole : the ship-gun flashed and roared.

" In the name of Progress, Humanity, and Civilisation," proclaimed Hermon Rackstraw, " Port Rackstraw annexes to the British Empire for ever the Island of New Gotham, formerly Apahu ! "

CHAPTER XXXVI.

What help's for hurts, if valour cannot mend 'em ?
What good in virtues, if we can't defend 'em ?

WHATEVER warrant he may or may not have had for his proceeding, a deed was done at which no true Briton can fairly cavil, seeing that in this straightforward and simple manner, Dr. Hermon Rackstraw had opened up to British enterprise an island that bore rubies. Well had it been that Rosamond had fallen under the guidance of so competent a man. While the Queen had been vexing her mind whether to bring her lost Eden into the line of progress and the circle of civilisation, or whether to leave to Nature what Nature herself had left alone, Dr. Rackstraw, with manly energy, had solved the problem at a bold stroke, once for all.

But the prospect that Apahu was already provided with whisky and gunpowder, and that a New Gotham Advertiser, and a mission station, and a steamer to Port Rackstraw, and a Ruby Mines Railroad Company, and a gaol, would shortly follow—this prospect, clear as it was, gave no comfort to Queen Ngahoung. Sick at heart, she turned away. She had fled to Apahu from all these things—and this was what she had found!

The bitterness of it all was too great even to leave room for indignation at Hermon Rackstraw's treachery. So it was for this he had wormed himself into her intimacy, and, while pretending to teach, had learned her all—how many days' journey from Port Rackstraw lay Apahu, and by what wind she had sailed, and all else needful for discovery.

After all, she upbraided her trusting folly, why should Hermon Rackstraw differ from the rest of civilised mankind? It was no moment for even so much thought as belongs to anger. She drew back yet farther among the trees, and buried her face in her hands. It was not a little thing, that she felt herself no longer a Queen. And yet that feeling was the least of all.

Not till a minute had passed did she become aware that it had contained one mad moment of impulse when she had been on the point of stepping forward to the flag-post, asserting her sovereignty defying the invaders, and bidding them begone. When she became conscious that this impulse had possessed her, she almost repented that she had not yielded to it, and taken the consequences, whatever they might be, from those who had robbed her of all she had left to live for. Now that the moment had passed, it left her too weak and too numbed to call it back again.

The echo of the shouting was still in her ears, when she started afresh : for a hand, and no light one, was laid on her arm, and a strong, deep voice was speaking, but too low to be heard beyond her screen of trees.

" Don't start," it half whispered : " Don't move. I know every thought in your heart: for half of them are my own. We may speak plainly out here yet awhile, thank Heaven : they've not yet brought Lowmoor here: but they will. You saved me once, Miss Fane : and I paid you ill: but it *shall* be paid—that debt and all. Do you remember an escaped convict who once told you that you were born to be a queen? Well, I have had to fly again, for defending a guiltless man's liberty : murder, the law would call it, but only the law. *That* doesn't trouble me. But I had my reasons for making my escape square with a visit to the Agent-General for the Goblin Islands: and for that reason where he is, there am I. Come quite out of hearing, if you please——"

Was this man, this demon, bound to follow her, and blight her

life even here? Was she not safe from him, even in Apahu?
Was Apahu itself to be cursed by her, because of him?

"This is too much—too horrible!" she cried out, heedless of
her voice being heard. " Guilty or guiltless, what is it to me?
I never harmed you; I never heard of you: yet you tore me
from my home, you made me dead to my dearest, and made them
dead to me: you haunt me when I escape to England: you come
to gloat over my escape back again; and the ruin of the one spot
of heaven left on earth, that men like you have done. To rid my
life of you, must I kill you, or you me?"

" Come farther. Did I not tell you, in London, what I want of
you? And, there or here, it is the same. Listen, for your own
sake: and for Heaven's sake don't let us be overheard. You know
what I am—rich enough in the new world: but in the only world
I care about hunted and driven to bay by wolves: and Hermon
Rackstraw is the chief of them. Yes: that is what I am—and
you are a dethroned queen: and our enemy is the same—there he
stands. What are all my silver mines, and all your rubies, to such
a cause: my liberty and your throne? You need me as much as
I need you. . . . Your people (I have seen something of them
these days) could drive this handful of invaders into the sea. But
the fools don't know how to fight: and they have never till to-day
heard the sound of a gun. They want a general to-day; not a
queen, I know something of savage warfare, and how it ought to
be carried on: and I will wager all my silver to your smallest
ruby, that in three days I . will be at the head of such an army as
shall not leave one of Rackstraw's pirates and filibusters alive to
tell the tale. You shall be queen again: and all the world shall
ring with your cause, and then, with a people who can fight, let a
hundred Rackstraws meddle with you if they dare. . . . Good
God, Miss Fane, we ought to found a kingdom, an empire, you and
I. What have we to do with the old ways of an old world?
You will thank me for having led you here—and for my reward
—you know it will not be your crown: but the Queen must have
a King."

Claimants to thrones are on record who have thought nothing
of plunging, for their own sakes, whole nations into war. Rosamond shuddered at Lawrence Derwent's touch (for she guessed
now who had struck down Oswald): but Queen Ngahoung was
bound to listen: for she thought, shall my people be robbed and
ruined without a blow? Is it not my part to lead them, conquer

21

with them, or die with them, as their Queen? And if this man
can help *them*, has not Heaven sent him to undo what I have done?
What she felt towards him was terribly like hate, but if he could
save her people from the horrors of civilisation, was any sacrifice
too great to make—any price to pay?

He saw her hesitate: and, though he misread from first to last
the motives that influenced her doubts, he read the result, and that
was enough for him.

"Come," said Lawrence Derwent. "I learned something of
this work, out west: and we must lose no time."

"Where are my people? I have not met with one—not one."

"Are you not with them?" he asked, in some surprise.

"This is my first hour here—Heaven forgive me for leaving
them, if it can—but I have been punished, Heaven knows. If you
know what to do—do it: worst enemy of me and mine though you
are."

"Never mind that now. We shall be friends in time. Hush,
go behind that bush; somebody is coming, and you had best not
be seen, especially with me." She obeyed: for the very shudder
which his presence inspired in her meant subjection to mastery.
"Holloa, Green," said Lawrence, "aren't you at the show?"

"Not I," said the man, in a grey flannel shirt, straw hat, and
high boots, who approached them from the direction of the glade.
Though dressed for rough business, his appearance did not correspond with his costume, for he was small, fat, and elderly, with a
long, thin, white beard, a vulture's beak for a nose, and a moist,
bright eye: he had nervous ways with his fingers, and a choking
snuffle in his voice, and his shoulders, though round and bent, did
not look used to toil. And he also was the type of a pioneer: for
even the march of civilisation must have its camp followers, its
sutlers, and its people who buy and sell. "They'll shout thebselves
dry; anthed cubs *by* show," said Jacob Green. "They bust be quick,
though: or by cask'll sood be as dry as theb. If you want to see a
bit o' fud ; you cub alog o' be."

"Niggers, eh?" asked Lawrence, making a sign to the Queen to
follow invisibly: and she obeyed.

Mr. Green led the way to the nearest corner of the clearing, and
pointed. The Queen also looked: and turned away again in
despair.

"Good business, eh?" chuckled Mr. Green.

It was good business, indeed—from the invaders' point of view.

But the sight shall not be described. It was an assembly of Apahuacs, who had become Mr. Green's customers, and all as drunk as if they had been civilised all their lives.

" And the rest ? " asked Lawrence ; with a gloomy frown.

"Off to the Ruby Bides ! *They're* cute, those diggers. They're foud out what Bister Rackstraw's after, and they're off for first haul ! "

Rosamond came forward, unconcealed. Mr. Green stared : but it was not Goblin Islands' fashion to lift one's hat, even to a lady. But for a remnant of Oriental courtesy, he would probably have done more than stare.

" Have you been long here, sir ? " she asked, abruptly.

" Cabe with the first lot, ma'am. Will you drink anything, ma'am ? It's close by."

" Can you tell me what has become of a very old man, a priest, who lived in the house which was burned down to set up a flag pole ? "

" Oh, I know the old digger you bead. The others was putting him into a hole when Bister Rackstraw came an' scuttled 'em ! for he was as dead as a dail. I saw his corpus : must have been as old as Adab. But who, ma'am, are you ? *You* don't want rubies nor diabods, with eyes like theb. Yes : as dead as a dail."

" Then *he* never knew——"

"Of the addexation ? How could he, when he was dead as a dail ? "

" Thank God ! " said Rosamond, and turned away.

" Who is she, Bister ? " asked Mr. Green.

" A friend of Rackstraw's," said Lawrence, following her. They returned into the strip of brush, and walked on silently, side by side. There was no need to tell one another that a nation which has all virtues save the soldiers' may just as well have no virtues at all.

" And *I* have done all this ! " she moaned.

"You ? No," he answered her, gloomily. "You didn't make the world's ways—nor I. If I had—but all that's over now. I can't offer you a kingdom. But I will give up even vengeance, if——"

" Never," said Rosamond. " I won't pretend to know what you mean. This is too awful a moment for pretence and play. We have been saved from a sin. Let us forgive one another, and meet no more."

He strode on in silence for awhile.. He thought it the dignity of the dethroned Queen that awed him : for he knew not, nor could know, how the woman, through him, had lost her all. Only he did know that not she herself had lost more than he.

" *You* must have some plans, for yourself," he said, " even if you leave me none. What are they ? "

" How should *I* have plans ? You know I can have none. And if I had—are you not the last creature on earth to whom I would tell them ? Perhaps you never meant to injure me. I think you come from Nevada. Go there: and then I shall know where not to go."

" Do you know how you are revenging yourself ? By God, if I could be half as well revenged on Rackstraw, and on Horace Derwent——"

" Revenge—on your own brother? On the only true and honest being I ever met on earth—on him who is seeking you because he thinks he has done you wrong ? As if the wrong could ever be on his side, between him and you ! "

" Miss Fane ! Think what you are saying—this is more than life and death to me ! "

" Then know from me, whose life you have cursed, that the brother you hate is striving to give you back your inheritance and your good name : and that he whom you sought to murder at my door held the proofs, for your brother, even while you struck him down : and that she tells you this, who——"

" What !—Why did you not tell me this before ? "

" Why should *I* think of *you?*—when my people : God help ~~them now~~ ! "

THE END.

. . . . But best of all the gleam,
When forth on Faith, at every turn dismayed,
And high on Hope, that ne'er to harvest grew,
And clear on Love, that mocked us as we strayed,
Shines full the sun, and all things find we true
That seemed but a dream.

AND so Apahu also had vanished like another dream. All Rosamond's dreams had vanished now : and the passing of the last was perhaps the bitterest of all.

She sought no interview with Dr. Rackstraw, who indeed, had she done so, would have treated her with but scant courtesy, and have sent a possible firebrand out of the island even more quickly than she departed of her own accord. All was lost there, and she knew it : and she carried away with her no more than a single bouquet of leaves from the precincts of the sacred college to remind her of what had been, and could never be again. She embarked, as an ordinary passenger, on a small steamer that was carrying to Port Rackstraw the news of the successful annexation. Lawrence Derwent travelled in her company: but held aloof from her as if they were strangers. He knew that he had influenced her once : but he no less knew now that his influence was as dead as the High Priest of New Gotham.

Of his plans, therefore, she knew nothing : and plans for herself she had none. She would not disturb Sophy again: and yet she had no other home. There was no more lonely ghost under heaven than she : and yet she had always meant so well! And she had so many years yet to live—what could she do with them all? Find out and help the poor, and her brothers and sisters in loneliness, of course : but they must be cold of spirit and feeble of heart indeed, or angels before their time, who at five and twenty can have no desires left for themselves.

*   *   *   *   *

They who can trace in this history, as in the life to which it may seem—but only seem—so lacking in likeness, how event led to event, and how there was no such thing as evitable accident from beginning to end, will see that as surely as Apahu could not remain for ever undiscovered, so surely was Lawrence Derwent bound to meet with an adventure which only a prodigy of accidents could postpone.

The Hotel of Port Rackstraw was an establishment by no means in accordance with the aspirations of the place in point of accommodation, though far beyond them in point of charges : but it was the only one in the place, and there all travellers were compelled to put up, for want of a better. Oswald Hargrave himself was not wholly a stranger there : for some ancient and broken clue had led him years ago to the Goblin Islands, whither, even before his strength had returned, he followed such traces of Senhora Miranda as he could gather, with Horace Derwent's help, from Sophy, from lists of passenger vessels, and from all other sources that were open to him. And he had succeeded in tracking the Senhora to Port Rackstraw, but there had lost sight of her again. But at last came the news, kept dark till the last moment, of the expedi-

tion to Apahu, and of its projected annexation by the Goblins:
and thus almost the one corner of the earth he had never searched
and in whose very existence he more than half disbelieved, was
revealed to him.   Was he following Rosamond or the Senhora ?
He hardly knew : nor did he much care to distinguish, seeing that
they were one and the same.   Nor did he ask himself very carefully what the result of his search was to be.   The search had
been for so long its own end that—in short, he simply followed
the steps of a woman : and it would be folly to ask the wherefore
of so common a thing.

He had just been enquiring as to the means of following the
New Gotham expedition, and had returned to the hotel, when, in
the long saloon of timber answering to the coffee room, and partly
to the general dormitory, and now empty save for himself and
another guest, he found himself, suddenly and at last, face to face,
with the man who had given him the slip at Crossmarsh—or
rather everywhere in the world.

There was no time for either to fence or to consider.   But it was
Lawrence Derwent alone who started and hesitated, and so gave
Oswald the first word.   Oswald did not start : he knew he must
meet this man again in time : he would not have wondered at
meeting him in a far less likely place than here.   But—then
Lawrence Derwent was with Rosamond still !

" You shall know the face of the man you tried to kill, Lawrence
Derwent," said he, " and who knows you as the actual murderer
of another man.   Well—you will not have the chance a second
time.   Where is Rosamond Fane ? "

" You are Mr. Hargrave ? " said Lawrence.   " It was you, then
that stopped my escape, and who took the most natural consequence
in the world ?   As for Moldwarp—*his* ghost won't haunt me.   I
have killed too many snakes without legs to mind one more just
because it happens to have two.   To you, Mr. Hargrave, I do owe
an apology for a mistake : and it is yours, since you consider life
so precious a thing.   As for the Queen—I at least will still call
her so—are you her enemy, or her friend ? "

" She *is* here ?   Is she your wife, Lawrence Derwent ?   If she
is—then I will seek neither her nor you more."

Lawrence flushed, and then turned pale.   " Do you mean to doubt
her honour, sir.   And by reason of *me ?*   By all I believe in—and
if that isn't much it is my all to swear by—if you think she would
marry me, or be else than married to any man on earth, I will

think no more of dealing with you than with a Moldwarp, or any other creeping thing. If I can be nothing else, I can be her champion: and I will."

Oswald flushed hotly, in his turn. "I know her story from her sister," said he. "But there is always something untold. If I have wronged her, I—Lawrence Derwent, we are enemies, you and I. But I wish to be just: and above all to you. You have been cruelly wronged, as all the world now knows. And it may be that if you had stood in my path to liberty, I should have done by you as you did by me. Think what it costs me to speak like this: and if you care for Rosamond's, Miss Fane's, welfare, tell me where she is now."

"Wait. . . . Is it true what I have heard: that it is my brother who found my father's will and is seeking to make me rich again and himself poor?"

"There is but one who could have told you so. It was she who found the will—and what else should he do, when it came into his hands?"

"Do? Destroy it, to be sure. I thought my brother a robber. Is he a fool? How can I talk to you about women, and such stuff, till I know what has become of my wrongs? If only I could see that will——"

"Your brother," said Oswald, with cold contempt, "was so jealous of your rights that he would not even keep your father's will under his own control. I gave him my promise not to let it go out of my own hands: nor have I: for I had learned where Miss Fane had gone: and where she was, we feared—But, in short here is the will. You will acknowledge that there has been no delay in placing it in your hands."

"Why did you not place it in safety? Voyages are dangerous things."

"There are those who would have made any hands unsafe but mine. And if I and it were lost, none would have contradicted your brother when he swore to his own ruin and to your gain. Here is the will. It was on me when you tried to kill me: it has never left my hands, night or day."

Lawrence Derwent took the will, with affected nonchalance, and glanced over it as coolly, though there was an eager light in his eyes. "Now, Mr. Hargrave," said he. "All the world has persisted in thinking me a scoundrel until, I think, it has made me so. A man who would rob his own father, and cheat his brother, and

who has actually killed a Moldwarp, would naturally betray and
corrupt an innocent girl. However, as my name is cleared from
all but the Moldwarp matter—which I would gladly do over again
—and as the only woman I ever loved will have none of me, and
as I am richer than I care to be, and as my brother has given me
the last lesson I ever looked to learn, I will give him one in return.
When that will came into his hands, he should have done this—"
and he tore the paper into fragments and threw them out to the
wind. "There's no law against destroying wills in the Goblins.
Rackstraw passes all the laws out her."

The end has been long in coming: but it came. There is much
that might still be told if this were the story of Lawrence Derwent, and not of Rosamond Fane. For him, now that he had at
last achieved his revenge in order to feel that he had done the
only thing that for Rosamond's sake was left him to do, he still had
all the world before him, and time enough to bury a hundred
passions, even if a thousand had not been buried in one generous
deed. He knew how to live strongly—

"And it is not such," said Oswald, on the deck of the *Southern
Cross*, northward and westward bound, "who go to the wall. He
will have some shock of conviction, or conversion, or whatever it
may be called: and it will be a violent one. He was already
planning an expedition of his own to New Gotham, to watch the
new treatment of the people, and to help them to make the best
of things as they are. . . . Rosamond. . . Where are we
going : you and I? Are only we to be left alone, all our lives?
Ten years ago, before your poor uncle, I vowed myself to
you : and am I to wait for ever, because I have waited ten
years ?"

"It is not that, Oswald," said she, gently : for she misjudged
him no longer : and if love had still to force its way through an
over-crowded heart, still it was the one real thing that was left at
the end of a journey through a wilderness of dreams.

"What is it? Do you regret your crown?"

"I hated my crown. I wanted it, because—because it seemed
the only thing left me. I was a bad queen : I should have seen
what end was bound to come——"

"What is it, then?"

"Oswald," she said, turning her face away, "you have earned
one right over me—that I should tell you what it is, and why.
If when I came home again, where all forgot me, you had said—

what you have been saying now : then—but when you were in your fever——"

" What happened then ?   What could I have done ? "

" You dreamed only of——"

" Well ? "

" Of—Miranda."

"Great heaven! and is that all ?   Are we to do nothing but live all our years in dreams ?   You *are* Miranda : and you are Rosamond : and you are that terrible name you bore as Queen of Apahu. And the lover of Rosamond is the lover of you all. Shall I be false to Miranda, and think only of the Rosamond who died ? "

" If she had died——"

" Then the Oswald who vowed to make her his wife is dead too.   Will this Rosamond take this Oswald—and begin life again ? "

" If——"

" If I never make you jealous of even yourself again ?   If you are loved as that other Oswald could never have loved the Rosamond of old time ? "

She now knew why, when she found herself forgotten by this one friend, she had begun to despair, and to clutch at dreams and straws, and crowns.   She had been jealous of herself—but such jealousy as that does not keep heart from heart, or hand from hand.

" At last ! " he said, drawing her towards him. And so, at last, this empress of vanished shadows became a Real Queen, with a Real crown.

THE END

PRINTED BY
KELLY AND CO., GATE STREET, LINCOLN'S INN FIELDS,
AND KINGSTON-ON-THAMES

AN ALPHABETICAL CATALOGUE
OF BOOKS IN FICTION AND
GENERAL LITERATURE
PUBLISHED BY
CHATTO & WINDUS
111 ST. MARTIN'S LANE
CHARING CROSS
LONDON, W.C.
[MAY, 1903.]

A B C (The) of Cricket: a Black View of the Game. (26 Illustrations.) By HUGH FIELDING. Demy 8vo, 1s.

Adams (W. Davenport), Works by.
A Dictionary of the Drama: being a comprehensive Guide to the Plays, Playwrights, Players, and Playhouses of the United Kingdom and America, from the Earliest Times to the Present Day. Crown 8vo, half-bound, 12s. 6d. *[Preparing.*
Quips and Quiddities. Selected by W. DAVENPORT ADAMS. Post 8vo, cloth limp, 2s. 6d.

Agony Column (The) of 'The Times,' from 1800 to 1870. Edited, with an Introduction, by ALICE CLAY. Post 8vo, cloth limp, 2s. 6d.

Alden (W. L.).—Drewitt's Dream. Crown 8vo, cloth, gilt top, 6s.

Alexander (Mrs.), Novels by. Post 8vo, illustrated boards, 2s. each.
Maid, Wife, or Widow? | Blind Fate.

Crown 8vo, cloth, 3s. 6d. each; post 8vo, picture boards, 2s. each.
Valerie's Fate. | A Life Interest. | Mona's Choice. | By Woman's Wit.

Crown 8vo, cloth 3s. 6d. each.
The Cost of her Pride. | Barbara, Lady's Maid and Peeress. | A Fight with Fate.
A Golden Autumn. | Mrs. Crichton's Creditor, | The Step-mother.
 | A Missing Hero. |

Allen (F. M.).—Green as Grass. Crown 8vo, cloth, 3s. 6d.

Allen (Grant), Works by. Crown 8vo, cloth, 6s. each.
The Evolutionist at Large. | Moorland Idylls.
Post-Prandial Philosophy. Crown 8vo, art linen, 3s. 6d.

Crown 8vo, cloth extra, 3s. 6d. each; post 8vo, illustrated boards, 2s. each.
Babylon. 12 Illustrations. | The Devil's Die. | The Duchess of Powysland.
Strange Stories. | This Mortal Coil. | Blood Royal.
The Beckoning Hand. | The Tents of Shem. | Ivan Greet's Masterpiece.
For Maimie's Sake. | The Great Taboo. | The Scallywag. 24 Illusts.
Philistia. | Dumaresq's Daughter. | At Market Value.
In all Shades. | Under Sealed Orders. |

The Tents of Shem. POPULAR EDITION, medium 8vo, 6d.

Anderson (Mary).—Othello's Occupation. Crown 8vo, cloth, 3s. 6d.

Antrobus (C. L.), Novels by. Crown 8vo, cloth, gilt top, 6s. each.
Quality Corner. | Wildersmoor. | The Wine of Finvarra.

Appleton (G. Webb).—Rash Conclusions. Crown 8vo, cloth, 3s. 6d.

Arnold (Edwin Lester), Stories by.
The Wonderful Adventures of Phra the Phœnician. Crown 8vo, cloth extra, with 12 Illustrations by H. M. PAGET, 3s. 6d.; post 8vo, illustrated boards, 2s.
The Constable of St. Nicholas. With Frontispiece by S. L. WOOD. Crown 8vo, cloth, 3s. 6d.; picture cloth, flat back, 2s.

Art (The) of Amusing: A Collection of Graceful Arts, Games, Tricks, Puzzles, and Charades. By FRANK BELLEW. With 300 Illustrations. Crown 8vo, cloth extra, 4s. 6d.

Artemus Ward's Works. With Portrait and Facsimile. Crown 8vo, cloth extra, 3s. 6d.—Also a POPULAR EDITION post 8vo, picture boards, 2s.

Ashton (John), Works by. Crown 8vo, cloth extra, 7s. 6d. each.
Humour, Wit, and Satire of the Seventeenth Century. With 82 Illustrations.
English Caricature and Satire on Napoleon the First. With 115 Illustrations.
Social Life in the Reign of Queen Anne. With 85 Illustrations. Crown 8vo, cloth, 3s. 6d.

Crown 8vo, cloth, gilt top, 6s. each.
Social Life under the Regency. With 90 Illustrations.
Florizel's Folly: The Story of GEORGE IV. With Photogravure Frontispiece and 12 Illustrations.

Bacteria, Yeast Fungi, and Allied Species, A Synopsis of. By
W. B. GROVE, B.A. With 87 Illustrations. Crown 8vo, cloth extra, 3s. 6d.

Bardsley (Rev. C. Wareing, M.A.), Works by.
English Surnames : Their Sources and Significations. Crown 8vo, cloth, 7s. 6d.
Curiosities of Puritan Nomenclature. Crown 8vo, cloth, 3s. 6d.

Barr (Robert), Stories by. Crown 8vo, cloth, 3s. 6d. each.
In a Steamer Chair. With Frontispiece and Vignette by DEMAIN HAMMOND.
From Whose Bourne, &c. With 47 Illustrations by HAL HURST and others.
Revenge! With 12 Illustrations by LANCELOT SPEED and others.
A Woman Intervenes. With 8 Illustrations by HAL HURST.

Crown 8vo, cloth, gilt top, 6s. each.
The Unchanging East : Notes on a Visit to the Farther Edge of the Mediterranean.
A Prince of Good Fellows. With 15 Illustrations by EDMUND J. SULLIVAN.

Barrett (Frank), Novels by.
Post 8vo, illustrated boards, 2s. each; cloth, 2s. 6d. each.

The Sin of Olga Zassoulich.	**John Ford; and His Helpmate.**
Between Life and Death.	**A Recoiling Vengeance.**
Folly Morrison.	**Little Lady Linton.**	**Lieut. Barnabas.**	**Found Guilty.**
A Prodigal's Progress.	**Honest Davie.**	**For Love and Honour.**

Crown 8vo, cloth, 3s. 6d. each; post 8vo, picture boards, 2s. each; cloth limp, 2s. 6d. each.
Fettered for Life. | **The Woman of the Iron Bracelets.** | **The Harding Scandal**
A Missing Witness. With 8 Illustrations by W. H. MARGETSON.

Crown 8vo, cloth, 3s. 6d. each.
Under a Strange Mask. With 19 Illusts. by E. F. BREWTNALL. | **Was She Justified ?**

Besant (Sir Walter) and James Rice, Novels by.
Crown 8vo, cloth extra, 3s. 6d. each; post 8vo, illustrated boards, 2s. each; cloth limp, 2s. 6d. each.

Ready-Money Mortiboy.	**This Son of Vulcan.**	**The Seamy Side.**
The Golden Butterfly.	**The Monks of Thelema.**	**The Case of Mr. Lucraft.**
My Little Girl.	**By Celia's Arbour.**	**'Twas in Trafalgar's Bay.**
With Harp and Crown.	**The Chaplain of the Fleet.**	**The Ten Years' Tenant.**

. There are also LIBRARY EDITIONS of all excepting the first two. Large crown 8vo, cloth, 6s. each.

Besant (Sir Walter), Novels by.
Crown 8vo, cloth extra, 3s. 6d. each; post 8vo, illustrated boards, 2s. each; cloth limp, 2s. 6d. each.
All Sorts and Conditions of Men. With 12 Illustrations by FRED. BARNARD - Also the
  LARGE TYPE, FINE PAPER EDITION, pott 8vo, cloth, gilt top, 2s. net; leather, gilt edges, 3s. net.
The Captains' Room, &c. With Frontispiece by E. J. WHEELER.
All in a Garden Fair. With 6 Illustrations by HARRY FURNISS.
Dorothy Forster. With Frontispiece by CHARLES GREEN.
Uncle Jack, and other Stories. | **Children of Gibeon.**
The World Went Very Well Then. With 12 Illustrations by A. FORESTIER.
Herr Paulus: His Rise, his Greatness, and his Fall. | **The Bell of St. Paul's.**
For Faith and Freedom. With Illustrations by A. FORESTIER and F. WADDY.
To Call Her Mine, &c. With 9 Illustrations by A. FORESTIER.
The Holy Rose, &c. With Frontispiece by F. BARNARD.
Armorel of Lyonesse : A Romance of To-day. With 12 Illustrations by F. BARNARD.
St. Katherine's by the Tower. With 12 Illustrations by C. GREEN.—Also in picture cloth flat
  back, 2s.
Verbena Camellia Stephanotis, &c. With a Frontispiece by GORDON BROWNE.
The Ivory Gate. | **The Rebel Queen.**
Beyond the Dreams of Avarice. With 12 Illustrations by W. H. HYDE.
In Deacon's Orders, &c. With Frontispiece by A. FORESTIER. | **The Revolt of Man.**
The Master Craftsman. | **The City of Refuge.**

Crown 8vo, cloth, 3s. 6d. each.
A Fountain Sealed. | **The Changeling.** | **The Fourth Generation.**

Crown 8vo, cloth, gilt top, 6s. each.
The Orange Girl. With 8 Illustrations by F. PEGRAM.
The Lady of Lynn. With 12 Illustrations by G. DEMAIN-HAMMOND.
No Other Way. With 12 Illustrations by CHARLES D. WARD.

POPULAR EDITIONS, medium 8vo, 6d. each.
All Sorts and Conditions of Men. | **The Chaplain of the Fleet.**
The Golden Butterfly. | **The Orange Girl.**
Ready-Money Mortiboy. | **Children of Gibeon.**

The Charm, and other Drawing-room Plays. By Sir WALTER BESANT and WALTER H. POLLOCK.
  With 50 Illustrations by CHRIS HAMMOND and JULE GOODMAN. Crown 8vo, cloth, 3s. 6d.
Fifty Years Ago. With 144 Illustrations. Crown 8vo, cloth, 3s. 6d.
The Eulogy of Richard Jefferies. With Portrait. Crown 8vo, cloth, 6s.
Sir Richard Whittington. With Frontispiece. Crown 8vo, art linen, 3s. 6d.
Gaspard de Coligny. With a Portrait. Crown 8vo, art linen, 3s. 6d.
The Art of Fiction. Fcap. 8vo, cloth, red top, 1s. net.
As We Are and As We May Be. Crown 8vo, buckram. gilt top, 6s.
Essays and Historiettes. Crown 8vo, buckram, gilt top, 6s.

Demy 8vo, cloth, 7s. 6d. each.
London. With 125 Illustrations.
Westminster. With an Etched Frontispiece by F. S. WALKER, R.E., and 130 Illustrations by
  WILLIAM PATTEN and others.
South London. With an Etched Frontispiece by F. S. WALKER, R.E., and 118 Illustrations.
East London. With an Etched Frontispiece by F. S. WALKER, and 55 Illustrations by PHIL
  MAY, L. RAVEN HILL, and JOSEPH PENNELL.
Jerusalem : The City of Herod and Saladin. By WALTER BESANT and E. H. PALMER. Fourth
  Edition. With a new Chapter, a Map, and 11 Illustrations.

Baring Gould (Sabine, Author of 'John Herring,' &c.), Novels by.
Crown 8vo, cloth extra, 3s. 6d. each; post 8vo, Illustrated boards, 2s. each.
Red Spider. | Eve.

Beaconsfield, Lord. By T. P. O'CONNOR, M.P. Cr. 8vo, cloth, 5s.

Bechstein (Ludwig).—As Pretty as Seven, and other German
Stories. With Additional Tales by the Brothers GRIMM, and 98 Illustrations by RICHTER. Square
8vo, cloth extra, 6s. 6d.; gilt edges, 7s. 6d.

Bennett (Arnold), Novels by. Crown 8vo, cloth, 6s. each.
The Grand Babylon Hotel: A Fantasia on Modern Themes. | **Anna of the Five Towns.**
The Gates of Wrath. Crown 8vo, cloth, 3s. 6d.

Bennett (W. C., LL.D.).—Songs for Sailors. Post 8vo. cl. limp, 2s.

Bewick (Thomas) and his Pupils. By AUSTIN DOBSON. With 95
Illustrations. Square 8vo, cloth extra, 3s. 6d.

Bierce (Ambrose).—In the Midst of Life: Tales of Soldiers and
Civilians. Crown 8vo, cloth extra, 3s. 6d.; post 8vo, illustrated boards, 2s.

Bill Nye's Comic History of the United States. With 146 Illustrations by F. OPPER. Crown 8vo, cloth extra, 3s. 6d.

Bindloss (Harold), Novels by. Crown 8vo, cloth, gilt top, 6s. each.
A Sower of Wheat. | **The Concession-Hunters.**
Ainslie's Ju-Ju: A Romance of the Hinterland. Cr. 8vo, cloth, 3s. 6d.; picture cloth, flat back 2s.

Bodkin (M. McD., K.C.), Books by.
Dora Myrl, the Lady Detective. Crown 8vo, cloth, 3s. 6d.; picture cloth, flat back. 2s.
Shillelagh and Shamrock. Crown 8vo, cloth, 3s. 6d.

Bourget (Paul).—A Living Lie. Translated by JOHN DE VILLIERS.
With special Preface for the English Edition. Crown 8vo, cloth, 3s. 6d.

Bourne (H. R. Fox), Books by.
English Merchants: Memoirs in Illustration of the Progress of British Commerce. With 32 Illus-
trations. Crown 8vo, cloth, 3s. 6d.
English Newspapers: Chapters in the History of Journalism. Two Vols., demy 8vo, cloth, 25s.
The Other Side of the Emin Pasha Relief Expedition. Crown 8vo, cloth, 6s.

Boyd.—A Versailles Christmas-tide. By MARY STUART BOYD. With
53 Illustrations by A. S. BOYD. Fcap. 4to. cloth gilt and gilt top, 6s.

Boyle (Frederick), Works by. Post 8vo, illustrated bds., 2s. each.
Chronicles of No-Man's Land. | **Camp Notes.** | **Savage Life.**

Brand (John).—Observations on Popular Antiquities; chiefly
illustrating the Origin of our Vulgar Customs, Ceremonies, and Superstitions. With the Additions of Sir
HENRY ELLIS. Crown 8vo, cloth, 3s. 6d.

Brayshaw (J. Dodsworth).—Slum Silhouettes: Stories of London
Life. Crown 8vo, cloth, 3s. 6d.

Brewer's (Rev. Dr.) Dictionaries. Crown 8vo, cloth, 3s. 6d. each.
**The Reader's Handbook of Famous Names in Fiction, Allusions, References,
Proverbs, Plots, Stories, and Poems.** A New Edition, Revised.
A Dictionary of Miracles: Imitative, Realistic, and Dogmatic.

Brewster (Sir David), Works by. Post 8vo, cloth, 4s. 6d. each.
More Worlds than One: The Creed of the Philosopher and Hope of the Christian. With Plates.
The Martyrs of Science: GALILEO, TYCHO BRAHE, and KEPLER. With Portraits.
Letters on Natural Magic. With numerous Illustrations.

Bright (Florence).—A Girl Capitalist. Cr. 8vo, cloth, gilt top, 6s.

Brillat-Savarin.—Gastronomy as a Fine Art. Translated by
R. E. ANDERSON, M.A. Post 8vo, half-bound, 2s.

Bryden (H. A.).—An Exiled Scot: A Romance. With a Frontispiece, by J. S. CROMPTON, R.I. Crown 8vo, cloth, 3s. 6d.

Brydges (Harold).—Uncle Sam at Home. With 91 Illustrations.
Post 8vo, illustrated boards, 2s.; cloth limp, 2s. 6d.

Burton (Robert).—The Anatomy of Melancholy. With Translations of the Quotations. Demy 8vo, cloth extra, 7s. 6d. BURTON'S ANATOMY.
Melancholy Anatomised: An Abridgment of BURTON'S ANATOMY. Post 8vo, half-cl., 2s. 6d.

Buchanan (Robert), Poems and Novels by.

The Complete Poetical Works of Robert Buchanan. 2 vols, crown 8vo, buckram, with Portrait Frontispiece to each volume, 12s.

Crown 8vo, cloth, 3s. 6d. each; post 8vo, illustrated boards, 2s. each.

The Shadow of the Sword.	**Love Me for Ever.** With Frontispiece.
A Child of Nature. With Frontispiece.	**Annan Water.** | **Foxglove Manor.**
God and the Man. With 11 Illustrations by	**The New Abelard.** | **Rachel Dene.**
Lady Kilpatrick. [FRED. BARNARD.	**Matt:** A Story of a Caravan. With Frontispiece.
The Martyrdom of Madeline. With	**The Master of the Mine.** With Frontispiece.
Frontispiece by A. W. COOPER.	**The Heir of Linne.** | **Woman and the Man.**

Crown 8vo, cloth, 3s. 6d. each.

Red and White Heather. | **Andromeda:** An Idyll of the Great River.

The Shadow of the Sword. POPULAR EDITION, medium 8vo, 6d.

The Charlatan. By ROBERT. BUCHANAN and HENRY MURRAY. Crown 8vo, cloth, with a Frontispiece by T. H. ROBINSON, 3s. 6d.; post 8vo, picture boards, 2s.

Caine (Hall), Novels by. Crown 8vo, cloth extra, 3s. 6d. each.; post

8vo, illustrated boards, 2s. each; cloth limp, 2s. 6d. each.
The Shadow of a Crime. | **A Son of Hagar.** | **The Deemster.**

Also LIBRARY EDITIONS of the three novels, set in new type, crown 8vo, bound uniform with **The Christian,** 6s. each; and CHEAP POPULAR EDITIONS, medium 8vo, portrait cover, 6d. each.—Also the FINE-PAPER EDITION of **The Deemster,** pott 8vo, cloth, gilt top, 2s. net; leather, gilt edges, 3s. net.

Cameron (Commander V. Lovett).—The Cruise of the 'Black
Prince' Privateer. Post 8vo, picture boards, 2s.

Canada (Greater) : The Past, Present, and Future of the Canadian
North-West. By E. B. OSBORN, B.A. With a Map. Crown 8vo, cloth, 3s. 6d.

Captain Coignet, Soldier of the Empire: An Autobiography.
Edited by LOREDAN LARCHEY. Translated by Mrs. CAREY. With 100 Illustrations. Crown 8vo, cloth, 3s. 6d.

Carlyle (Thomas).—On the Choice of Books. Post 8vo, cl., 1s. 6d.

Carruth (Hayden).—The Adventures of Jones. With 17 Illustra-
tions. Fcap. 8vo, cloth, 2s.

Chambers (Robert W.), Stories of Paris Life by.

The King in Yellow. Crown 8vo, cloth, 3s. 6d.; fcap. 8vo, cloth limp, 2s. 6d.
In the Quarter. Fcap. 8vo, cloth, 2s. 6d.

Chapman's (George), Works. Vol. I., Plays Complete, including the
Doubtful Ones.—Vol. II., Poems and Minor Translations, with Essay by A. C. SWINBURNE.—Vol. III., Translations of the Iliad and Odyssey. Three Vols., crown 8vo, cloth, 3s. 6d. each.

Chapple (J. Mitchell).—The Minor Chord: The Story of a Prima
Donna. Crown 8vo, cloth, 3s. 6d.

Chaucer for Children: A Golden Key. By Mrs. H. R. HAWEIS. With
8 Coloured Plates and 30 Woodcuts. Crown 4to, cloth extra, 3s. 6d.
Chaucer for Schools. With the Story of his Times and his Work. By Mrs. H. R. HAWEIS. A New Edition, revised. With a Frontispiece. Demy 8vo, cloth, 2s. 6d.

Chess, The Laws and Practice of. With an Analysis of the Open-
ings. By HOWARD STAUNTON. Edited by R. B. WORMALD. Crown 8vo, cl. 7b, 5s.
The Minor Tactics of Chess: A Treatise on the Deployment of the Forces in obedience to Strategic Principle. By F. K. YOUNG and E. C. HOWELL. Long fcap. 8vo, cloth, 2s. 6d.
The Hastings Chess Tournament. Containing the Authorised Account of the 230 Games played Aug.-Sept. 1895. With Annotations by PILLSBURY, LASKER, TARRASCH, STEINITZ, SCHIFFERS, TEICHMANN, BARDELEBEN, BLACKBURNE, GUNSBERG, TINSLEY, MASON, and ALBIN; Biographical Sketches of the Chess Masters, and 22 Portraits. Edited by H. F. CHESHIRE. Cheaper Edition. Crown 8vo, cloth, 5s.

Clare (Austin), Stories by.
For the Love of a Lass. Post 8vo, illustrated boards, 2s.; cloth, 2s. 6d.
By the Rise of the River: Tales and Sketches in South Tynedale. Crown 8vo, cloth, 3s. 6d.
The Tideway. Crown 8vo, cloth, gilt top, 6s.

Clive (Mrs. Archer), Novels by.
Post 8vo, cloth, 3s. 6d. each; picture boards, 2s. each.
Paul Ferroll. | **Why Paul Ferroll Killed his Wife.**

Clodd (Edward, F.R.A.S.).—Myths and Dreams. Cr. 8vo, 3s. 6d.

Coates (Anne).—Rie's Diary. Crown 8vo, cloth, 3s. 6d.

Cobban (J. Maclaren), Novels by.
The Cure of Souls. Post 8vo, Illustrated boards, 2s.
The Red Sultan. Crown 8vo, cloth extra, 3s. 6d. ; post 8vo, Illustrated boards, 2s.
The Burden of Isabel. Crown 8vo, cloth extra, 3s. 6d.

Collins (C. Allston).—The Bar Sinister. Post 8vo, boards, 2s.

Collins (John Churton, M.A.), Books by. Cr. 8vo, cl., 3s. 6d. each.
Illustrations of Tennyson.
Jonathan Swift. A Biographical and Critical Study.

Collins (Mortimer and Frances), Novels by.
Crown 8vo, cloth extra, 3s. 6d. each; post 8vo, illustrated boards, 2s. each.
From Midnight to Midnight. | Blacksmith and Scholar.
You Play me False. | The Village Comedy.

Post 8vo, Illustrated boards, 2s. each.
Transmigration. | Sweet Anne Page. | Frances.
A Fight with Fortune. | Sweet and Twenty.

Collins (Wilkie), Novels by.
Crown 8vo, cloth extra, many Illustrated, 3s. 6d. each ; post 8vo, picture boards, 2s. each;
cloth limp, 2s. 6d. each.

* Antonina. | My Miscellanies. | Jezebel's Daughter.
* Basil. | Armadale. | The Black Robe.
* Hide and Seek. | Poor Miss Finch. | Heart and Science.
* The Woman in White. | Miss or Mrs.? | 'I Say No.'
* The Moonstone. | The New Magdalen. | A Rogue's Life.
* Man and Wife. | The Frozen Deep. | The Evil Genius.
* The Dead Secret. | The Law and the Lady. | Little Novels.
After Dark. | The Two Destinies. | The Legacy of Cain.
The Queen of Hearts. | The Haunted Hotel. | Blind Love.
No Name. | The Fallen Leaves.
** Marked * have been reset in new type, in uniform style.

POPULAR EDITIONS, medium 8vo, 6d. each.
The Moonstone. | Antonina. | The Dead Secret.
The Woman in White. | The New Magdalen. | Man and Wife. | Armadale. [Shortly
The Woman in White. LARGE TYPE, FINE PAPER EDITION. Pott 8vo, cloth, gilt top, 2s.
net : leather, gilt edges, 3s. net.

Colman's (George) Humorous Works: 'Broad Grins,' 'My Night-
gown and Slippers,' &c. With Life and Frontispiece. Crown 8vo, cloth extra, 3s. 6d.

Colquhoun (M. J.).—Every Inch a Soldier. Crown 8vo, cloth,
3s. 6d. ; post 8vo, illustrated boards, 2s.

Colt-breaking, Hints on. By W. M. HUTCHISON. Cr. 8vo, cl., 3s. 6d.

Compton (Herbert), Novels by.
The Inimitable Mrs. Massingham. Crown 8vo, cloth, 3s. 6d.
The Wilful Way. Crown 8vo, cloth, gilt top, 6s.

Convalescent Cookery. By CATHERINE RYAN. Cr. 8vo, 1s. ; cl., 1s. 6d.

Cooper (Edward H.).—Geoffory Hamilton. Cr. 8vo, cloth, 3s. 6d.

Cornish (J. F.).—Sour Grapes : A Novel. Cr. 8vo, cloth, gilt top, 6s.

Cornwall.—Popular Romances of the West of England; or, The
Drolls, Traditions, and Superstitions of Old Cornwall. Collected by ROBERT HUNT, F.R.S. With
two Steel Plates by GEORGE CRUIKSHANK. Crown 8vo, cloth, 7s. 6d.

Cotes (V. Cecil).—Two Girls on a Barge. With 44 Illustrations by
F. H. TOWNSEND. Crown 8vo, cloth extra, 3s. 6d. ; post 8vo, cloth, 2s. 6d.

Craddock (C. Egbert), Stories by.
The Prophet of the Great Smoky Mountains. Crown 8vo, cloth, 3s. 6d. ; post 8vo,
illustrated boards, 2s.
His Vanished Star. Crown 8vo, cloth, 3s. 6d.

Crellin (H. N.), Books by.
Romances of the Old Seraglio. With 28 Illustrations by S. L. WOOD. Crown 8vo, cloth, 3s. 6d.
Tales of the Caliph. Crown 8vo, cloth, 2s.
The Nazarenes: A Drama. Crown 8vo, 1s.

Crim (Matt.).—Adventures of a Fair Rebel. Crown 8vo, cloth
extra, with a Frontispiece by DAN. BEARD, 3s. 6d. ; post 8vo, illustrated boards, 2s.

Crockett (S. R.) and others. — Tales of Our Coast. By S. R.
CROCKETT, GILBERT PARKER, HAROLD FREDERIC, 'Q,' and W. CLARK RUSSELL. With 8
Illustrations by FRANK BRANGWYN. Crown 8vo, cloth, 3s. 6d.

Croker (Mrs. B. M.), Novels by. Crown 8vo, cloth extra, 3s. 6d,

each; post 8vo, illustrated boards, 2s. each; cloth limp, 2s. 6d. each.

Pretty Miss Neville.	Interference.	Village Tales & Jungle
Proper Pride.	A Family Likeness.	Tragedies.
A Bird of Passage.	A Third Person.	The Real Lady Hilda.
Diana Barrington.	Mr. Jervis.	Married or Single ?
Two Masters.		

Crown 8vo, cloth extra, 3s. 6d each.

Some One Else.	Miss Balmaine's Past.	Beyond the Pale.
In the Kingdom of Kerry.	Jason, &c.	Infatuation.

Terence. With 6 Illustrations by SIDNEY PAGET.

'To Let,' &c. Post 8vo, picture boards, 2s.; cloth limp, 2s. 6d.
The Cat's-paw. With 12 Illustrations by FRED. PEGRAM. Crown 8vo, cloth, gilt top, 6s.
Diana Barrington. POPULAR EDITION, medium 8vo, 6d.

Cruikshank's Comic Almanack. Complete in Two SERIES: The

FIRST, from 1835 to 1843; the SECOND, from 1844 to 1853. A Gathering of the Best Humour of
THACKERAY, HOOD, MAYHEW, ALBERT SMITH, A'BECKETT, ROBERT BROUGH, &c. With
numerous Steel Engravings and Woodcuts by GEORGE CRUIKSHANK, HINE, LANDELLS, &c.
Two Vols., crown 8vo, cloth gilt, 7s. 6d. each.
The Life of George Cruikshank. By BLANCHARD JERROLD. With 84 Illustrations and a
Bibliography. Crown 8vo, cloth extra, 3s. 6d.

Cumming (C. F. Gordon), Works by. Large cr. 8vo, cloth, 6s. each.

In the Hebrides. With an Autotype Frontispiece and 23 Illustrations.
In the Himalayas and on the Indian Plains. With 42 Illustrations.
Two Happy Years in Ceylon. With 28 Illustrations.
Via Cornwall to Egypt. With a Photogravure Frontispiece.

Cussans (John E.).—A Handbook of Heraldry; with Instructions

for Tracing Pedigrees and Deciphering Ancient MSS., &c. Fourth Edition, revised, with 408 Woodcuts
and 2 Coloured Plates. Crown 8vo, cloth extra, 6s.

Daudet (Alphonse).—The Evangelist; or, Port Salvation. Crown

8vo, cloth extra, 3s. 6d.; post 8vo, illustrated boards, 2s.

Davenant (Francis, M.A.).—Hints for Parents on the Choice of

a Profession for their Sons when Starting in Life. Crown 8vo, cloth, 1s. 6d.

Davidson (Hugh Coleman).—Mr. Sadler's Daughters. With a

Frontispiece by STANLEY WOOD. Crown 8vo, cloth extra, 3s. 6d.

Davies (Dr. N. E. Yorke-), Works by. Cr. 8vo, 1s. ea.; cl., 1s. 6d. ea.

One Thousand Medical Maxims and Surgical Hints.
Nursery Hints: A Mother's Guide in Health and Disease.
Foods for the Fat: The Dietetic Cure of Corpulency and of Gout.

Aids to Long Life. Crown 8vo, 2s.; cloth limp, 2s. 6d.

Davies' (Sir John) Complete Poetical Works. Collected and Edited,

with Introduction and Notes, by Rev. A. B. GROSART, D.D. Two Vols., crown 8vo, cloth, 3s. 6d. each.

De Guerin (Maurice), The Journal of. Edited by G. S. TREBUTIEN.

With a Memoir by SAINTE-BEUVE. Translated from the 20th French Edition by JESSIE P. FROTH-
INGHAM. Fcap. 8vo, half-bound, 2s. 6d.

De Maistre (Xavier).—A Journey Round my Room. Translated

by HENRY ATTWELL. Post 8vo, cloth limp, 2s. 6d.

Derby (The): The Blue Ribbon of the Turf. With Brief Accounts

of THE OAKS. By LOUIS HENRY CURZON. Crown 8vo, cloth limp, 2s. 6d.

Dewar (T. R.).—A Ramble Round the Globe. With 220 Illustra-

tions. Crown 8vo, cloth extra, 7s. 6d.

De Windt (Harry), Books by.

Through the Gold-Fields of Alaska to Bering Straits. With Map and 33 full-page Illustrations. Cheaper Issue. Demy 8vo, cloth, 6s.
True Tales of Travel and Adventure. Crown 8vo, cloth, 3s. 6d.

Dickens (Charles), About England with. By ALFRED RIMMER.

With 57 Illustrations by C. A. VANDERHOOP and the AUTHOR. Square 8vo, cloth, 3s. 6d.

Dictionaries.

The Reader's Handbook of Famous Names in Fiction, Allusions, References,
Proverbs, Plots, Stories, and Poems. By Rev. E. C. BREWER, LL.D. A New Edi-
tion. Revised. Crown 8vo, cloth, 3s. 6d.
A Dictionary of Miracles: Imitative, Realistic, and Dogmatic. By the Rev. E. C. BREWER,
LL.D. Crown 8vo, cloth, 3s. 6d.
Familiar Short Sayings of Great Men. With Historical and Explanatory Notes by SAMUEL
A. BENT. A.M. Crown 8vo, cloth extra, 7s. 6d.
The Slang Dictionary: Etymological, Historical, and Anecdotal. Crown 8vo, cloth, 6s. 6d.
Words, Facts, and Phrases: A Dictionary of Curious, Quaint, and Out-of-the-Way Matters. By
ELIEZER EDWARDS. Crown 8vo, cloth extra, 3s 6d.

Dilke (Rt. Hon. Sir Charles, Bart., M.P.).—The British Empire.

Crown 8vo, buckram, 3s. 6d.

Dobson (Austin), Works by.

Thomas Bewick and his Pupils. With 95 Illustrations. Square 8vo, cloth, 3s. 6d.
Four Frenchwomen. With Four Portraits. Crown 8vo, buckram, gilt top, 6s.
Eighteenth Century Vignettes. IN THREE SERIES. Crown 8vo, buckram, 6s. each.
A Paladin of Philanthropy, and other Papers. With 2 Illusts. Cr 8vo, buckram, 6s.
Side-walk Studies. With 5 Illustrations. SECOND EDITION. Crown 8vo, buckram, gilt top, 6s.

Dobson (W. T.).—Poetical Ingenuities and Eccentricities. Post
8vo, cloth limp, 2s. 6d.

Donovan (Dick), Detective Stories by.

Post 8vo, illustrated boards, 2s. each : cloth limp, 2s. 6d. each.

The Man-Hunter.	Wanted!
Caught at Last.	Tracked to Doom.
Tracked and Taken.	Link by Link.
Who Poisoned Hetty Duncan?	

Suspicion Aroused.   Riddles Read.
A Detective's Triumphs.
In the Grip of the Law.
From Information Received.

Crown 8vo, cloth extra, 3s. 6d. each : post 8vo, illustrated boards, 2s. each : cloth, 2s. 6d. each.
The Man from Manchester. With 23 Illustrations.
The Mystery of Jamaica Terrace. | **The Chronicles of Michael Danevitch.**

Crown 8vo, cloth, 3s. 6d. each.
The Records of Vincent Trill, of the Detective Service.—Also picture cloth, flat back, 2s.
The Adventures of Tyler Tatlock, Private Detective.
Deacon Brodie; or, Behind the Mask. | **Tales of Terror.**
Dark Deeds. Crown 8vo, picture cloth, flat back, 2s.

Dowling (Richard).—Old Corcoran's Money. Crown 8vo, cl., 3s. 6d.

Doyle (A. Conan).—The Firm of Girdlestone. Cr. 8vo, cl., 3s. 6d.

Dramatists, The Old. Cr. 8vo, cl. ex., with Portraits, 3s. 6d. per Vol.

Ben Jonson's Works. With Notes, Critical and Explanatory, and a Biographical Memoir by
WILLIAM GIFFORD. Edited by Colonel CUNNINGHAM. Three Vols.
Chapman's Works. Three Vols. Vol. I. contains the Plays complete ; Vol. II., Poems and Minor
Translations, with an Essay by A. C. SWINBURNE ; Vol. III., Translations of the Iliad and Odyssey.
Marlowe's Works. Edited, with Notes, by Colonel CUNNINGHAM. One Vol.
Massinger's Plays. From GIFFORD'S Text. Edited by Colonel CUNNINGHAM. One Vol.

Dublin Castle and Dublin Society, Recollections of. By A
NATIVE. Crown 8vo, cloth, gilt top 6s.

Duncan (Sara Jeannette: Mrs. EVERARD COTES), Books by.

Crown 8vo, cloth extra, 7s. 6d. each.
A Social Departure. With 111 Illustrations by F. H. TOWNSEND.
An American Girl in London. With 80 Illustrations by F. H. TOWNSEND.
The Simple Adventures of a Memsahib. With 37 Illustrations by F. H. TOWNSEND.

Crown 8vo, cloth extra, 3s. 6d. each.
A Daughter of To-Day. | **Vernon's Aunt.** With 47 Illustrations by HAL HURST.

Dutt (Romesh C.).—England and India: A Record of Progress
during One Hundred Years. Crown 8vo, cloth, 2s.

Early English Poets. Edited, with Introductions and Annotations,
by Rev. A. B. GROSART, D.D. Crown 8vo, cloth boards, 3s. 6d. per Volume.
Fletcher's (Giles) Complete Poems. One Vol.
Davies' (Sir John) Complete Poetical Works. Two Vols.
Sidney's (Sir Philip) Complete Poetical Works. Three Vols.

Edgcumbe (Sir E. R. Pearce).—Zephyrus: A Holiday in Brazil
and on the River Plate. With 41 Illustrations. Crown 8vo, cloth extra, 5s.

Edwardes (Mrs. Annie), Novels by.

A Point of Honour. Post 8vo, illustrated boards, 2s. | **A Plaster Saint.** Cr. 8vo, cl., 3s. 6d.
Archie Lovell. Crown 8vo, cloth, 3s. 6d. ; illustrated boards, 2s.

Edwards (Eliezer).—Words, Facts, and Phrases: A Dictionary
of Curious, Quaint, and Out-of-the-Way Matters. Cheaper Edition. Crown 8vo, cloth, 3s. 6d.

Egerton (Rev. J. C., M.A.). — Sussex Folk and Sussex Ways.
With Introduction by Rev. Dr. H. WACE, and Four Illustrations. Crown 8vo, cloth extra, 5s.

Eggleston (Edward).—Roxy: A Novel. Post 8vo, illust. boards, 2s.

Englishman (An) in Paris. Notes and Recollections during the
Reign of Louis Philippe and the Empire. Crown 8vo, cloth, 3s. 6d.

Englishman's House, The: A Practical Guide for Selecting or Build-
ing a House. By C. J. RICHARDSON. Coloured Frontispiece and 534 Illusts. Cr. 8vo, cloth, 3s. 6d.

Eyes, Our: How to Preserve Them. By JOHN BROWNING. Cr. 8vo, 1s.

Familiar Short Sayings of Great Men. By SAMUEL ARTHUR BENT,
A.M. Fifth Edition, Revised and Enlarged. Crown 8vo, cloth extra, 7s. 6d.

Faraday (Michael), Works by. Post 8vo, cloth extra, 4s. 6d. each.

The Chemical History of a Candle: Lectures delivered before a Juvenile Audience. Edited by WILLIAM CROOKES, F.C.S. With numerous Illustrations.

On the Various Forces of Nature, and their Relations to each other. Edited by WILLIAM CROOKES, F.C.S. With Illustrations.

Farrer (J. Anson).—War: Three Essays. Crown 8vo, cloth, 1s. 6d.

Fenn (G. Manville), Novels by.

♥ Crown 8vo, cloth extra, 3s. 6d. each; post 8vo, illustrated boards, 2s. each.

The New Mistress. | **Witness to the Deed.** | **The Tiger Lily.** | **The White Virgin.**

Crown 8vo, cloth 3s. 6d. each.

A Woman Worth Winning.	Double Cunning.	The Story of Antony Grace
Cursed by a Fortune.	A Fluttered Dovecote.	The Man with a Shadow.
The Case of Ailsa Gray.	King of the Castle.	One Maid's Mischief.
Commodore Junk.	The Master of the Cere-	This Man's Wife.
Black Blood.	monies.	In Jeopardy.

Crown 8vo, cloth, gilt top, 5s. each.

The Bag of Diamonds, and Three Bits of Paste.
Running Amok: a Story of Adventure.
The Cankerworm: being Episodes of a Woman's Life. | **Black Shadows.**
A Crimson Crime. Crown 8vo, cloth, gilt top, 6s.; picture cloth, flat back, 2s.

Fiction, A Catalogue of, with Descriptive Notices and Reviews of

over NINE HUNDRED NOVELS, will be sent free by Messrs. CHATTO & WINDUS upon application.

Fin-Bec.—The Cupboard Papers: Observations on the Art of Living

and Dining. Post 8vo, cloth limp, 2s. 6d.

Firework-Making, The Complete Art of; or, The Pyrotechnist's

Treasury. By THOMAS KENTISH. With 267 Illustrations. Crown 8vo, cloth, 3s. 6d.

First Book, My. By WALTER BESANT, JAMES PAYN, W. CLARK RUS-

SELL, GRANT ALLEN, HALL CAINE, GEORGE R. SIMS, RUDYARD KIPLING, A. CONAN DOYLF,
M. E. BRADDON, F. W. ROBINSON, H. RIDER HAGGARD, R. M. BALLANTYNE, I. ZANGWILL,
MORLEY ROBERTS, D. CHRISTIE MURRAY, MARY CORELLI, J. K. JEROME, JOHN STRANGE
WINTER, BRET HARTE, 'Q.,' ROBERT BUCHANAN, and R. L. STEVENSON. With a Prefatory Story
by JEROME K. JEROME, and 185 Illustrations. A New Edition. Small demy 8vo, art linen, 3s. 6d.

Fitzgerald (Percy), Works by.

Little Essays: Passages from the Letters of CHARLES LAMB. Post 8vo, cloth, 2s. 6d.
Fatal Zero. Crown 8vo, cloth extra, 3s. 6d. | post 8vo, illustrated boards, 2s.

Post 8vo, illustrated boards, 2s. each.

Bella Donna.	The Lady of Brantome.	The Second Mrs. Tillotson.
Polly.	Never Forgotten.	Seventy-five Brooke Street.

Sir Henry Irving: Twenty Years at the Lyceum. With Portrait. Crown 8vo, cloth, 1s. 6d.

Flammarion (Camille), Works by.

Popular Astronomy: A General Description of the Heavens. Translated by J. ELLARD GORE,
F.R.A.S. With Three Plates and 288 Illustrations. Medium 8vo, cloth, 10s. 6d.
Urania: A Romance. With 87 Illustrations. Crown 8vo, cloth extra, 5s.

Fletcher's (Giles, B.D.) Complete Poems: Christ's Victorie in

Heaven, Christ's Victorie on Earth, Christ's Triumph over Death, and Minor Poems. With Notes by
Rev. A. B. GROSART, D.D. Crown 8vo, cloth boards, 3s. 6d.

Forbes (Archibald).—The Life of Napoleon III. With Photo-

gravure Frontispiece and Thirty-six full-page Illustrations. Cheaper Issue. Demy 8vo, cloth, 6s.

Forbes (Hon. Mrs. Walter R. D.).—Dumb. Crown 8vo, cl., 3s. 6d.

Francillon (R. E.), Novels by.

Crown 8vo, cloth extra, 3s. 6d. each; post 8vo, illustrated boards, 2s. each.

One by One. | **A Real Queen.** | **A Dog and his Shadow.** | **Ropes of Sand.** Illust.

Post 8vo, illustrated boards, 2s. each.

Queen Cophetua. | **Olympia.** | **Romances of the Law.** | **King or Knave?**
Jack Doyle's Daughter. Crown 8vo, cloth, 3s. 6d.

Frederic (Harold), Novels by. Post 8vo, cloth extra, 3s. 6d. each;

illustrated boards, 2s. each.

Seth's Brother's Wife. | **The Lawton Girl.**

Fry's (Herbert) Royal Guide to the London Charities, 1903.

Edited by JOHN LANE. Published Annually. Crown 8vo, cloth, 1s. 6d.

Gardening Books. Post 8vo, 1s. each; cloth limp, 1s. 6d. each.

A Year's Work in Garden and Greenhouse. By GEORGE GLENNY.
Household Horticulture. By TOM and JANE JERROLD. Illustrated.
The Garden that Paid the Rent. By TOM JERROLD.

Gaulot (Paul).—The Red Shirts: A Tale of 'The Terror.' Trans-

lated by JOHN DE VILLIERS. With a Frontispiece by STANLEY WOOD. Crown 8vo, cloth, 3s. 6d.;
picture cloth, flat back, 2s.

Gentleman's Magazine, The. 1s. Monthly. Contains Stories,
Articles upon Literature, Science, Biography, and Art, and 'Table Talk' by SYLVANUS URBAN.
• *Bound Volumes for recent years kept in stock,* 8s. 6d. *each. Cases for binding,* 2s. *each.*

German Popular Stories. Collected by the Brothers GRIMM and
Translated by EDGAR TAYLOR. With Introduction by JOHN RUSKIN, and 22 Steel Plates after
GEORGE CRUIKSHANK. Square 8vo, cloth, 6s. 6d.; gilt edges, 7s. 6d.

Gibbon (Chas.), Novels by. Cr. 8vo, cl., 3s. 6d. ea.; post 8vo, bds., 2s. ea.

Robin Gray. With Frontispiece.	Loving a Dream.	The Braes of Yarrow.
The Golden Shaft. With Frontispiece.	Of High Degree.
The Flower of the Forest.	Queen of the Meadow.

Post 8vo, Illustrated boards, 2s. each.

The Dead Heart.	In Pastures Green.	In Honour Bound.
For Lack of Gold.	In Love and War.	Heart's Delight.
What Will the World Say?	A Heart's Problem.	Blood-Money.
For the King.	By Mead and Stream.	
A Hard Knot.	Fancy Free.	

Gibney (Somerville).—Sentenced ! Crown 8vo, cloth, 1s. 6d.

Gilbert's (W. S.) Original Plays. In 3 Series, post 8vo, 2s. 6d. each.
The FIRST SERIES contains: The Wicked World—Pygmalion and Galatea—Charity—The Princess—
The Palace of Truth—Trial by Jury—Iolanthe.
The SECOND SERIES : Broken Hearts—Engaged—Sweethearts—Gretchen—Dan'l Druce—Tom Cobb
—H.M.S. 'Pinafore'—The Sorcerer—The Pirates of Penzance.
The THIRD SERIES: Comedy and Tragedy—Foggerty's Fairy—Rosencrantz and Guildenstern -
Patience—Princess Ida—The Mikado—Ruddigore—The Yeomen of the Guard—The Gondoliers—
The Mountebanks—Utopia.

Eight Original Comic Operas written by W. S. GILBERT. Two Series, demy 8vo, cloth, 2s. 6d.
each. The FIRST SERIES contains: The Sorcerer—H.M.S. 'Pinafore'—The Pirates of Penzance—
Iolanthe—Patience—Princess Ida—The Mikado—Trial by Jury.
The SECOND SERIES contains: The Gondoliers—The Grand Duke—The Yeomen of the Guard—
His Excellency—Utopia, Limited—Ruddigore—The Mountebanks—Haste to the Wedding.
The Gilbert and Sullivan Birthday Book: Quotations for Every Day in the Year, selected
from Plays by W. S. GILBERT set to Music by Sir A. SULLIVAN. Compiled by ALEX. WATSON
Royal 16mo, Japanese leather, 2s. 6d.

Gilbert (William).— James Duke, Costermonger. Post 8vo,
Illustrated boards, 2s.

Gissing (Algernon), Novels by. Crown 8vo, cloth, gilt top, 6s. each.
A Secret of the North Sea. | The Wealth of Mallerstang.
Knitters in the Sun.

Glanville (Ernest), Novels by.
Crown 8vo, cloth extra, 3s. 6d. each; post 8vo, illustrated boards, 2s. each.
The Lost Heiress: A Tale of Love, Battle, and Adventure. With Two Illustrations by H. NISBET.
The Fossicker: A Romance of Mashonaland. With Two Illustrations by HUME NISBET.
A Fair Colonist. With a Frontispiece by STANLEY WOOD.

The Golden Rock. With a Frontispiece by STANLEY WOOD. Crown 8vo, cloth extra, 3s. 6d.
Kloof Yarns. Crown 8vo cloth, 1s. 6d.
Tales from the Veld. With Twelve Illustrations by M. NISBET. Crown 8vo, cloth, 3s. 6d.
Max Thornton. With 8 Illustrations by J. S. CROMPTON, R.I. Large crown 8vo, cloth, gilt
edges, 5s.; cloth, gilt top, 6s.

Glenny (George).—A Year's Work in Garden and Greenhouse:
Practical Advice as to the Management of the Flower, Fruit, and Frame Garden. Post 8vo, 1s.; cloth, 1s. 6d.

Godwin (William).—Lives of the Necromancers. Post 8vo, cl., 2s.

Golden Treasury of Thought, The: A Dictionary of Quotations
from the Best Authors. By THEODORE TAYLOR. Crown 8vo, cloth, 3s. 6d.

Goodman (E. J.).—The Fate of Herbert Wayne. Cr. 8vo, 3s. 6d.

Gore (J. Ellard, F.R.A.S.).—The Stellar Heavens: an Introduc-
tion to the Study of the Stars and Nebulæ. Crown 8vo, cloth, 2s. net.

Grace (Alfred A.).—Tales of a Dying Race. Cr. 8vo, cloth, 3s. 6d.

Greeks and Romans, The Life of the, described from Antique
Monuments. By ERNST GUHL and W. KONER. Edited by Dr. F. HUEFFER. With 545 Illustrations. Large crown 8vo, cloth extra, 7s. 6d.

Greenwood (James: "The Amateur Casual").—The Prisoner
in the Dock; My Four Years' Daily Experiences in the London Police Courts. Cr. 8vo, cl., 3s. 6d.

Grey (Sir George).—The Romance of a Proconsul: Being the
Personal Life and Memoirs of Sir GEORGE GREY, K.C.B. By JAMES MILNE. With Portrait. SECOND
EDITION. Crown 8vo, buckram, 6s.

*

Griffith (Cecil).—Corinthia Marazion : A Novel. Crown 8vo, cloth extra, 3s. 6d.

Gunter (A. Clavering, Author of ' Mr. Barnes of New York ').—
A Florida Enchantment. Crown 8vo, cloth, 3s. 6d.

Guttenberg (Violet), Novels by.
Neither Jew nor Greek. | **The Power of the Palm'st.**

Hair, The: Its Treatment in Health, Weakness, and Disease. Translated from the German of Dr. J. PINCUS. Crown 8vo, 1s. ; cloth, 1s. 6d.

Hake (Dr. Thomas Gordon), Poems by. Cr. 8vo, cl. ex., 6s. each.
New Symbols. | **Legends of the Morrow.** | **The Serpent Play.**
Maiden Ecstasy. Small 4to, cloth extra, 8s.

Halifax (C.).—Dr. Rumsey's Patient. By Mrs. L. T. MEADE and CLIFFORD HALIFAX, M.D. Crown 8vo, cloth, 3s. 6d.

Hall (Mrs. S. C.).—Sketches of Irish Character. With numerous Illustrations on Steel and Wood by MACLISE, GILBERT, HARVEY, and GEORGE CRUIKSHANK. Small demy 8vo, cloth extra, 7s. 6d.

Hall (Owen), Novels by.
The Track of a Storm. Crown 8vo, cloth, 3s. 6d. ; picture cloth, flat back, 2s.
Jetsam. Crown 8vo, cloth, 3s. 6d.

Crown 8vo, cloth, gilt top, 6s. each.
Eureka. | **Hernando.**

Halliday (Andrew).—Every-day Papers. Post 8vo, picture bds., 2s.

Hamilton (Cosmo), Stories by. Crown 8vo, cloth gilt, 3s. 6d. each.
The Glamour of the Impossible. | **Through a Keyhole.**
₊ The two stories may also be had bound together in one volume, crown 8vo, cloth, 3s. 6d.

Harte's (Bret) Collected Works. Revised by the Author. LIBRARY EDITION, in Ten Volumes, crown 8vo, cloth extra, 6s. each.
Vol. I. COMPLETE POETICAL AND DRAMATIC WORKS. With Steel-plate Portrait.
" II. THE LUCK OF ROARING CAMP—BOHEMIAN PAPERS—AMERICAN LEGEND.
" III. TALES OF THE ARGONAUTS—EASTERN SKETCHES.
" IV. GABRIEL CONROY. | Vol. V. STORIES—CONDENSED NOVELS, &c.
" VI. TALES OF THE PACIFIC SLOPE.
" VII. TALES OF THE PACIFIC SLOPE—II. With Portrait by JOHN PETTIE, R.A.
" VIII. TALES OF THE PINE AND THE CYPRESS.
" IX. BUCKEYE AND CHAPPAREL.
" X. TALES OF TRAIL AND TOWN, &c.
Bret Harte's Choice Works, in Prose and Verse. With Portrait of the Author and 40 Illustrations. Crown 8vo, cloth, 3s. 6d.
Bret Harte's Poetical Works. Printed on hand-made paper. Crown 8vo, buckram, 4s. 6d.
Some Later Verses. Crown 8vo, linen gilt, 5s.
In a Hollow of the Hills. Crown 8vo, picture cloth, flat back, 2s.
Condensed Novels. (The Two Series in One Volume.) Pott 8vo, cloth, gilt top, 2s. net ; leather, gilt edges, 3s. net.

Crown 8vo, cloth, 6s. each.
On the Old Trail. | **From Sandhill to Pine.**
Under the Redwoods. | **Stories in Light and Shadow.**
Mr. Jack Hamlin's Mediation.

Crown 8vo, cloth extra, 3s. 6d. each ; post 8vo, picture boards, 2s. each.
Gabriel Conroy.
A Waif of the Plains. With 60 Illustrations by STANLEY L. WOOD.
A Ward of the Golden Gate. With 59 Illustrations by STANLEY L. WOOD.

Crown 8vo, cloth extra, 3s. 6d. each.
Susy : A Novel. With Frontispiece and Vignette by J. A. CHRISTIE.
Sally Dows, &c. With 47 Illustrations by W. D. ALMOND and others.
The Bell-Ringer of Angel's, &c. With 39 Illustrations by DUDLEY HARDY and others.
Clarence : A Story of the American War. With Eight Illustrations by A. JULE GOODMAN.
Barker's Luck, &c. With 39 Illustrations by A. FORESTIER, PAUL HARDY, &c.
Devil's Ford, &c. With a Frontispiece by W. H. OVEREND.
The Crusade of the "Excelsior." With a Frontispiece by J. BERNARD PARTRIDGE.
Three Partners ; or, The Big Strike on Heavy Tree Hill. With 8 Illustrations by J. GULICH.
Tales of Trail and Town. With Frontispiece by G. P. JACOMB-HOOD.
New Condensed Novels ; Burlesques.

Crown 8vo, cloth, 3s. 6d. each ; picture cloth, flat back, 2s. each.
The Luck of Roaring Camp, and **Sensation Novels Condensed.**
A Sappho of Green Springs. | **Colonel Starbottle's Client.**
A Protegee of Jack Hamlin's. With numerous Illustrations.

Post 8vo, illustrated boards, 2s. each.
An Heiress of Red Dog. | **The Luck of Roaring Camp.** | **Californian Stories.**

Post 8vo, illustrated boards, 2s. each ; cloth, 2s. 6d. each.
Flip. | **Maruja.** | **A Phyllis of the Sierras.**

Handwriting, The Philosophy of. With over 100 Facsimiles and Explanatory Text. By DON FELIX DE SALAMANCA. Post 8vo, half-cloth, 2s. 6d.

Hanky-Panky: Easy and Difficult Tricks, White Magic, Sleight of Hand, &c. Edited by W. H. CREMER. Crown 8vo, cloth extra, 4s. 6d.

Hardy (Rev. E. J., Author of ' How to be Happy though Married ').— Love, Courtship, and Marriage. Crown 8vo, cloth, 3s. 6d.

Hardy (Iza Duffus), Novels by. Crown 8vo, cloth, gilt top, 6s. each.
The Lesser Evil. | Man, Woman, and Fate.

Hardy (Thomas).—Under the Greenwood Tree. Post 8vo, cloth extra, 3s. 6d.; illustrated boards, 2s.; cloth limp, 2s. 6d.—Also the FINE PAPER EDITION, pott 8vo, cloth, gilt top, 2s. net; leather, gilt edges, 3s. net.

Haweis (Mrs. H. R.), Books by.
The Art of Beauty. With Coloured Frontispiece and 91 Illustrations. Square 8vo, cloth late, 6s.
The Art of Decoration. With Coloured Frontispiece and 74 Illustrations. Sq. 8vo, cloth bds., 6s.
The Art of Dress. With 32 Illustrations. Post 8vo, 1s.; cloth, 1s. 6d.
Chaucer for Schools. With the Story of his Times and his Work. A New Edition, revised. With a Frontispiece. Demy 8vo, cloth, 2s. 6d.
Chaucer for Children. With 38 Illustrations (8 Coloured). Crown 4to, cloth extra, 3s. 6d.

Haweis (Rev. H. R., M.A.).—American Humorists: WASHINGTON IRVING, OLIVER WENDELL HOLMES, JAMES RUSSELL LOWELL, ARTEMUS WARD, MARK TWAIN, and BRET HARTE. Crown 8vo, cloth, 6s.

Hawthorne (Julian), Novels by.
Crown 8vo, cloth extra, 3s. 6d. each; post 8vo, illustrated boards, 2s. each.
Garth. | Ellice Quentin. | Beatrix Randolph. With Four Illusts.
Fortune's Fool. | Dust. Four Illusts. | David Poindexter's Disappearance.
| | The Spectre of the Camera.

Post 8vo, illustrated boards, 2s. each.
Miss Cadogna. | Love—or a Name.

Sebastian Strome. Crown 8vo, cloth, 3s. 6d.

Heckethorn (C. W.), Books by.
London Souvenirs. | London Memories: Social, Historical, and Topographical

Helps (Sir Arthur), Books by. Post 8vo, cloth limp, 2s. 6d. each.
Animals and their Masters. | Social Pressure.
Ivan de Biron: A Novel. Crown 8vo, cloth extra, 3s. 6d.; post 8vo, illustrated boards, 2s.

Henderson (Isaac). — Agatha Page: A Novel. Cr. 8vo, cl., 3s. 6d.

Henty (G. A.), Novels by.
Rujub, the Juggler. Post 8vo, cloth, 3s. 6d.; illustrated boards, 2s.
Colonel Thorndyke's Secret. With a Frontispiece by STANLEY L. WOOD. Small demy 8vo, cloth, gilt edges, 5s.
Crown 8vo, cloth, 3s. 6d. each.
The Queen's Cup. | Dorothy's Double.

Herman (Henry).—A Leading Lady. Post 8vo, cloth, 2s. 6d.

Hertzka (Dr. Theodor).—Freeland: A Social Anticipation. Translated by ARTHUR RANSOM. Crown 8vo, cloth extra, 6s.

Hesse-Wartegg (Chevalier Ernst von).— Tunis: The Land and the People. With 22 Illustrations. Crown 8vo, cloth extra, 3s. 6d.

Hill (Headon).—Zambra the Detective. Crown 8vo, cloth, 3s. 6d.; post 8vo, picture boards, 2s.

Hill (John), Works by.
Treason-Felony. Post 8vo, boards, 2s. | The Common Ancestor. Cr. 8vo, cloth, 3s. 6d.

Hinkson (H. A.), Novels by. Crown 8vo, cloth, gilt top, 6s. each.
Fan Fitzgerald. | Silk and Steel.

Hoey (Mrs. Cashel).—The Lover's Creed. Post 8vo, boards, 2s.

Holiday, Where to go for a. By E. P. SHOLL, Sir H. MAXWELL, Bart., M.P., JOHN WATSON, JANE BARLOW, MARY LOVETT CAMERON, JUSTIN H. MCCARTHY, PAUL LANGE, J. W. GRAHAM, J. H. SALTER, PHŒBE ALLEN, S. J. BECKETT, L. RIVERS VINE, and C. F. GORDON CUMMING. Crown 8vo, cloth, 1s. 6d.

Holmes (Oliver Wendell), Works by.
The Autocrat of the Breakfast-Table. Illustrated by J. GORDON THOMSON. Post 8vo, cloth limp, 2s. 6d. Another Edition, post 8vo, cloth, 2s.
The Autocrat of the Breakfast-Table and The Professor at the Breakfast-Table. In One Vol. Post 8vo, half-bound, 2s.

Hooper (Mrs. Geo.).—The House of Raby. Post 8vo, boards, 2s.

Hood's (Thomas) Choice Works in Prose and Verse. With Life of the Author, Portrait, and 200 Illustrations. Crown 8vo, cloth, 3s. 6d.
Hood's Whims and Oddities. With 85 Illustrations. Post 8vo, half-bound. 2s.

Hook's (Theodore) Choice Humorous Works ; including his Ludicrous Adventures, Bons Mots, Puns, and Hoaxes. With a Life. A New Edition, with a Frontispiece. Crown 8vo, cloth, 3s. 6d.

Hopkins (Tighe), Novels by.
For Freedom. Crown 8vo, cloth, 6s.
    Crown 8vo, cloth, 3s. 6d. each.
Twixt Love and Duty. With a Frontispiece. | **The Incomplete Adventurer.**
The Nugents of Carriconna. | **Nell Haffenden.** With 8 Illustrations by C. GREGORY.

Horne (R. Hengist).—Orion : An Epic Poem. With Photograph Portrait by SUMMERS. Tenth Edition. Crown 8vo, cloth extra, 7s.

Hornung (E. W.).—The Shadow of the Rope. Crown 8vo, cloth, gilt top, 6s.

Hugo (Victor).—The Outlaw of Iceland (Han d'Islande). Translated by Sir GILBERT CAMPBELL. Crown 8vo, cloth, 3s. 6d.

Hume (Fergus), Novels by.
The Lady from Nowhere. Crown 8vo, cloth, 3s. 6d. ; picture cloth, flat back, 2s
The Millionaire Mystery. Crown 8vo, cloth, 3s. 6d.

Hungerford (Mrs., Author of ' Molly Bawn '), Novels by.
Crown 8vo, cloth extra, 3s. 6d. each ; post 8vo, illustrated boards, 2s. each ; cloth limp, 2s. 6d. each.

A Maiden All Forlorn.	**Peter's Wife.**	**An Unsatisfactory Lover.**
In Durance Vile.	**Lady Patty.**	**The Professor's Experiment.**
Marvel.	**Lady Verner's Flight.**	**The Three Graces.**
A Modern Circe.	**The Red-House Mystery.**	**Nora Creina.**
April's Lady.		**A Mental Struggle.**

Crown 8vo, cloth extra, 3s. 6d. each.
An Anxious Moment. | **The Coming of Chloe.** | **A Point of Conscience.** | **Lovice.**

Hunt's (Leigh) Essays: A Tale for a Chimney Corner, &c. Edited by EDMUND OLLIER. Post 8vo, half-bound. 2s.

Hunt (Mrs. Alfred), Novels by.
Crown 8vo, cloth extra, 3s. 6d. each ; post 8vo, illustrated boards, 2s. each.
The Leaden Casket. | **Self-Condemned.** | **That Other Person.**
Mrs. Juliet. Crown 8vo, cloth extra, 3s. 6d.

Hutchison (W. M.).—Hints on Colt-breaking. With 25 Illustrations. Crown 8vo, cloth extra, 3s. 6d.

Hydrophobia : An Account of M. PASTEUR'S System ; The Technique of his Method, and Statistics. By RENAUD SUZOR, M.B. Crown 8vo, cloth extra, 6s.

Idler Magazine (The). Edited by ROBERT BARR. Profusely Illustrated. 6d. Monthly.

Impressions (The) of Aureole. Post 8vo, cloth, 2s. 6d.

Indoor Paupers. By ONE OF THEM. Crown 8vo, 1s. ; cloth, 1s. 6d.

Inman (Herbert) and Hartley Aspden.—The Tear of Kalee. Crown 8vo, cloth, gilt top, 6s.

In Memoriam : Verses for every Day in the Year. Selected and arranged by LUCY RIDLEY. Small square 8vo, cloth, 2s. 6d. net : leather, 3s. 6d. net.

Innkeeper's Handbook (The) and Licensed Victualler's Manual. By J. TREVOR-DAVIES. A New Edition. Crown 8vo, cloth, 2s.

Irish Wit and Humour, Songs of. Collected and Edited by A. PERCEVAL GRAVES. Post 8vo, cloth limp, 2s. 6d.

Irving (Sir Henry) : A Record of over Twenty Years at the Lyceum. By PERCY FITZGERALD. With Portrait. Crown 8vo, cloth, 1s. 6d.

James (C. T. C.). — A Romance of the Queen's Hounds. Post 8vo, cloth limo, 1s. 6d.

Jameson (William).—My Dead Self. Post 8vo, cloth, 2s. 6d.

Japp (Alex. H., LL.D.).—Dramatic Pictures, &c. Cr. 8vo, cloth, 5s.

Jennings (Henry J.), Works by.
Curiosities of Criticism. Post 8vo, cloth limp, 2s. 6d.
Lord Tennyson : A Biographical Sketch. With Portrait. Post 8vo, cloth, 1s. 6d.

Jefferies (Richard), Books by.
The Open Air. Post 8vo, cloth, 2s. 6d.

Nature near London. Crown 8vo, buckram, 6s. each ; post 8vo, cloth limp, 2s. 6d. each.

Also, the LARGE TYPE, FINE PAPER EDITION of **The Life of the Fields.** | **The Life of the Fields.** gilt top, 2s. net; leather, gilt edges, 3s. net. of Pott 8vo, cloth.

The Eulogy of Richard Jefferies. By Sir WALTER BESANT. With a Photograph Portrait. Crown 8vo, cloth extra, 6s.

Jerome (Jerome K.), Books by.
Stageland. With 64 Illustrations by J. BERNARD PARTRIDGE. Fcap. 4to, picture cover, 1s.
John Ingerfield, &c. With 9 Illusts. by A. S. BOYD and JOHN GULICH. Fcap. 8vo, pic. cov. 1s. 6d.

Jerrold (Douglas).—The Barber's Chair; and The Hedgehog
Letters. Post 8vo, printed on laid paper and half-bound, 2s.

Jerrold (Tom), Works by. Post 8vo, 1s. ea.; cloth limp, 1s. 6d. each.
The Garden that Paid the Rent.
Household Horticulture: A Gossip about Flowers. Illustrated.

Jesse (Edward).—Scenes and Occupations of a Country Life.
Post 8vo, cloth limp, 2s.

Jones (William, F.S.A.), Works by. Cr. 8vo, cl. extra, 3s. 6d. each.
Finger-Ring Lore: Historical, Legendary, and Anecdotal. With Hundreds of Illustrations.
Crowns and Coronations: A History of Regalia. With 91 Illustrations.

Jonson's (Ben) Works. With Notes Critical and Explanatory, and
a Biographical Memoir by WILLIAM GIFFORD. Edited by Colonel CUNNINGHAM. Three Vols. crown 8vo, cloth extra, 3s. 6d. each.

Josephus, The Complete Works of. Translated by WHISTON. Con-
taining 'The Antiquities of the Jews' and 'The Wars of the Jews.' With 52 Illustrations and Maps. Two Vols., demy 8vo, half-cloth, 12s. 6d.

Kempt (Robert).—Pencil and Palette: Chapters on Art and Artists.
Post 8vo, cloth limp, 2s. 6d.

Kershaw (Mark). — Colonial Facts and Fictions: Humorous
Sketches. Post 8vo, illustrated boards, 2s.; cloth, 2s. 6d.

King (R. Ashe), Novels by. Post 8vo, illustrated boards, 2s. each.
'The Wearing of the Green.' | **Passion's Slave.** | **Bell Barry.**

A Drawn Game. Crown 8vo, cloth, 3s. 6d.; post 8vo, illustrated boards, 2s.

Kipling Primer (A). Including Biographical and Critical Chapters,
an Index to Mr. Kipling's principal Writings, and Bibliographies. By F. L. KNOWLES, Editor of 'The Golden Treasury of American Lyrics.' With Two Portraits. Crown 8vo, cloth, 3s. 6d.

Knight (William, M.R.C.S., and Edward, L.R.C.P.). — The
Patient's Vade Mecum: How to Get Most Benefit from Medical Advice. Cr. 8vo, cloth, 1s. 6d.

Knights (The) of the Lion: A Romance of the Thirteenth Century.
Edited, with an Introduction, by the MARQUESS OF LORNE, K.T. Crown 8vo, cloth extra, 6s.

Lambert (George).—The President of Boravia. Crown 8vo, cl., 3s. 6d.

Lamb's (Charles) Complete Works in Prose and Verse, including
'Poetry for Children' and 'Prince Dorus.' Edited, with Notes and Introduction, by R. H. SHEP-HERD. With Two Portraits and Facsimile of the 'Essay on Roast Pig.' Crown 8vo, cloth, 3s. 6d.
The Essays of Elia. Post 8vo, printed on laid paper and half-bound, 2s.
Little Essays: Sketches and Characters by CHARLES LAMB, selected from his Letters by PERCY FITZGERALD. Post 8vo, cloth limp, 2s. 6d.
The Dramatic Essays of Charles Lamb. With Introduction and Notes by BRANDER MAT-THEWS, and Steel-plate Portrait. Fcap. 8vo, half-bound, 2s. 6d.

Landor (Walter Savage).—Citation and Examination of William
Shakspeare, &c. Before Sir Thomas Lucy, touching Deer-stealing, 19th September, 1582. To which is added, **A Conference of Master Edmund Spenser** with the Earl of Essex, touching the State of Ireland, 1595. Fcap. 8vo, half-Roxburghe, 2s. 6d.

Lane (Edward William).—The Thousand and One Nights, com-
monly called in England The Arabian Nights' Entertainments. Translated from the Arabic, with Notes. Illustrated with many hundred Engravings from Designs by HARVEY. Edited by EDWARD STANLEY POOLE. With Preface by STANLEY LANE-POOLE. Three Vols., demy 8vo, cloth, 7s. 6d. ea.

Larwood (Jacob), Works by.
Anecdotes of the Clergy. Post 8vo, laid paper, half cloth, 2s.
Theatrical Anecdotes. Post 8vo, cloth limp, 2s. 6d.
Humo r of the Law: Forensic Anecdotes. Post 8vo, cloth, 2s.

Lehmann (R. C.), Works by. Post 8vo, cloth, 1s. 6d. each.
Harry Fludyer at Cambridge.
Conversational Hints for Young Shooters: A Guide to Polite Talk.

Leigh (Henry S.).—Carols of Cockayne. Printed on hand-made
paper, bound in buckram. 5s.

Leland (C. Godfrey).—A Manual of Mending and Repairing.
With Diagrams. Crown 8vo, cloth, 5s.

Lepelletier (Edmond). — Madame Sans-Gêne. Translated from
the French by JOHN DE VILLIERS. Post 8vo, cloth, 3s. 6d. ; picture boards, 2s.

Leys (John K.), Novels by.
The Lindsays. Post 8vo, picture bds., 2s. | **A Sore Temptation.** Cr. 8vo, cloth, gilt top, 6s.

Lilburn (Adam).—A Tragedy in Marble. Crown 8vo, cloth, 3s. 6d.

Lindsay (Harry, Author of 'Methodist Idylls'), Novels by.
Crown 8vo, cloth, 3s. each.
Rhoda Roberts. | **The Jacobite:** A Romance of the Conspiracy of 'The Forty.'
Crown 8vo, cloth, gilt top, 6s. each.
Judah Pyecroft, Puritan. | **The Story of Leah.**

Linton (E. Lynn), Works by.
An Octave of Friends. Crown 8vo, cloth, 3s. 6d.
Crown 8vo, cloth extra, 3s. 6d. each ; post 8vo, illustrated boards, 2s. each.
Patricia Kemball. | **Ione.** **Under which Lord?** With 12 Illustrations.
The Atonement of Leam Dundas. 'My Love!' | **Sowing the Wind.**
The World Well Lost. With 12 Illusts. **Paston Carew,** Millionaire and Miser
The One Too Many. **Dulcie Everton.** | **With a Silken Thread.**
The Rebel of the Family.
Post 8vo, cloth limp, 2s. 6d. each.
Witch Stories. | **Ourselves:** Essays on Women.
Freeshooting: Extracts from the Works of Mrs. LYNN LINTON.

Lowe (Charles, M.A.),—Our Greatest Living Soldiers. With
8 Portraits. Crown 8vo, cloth, 3s. 6d.

Lucy (Henry W.).—Gideon Fleyce: A Novel. Crown 8vo, cloth
extra, 3s. 6d. ; post 8vo, illustrated boards, 2s.

McCarthy (Justin), Works by.
A History of Our Own Times, from the Accession of Queen Victoria to the General Election of
1880. LIBRARY EDITION. Four Vols., demy 8vo, cloth extra, 12s. each.—Also a POPULAR
EDITION, in Four Vols., crown 8vo, cloth extra, 6s. each.—And the JUBILEE EDITION, with an
Appendix of Events to the end of 1886, in Two Vols., large crown 8vo, cloth extra, 7s. 6d. each.
A History of Our Own Times, from 1880 to the Diamond Jubilee. Demy 8vo, cloth extra,
12s. ; or crown 8vo, cloth, 6s.
A Short History of Our Own Times. One Vol., crown 8vo, cloth extra, 6s.—Also a CHEAP
POPULAR EDITION, post 8vo, cloth limp, 2s. 6d.
A History of the Four Georges and of William the Fourth. By JUSTIN MCCARTHY
and JUSTIN HUNTLY MCCARTHY. Four Vols., demy 8vo, cloth extra, 12s. each.
The Reign of Queen Anne. 2 vols., demy 8vo, cloth, 12s each.
Reminiscences. With a Portrait. Two Vols., demy 8vo, cloth, 24s.
Crown 8vo, cloth extra, 3s. 6d. each; post 8vo, illustrated boards, 2s. each; cloth limp, 2s. 6d. each
The Waterdale Neighbours. **Donna Quixote.** With 12 Illustrations.
My Enemy's Daughter. **The Comet of a Season.**
A Fair Saxon. | **Linley Rochford.** **Maid of Athens.** With 12 Illustrations.
Dear Lady Disdain. | **The Dictator.** **Camiola:** A Girl with a Fortune.
Miss Misanthrope. With 12 Illustrations. **Red Diamonds.** | **The Riddle Ring.**
Crown 8vo, cloth, 3s. 6d. each.
The Three Disgraces, and other Stories. | **Mononia:** A Love Story of 'Forty-eight.'
'The Right Honourable.' By JUSTIN MCCARTHY and Mrs. CAMPBELL PRAED. Crown 8vo,
cloth extra, 6s.

McCarthy (Justin Huntly), Works by.
The French Revolution. (Constituent Assembly, 1-89 91). Four Vols., demy 8vo, cloth, 12s. each.
An Outline of the History of Ireland. Crown 8vo, 1s. ; cloth, 1s. 6d.
Ireland Since the Union: Sketches of Irish History, 1798-1886. Crown 8vo, cloth, 6s.
Hafiz in London: Poems. Small 8vo, gold cloth, 3s. 6d.
Our Sensation Novel. Crown 8vo, picture cover, 1s. ; cloth limp, 1s. 6d.
Doom! An Atlantic Episode. Crown 8vo, picture cover, 1s.
Dolly: A Sketch. Crown 8vo, picture cover, 1s.
Lily Lass: A Romance. Crown 8vo, picture cover, 1s. ; cloth limp, 1s. 6d.
A London Legend. Crown 8vo, cloth, 3s. 6d.
The Royal Christopher. Crown 8vo, cloth, 3s. 6d.

MacColl (Hugh), Novels by.
Mr. Stranger's Sealed Packet. Post 8vo, illustrated boards, 2s.
Ednor Whitlock. Crown 8vo, cloth, 6s.

Macdonell (Agnes).—Quaker Cousins. Post 8vo, boards, 2s.

MacGregor (Robert).—Pastimes and Players. Notes on Popular
Games. Post 8vo, cloth limp, 2s. 6d.

Machray (Robert).—A Blow over the Heart. Crown 8vo, cloth,
gilt top, 6s.

MacDonald (George, LL.D.), Books by.

Works of Fancy and Imagination. Ten Vols., 16mo, cloth, gilt edges, in cloth case, 21s.; or the Volumes may be had separately, in Grolier cloth, at 2s. 6d. each.
Vol. I. WITHIN AND WITHOUT.—THE HIDDEN LIFE.
,, II. THE DISCIPLE.—THE GOSPEL WOMEN.—BOOK OF SONNETS.—ORGAN SONGS.
,, III. VIOLIN SONGS.—SONGS OF THE DAYS AND NIGHTS.—A BOOK OF DREAMS.—ROADSIDE
POEMS.—POEMS FOR CHILDREN.
,, IV. PARABLES.—BALLADS.—SCOTCH SONGS.
,, V. & VI. PHANTASTES: A Faerie Romance. | Vol. VII. THE PORTENT.
,, VIII. THE LIGHT PRINCESS.—THE GIANT'S HEART.—SHADOWS.
,, IX. CROSS PURPOSES.—THE GOLDEN KEY.—THE CARASOYN.— LITTLE DAYLIGHT
,, X. THE CRUEL PAINTER.—THE WOW O' RIVVEN.—THE CASTLE.—THE BROKEN SWORDS.
—THE GRAY WOLF.—UNCLE CORNELIUS.

Poetical Works of George MacDonald. Collected and Arranged by the Author. Two Vols. crown 8vo, buckram, 12s.

A Threefold Cord. Edited by GEORGE MACDONALD. Post 8vo, cloth, 5s.

Phantastes: A Faerie Romance. With 25 Illustrations by J. BELL. Crown 8vo, cloth extra, 3s 6d.
Heather and Snow: A Novel. Crown 8vo, cloth extra, 3s. 6d.; post 8vo, illustrated boards, 2s.
Lilith: A Romance. SECOND EDITION. Crown 8vo, cloth extra, 6s.

Mackay (Charles, LL.D.). — Interludes and Undertones; or, Music at Twilight. Crown 8vo, cloth extra 6s.

Mackenna (Stephen J.) and J. Augustus O'Shea.—Brave Men in Action: Thrilling Stories of the British Flag. With 8 Illustrations by STANLEY L. WOOD. Small demy 8vo, cloth, gilt edges, 5s.

Maclise Portrait Gallery (The) of Illustrious Literary Characters: 85 Portraits by DANIEL MACLISE: with Memoirs—Biographical, Critical, Bibliographical, and Anecdotal—illustrative of the Literature of the former half of the Present Century, by WILLIAM BATES, B.A. Crown 8vo, cloth extra, 3s. 6d.

Macquoid (Mrs.), Works by. Square 8vo, cloth extra, 6s. each.

In the Ardennes. With 50 Illustrations by THOMAS R. MACQUOID.
Pictures and Legends from Normandy and Brittany. 34 Illusts. by T. R. MACQUOID.
Through Normandy. With 92 Illustrations by T. R. MACQUOID, and a Map.
About Yorkshire. With 67 Illustrations by T. R. MACQUOID.

Magician's Own Book, The: Performances with Eggs, Hats, &c. Edited by W. H. CREMER. With 200 Illustrations. Crown 8vo, cloth extra, 4s. 6d.

Magic Lantern, The, and its Management : Including full Practical Directions. By T. C. HEPWORTH. With 10 Illustrations. Crown 8vo, 1s.; cloth, 1s. 6d.

Magna Charta: An Exact Facsimile of the Original in the British Museum, 3 feet by 2 feet, with Arms and Seals emblazoned in Gold and Colours, 5s.

Mallory (Sir Thomas). — Mort d'Arthur: The Stories of King Arthur and of the Knights of the Round Table. (A Selection.) Edited by B. MONTGOMERIE RANKING. Post 8vo, cloth limp, 2s.

Mallock (W. H.), Works by.

The New Republic. Post 8vo, cloth, 2s. 6d.; picture boards, 2s.
The New Paul and Virginia: Positivism on an Island. Post 8vo, cloth, 2s. 6d.

Poems. Small 4to, parchment, 8s. | **Is Life Worth Living?** Crown 8vo, cloth extra, 6s.

Margueritte (Paul and Victor).—The Disaster. Translated by FREDERIC LEES. Crown 8vo, cloth, 3s. 6d.

Marlowe's Works. Including his Translations. Edited, with Notes and Introductions, by Colonel CUNNINGHAM. Crown 8vo, cloth extra, 3s. 6d.

Mason (Finch).—Annals of the Horse-Shoe Club. With 5 Illustrations by the AUTHOR. Crown 8vo, cloth, gilt top, 6s.

Massinger's Plays. From the Text of WILLIAM GIFFORD. Edited by Col. CUNNINGHAM. Crown 8vo, cloth extra, 3s. 6d.

Matthews (Brander).—A Secret of the Sea, &c. Post 8vo, illustrated boards, 2s.; cloth limp, 2s. 6d.

Max O'Rell, Books by. Crown 8vo, cloth, 3s. 6d. each.

Her Royal Highness Woman. | **Between Ourselves.**
Rambles in Womanland.

Meade (L. T.), Novels by.

A Soldier of Fortune. Crown 8vo, cloth, 3s. 6d.; post 8vo, illustrated boards, 2s.

Crown 8vo, cloth, 3s. 6d. each.		
The Voice of the Charmer. With 8 Illustrations.		**An Adventuress.**
In an Iron Grip.	**On the Brink of a Chasm.**	**The Blue Diamond.**
The Siren.	**The Way of a Woman.**	**A Stumble by the Way.**
Dr. Rumsey's Patient.	**A Son of Ishmael.**	

Crown 8vo, cloth, gilt top, 6s. each.
This Troublesome World. | **Rosebury.**

Merivale (Herman).—Bar, Stage, and Platform: Autobiographic Memories. With a Portrait. Crown 8vo, cloth, gilt top, 6s.

Merrick (Leonard), Novels by.
The Man who was Good. Post 8vo, picture boards, 2s.
Crown 8vo. cloth, 3s. 6d. each.
This Stage of Fools. | **Cynthia:** A Daughter of the Philistines.

Mexican Mustang (On a), through Texas to the Rio Grande. By
A. E. SWEET and J. ARMOY KNOX. With 265 Illustrations. Crown 8vo, cloth extra, 7s. 6d.

Miller (Mrs. F. Fenwick).—Physiology for the Young; or, The
House of Life. With numerous Illustrations. Post 8vo, cloth limp, 2s. 6d.

Milton (J. L.).—The Bath in Diseases of the Skin. Post 8vo,
1s. ; cloth, 1s. 6d.

Minto (Wm.).—Was She Good or Bad? Crown 8vo, cloth, 1s. 6d.

Mitchell (Edmund), Novels by.
The Lone Star Rush. With 8 Illustrations by NORMAN H. HARDY. Crown 8vo, cloth, 3s. 6d.
Crown 8vo, cloth, gilt top, 6s. each.
Only a Nigger. | **The Belforts of Culben.**
Crown 8vo, picture cloth, flat backs, 2s. each.
Plotters of Paris. | **The Temple of Death.** | **Towards the Eternal Snows.**

Mitford (Bertram), Novels by. Crown 8vo, cloth extra, 3s. 6d. each.
The Gun-Runner: A Romance of Zululand. With a Frontispiece by STANLEY L. WOOD.
Renshaw Fanning's Quest. With a Frontispiece by STANLEY L. WOOD.
The Triumph of Hilary Blachland.
Crown 8vo, cloth, 3s. 6d. each ; picture cloth, flat backs, 2s. each.
The Luck of Gerard Ridgeley.
The King's Assegai. With Six full-page Illustrations by STANLEY L. WOOD.
Haviland's Chum. Crown 8vo, cloth, gilt top, 6s.

Molesworth (Mrs.).—Hathercourt Rectory. Crown 8vo, cloth,
3s. 6d.; post 8vo, illustrated boards, 2s.

Moncrieff (W. D. Scott-).—The Abdication: An Historical Drama.
With Seven Etchings by JOHN PETTIE. W. Q ORCHARDSON, J. MACWHIRTER, COLIN HUNTER,
R. MACBETH and TOM GRAHAM. Imperial 4to, buckram, 21s.

Montagu (Irving).—Things I Have Seen in War. With 16 full-
page Illustrations. Crown 8vo, cloth, 6s.

Moore (Thomas), Works by.
The Epicurean ; and **Alciphron.** Post 8vo, half-bound, 2s.
Prose and Verse; including Suppressed Passages from the MEMOIRS OF LORD BYRON. Edited
by R. H. SHEPHERD. With Portrait. Crown 8vo, cloth extra, 7s. 6d.

Morrow (W. C.).—Bohemian Paris of To-Day. With 106 Illustra-
tions by EDOUARD CUCUEL. Small demy 8vo, cloth, gilt top, 6s.

Muddock (J. E.), Stories by. Crown 8vo, cloth, 3s. 6d. each.
Basile the Jester. With Frontispiece by STANLEY WOOD.
Young Lochinvar. | **The Golden Idol.**
Post 8vo, illustrated boards, 2s. each.
The Dead Man's Secret. | **From the Bosom of the Deep.**
Stories Weird and Wonderful. Post 8vo. illustrated boards, 2s.; cloth, 2s. 6d.
Maid Marian and Robin Hood. With 12 Illustrations by S. L. WOOD. Crown 8vo, cloth extra,
3s. 6d.; picture cloth, flat back, 2s.

Murray (D. Christie), Novels by.
Crown 8vo, cloth extra, 3s. 6d. each ; post 8vo, illustrated boards, 2s. each.

A Life's Atonement.	A Model Father.	Bob Martin's Little Girl.
Joseph's Coat. 12 Illusts.	Old Blazer's Hero.	Time's Revenges.
Coals of Fire. 3 Illusts.	Cynic Fortune. Frontisp.	A Wasted Crime.
Val Strange.	By the Gate of the Sea.	In Direst Peril.
Hearts.	A Bit of Human Nature.	Mount Despair.
The Way of the World.	First Person Singular.	A Capful o' Nails.

The Making of a Novelist : An Experiment in Autobiography. With a Collotype Portrait. Cr.
8vo. buckram, 3s. 6d.
My Contemporaries in Fiction. Crown 8vo, buckram, 3s. 6d.
His Own Ghost. Crown 8vo, cloth, 3s. 6d.; picture cloth, flat back, 2s.
Crown 8vo, cloth, 2s. 6d. each.
This Little World. | **A Race for Millions.** | **The Church of Humanity.**
Tales in Prose and Verse. With Frontispiece by ARTHUR HOPKINS.
Despair's Last Journey. Crown 8vo. cloth, gilt top, 6s.
Joseph's Coat. POPULAR EDITION, medium 8vo, 6d.

Murray (D. Christie) and Henry Herman, Novels by.
Crown 8vo, cloth extra, 3s. 6d. each; post 8vo, illustrated boards, 2s. each.
One Traveller Returns. | **The Bishops' Bible.**
Paul Jones's Alias, &c. With Illustrations by A. FORESTIER and G. NICOLET.

Murray (Henry), Novels by.
Post 8vo, cloth, 2s. 6d. each.
A Game of Bluff. | **A Song of Sixpence.**

Newbolt (H.).—Taken from the Enemy. Post 8vo, leatherette, 1s.

Nisbet (Hume), Books by.
'**Ball Up.**' Crown 8vo, cloth extra, 3s. 6d.; post 8vo, Illustrated boards, 2s.
Dr. Bernard St. Vincent. Post 8vo, illustrated boards, 2s.
Lessons in Art. With 21 Illustrations. Crown 8vo, cloth extra, 2s. 6d.

Norris (W. E.), Novels by. Crown 8vo, cloth, 3s. 6d. each ; post 8vo, picture boards, 2s. each.
Saint Ann's. | **Billy Bellew.** With a Frontispiece by F. H. TOWNSEND.
Miss Wentworth's Idea. Crown 8vo, cloth, 3s. 6d.

Ohnet (Georges), Novels by. Post 8vo, illustrated boards, 2s. each.
Doctor Rameau. | **A Last Love.**
A Weird Gift. Crown 8vo, cloth, 3s. 6d.; post 8vo, picture boards, 2s.
Love's Depths. Translated by F. ROTHWELL. Crown 8vo, cloth, 3s. 6d.
The Woman of Mystery. Translated by F. ROTHWELL. Crown 8vo, cloth, gilt top, 6s.

Oliphant (Mrs.), Novels by. Post 8vo, illustrated boards, 2s. each.
The Primrose Path. | **Whiteladies.** | **The Greatest Heiress in England.**
The Sorceress. Crown 8vo, cloth, 3s. 6d.

O'Shaughnessy (Arthur), Poems by:
Fcap. 8vo, cloth extra, 7s. 6d. each.
Music and Moonlight. | **Songs of a Worker.**
Lays of France. Crown 8vo, cloth extra, 10s. 6d.

Ouida, Novels by. Cr. 8vo, cl., 3s. 6d. ea.; post 8vo, illust. bds., 2s. ea.

Held in Bondage.	A Dog of Flanders.	In Maremma. ! Wanda.
Tricotrin.	Pascarel.	Signa.	Bimbi.	Syrlin.
Strathmore.	Chandos.	Two Wooden Shoes.	Frescoes.	Othmar.
Cecil Castlemaine's Gage	In a Winter City.	Princess Napraxine.
Under Two Flags.	Ariadne.	Friendship.	Guilderoy.	Ruffino.
Puck.	Idalia.	A Village Commune.	Two Offenders.
Folle-Farine.	Moths. ! Pipistrello.	Santa Barbara.

POPULAR EDITIONS, medium 8vo, 6d. each.
Under Two Flags. | **Moths.** | **Held in Bondage.** | **Puck.** | **Strathmore.** [Shortly.
The Waters of Edera. Crown 8vo, cloth, 3s. 6d.; picture cloth, flat back, 2s.
Wisdom, Wit, and Pathos, selected from the Works of OUIDA by F. SYDNEY MORRIS. Post 8vo, cloth extra, 5s.—CHEAP EDITION, illustrated boards, 2s.

Palmer (W. T.).—Lake-Country Rambles. With a Frontispiece.
Crown 8vo, linen, gilt top, 6s.

Pandurang Hari; or, Memoirs of a Hindoo. With Preface by Sir
BARTLE FRERE. Post 8vo, illustrated boards, 2s.

Paris Salon, The Illustrated Catalogue of the, for 1902. (Twenty-
fourth Year.) With over 300 Illustrations. Demy 8vo, 3s.

Pascal's Provincial Letters. A New Translation, with Historical
Introduction and Notes by T. M'CRIE, D.D. Post 8vo, half-cloth, 2s.

Payn (James), Novels by.
Crown 8vo, cloth extra, 3s. 6d. each ; post 8vo, illustrated boards, 2s. each.

Lost Sir Massingberd.	The Family Scapegrace.
A County Family.	Holiday Tasks.
Less Black than We're Painted.	The Talk of the Town. With 12 Illusts.
By Proxy.	For Cash Only.	The Mystery of Mirbridge.
High Spirits.	The Word and the Will.
A Confidential Agent. With 12 Illusts.	The Burnt Million.
A Grape from a Thorn. With 12 Illusts.	Sunny Stories.	A Trying Patient.

Post 8vo illustrated boards, 2s. each.

Humorous Stories.	From Exile.	Found Dead.	Gwendoline's Harvest.
The Foster Brothers.	Mirk Abbey.	A Marine Residence.
Married Beneath Him.	The Canon's Ward.
Bentinck's Tutor.	Walter's Word.	Not Wooed, But Won.
A Perfect Treasure.	Two Hundred Pounds Reward.
Like Father, Like Son.	The Best of Husbands.
A Woman's Vengeance.	Halves.	What He Cost Her.
Carlyon's Year.	Cecil's Tryst.	Fallen Fortunes.	Kit: A Memory.
Murphy's Master.	At Her Mercy.	Under One Roof.	Glow-worm Tales.
The Clyffards of Clyffe.	A Prince of the Blood.
Some Private Views.	

A Modern Dick Whittington; or, A Patron of Letters. With a Portrait of the Author. Crown 8vo, cloth, 3s. 6d.; picture cloth, flat back, 2s.
In Peril and Privation. With 17 Illustrations. Crown 8vo, cloth, 3s. 6d.
Notes from the 'News.' Crown 8vo, cloth, 1s. 6d.

Payne (Will).—Jerry the Dreamer. Crown 8vo, cloth, 3s. 6d.

Paul (Margaret A.).—Gentle and Simple. Crown 8vo, cloth, with
Frontispiece by HELEN PATERSON, 3s. 6d.; post 8vo, illustrated boards, 2s.

**Pennell-Elmhirst (Captain E. : " Brooksby ").—The Best of the
Fun.** With Coloured and Plain Illustrations by JOHN STURGESS. Royal 8vo, cloth. Shortly.

Pennell (H. Cholmondeley), Works by. Post 8vo, cloth, 2s. 6d. ea.
Puck on Pegasus. With Illustrations.
Pegasus Re-Saddled. With Ten full-page Illustrations by G. DU MAURIER.
The Muses of Mayfair : Vers de Société. Selected by H. C. PENNELL.

Phelps (E. Stuart), Works by. Post 8vo, cloth, 1s. 6d. each.
An Old Maid's Paradise. | Burglars in Paradise.
Beyond the Gates. Post 8vo, picture cover, 1s.; cloth, 1s. 6d.
Jack the Fisherman. Illustrated by C. W. REED. Crown 8vo, cloth, 1s 6d.

Phil May's Sketch-Book. Containing 54 Humorous Cartoons. Crown
folio, cloth, 2s. 6d.

Phipson (Dr. T. L.), Books by. Crown 8vo, canvas, gilt top 5s. each.
Famous Violinists and Fine Violins. | The Confessions of a Viol nist.
Voice and Violin: Sketches, Anecdotes, and Reminiscences.

Pilkington (Lionel L.).—Mallender's Mistake. Crown 8vo, cloth,
gilt top, 6s.

Planche (J. R.), Works by.
The Pursuivant of Arms. With Six Plates and 209 Illustrations. Crown 8vo, cloth, 7s. 6d.
Songs and Poems, 1819-1879. With Introduction by Mrs. MACKARNESS. Crown 8vo, cloth, 6s.

Plutarch's Lives of Illustrious Men. With Notes and a Life of
Plutarch by JOHN and WM. LANGHORNE, and Portraits. Two Vols., demy 8vo, half-cloth 10s. 6d.

Poe's (Edgar Allan) Choice Works: Poems, Stories, Essays.
With an Introduction by CHARLES BAUDELAIRE. Crown 8vo, cloth, 3s. 6d.

Pollock (W. H.).—The Charm, and other Drawing-room Plays. By
Sir WALTER BESANT and WALTER H. POLLOCK. With 50 Illustrations. Crown 8vo, cloth gilt, 6s.

Pope's Poetical Works. Post 8vo, cloth limp, 2s.

Porter (John).—Kingsclere. Edited by BYRON WEBBER. With 19
full-page and many smaller Illustrations. Cheaper Edition. Demy 8vo, cloth, 7s. 6d.

Praed (Mrs. Campbell), Novels by. Post 8vo, illust. bds., 2s. each.
The Romance of a Station. | The Soul of Countess Adrian.

Crown 8vo, cloth, 3s. 6d. each; post 8vo, boards, 2s. each.
Outlaw and Lawmaker. | Christina Chard. With Frontispiece by W PAGET.
Mrs. Tregaskiss. With 8 Illustrations by ROBERT SAUBER.

Crown 8vo, cloth, 3s. 6d. each.
Nulma. | Madame Izan. | 'As a Watch in the Night.'

Price (E. C.).—Valentina. Crown 8vo. cloth, 3s. 6d.

Princess Olga.—Radna : A Novel. Crown 8vo, cloth extra, 6s.

Pryce (Richard).—Miss Maxwell's Affections. Crown 8vo, cloth,
with Frontispiece by HAL LUDLOW, 3s. 6d.; post 8vo, illustrated boards, 2s.

Proctor (Richard A.), Works by.
Flowers of the Sky. With 55 Illustrations. Small crown 8vo, cloth extra, 3s. 6d.
Easy Star Lessons. With Star Maps for every Night in the Year. Crown 8vo, cloth, 6s.
Familiar Science Studies. Crown 8vo, cloth extra, 6s.
Saturn and its System. With 13 Steel Plates. Demy 8vo, cloth extra, 10s. 6d.
Mysteries of Time and Space. With numerous Illustrations. Crown 8vo, cloth extra, 6s.
The Universe of Suns, &c. With numerous Illustrations. Crown 8vo, cloth extra, 6s.
Wages and Wants of Science Workers. Crown 8vo, 1s. 6d.

Rambosson (J.).—Popular Astronomy. Translated by C. B. PITMAN.
With 10 Coloured Plates and 63 Woodcut Illustrations. Crown 8vo, cloth, 7s. 6d.

Randolph (Col. G.).—Aunt Abigail Dykes. Crown 8vo, cloth, 7s. 6d.

Richardson (Frank), Novels by.
The Man who Lost his Past. With 50 Illusts. by TOM BROWNE, R.I. Cr. 8vo, cloth, 3s. 6d.

Crown 8vo, cloth, gilt top, 6s. each.
The King's Counsel. | Semi Society.

Riddell (Mrs. J. H.), Novels by.
A Rich Man's Daughter. Crown 8vo, cloth, 3s. 6d.
Weird Stories. Crown 8vo, cloth extra, 3s. 6d.; post 8vo, illustrated boards, 2s.

Post 8vo, illustrated boards, 2s. each
The Uninhabited House. | Fairy Water.
The Prince of Wales's Garden Party. | Her Mother's Darling.
The Mystery in Palace Gardens. | The Nun's Curse. | Idle Tales.

Reade's (Charles) Novels.

The New Collected LIBRARY EDITION, complete in Seventeen Volumes, set in new long primer type, printed on laid paper, and elegantly bound in cloth, price 3s. 6d. each.

1. Peg Woffington; and Christie John-stone.
2. Hard Cash.
3. The Cloister and the Hearth. With a Preface by Sir WALTER BESANT.
4. 'It is Never Too Late to Mend.'
5. The Course of True Love Never Did Run Smooth; and Singleheart and Doubleface.
6. The Autobiography of a Thief; Jack of all Trades; A Hero and a Martyr; and The Wandering Heir.

7. Love Me Little, Love me Long.
8. The Double Marriage.
9. Griffith Gaunt.
10. Foul Play.
11. Put Yourself In His Place.
12. A Terrible Temptation.
13. A Simpleton.
14. A Woman-Hater.
15. The Jilt, and other Stories and Good Stories of Man and other Animals.
16. A Perilous Secret.
17. Readiana; and Bible Characters.

In Twenty-one Volumes, post 8vo, illustrated boards, 2s. each.

Peg Woffington. | Christie Johnstone.
'It is Never Too Late to Mend.'
The Course of True Love Never Did Run Smooth.
The Autobiography of a Thief; Jack of all Trades; and James Lambert.
Love Me Little, Love Me Long.
The Double Marriage.
The Cloister and the Hearth.

Hard Cash. | Griffith Gaunt.
Foul Play. | Put Yourself in His Place.
A Terrible Temptation.
A Simpleton. | The Wandering Heir.
A Woman-Hater.
Singleheart and Doubleface.
Good Stories of Man and other Animals.
The Jilt, and other Stories.
A Perilous Secret. | Readiana.

LARGE TYPE, FINE PAPER EDITIONS. Pott 8vo, cl., gilt top, 2s. net ea.; leather, gilt edges, 3s. net ea.
The Cloister and the Hearth. | 'It is Never Too Late to Mend.'

POPULAR EDITIONS, medium 8vo, 6d. each.
'It is Never Too Late to Mend.' | The Cloister and the Hearth. | Foul Play.
Peg Woffington; and Christie Johnstone. | Hard Cash. | Griffith Gaunt.

Christie Johnstone. With Frontispiece. Choicely printed in Elzevir style. Fcap. 8vo, half-Roxb 2s. 6d.
Peg Woffington. Choicely printed in Elzevir style. Fcap. 8vo, half-Roxburghe, 2s. 6d.
The Cloister and the Hearth. NEW ILLUSTRATED EDITION, with 16 Photogravure and 84 half-tone Illustrations by MATT B. HEWERDINE. Small 4to, cloth gilt and gilt top, 1s. 6d. net —
Also in Four Vols., post 8vo, with an Introduction by Sir WALTER BESANT, and a Frontispiece to each Vol., buckram, gilt top, 6s. the set.
Bible Characters. Fcap. 8vo, leatherette, 1s.

Selections from the Works of Charles Reade. With an Introduction by Mrs. ALEX. IRELAND. Post 8vo, cloth limp, 2s. 6d.

Rimmer (Alfred), Works by. Large crown 8vo, cloth, 3s. 6d. each.
Rambles Round Eton and Harrow. With 52 Illustrations by the Author.
About England with Dickens. With 58 Illustrations by C. A. VANDERHOOF and A. RIMMER.

Rives (Amelie), Stories by. Crown 8vo, cloth, 3s. 6d. each.
Barbara Dering. | Meriel: A Love Story.

Robinson Crusoe. By DANIEL DEFOE. With 37 Illustrations by
GEORGE CRUIKSHANK. Post 8vo, half-cloth, 2s.

Robinson (F. W.), Novels by.
Women are Strange. Post 8vo, illustrated boards, 2s.
The Hands of Justice. Crown 8vo, cloth extra, 3s. 6d.; post 8vo illustrated boards, 2s.
The Woman in the Dark. Crown 8vo, cloth, 3s. 6d.; post 8vo, illustrated boards, 2s.

Robinson (Phil), Works by. Crown 8vo, cloth extra, 6s. each
The Poets' Birds. | The Poets' Beasts. | The Poets' Reptiles, Fishes, and Insects.

Roll of Battle Abbey, The: A List of the Principal Warriors who
came from Normandy with William the Conqueror, 1066. Printed in Gold and Colours, 5s.

Rosengarten (A.).—A Handbook of Architectural Styles. Trans-
lated by W. COLLETT-SANDARS. With 639 Illustrations. Crown 8vo, cloth extra, 7s. 6d.

Ross (Albert).—A Sugar Princess. Crown 8vo, cloth, 3s. 6d

Rowley (Hon. Hugh). Post 8vo, cloth. 2s. 6d. each.
Puniana: or, Thoughts Wise and Other-wise: a Collection of the Best Riddles, Conundrums, Jokes, Sells, &c., with numerous Illustrations by the Author.
More Puniana: A Second Collection of Riddles, Jokes, &c. With numerous Illustrations.

Runciman (James), Stories by.
Schools and Scholars. Post 8vo, cloth, 2s 6d.
Skippers and Shellbacks. Crown 8vo, cloth, 3s. 6d.

Russell (Dora), Novels by.
A Country Sweetheart. Post 8vo, picture boards, 2s.; picture cloth, flat back, 2s.
The Drift of Fate. Crown 8vo, cloth, 3s. 6d.; picture cloth, flat back, 2s

Russell (Herbert).—True Blue; or, 'The Lass that Loved a Sailor.
Crown 8vo, cloth, 3s. 6d.

Russell (Rev. John) and his Out-of-door Life. By E. W. L.
DAVIES. A New Edition, with Illustrations coloured by hand. Royal 8vo, cloth, 16s. net.

Russell (W. Clark), Novels, &c., by.
Crown 8vo, cloth extra, 3s. 6d. each; post 8vo, illustrated boards, 2s. each; cloth limp, 2s. 6d. each.

Round the Galley-Fire. | An Ocean Tragedy.
In the Middle Watch. | My Shipmate Louise.
On the Fo'k'sle Head. | Alone on a Wide Wide Sea.
A Voyage to the Cape. | The Good Ship 'Mohock.'
A Book for the Hammock. | The Phantom Death.
The Mystery of the 'Ocean Star.' | Is He the Man? | The Convict Ship.
The Romance of Jenny Harlowe. | Heart of Oak. | The Last Entry.

The Tale of the Ten.
Crown 8vo, cloth, 3s. 6d. each.
A Tale of Two Tunnels. | The Death Ship.

The Ship: Her Story. With 50 Illustrations by H. C. SEPPINGS WRIGHT. Small 4to, cloth, 6s.
The 'Pretty Polly': A Voyage of Incident. With 12 Illustrations by G. E. ROBERTSON.
Large crown 8vo, cloth, gilt edges, 5s.
Overdue. Crown 8vo, cloth, gilt top, 6s.

Saint Aubyn (Alan), Novels by.
Crown 8vo, cloth extra, 3s. 6d. each; post 8vo, illustrated boards, 2s. each.
A Fellow of Trinity. With a Note by OLIVER WENDELL HOLMES and a Frontispiece.
The Junior Dean. | The Master of St. Benedict's. | To His Own Master.
Orchard Damerel. | In the Face of the World. | The Tremlett Diamonds.

Crown 8vo, cloth, 3s. 6d. each.
The Wooing of May. | A Tragic Honeymoon. | A Proctor's Wooing.
Fortune's Gate. | Gallantry Bower. | Bonnie Maggie Lauder.
Mary Unwin. With 8 Illustrations by PERCY TARRANT. | Mrs. Dunbar's Secret.

Saint John (Bayle).—A Levantine Family. A New Edition.
Crown 8vo, cloth, 3s. 6d.

Sala (George A.).—Gaslight and Daylight. Post 8vo, boards, 2s.

Scotland Yard, Past and Present: Experiences of Thirty-seven Years.
By Ex-Ch.-Inspector CAVANAGH. Post 8vo, illustrated boards, 2s.; cloth, 2s. 6d.

Secret Out, The: One Thousand Tricks with Cards: with Entertaining Experiments in Drawing-room or 'White' Magic. By W. H. CREMER. With 300 Illustrations. Crown 8vo, cloth extra, 4s. 6d.

Seguin (L. G.), Works by.
The Country of the Passion Play (Oberammergau) and the Highlands of Bavaria. With Map and 37 Illustrations. Crown 8vo, cloth extra, 3s. 6d.
Walks in Algiers. With Two Maps and 16 Illustrations. Crown 8vo, cloth extra, 6s.

Senior (Wm.).—By Stream and Sea. Post 8vo, cloth, 2s. 6d.

Sergeant (Adeline), Novels by. Crown 8vo, cloth, 3s. 6d. each.
Under False Pretences. | Dr. Endicott's Experiment.

Seymour (Cyril).—The Magic of To-Morrow. Crown 8vo, cloth, gilt top, 6s.

Shakespeare for Children: Lamb's Tales from Shakespeare.
With Illustrations, coloured and plain, by J. MOYR SMITH. Crown 4to, cloth gilt, 3s. 6d.

Shakespeare the Boy. With Sketches of the Home and School Life, the Games and Sports, the Manners, Customs, and Folk-lore of the Time. By WILLIAM J. ROLFE, Litt.D. A New Edition, with 42 Illustrations, and an INDEX OF PLAYS AND PASSAGES REFERRED TO. Crown 8vo, cloth gilt, 3s. 6d.

Sharp (William).—Children of To-morrow. Crown 8vo, cloth, 6s.

Shelley's (Percy Bysshe) Complete Works in Verse and Prose.
Edited, Prefaced, and Annotated by R. HERNE SHEPHERD. Five Vols., crown 8vo, cloth, 3s. 6d. each.
Poetical Works, in Three Vols.:
Vol. I. Introduction by the Editor: Posthumous Fragments of Margaret Nicholson; Shelley's Correspondence with Stockdale; The Wandering Jew; Queen Mab, with the Notes; Alastor, and other Poems; Rosalind and Helen; Prometheus Unbound; Adonais, &c.
II. Laon and Cythna: The Cenci; Julian and Maddalo; Swellfoot the Tyrant; The Witch of Atlas; Epipsychidion; Hellas.
,, III. Posthumous Poems; The Masque of Anarchy; and other Pieces.
Prose Works, in Two Vols.:
Vol. I. The Two Romances of Zastrozzi and St. Irvyne: the Dublin and Marlow Pamphlets; A Refutation of Deism: Letters to Leigh Hunt, and some Minor Writings and Fragments.
II. The Essays; Letters from Abroad; Translations and Fragments, edited by Mrs. SHELLEY. With a Biography of Shelley, and an Index of the Prose Works.

Sherard (R. H.).—Rogues: A Novel. Crown 8vo, cloth, 1s. 6d.

Sheridan's (Richard Brinsley) Complete Works, with Life and Anecdotes. Including his Dramatic Writings, his Works in Prose and Poetry, Translations, Speeches, and Jokes. Crown 8vo, cloth, 3s. 6d.
The Rivals, The School for Scandal, and other Plays. Post 8vo, half-bound, 2s.
Sheridan's Comedies: The Rivals and The School for Scandal. Edited, with an Introduction and Notes to each Play, and a Biographical Sketch, by BRANDER MATTHEWS. With Illustrations. Demy 8vo, buckram, gilt top, 12s. 6d.

Shiel (M. P.).—The Purple Cloud. Crown 8vo, cloth, 3s. 6d.

Sidney's (Sir Philip) Complete Poetical Works, including all those in 'Arcadia.' With Portrait, Memorial-Introduction, Notes, &c., by the Rev. A. B. GROSART, D.D. Three Vols., crown 8vo, cloth boards, 3s. 6d. each.

Signboards: Their History, including Anecdotes of Famous Taverns and Remarkable Characters. By JACOB LARWOOD and JOHN CAMDEN HOTTEN. With Coloured Frontispiece and 94 Illustrations. Crown 8vo, cloth extra, 3s. 6d.

Sims (George R.), Works by.
Post 8vo, illustrated boards, 2s. each; cloth limp, 2s. 6d. each.
The Ring o' Bells. | **My Two Wives.** | **Memoirs of a Landlady.**
Tinkletop's Crime. | **Tales of To-day.** | **Scenes from the Show.**
Zeph: A Circus Story, &c. | **The Ten Commandments: Stories.**
Dramas of Life. With 60 Illustrations.
Crown 8vo, picture cover, 1s. each; cloth, 1s. 6d. each.
The Dagonet Reciter and Reader: Being Readings and Recitations in Prose and Verse selected from his own Works by GEORGE R. SIMS.
The Case of George Candlemas. | **Dagonet Ditties.** (From The Referee
How the Poor Live; and **Horrible London.** With a Frontispiece by F. BARNARD. Crown 8vo, leatherette, 1s. | **Dagonet Dramas of the Day.** Crown 8vo, 1s.
Crown 8vo, cloth, 3s. 6d. each; post 8vo, picture boards, 2s. each; cloth limp, 2s. 6d. each.
Mary Jane's Memoirs. | **Mary Jane Married.** | **Rogues and Vagabonds.**
Dagonet Abroad.
Crown 8vo, cloth, 3s. 6d. each.
Once upon a Christmas Time. With 8 Illustrations by CHARLES GREEN, R.I.
In London's Heart: A Story of To-day.—Also in picture cloth, flat back, 2s | **A Blind Marriage.**
Without the Limelight: Theatrical Life as it is. | **The Small-part Lady, &c.**
Biographs of Babylon: Life Pictures of London's Moving Scenes.

Sister Dora: A Biography. By MARGARET LONSDALE. With Four Illustrations. Demy 8vo, picture cover, 4d.; cloth, 6d.

Sketchley (Arthur).—A Match in the Dark. Post 8vo, boards, 2s.

Slang Dictionary (The): Etymological, Historical, and Anecdotal. Crown 8vo, cloth extra, 6s. 6d.

Smart (Hawley), Novels by.
Crown 8vo, cloth 3s. 6d. each; post 8vo, picture boards, 2s. each.
Beatrice and Benedick. | **Long Odds.**
Without Love or Licence. | **The Master of Rathkelly.**
Crown 8vo, cloth, 3s. 6d. each.
The Outsider | **A Racing Rubber.**
The Plunger. Post 8vo, picture boards, 2s.

Smith (J. Moyr), Works by.
The Prince of Argolis. With 130 Illustrations. Post 8vo, cloth extra, 3s. 6d.
The Wooing of the Water Witch. With numerous Illustrations. Post 8vo, cloth, 6s.

Snazelleparilla. Decanted by G. S. EDWARDS. With Portrait of G. H. SNAZELLE and 65 Illustrations by C. LYALL. Crown 8vo, cloth, 3s. 6d.

Society in London. Crown 8vo, 1s.; cloth, 1s. 6d.

Somerset (Lord Henry).—Songs of Adieu. Small 4to Jap. vel., 6s.

Spalding (T. A., LL.B.).—Elizabethan Demonology: An Essay on the Belief in the Existence of Devils. Crown 8vo, cloth extra, 5s.

Speight (T. W.), Novels by.
Post 8vo, illustrated boards, 2s. each.
The Mysteries of Heron Dyke. | **The Loudwater Tragedy.**
By Devious Ways, &c. | **Borgo's Romance.**
Hoodwinked; & Sandycroft Mystery. | **Quittance in Full.**
The Golden Hoop. | **Back to Life.** | **A Husband from the Sea.**
Post 8vo, cloth limp, 1s. 6d. each.
A Barren Title. | **Wife or No Wife?**
Crown 8vo, cloth extra, 3s. 6d. each.
A Secret of the Sea. | **The Grey Monk.** | **The Master of Trenance.**
A Minion of the Moon: A Romance of the King's Highway | **Her Ladyship.**
The Secret of Wyvern Towers. | **The Doom of Siva.** | **The Web of Fate.**
The Strange Experiences of Mr. Verschoyle. | **As it was Written.**

Spenser for Children. By M. H. TOWRY. With Coloured Illustrations by WALTER J. MORGAN. Crown 4to, cloth extra, 3s. 6d.

Sprigge (S. Squire).—An Industrious Chevalier. Crown 8vo, cloth, gilt top, 6s.

Spettigue (H. H.).—The Heritage of Eve. Crown 8vo, cloth, 6s

Stafford (John), Novels by.
Doris and I. Crown 8vo, cloth, 3s. 6d. | **Carlton Priors.** Crown 8vo, cloth, gilt top, 6s

Starry Heavens (The): A POETICAL BIRTHDAY BOOK. Royal 16mo, cloth extra, 2s. 6d.

Stag-Hunting with the 'Devon and Somerset.' An Account of the Chase of the Wild Red Deer on Exmoor, 1887-1901. By PHILIP EVERED. With 70 Illustrations by H. M. LOMAS. Crown 4to, cloth gilt, 16s. net.

Stedman (E. C.).—Victorian Poets. Crown 8vo, cloth extra, 9s.

Stephens (Riccardo, M.B.).—The Cruciform Mark: The Strange Story of RICHARD TREGENNA, Bachelor of Medicine (Univ. Edinb.) Crown 8vo, cloth, 3s. 6d.

Stephens (Robert Neilson).—Philip Winwood: A Sketch of the Domestic History of an American Captain in the War of Independence. Crown 8vo, cloth, 3s. 6d.

Sterndale (R. Armitage).—The Afghan Knife: A Novel. Post 8vo, cloth, 3s. 6d.; illustrated boards, 2s.

Stevenson (R. Louis), Works by.
Crown 8vo, buckram, gilt top, 6s. each.

Travels with a Donkey. With a Frontispiece by WALTER CRANE.
An Inland Voyage. With a Frontispiece by WALTER CRANE.
Familiar Studies of Men and Books.
The Silverado Squatters. With Frontispiece by J. D. STRONG.
The Merry Men. | **Underwoods:** Poems. | **Memories and Portraits.**
Virginibus Puerisque, and other Papers. | **Ballads.** | **Prince Otto.**
Across the Plains, with other Memories and Essays.
Weir of Hermiston. | **In the South Seas.**

An Inland Voyage. PRESENTATION EDITION, with 12 Illustrations. Fcap. 8vo, leather, gilt edges, 6s. net.
Songs of Travel. Crown 8vo, buckram, 5s.
New Arabian Nights. Crown 8vo, buckram, gilt top, 6s.; post 8vo, illustrated boards, 2s. —POPULAR EDITION, medium 8vo, 6d.
The Suicide Club; and The Rajah's Diamond. (From NEW ARABIAN NIGHTS.) With Eight Illustrations by W. J. HENNESSY. Crown 8vo, cloth, 3s. 6d.
The Stevenson Reader: Selections from the Writings of ROBERT LOUIS STEVENSON. Edited by LLOYD OSBOURNE. Post 8vo, cloth, 2s. 6d.; buckram, gilt top, 3s. 6d.
The Pocket R.L.S.: Favourite Passages from the Works of STEVENSON. Small 16mo, cloth, 2s. net; leather, 3s. net.
LARGE TYPE, FINE PAPER EDITIONS. Pott 8vo, cl., gilt top, 2s. net each; leather, gilt edges, 3s. net each.
Familiar Studies of Men and Books. | **New Arabian Nights.**
Robert Louis Stevenson: A Life Study in Criticism. By H. BELLYSE BAILDON. With 2 Portraits. SECOND EDITION, REVISED. Crown 8vo, buckram, gilt top, 6s.

Stockton (Frank R.).—The Young Master of Hyson Hall. With 36 Illustrations by VIRGINIA H. DAVISSON and C. H. STEPHENS. Crown 8vo, cloth, 3s. 6d.; picture cloth, flat back, 2s.

Stories from Foreign Novelists. With Notices by HELEN and ALICE ZIMMERN. Crown 8vo, cloth extra, 3s. 6d.

Strange Manuscript (A) Found in a Copper Cylinder. Crown 8vo, cloth extra, with 19 Illustrations by GILBERT GAUL, 3s. 6d.; post 8vo, illustrated boards, 2s.

Strange Secrets. Told by PERCY FITZGERALD, CONAN DOYLE, FLORENCE MARRYAT, &c. Post 8vo, illustrated boards, 2s.

Strutt (Joseph). — The Sports and Pastimes of the People of England; including the Rural and Domestic Recreations, May Games, Mummeries, Shows, &c., from the Earliest Period. Edited by WILLIAM HONE. With 140 Illustrations. Cr. 8vo, cloth extra, 3s. 6d.

Sundowner, Stories by.
Told by the Taffrail. Cr. 8vo, cl., 3s. 6d. | **The Tale of the Serpent.** Cr. 8vo, cl., flat back, 2s.

Surtees (Robert).—Handley Cross; or, Mr. Jorrocks's Hunt. With 79 Illustrations by JOHN LEECH. A New Edition. Post 8vo, cloth, 2s.

Swinburne's (Algernon Charles) Works.

Selections from the Poetical Works of A. C. Swinburne. Fcap. 8vo, 6s.
Atalanta in Calydon. Crown 8vo, 6s.
Chastelard: A Tragedy. Crown 8vo, 7s.
Poems and Ballads. FIRST SERIES. Crown 8vo, or fcap. 8vo, 9s.
Poems and Ballads. SECOND SER. Cr. 8vo, 9s.
Poems & Ballads. THIRD SERIES. Cr. 8vo, 7s.
Songs before Sunrise. Crown 8vo, 10s. 6d.
Bothwell: A Tragedy. Crown 8vo, 12s. 6d.
Songs of Two Nations. Crown 8vo, 6s.
George Chapman. (See Vol. II. of G. CHAPMAN'S Works.) Crown 8vo, 3s. 6d.
Essays and Studies. Crown 8vo, 12s.
Erechtheus: A Tragedy. Crown 8vo, 6s.
A Note on Charlotte Bronte. Cr. 8vo, 6s.
A Study of Shakespeare. Crown 8vo, 8s.
Songs of the Springtides. Crown 8vo, 6s.

Studies in Song. Crown 8vo, 7s.
Mary Stuart: A Tragedy. Crown 8vo, 8s.
Tristram of Lyonesse. Crown 8vo, 9s.
A Century of Roundels. Small 4to, 8s.
A Midsummer Holiday. Crown 8vo, 7s.
Marino Faliero: A Tragedy. Crown 8vo, 6s.
A Study of Victor Hugo. Crown 8vo, 6s.
Miscellanies. Crown 8vo, 12s.
Locrine: A Tragedy. Crown 8vo, 6s.
A Study of Ben Jonson. Crown 8vo, 7s.
The Sisters: A Tragedy. Crown 8vo, 6s.
Astrophel, &c. Crown 8vo, 7s.
Studies in Prose and Poetry. Cr. 8vo, 9s.
The Tale of Balen. Crown 8vo, 7s.
Rosamund, Queen of the Lombards: A Tragedy. Crown 8vo, 6s.
A New Volume of Poems. Cr. 8vo. [Shortly.

Swift's (Dean) Choice Works, in Prose and Verse. With Memoir,
Portrait, and Facsimiles of the Maps in 'Gulliver's Travels.' Crown 8vo, cloth, 3s. 6d.
Gulliver's Travels, and **A Tale of a Tub.** Post 8vo, half-bound, 2s.
Jonathan Swift: A Study. By J. CHURTON COLLINS. Crown 8vo, cloth extra, 8s.

Syntax's (Dr.) Three Tours: In Search of the Picturesque, in Search
of Consolation, and in Search of a Wife. With ROWLANDSON'S Coloured Illustrations, and Life of the
Author by J. C. HOTTEN. Crown 8vo, cloth extra, 7s. 6d.

Taine's History of English Literature. Translated by HENRY VAN
LAUN. Four Vols., small demy 8vo, cloth boards, 30s.—POPULAR EDITION, Two Vols., large crown
8vo, cloth extra, 15s.

Taylor (Bayard). — Diversions of the Echo Club: Burlesques of
Modern Writers. Post 8vo, cloth limp, 2s.

Taylor (Tom).—Historical Dramas: 'JEANNE DARC,' ''TWIXT AXE
AND CROWN,' 'THE FOOL'S REVENGE,' 'ARKWRIGHT'S WIFE,' 'ANNE BOLEYNE,' 'PLOT AND
PASSION.' Crown 8vo, 1s. each.

Temple (Sir Richard, G.C.S.I.).—A Bird's-eye View of Pictur-
esque India. With 32 Illustrations by the Author. Crown 8vo, cloth, gilt top, 6s.

Thackerayana: Notes and Anecdotes, With Coloured Frontispiece and
Hundreds of Sketches by WILLIAM MAKEPEACE THACKERAY. Crown 8vo, cloth extra, 3s. 6d.

Thames, A New Pictorial History of the. By A. S. KRAUSSE.
With 340 Illustrations. Post 8vo, cloth, 1s. 6d.

Thomas (Annie), Novels by.
The Siren's Web: A Romance of London Society. Crown 8vo, cloth, 3s. 6d.
Comrades True. Crown 8vo, cloth, gilt top, 6s.

Thomas (Bertha), Novels by. Crown 8vo, cloth, 3s. 6d. each,
The Violin-Player. | **In a Cathedral City.**
Crown 8vo, cloth, gilt top, 6s. each.
The House on the Scar: a Tale of South Devon. | **The Son of the House.**

Thomson's Seasons, and The Castle of Indolence. With Introduction by ALLAN CUNNINGHAM, and 48 Illustrations. Post 8vo, half-bound, 2s.

Thoreau: His Life and Aims. By H. A. PAGE. With a Portrait
and View. Post 8vo buckram, 3s. 6d.

Thornbury (Walter), Books by.
The Life and Correspondence of J. M. W. Turner. With Eight Illustrations in Colours and
Two Woodcuts. New and Revised Edition. Crown 8vo, cloth, 3s. 6d.
Tales for the Marines. Post 8vo, illustrated boards, 2s.

Timbs (John), Works by. Crown 8vo, cloth, 3s. 6d. each.
Clubs and Club Life in London: Anecdotes of its Famous Coffee-houses, Hostelries, and
Taverns. With 41 Illustrations.
English Eccentrics and Eccentricities: Stories of Delusions, Impostures, Sporting Scenes,
Eccentric Artists, Theatrical Folk, &c. With 48 Illustrations.

Twain's (Mark) Books.
The Author's Edition de Luxe of the Works of Mark Twain, in 22 Volumes (limited
to 600 Numbered Copies for sale in Great Britain and its Dependencies), price £11 15s. net the
Set ; or, 12s. 6d. net per Volume, is now complete, and a detailed Prospectus may be had. The
First Volume of the Set is SIGNED BY THE AUTHOR. (Sold only in Sets.)
UNIFORM LIBRARY EDITION OF MARK TWAIN'S WORKS.
Crown 8vo, cloth extra, 3s. 6d. each.
Mark Twain's Library of Humour. With 197 Illustrations by E. W. KEMBLE.
Roughing It; and The Innocents at Home. With 200 Illustrations by F. A. FRASER.
The American Claimant. With 81 Illustrations by HAL HURST and others.
The Adventures of Tom Sawyer. With 111 Illustrations.
Tom Sawyer Abroad. With 26 Illustrations by DAN BEARD.
Tom Sawyer, Detective, &c. With Photogravure Portrait of the Author.
Pudd'nhead Wilson. With Portrait and Six Illustrations by LOUIS LOEB.
A Tramp Abroad. With 314 Illustrations.
The Innocents Abroad; or, The New Pilgrim's Progress. With 234 Illustrations. (The Two Shil-
ling Edition is entitled **Mark Twain's Pleasure Trip.**)
The Gilded Age. By MARK TWAIN and C. D. WARNER. With 212 Illustrations.
The Prince and the Pauper. With 190 Illustrations.
Life on the Mississippi. With 300 Illustrations.
The Adventures of Huckleberry Finn. With 174 Illustrations by E. W. KEMBLE.
A Yankee at the Court of King Arthur. With 220 Illustrations by DAN BEARD.
The Stolen White Elephant. | **The £1,000,000 Bank-Note.**
A Double-barrelled Detective Story. With 7 Illustrations by LUCIUS HITCHCOCK.
The Choice Works of Mark Twain. Revised and Corrected throughout by the Author. With
Life, Portrait, and numerous Illustrations.
, The books marked * may be had also in post 8vo. picture boards, at 2s. each.
Crown 8vo, cloth, gilt top, 6s. each.
Personal Recollections of Joan of Arc. With Twelve Illustrations by F. V. DU MOND.
More Tramps Abroad.
The Man that Corrupted Hadleyburg, and other Stories and Sketches. With a Frontispiece
Mark Twain's Sketches. Pott 8vo, cloth, gilt top, 2s.; leather, gilt edges, 3s. net.

Treeton (Ernest A.).—The Instigator. Cr. 8vo, cloth, gilt top, 6s.

Trollope (Anthony), Novels by.
Crown 8vo, cloth extra, 3s. 6d. each; post 8vo, illustrated boards, 2s. each.

The Way We Live Now.	**Mr. Scarborough's Family.**
Frau Frohmann.	**Marion Fay.**	**The Land-Leaguers.**

Post 8vo, illustrated boards, 2s. each.
Kept in the Dark. | **The American Senator.** | **The Golden Lion of Granpere.**

Trollope (Frances E.), Novels by.
Crown 8vo, cloth extra, 3s. 6d. each; post 8vo, illustrated boards, 2s. each.
Like Ships upon the Sea. | **Mabel's Progress.** | **Anne Furness.**

Trollope (T. A.).—Diamond Cut Diamond. Post 8vo, illust. bds., 2s.

Tytler (C. C. Fraser-).—Mistress Judith: A Novel. Crown 8vo, cloth extra, 3s. 6d.; post 8vo, illustrated boards, 2s.

Tytler (Sarah), Novels by.
Crown 8vo, cloth extra, 3s. 6d. each; post 8vo, illustrated boards, 2s. each.
Buried Diamonds. | **The Blackhall Ghosts.** | **What She Came Through.**

Post 8vo, illustrated boards, 2s. each.
The Bride's Pass.	**The Huguenot Family.**	**Noblesse Oblige.**	**Disappeared.**
Saint Mungo's City.	**Lady Bell.**	**Beauty and the Beast.**

Crown 8vo, cloth, 3s. 6d. each.
The Macdonald Lass. With Frontispiece.	**Mrs. Carmichael's Goddesses.**
The Witch-Wife.	**Rachel Langton.**	**Sapphira.**	**A Honeymoon's Eclipse.**
A Young Dragon.

Citoyenne Jacqueline. Crown 8vo, picture cloth, flat back, 2s.

Crown 8vo, cloth, gilt top, 6s. each.
Three Men of Mark. | **In Clarissa's Day.**

Upward (Allen).—The Queen Against Owen. Crown 8vo, cloth, 3s. 6d.; picture cloth, flat back, 2s.; post 8vo, picture boar 1s, 2s.

Vandam (Albert D.).—A Court Tragedy. With 6 Illustrations by J. BARNARD DAVIS. Crown 8vo, cloth, 3s. 6d.

Vashti and Esther. By 'Belle' of *The World.* Cr. 8vo, cloth, 3s. 6d.

Vizetelly (Ernest A.), Books by. Crown 8vo, cloth, 3s. 6d. each.
The Scorpion: A Romance of Spain. With a Frontispiece. | **The Lover's Progress.**
With Zola in England: A Story of Exile. With 4 Portraits.
A Path of Thorns. Crown 8vo, cloth, gilt top, 6s.
Bluebeard: An Account of Comorre the Cursed and Gilles de Rais; with a Summary of various Tales and Traditions. With 9 Illustrations. Demy 8vo, cloth, 9s. net.

Wade (Claude F.).—Exmoor Streams: Notes and Jottings, with Practical Hints for Anglers. With 16 Full-page Illustrations. Crown 8vo, cloth, 5s. net.

Wagner (Leopold).—How to Get on the Stage, and how to Succeed there. Crown 8vo, cloth, 2s. 6d.

Walford's County Families of the United Kingdom (1903).
Containing Notices of the Descent, Birth, Marriage, Education, &c., of more than 12,000 Distinguished Heads of Families, their Heirs Apparent or Presumptive, the Offices they hold or have held, their Town and Country Addresses, Clubs, &c. Royal 8vo, cloth gilt, 50s. [*Preparing.*]

Waller (S. E.).—Sebastiani's Secret. With 9 Illusts. Cr. 8vo, cl., 6s.

Walton and Cotton's Complete Angler. With Memoirs and Notes by Sir HARRIS NICOLAS. Post 8vo, cloth, gilt top, 2s. net; leather, gilt edges, 3s. net.

Walt Whitman, Poems by. Edited, with Introduction, by WILLIAM M. ROSSETTI. With Portrait. Crown 8vo, hand-made paper and buckram, 6s.

Warden (Florence), Novels by.
Joan, the Curate. Crown 8vo, cloth, 3s. 6d.; picture cloth, flat back, 2s.
A Fight to a Finish. Crown 8vo, cloth, 3s. 6d.
The Heart of a Girl. With 8 Illustrations by FRANCES EWAN. Crown 8vo, cloth, gilt top, 6s.

Warman (Cy).—The Express Messenger. Crown 8vo, cloth, 3s. 6d.

Warner (Chas. Dudley).—A Roundabout Journey. Cr. 8vo, cl., 6s.

Warrant to Execute Charles I. A Facsimile, with the 59 Signatures and Seals. Printed on paper 22 in. by 14 in. 2s.
Warrant to Execute Mary Queen of Scots. A Facsimile, including Queen Elizabeth's Signature and the Great Seal. 2s.

Wassermann (Lillias).—The Daffodils. Crown 8vo, cloth, 1s. 6d.

Weather, How to Foretell the, with the Pocket Spectroscope.
By F. W. CORY. With Ten Illustrations. Crown 8vo, 1s.; cloth, 1s. 6d.

Webber (Byron).—Sport and Spangles. Crown 8vo, cloth, 2s.

Werner (A.).—Chapenga's White Man. Crown 8vo, cloth, 3s. 6d.

Westbury (Atha).—The Shadow of Hilton Fernbrook: A Romance of Maoriland. Crown 8vo, cloth, 3s. 6d.

Westall (William), Novels by.
Trust Money. Crown 8vo, cloth, 3s. 6d. ; post 8vo, illustrated boards, 2s.

Crown 8vo, cloth, 6s. each.

As a Man Sows.	As Luck would have It.	The Sacred Crescents.
Her Ladyship's Secret.	The Old Bank.	

Crown 8vo, cloth, 3s. 6d. each.

A Woman Tempted Him.	Nigel Fortescue.	The Phantom City.
For Honour and Life.	Ben Clough. | Birch Dene.	Ralph Norbreck's Trust.
Her Two Millions.	The Old Factory (also at 6d.)	A Queer Race.
Two Pinches of Snuff.	Sons of Belial.	Red Ryvington.
With the Red Eagle.	Strange Crimes.	Roy of Roy's Court.
A Red Bridal.		

Wheelwright (E. Gray).—A Slow Awakening. Crown 8vo, 6s.

Whishaw (Fred.), Novels by.
A Forbidden Name: A Story of the Court of Catherine the Great. Crown 8vo, cloth, 3s. 6d.

Crown 8vo, cloth, gilt top, 6s. each.

Mazeppa.	Near the Tsar, near Death.

White (Gilbert).—Natural History of Selborne. Post 8vo, 2s.

Wilde (Lady). — **The Ancient Legends, Mystic Charms, and** Superstitions of Ireland ; with Sketches of the Irish Past. Crown 8vo, cloth, 3s. 6d.

Williams (W. Mattieu, F.R.A.S.), Works by.
Science in Short Chapters. Crown 8vo, cloth extra, 7s. 6d.
A Simple Treatise on Heat. With Illustrations. Crown 8vo, cloth, 2s. 6d.
The Chemistry of Cookery. Crown 8vo, cloth extra, 6s.

Williamson (Mrs. F. H.).—A Child Widow. Post 8vo, bds., 2s.

Wills (C. J.), Novels by.
An Easy-going Fellow. Crown 8vo, cloth, 3s. 6d. \| His Dead Past. Crown 8vo, cloth, 6s.

Wilson (Dr. Andrew, F.R.S.E.), Works by.
Chapters on Evolution. With 259 Illustrations. Crown 8vo, cloth extra, 7s. 6d.
Leisure-Time Studies. With Illustrations. Crown 8vo, cloth extra, 6s.
Studies in Life and Sense. With 36 Illustrations. Crown 8vo, cloth 3s. 6d.
Common Accidents: How to Treat Them. With Illustrations. Crown 8vo, 1s.; cloth, 1s. 6d.
Glimpses of Nature. With 35 Illustrations. Crown 8vo, cloth extra, 3s. 6d.

Winter (John Strange), Stories by. Post 8vo, illustrated boards, 2s. each ; cloth limp, 2s. 6d. each.

Cavalry Life.	Regimental Legends.

Cavalry Life and Regimental Legends. Cr. 8vo, cloth, 3s. 6d. ; picture cloth, flat back, 2s

Wood (H. F.), Detective Stories by. Post 8vo, boards, 2s. each.

The Passenger from Scotland Yard.	The Englishman of the Rue Cain.

Woolley (Celia Parker).—Rachel Armstrong; or, Love and The- ology. Post 8vo, cloth, 2s. 6d.

Wright (Thomas, F.S.A.), Works by.
Caricature History of the Georges; or, Annals of the House of Hanover. Compiled from Squibs, Broadsides, Window Pictures, Lampoons, and Pictorial Caricatures of the Time. With over 300 Illustrations. Crown 8vo, cloth, 3s. 6d.
History of Caricature and of the Grotesque in Art, Literature, Sculpture, and Painting. Illustrated by F. W. FAIRHOLT, F.S.A. Crown 8vo, cloth, 7s. 6d.

Wynman (Margaret).—My Flirtations. With 13 Illustrations by J. BERNARD PARTRIDGE. Post 8vo, cloth limp, 2s.

Zola's (Emile) Novels. UNIFORM EDITION. Translated or Edited, with Introductions, by ERNEST A. VIZETELLY. Crown 8vo, cloth, 3s. 6d. each.

His Masterpiece.	The Fat and the Thin.	Money.
The Joy of Life.	His Excellency.	
Germinal: Master and Man.	The Dream.	
The Honour of the Army.	The Downfall.	
Abbe Mouret's Transgression.	Doctor Pascal.	
The Fortune of the Rougons.	Lourdes.	Fruitfulness.
The Conquest of Plassans.	Rome.	Work.
The Dram-Shop.	Paris.	Truth.

POPULAR EDITIONS, medium 8vo, 6d. each.

The Dram-Shop.	The Downfall.

With Zola in England. By ERNEST A. VIZETELLY. With Four Portraits. Crown 8vo, cloth, 3s. 6d.

'ZZ' (L. Zangwill).—A Nineteenth Century Miracle. Cr. 8vo. 3s. 6d.

SOME BOOKS CLASSIFIED IN SERIES.

The St. Martin's Library. Pott 8vo, cloth, 2s. net each; leather, 3s. net each
The Woman in White. By WILKIE COLLINS.
All Sorts and Conditions of Men. By Sir WALTER BESANT.
The Cloister and the Hearth. By CHAS. READE. | 'It is Never Too Late to Mend.' By CH. READE.
Familiar Studies of Men and Books. By ROBERT LOUIS STEVENSON.
The Pocket R.L.S.: Favourite Passages from STEVENSON'S Works.
New Arabian Nights. By ROBERT LOUIS STEVENSON. | The Deemster. By HALL CAINE.
Under the Greenwood Tree. By THOMAS HARDY. | The Life of the Fields. By RICHARD JEFFERIES.
Walton and Cotton's Complete Angler. | Mark Twain's Sketches.
Condensed Novels. (The Two Series in One Volume.) By BRET HARTE.

The Mayfair Library. Post 8vo, cloth limp, 2s. 6d. per Volume.
Quips and Quiddities. By W. D. ADAMS.
The Agony Column of 'The Times.'
A Journey Round My Room. By X. DE MAISTRE.
Poetical Ingenuities. By W. T. DOBSON.
The Cupboard Papers. By FIN-BEC.
Songs of Irish Wit and Humour.
Animals and their Masters. By Sir A. HELPS.
Social Pressure. By Sir A. HELPS.
Autocrat of Breakfast-Table. By O. W. HOLMES.
Curiosities of Criticism. By H. J. JENNINGS.
Pencil and Palette. By R. KEMPT.

Little Essays: from LAMB'S LETTERS.
Forensic Anecdotes. By JACOB LARWOOD.
Theatrical Anecdotes. By JACOB LARWOOD.
Ourselves. By E. LYNN LINTON.
Witch Stories. By E. LYNN LINTON.
Pastimes and Players. By R. MACGREGOR.
New Paul and Virginia. By W. H. MALLOCK.
Puck on Pegasus. By H. C. PENNELL.
Pegasus Re-saddled. By H. C. PENNELL.
The Muses of Mayfair. By H. C. PENNELL.
By Stream and Sea. By WILLIAM SENIOR.

The Golden Library. Post 8vo, cloth limp, 2s. per Volume.
Songs for Sailors. By W. C. BENNETT.
Lives of the Necromancers. By W. GODWIN.
The Autocrat of the Breakfast Table. By OLIVER WENDELL HOLMES.

Scenes of Country Life. By EDWARD JESSE.
La Mort d'Arthur: Selections from MALLORY.
The Poetical Works of Alexander Pope.
Diversions of the Echo Club. BAYARD TAYLOR.

My Library. Printed on laid paper, post 8vo, half-Roxburghe, 2s. 6d. each.
The Journal of Maurice de Guerin.
The Dramatic Essays of Charles Lamb.
Citation of William Shakspeare. W. S. LANDOR.

Christie Johnstone. By CHARLES READE.
Peg Woffington. By CHARLES READE.

The Pocket Library. Post 8vo, printed on laid paper and hf.-bd., 2s. each.
Gastronomy. By BRILLAT-SAVARIN.
Robinson Crusoe. Illustrated by G. CRUIKSHANK
Autocrat and Professor. By O. W. HOLMES.
Provincial Letters of Blaise Pascal.
Whims and Oddities. By THOMAS HOOD.
Leigh Hunt's Essays. Edited by E. OLLIER.
The Barber's Chair. By DOUGLAS JERROLD.

The Essays of Elia. By CHARLES LAMB.
Anecdotes of the Clergy. By JACOB LARWOOD.
The Epicurean, &c. By THOMAS MOORE.
Plays by RICHARD BRINSLEY SHERIDAN.
Gulliver's Travels, &c. By Dean SWIFT.
Thomson's Seasons. Illustrated.
White's Natural History of Selborne.

POPULAR SIXPENNY NOVELS.
The Tents of Shem By GRANT ALLEN.
The Orange Girl. By WALTER BESANT.
All Sorts and Conditions of Men. WALT. BESANT.
Children of Gibeon. By WALTER BESANT.
The Chaplain of the Fleet. BESANT and RICE.
Ready-Money Mortiboy. BESANT and RICE.
The Golden Butterfly. BESANT and RICE.
Shadow of the Sword. By R. BUCHANAN.
The Deemster. By HALL CAINE.
The Shadow of a Crime. By HALL CAINE.
A Son of Hagar. By HALL CAINE.
Antonina. By WILKIE COLLINS.
Armadale. By WILKIE COLLINS.
The Moonstone. By WILKIE COLLINS.
The Woman in White. By WILKIE COLLINS.
The Dead Secret. By WILKIE COLLINS.
Man and Wife. By WILKIE COLLINS.
The New Magdalen. By WILKIE COLLINS.

Diana Barrington. By B. M. CROKER.
Joseph's Coat. By D. CHRISTIE MURRAY.
Held in Bondage. By OUIDA.
Moths. By OUIDA. | Puck. By OUIDA.
Under Two Flags. By OUIDA.
Strathmore. By OUIDA.
Peg Woffington; and Christie Johnstone. By CHARLES READE.
The Cloister and the Hearth. By CHARLES READE.
Griffith Gaunt. By CHARLES READE.
It is Never Too Late to Mend. CHARLES READE.
Hard Cash. By CHARLES READE.
Foul Play. By CHARLES READE.
New Arabian Nights. By R. L. STEVENSON.
The Old Factory. By WILLIAM WESTALL.
The Downfall. By EMILE ZOLA.
The Dram-Shop. By EMILE ZOLA.

THE PICCADILLY NOVELS.
LIBRARY EDITIONS OF NOVELS, many Illustrated, crown 8vo, cloth extra, 3s. 6d. each.

By Mrs. ALEXANDER.
Valerie's Fate.
A Life Interest.
Mona's Choice.
By Woman's Wit.
The Cost of Her Pride.
A Missing Hero.

Barbara.
A Fight with Fate.
A Golden Autumn.
Mrs Crichton's Creditor.
The Step-mother.

By M. ANDERSON.—Othello's Occupation.

By G. WEBB APPLETON.
Rash Conclusions.

By EDWIN L. ARNOLD.
Phra the Phoenician. | Constable of St. Nicholas.

By ARTEMUS WARD.
Artemus Ward Complete.

By F. M. ALLEN.—Green as Grass.

By GRANT ALLEN.
Philistia.
Babylon.
Strange Stories.
For Maimie's Sake.
In all Shades.
The Beckoning Hand.
The Devil's Die.
This Mortal Coil.
The Tents of Shem.
The Great Taboo.
Dumaresq's Daughter.
Duchess of Powysland.
Blood Royal.
I. Greet's Masterpiece.
The Scallywag.
At Market Value.
Under Sealed Orders.

By ROBERT BARR.
In a Steamer Chair. | A Woman Intervenes.
From Whose Bourne. | Revenge!

THE PICCADILLY (3/6) NOVELS—continued.
By OWEN HALL.
The Track of a Storm. | Jetsam.
By COSMO HAMILTON.
Glamour of Impossible. | Through a Keyhole.
By THOMAS HARDY.
Under the Greenwood Tree.
By JULIAN HAWTHORNE.
Garth. | Dust.
Ellice Quentin.
Sebastian Strome.
Fortune's Fool.
Beatrix Randolph.
David Poindexter's Disappearance.
Spectre of Camera.
By Sir A. HELPS.—Ivan de Biron.
By I. HENDERSON.—Agatha Page.
By G. A. HENTY.
Dorothy's Double. | The Queen's Cup.
Rujub, the Juggler.
HEADON HILL.—Zambra the Detective.
By JOHN HILL.—The Common Ancestor.
By TIGHE HOPKINS.
Twixt Love and Duty. | Nugents of Carriconna.
The Incomplete Adventurer. | Nell Haffenden.
VICTOR HUGO.—The Outlaw of Iceland.
By FERGUS HUME.
Lady from Nowhere. | The Millionaire Mystery
By Mrs. HUNGERFORD.
Marvel.
Unsatisfactory Lover.
In Durance Vile.
A Modern Circe.
Lady Patty.
A Mental Struggle.
Lady Verner's Flight.
The Red-House Mystery
The Three Graces.
Professor's Experiment
A Point of Conscience.
A Maiden all Forlorn.
The Coming of Chloe.
Nora Creina.
An Anxious Moment.
April's Lady.
Peter's Wife.
Lovice.
By Mrs. ALFRED HUNT.
The Leaden Casket. | Self Condemned.
That Other Person. | Mrs. Juliet.
By R. ASHE KING.—A Drawn Game.
By GEORGE LAMBERT.
The President of Boravia.
By EDMOND LEPELLETIER.
Madame Sans Gene.
By ADAM LILBURN, A Tragedy in Marble
By HARRY LINDSAY.
Rhoda Roberts. | The Jacobite.
By HENRY W. LUCY.—Gideon Fleyce.
By E. LYNN LINTON.
Patricia Kemball.
Under which Lord?
'My Love!' | Ione.
Paston Carew.
Sowing the Wind.
With a Silken Thread.
The World Well Lost.
The Atonement of Leam Dundas.
The One Too Many.
Dulcie Everton.
Rebel of the Family.
An Octave of Friends.
By JUSTIN McCARTHY.
A Fair Saxon.
Linley Rochford.
Dear Lady Disdain.
Camiola | Mononia.
Waterdale Neighbours.
My Enemy's Daughter.
Miss Misanthrope.
Donna Quixote.
Maid of Athens.
The Comet of a Season.
The Dictator.
Red Diamonds.
The Riddle Ring.
The Three Disgraces.
By JUSTIN H. McCARTHY.
A London Legend. | The Royal Christopher
By GEORGE MACDONALD.
Heather and Snow. | Phantastes.
W. H. MALLOCK.—The New Republic.
P. & V. MARGUERITTE.—The Disaster.
By L. T. MEADE.
A Soldier of Fortune.
In an Iron Grip.
Dr. Rumsey's Patient.
The Voice of the Charmer.
An Adventuress.
On Brink of a Chasm.
The Siren.
The Way of a Woman.
A Son of Ishmael.
The Blue Diamond.
A Stumble by the Way.
By LEONARD MERRICK.
This Stage of Fools. | Cynthia.
By EDMUND MITCHELL
The Lone Star Rush.

By BERTRAM MITFORD.
The Gun Runner.
Luck of Gerard Ridgeley.
The King's Assegai.
Renshaw Fanning's Quest.
The Triumph of Hilary Blachland.
By Mrs. MOLESWORTH.
Hathercourt Rectory.
By J. E. MUDDOCK.
Maid Marian and Robin Hood. | Golden Idol.
Basile the Jester. | Young Lochinvar.
By D. CHRISTIE MURRAY.
A Life's Atonement.
Joseph's Coat.
Coals of Fire.
Old Blazer's Hero.
Val Strange. | Hearts.
A Model Father.
By the Gate of the Sea.
A Bit of Human Nature.
First Person Singular.
Cynic Fortune.
The Way of the World.
Bob Martin's Little Girl
Time's Revenges.
A Wasted Crime.
In Direst Peril.
Mount Despair.
A Capful o' Nails.
Tales in Prose & Verse
A Race for Millions.
This Little World.
His Own Ghost.
Church of Humanity.
By MURRAY and HERMAN.
The Bishops' Bible. | Paul Jones's Alias.
One Traveller Returns.
By HUME NISBET.—'Bail Up!'
By W. E. NORRIS.
Saint Ann's. | Billy Bellew.
Miss Wentworth's Idea.
By G. OHNET.
A Weird Gift. | Love's Depths.
By Mrs. OLIPHANT.—The Sorceress.
By OUIDA.
Held in Bondage.
Strathmore. | Chandos.
Under Two Flags.
Idalia. | Gage.
Cecil Castlemaine's
Tricotrin. | Puck.
Folle Farine.
A Dog of Flanders.
Pascarel. | Signa.
Princess Napraxine.
Two Wooden Shoes.
In a Winter City.
Friendship.
Moths. | Ruffino.
Pipistrello. | Ariadne.
A Village Commune.
Bimbi. | Wanda.
Frescoes. | Othmar.
In Maremma.
Syrlin. | Guilderoy.
Santa Barbara.
Two Offenders.
The Waters of Edera.
By MARGARET A. PAUL.
Gentle and Simple.
By JAMES PAYN.
Lost Sir Massingberd.
The Family Scapegrace
A Country Family.
Less Black than We're Painted.
A Confidential Agent.
A Grape from a Thorn.
In Peril and Privation.
Mystery of Mirbridge.
High Spirits. By Proxy.
The Talk of the Town.
Holiday Tasks.
For Cash Only.
The Burnt Million.
The Word and the Will.
Sunny Stories.
A Trying Patient.
A Modern Dick Whittington.
By WILL PAYNE.—Jerry the Dreamer.
By Mrs. CAMPBELL PRAED.
Outlaw and Lawmaker. | Mrs. Tregaskiss.
Christina Chard. | Nulma. | Madame Izan.
'As a Watch in the Night.'
By E. C. PRICE.—Valentina.
By RICHARD PRYCE.
Miss Maxwell's Affections.
By CHARLES READE.
Peg Woffington; and | Griffith Gaunt.
Christie Johnstone.
Hard Cash.
Cloister & the Hearth.
Never Too Late to Mend
The Course of True
Love; and Single-
heart & Doubleface.
Autobiography of a
Thief; Jack of all
Trades; A Hero and
a Martyr; and The
Wandering Heir.
Love Little, Love Long.
The Double Marriage.
Foul Play.
Put Yrself in His Place
A Terrible Temptation.
A Simpleton.
A Woman-Hater.
The Jilt, & other Stories;
& Good Stories of Man.
A Perilous Secret.
Readiana; and Bible
Characters.
By FRANK RICHARDSON.
The Man who Lost His Past.
By Mrs. J. H. RIDDELL.
Weird Stories. | A Rich Man's Daughter.

Two-Shilling Novels—continued.

BY FRANK BARRETT.
Fettered for Life.
Little Lady Linton.
Between Life & Death.
Sin of Olga Zassoulich.
Folly Morrison.
Lieut. Barnabas.
Honest Davie.
A Prodigal's Progress.

Found Guilty.
A Recoiling Vengeance.
For Love and Honour.
John Ford, &c.
Woman o' Iron Bracelets
The Harding Scandal.
A Missing Witness.

By Sir W. BESANT and J. RICE.
Ready-Money Mortiboy.
My Little Girl.
With Harp and Crown.
This Son of Vulcan.
The Golden Butterfly.
The Monks of Thelema.

By Celia's Arbour.
Chaplain of the Fleet.
The Seamy Side.
In Trafalgar's Bay.
The Ten Years' Tenant.

By Sir WALTER BESANT.
All Sorts and Conditions of Men.
The Captains' Room.
All in a Garden Fair.
Dorothy Forster.
Uncle Jack.
The World Went Very Well Then.
Children of Gibeon.
Herr Paulus.
For Faith and Freedom.
To Call Her Mine.
The Master Craftsman.

The Bell of St. Paul's.
The Holy Rose.
Armorel of Lyonesse.
S.Katherine's by Tower
Verbena Camellia Stephanotis.
The Ivory Gate.
The Rebel Queen.
Beyond the Dreams of Avarice.
The Revolt of Man.
In Deacon's Orders.
The City of Refuge.

By AMBROSE BIERCE.
In the Midst of Life.

By FREDERICK BOYLE.
Camp Notes.
Savage Life.

Chronicles of No man's Land.

BY BRET HARTE.
Californian Stories.
Gabriel Conroy.
Luck of Roaring Camp.
An Heiress of Red Dog.

Flip. | Maruja.
A Phyllis of the Sierras.
A Waif of the Plains.
Ward of Golden Gate.

By ROBERT BUCHANAN.
Shadow of the Sword.
A Child of Nature.
God and the Man.
Love Me for Ever.
Foxglove Manor.
The Master of the Mine.
Annan Water.

The Martyrdom of Madeline.
The New Abelard.
The Heir of Linne.
Woman and the Man.
Rachel Dene. | Matt.
Lady Kilpatrick.

By BUCHANAN and MURRAY.
The Charlatan.

By HALL CAINE.
The Shadow of a Crime. | The Deemster.
A Son of Hagar.

By Commander CAMERON.
The Cruise of the 'Black Prince.'

By HAYDEN CARRUTH.
The Adventures of Jones.

By AUSTIN CLARE.
For the Love of a Lass.

By Mrs. ARCHER CLIVE.
Paul Ferroll.
Why Paul Ferroll Killed his Wife.

By MACLAREN COBBAN.
The Cure of Souls. | The Red Sultan.

By WILKIE COLLINS.
Armadale. | After Dark.
No Name.
Antonina.
Basil.
Hide and Seek.
The Dead Secret.
Queen of Hearts.
Miss or Mrs.?
The New Magdalen.
The Frozen Deep.
The Law and the Lady.
The Two Destinies.
The Haunted Hotel.
A Rogue's Life.

My Miscellanies.
The Woman in White.
The Moonstone.
Man and Wife.
Poor Miss Finch.
The Fallen Leaves.
Jezebel's Daughter.
The Black Robe.
Heart and Science.
'I Say No!'
The Evil Genius.
Little Novels.
Legacy of Cain.
Blind Love.

By C. ALLSTON COLLINS.
The Bar Sinister.

By MORT. & FRANCES COLLINS
Sweet Anne Page.
Transmigration.
From Midnight to Midnight.
A Fight with Fortune.

Sweet and Twenty.
The Village Comedy.
You Play me False.
Blacksmith and Scholar.
Frances.

By M. J. COLQUHOUN.
Every Inch a Soldier.

By C. EGBERT CRADDOCK.
The Prophet of the Great Smoky Mountains.

By MATT CRIM.
The Adventures of a Fair Rebel.

By H. N. CRELLIN.—Tales of the Caliph.

By B. M. CROKER.
Pretty Miss Neville.
Diana Barrington.
'To Let.'
A Bird of Passage.
Proper Pride.
A Family Likeness.
A Third Person.

Village Tales and Jungle Tragedies.
Two Masters.
Mr. Jervis.
The Real Lady Hilda.
Married or Single?
Interference.

By ALPHONSE DAUDET.
The Evangelist; or, Port Salvation.

By DICK DONOVAN.
The Man-Hunter.
Tracked and Taken.
Caught at Last!
Wanted!
Who Poisoned Hetty Duncan?
Man from Manchester.
A Detective's Triumphs.
The Mystery of Jamaica Terrace.
The Chronicles of Michael Danevitch.

In the Grip of the Law.
From Information Received.
Tracked to Doom.
Link by Link.
Suspicion Aroused.
Riddles Read.

By Mrs. ANNIE EDWARDES.
A Point of Honour. | Archie Lovell.

By EDWARD EGGLESTON.
Roxy.

By G. MANVILLE FENN.
The New Mistress.
Witness to the Deed.

The Tiger Lily.
The White Virgin.

By PERCY FITZGERALD.
Bella Donna.
Never Forgotten.
Polly.
Fatal Zero.

Second Mrs. Tillotson.
Seventy-five Brooke Street.
The Lady of Brantome

By P. FITZGERALD and others.
Strange Secrets.

By R. E. FRANCILLON.
Olympia.
One by One.
A Real Queen.
Queen Cophetua.

King or Knave?
Romances of the Law
Ropes of Sand.
A Dog and his Shadow

By HAROLD FREDERIC.
Seth's Brother's Wife. | The Lawton Girl.

Prefaced by Sir BARTLE FRERE.
Pandurang Hari.

By GILBERT GAUL.
A Strange Manuscript.

By CHARLES GIBBON.
Robin Gray.
Fancy Free.
For Lack of Gold.
What will World Say?
In Love and War.
For the King.
In Pastures Green.
Queen of the Meadow.
A Heart's Problem.
The Dead Heart.

In Honour Bound.
Flower of the Forest.
The Braes of Yarrow.
The Golden Shaft.
Of High Degree.
By Mead and Stream.
Loving a Dream.
A Hard Knot.
Heart's Delight.
Blood-Money.

By WILLIAM GILBERT.
James Duke.

By ERNEST GLANVILLE
The Lost Heiress. | The Fossicker.
A Fair Colonist.

By Rev. S. BARING GOULD
Red Spider. | Eve.

TWO-SHILLING NOVELS—*continued.*

By ANDREW HALLIDAY.
Every-day Papers.

By THOMAS HARDY.
Under the Greenwood Tree.

By JULIAN HAWTHORNE.

Garth.	Love—or a Name.
Ellice Quentin.	David Poindexter's Dis-
Fortune's Fool.	appearance.
Miss Cadogna.	The Spectre of the
Dust.	Camera.
Beatrix Randolph.	

By Sir ARTHUR HELPS.
Ivan de Biron.

By G. A. HENTY.
Rujub the Juggler.

By HEADON HILL.
Zambra the Detective.

By JOHN HILL.
Treason Felony.

By Mrs. CASHEL HOEY.
The Lover's Creed.

By Mrs. GEORGE HOOPER.
The House of Raby.

By Mrs. HUNGERFORD.

A Maiden all Forlorn.	Lady Verner's Flight.
In Durance Vile.	The Red-House Mystery
Marvel.	The Three Graces.
A Mental Struggle.	Unsatisfactory Lover.
A Modern Circe.	Lady Patty.
April's Lady.	Nora Creina.
Peter's Wife.	Professor's Experiment.

By Mrs. ALFRED HUNT.
That Other Person. | The Leaden Casket.
Self Condemned. |

By MARK KERSHAW.
Colonial Facts and Fictions.

By R. ASHE KING.
A Drawn Game. | Passion's Slave.
'The Wearing of the | Bell Barry.
Green.' |

By EDMOND LEPELLETIER
Madame Sans-Gene.

By JOHN LEYS.
The Lindsays.

By E. LYNN LINTON.

Patricia Kemball.	The Atonement of Leam
The World Well Lost.	Dundas.
Under which Lord ?	Rebel of the Family.
Paston Carew.	Sowing the Wind.
'My Love!'	The One Too Many.
Ione.	Dulcie Everton.
With a Silken Thread.	

By HENRY W. LUCY.
Gideon Fleyce.

By JUSTIN McCARTHY.

Dear Lady Disdain.	Donna Quixote.
Waterdale Neighbours.	Maid of Athens.
My Enemy's Daughter	The Comet of a Season.
A Fair Saxon.	The Dictator.
Linley Rochford.	Red Diamonds.
Miss Misanthrope.	The Riddle Ring.
Camiola	

By HUGH MACCOLL.
Mr. Stranger's Sealed Packet.

By GEORGE MACDONALD.
Heather and Snow.

By AGNES MACDONELL.
Quaker Cousins.

By W. H. MALLOCK.
The New Republic.

By BRANDER MATTHEWS.
A Secret of the Sea.

By L. T. MEADE.
A Soldier of Fortune.

By LEONARD MERRICK.
The Man who was Good.

By Mrs. MOLESWORTH.
Hathercourt Rectory.

By J. E. MUDDOCK.
Stories Weird and Won- | From the Bosom of the
derful. | Deep.
The Dead Man's Secret. |

By D. CHRISTIE MURRAY.

A Model Father.	A Bit of Human Nature.
Joseph's Coat.	First Person Singular
Coals of Fire.	Bob Martin's Little-Girl.
Val Strange.	Hearts.	Time's Revenges.
Old Blazer's Hero.	A Wasted Crime.
The Way of the World	In Direct Peril.
Cynic Fortune.	Mount Despair
A Life's Atonement.	A Capful o' Nails
By the Gate of the Sea.	

By MURRAY and HERMAN.
One Traveller Returns. | The Bishops' Bible.
Paul Jones's Alias. |

By HUME NISBET.
Bail Up! | Dr. Bernard St. Vincent.

By W. E. NORRIS.
Saint Ann's | Billy Bellew.

By GEORGES OHNET.
Dr. Rameau. | A Weird Gift.
A Last Love. |

By Mrs. OLIPHANT.
Whiteladies. | The Greatest Heiress in
The Primrose Path. | England.

By OUIDA.

Held in Bondage.	Two Lit. Wooden Shoes
Strathmore.	Moths.
Chandos.	Bimbi.
Idalia.	Pipistrello.
Under Two Flags.	A Village Commune.
Cecil Castlemaine's Gage	Wanda
Tricotrin.	Othmar
Puck.	Frescoes.
Folle Farine.	In Maremma.
A Dog of Flanders.	Guilderoy.
Pascarel.	Ruffino.
Signa.	Syrlin.
Princess Napraxine.	Santa Barbara.
In a Winter City.	Two Offenders.
Ariadne.	Ouida's Wisdom, Wit.
Friendship.	and Pathos.

By MARGARET AGNES PAUL.
Gentle and Simple.

By Mrs. CAMPBELL PRAED.
The Romance of a Station.
The Soul of Countess Adrian.
Outlaw and Lawmaker. | Mrs. Tregaskiss
Christina Chard. |

By JAMES PAYN.

Bentinck's Tutor.	The Talk of the Town.
Murphy's Master.	Holiday Tasks.
A County Family.	A Perfect Treasure.
At Her Mercy.	What He Cost Her.
Cecil's Tryst.	A Confidential Agent.
The Clyffards of Clyffe.	Glow-worm Tales.
The Foster Brothers.	The Burnt Million.
Found Dead.	Sunny Stories.
The Best of Husbands.	Lost Sir Massingberd.
Walter's Word.	A Woman's Vengeance.
Halves.	The Family Scapegrace.
Fallen Fortunes.	Gwendoline's Harvest
Humorous Stories.	Like Father, Like Son.
£200 Reward.	Married Beneath Him.
A Marine Residence.	Not Wooed, but Won.
Mirk Abbey.	Less Black than We're
By Proxy.	Painted.
Under One Roof.	Some Private Views
High Spirits.	A Grape from a Thorn
Carlyon's Year.	The Mystery of Mir-
From Exile.	bridge.
For Cash Only.	The Word and the Will
Kit.	A Prince of the Blood.
The Canon's Ward.	A Trying Patient.

By RICHARD PRYCE.
Miss Maxwell's Affections.

TWO-SHILLING NOVELS—*continued.*

By CHARLES READE.

It is Never Too Late to | A Terrible Temptation.
Mend. | Foul Play.
Christie Johnstone. | The Wandering Heir.
The Double Marriage. | Hard Cash.
Put Yourself in His | Singleheart and Double-
Place | face.
Love Me Little, Love | Good Stories of Man and
Me Long. | other Animals.
The Cloister and the | Peg Woffington.
Hearth. | Griffith Gaunt.
Course of True Love | A Perilous Secret.
The Jilt. | A Simpleton.
The Autobiography of | Readiana.
a Thief. | A Woman-Hater.

By Mrs. J. H. RIDDELL.

Weird Stories. | The Uninhabited House.
Fairy Water. | The Mystery in Palace
Her Mother's Darling. | Gardens.
The Prince of Wales's | The Nun's Curse.
Garden Party. | Idle Tales.

By F. W. ROBINSON.

Women are Strange. | The Woman in the Dark
The Hands of Justice.

By W. CLARK RUSSELL.

Round the Galley Fire. | An Ocean Tragedy.
On the Fo'k'sle Head. | My Shipmate Louise.
In the Middle Watch. | Alone on Wide Wide Sea.
A Voyage to the Cape. | Good Ship 'Mohock.'
A Book for the Ham- | The Phantom Death.
mock. | Is He the Man?
The Mystery of the | Heart of Oak.
'Ocean Star.' | The Convict Ship
The Romance of Jenny | The Tale of the Ten.
Harlowe. | The Last Entry.

By DORA RUSSELL.

A Country Sweetheart.

By GEORGE AUGUSTUS SALA.

Gaslight and Daylight.

By GEORGE R. SIMS.

The Ring o' Bells. | Zeph.
Mary Jane's Memoirs. | Memoirs of a Landlady.
Mary Jane Married. | Scenes from the Show.
Tales of To-day. | The 10 Commandments.
Dramas of Life. | Dagonet Abroad.
Tinkletop's Crime. | Rogues and Vagabonds.
My Two Wives.

By HAWLEY SMART.

Without Love or Licence. | The Plunger
Beatrice and Benedick. | Long Odds.
The Master of Rathkelly.

By T. W. SPEIGHT.

The Mysteries of Heron | Back to Life.
Dyke. | The Loudwater Tragedy.
The Golden Hoop. | Burgo's Romance.
Hoodwinked. | Quittance in Full.
By Devious Ways. | A Husband from the Sea

By ARTHUR SKETCHLEY.

A Match in the Dark.

By R. A. STERNDALE.

The Afghan Knife.

By ALAN ST. AUBYN.

A Fellow of Trinity. | Orchard Damerel.
The Junior Dean. | In the Face of the World.
Master of St. Benedict's | The Tremlett Diamonds.
To His Own Master.

By R. LOUIS STEVENSON.

New Arabian Nights.

By ROBERT SURTEES.

Handley Cross.

By WALTER THORNBURY.

Tales for the Marines.

By T. ADOLPHUS TROLLOPE.

Diamond Cut Diamond.

By F. ELEANOR TROLLOPE.

Like Ships upon the | Anne Furness.
Sea. | Mabel's Progress.

By ANTHONY TROLLOPE.

Frau Frohmann. | The American Senator.
Marion Fay. | Mr. Scarborough's
Kept in the Dark. | Family.
The Way We Live Now. | Golden Lion of Granpere
The Land-Leaguers.

By MARK TWAIN.

A Pleasure Trip on the | Life on the Mississippi.
Continent. | The Prince and the
The Gilded Age. | Pauper.
Huckleberry Finn. | A Yankee at the Court
Tom Sawyer. | of King Arthur.
A Tramp Abroad. | £1,000,000 Bank-Note.
Stolen White Elephant.

By C. C. FRASER-TYTLER.

Mistress Judith.

By SARAH TYTLER.

Bride's Pass | Lady Bell | The Huguenot Family
Buried Diamonds. | The Blackhall Ghosts
St. Mungo's City. | What She Came Through
Noblesse Oblige. | Beauty and the Beast.
Disappeared.

By ALLEN UPWARD.

The Queen against Owen.

By WILLIAM WESTALL.

Trust-Money.

By Mrs. F. H. WILLIAMSON.

A Child Widow.

By J. S. WINTER.

Cavalry Life. | Regimental Legends.

By H. F. WOOD.

The Passenger from Scotland Yard.
The Englishman of the Rue Cain.

By MARGARET WYNMAN.

My Flirtations.

NEW SERIES OF TWO-SHILLING NOVELS.

Picture cloth, flat backs.

The Constable of St. Nicholas. By EDWIN
LESTER ARNOLD.
St. Katherine's by the Tower. By Sir WALTER
BESANT.
Ainslie's Ju Ju. By HAROLD BINDLOSS.
Dora Myrl, the Lady Detective. By McD.
BODKIN, K.C.
Vincent Trill, Detective. By DICK DONOVAN.
Dark Deeds. By DICK DONOVAN.
A Crimson Crime. By G. MANVILLE FENN.
The Red Shirts. By PAUL GAULOT.
The Track of a Storm. By OWEN HALL.
The Luck of Roaring Camp: and Sensation Novels
Condensed. By BRET HARTE.
In a Hollow of the Hills. By BRET HARTE.
Colonel Starbottle's Client. By BRET HARTE.
A Protegee of Jack Hamlin's. By BRET HARTE.
A Sappho of Green Springs. By BRET HARTE.
The Lady from Nowhere. By FERGUS HUME.
Plotters of Paris. By EDMUND MITCHELL.
The Temple of Death. By EDMUND MITCHELL.

Towards the Eternal Snows. By EDMUND
MITCHELL.
The Luck of Gerard Ridgeley. By BERTRAM
MITFORD.
The King's Assegai. By BERTRAM MITFORD.
Maid Marian and Robin Hood. By J.E.MUDDOCK.
His Own Ghost. By D. CHRISTIE MURRAY.
The Waters of Edera. By OUIDA.
A Modern Dick Whittington. By JAMES PAYN.
The Drift of Fate. By DORA RUSSELL.
A Country Sweetheart. By DORA RUSSELL.
In London's Heart. By G. R. SIMS.
The Young Master of Hyson Hall. By FRANK
STOCKTON. With 36 Illustrations.
The Tale of the Serpent. By SUNDOWNER.
Citoyenne Jacqueline. By SARAH TYTLER.
The Queen against Owen. By ALLEN UPWARD.
Joan the Curate. By FLORENCE WARDEN.
Sport and Spangles. By BYRON WEBBER.
Cavalry Life; and Regimental Legends. By
JOHN STRANGE WINTER.

UNWIN BROTHERS, LTD, Printers, 27, Pilgrim Street, London, E.C.